# PRACTICAL PSYCHOLOGY

Not Listed
only Copy

# PRACTICAL PSYCHOLOGY

**JAMES P. FLANDERS**
Florida International University

HARPER & ROW, PUBLISHERS
NEW YORK, HAGERSTOWN, SAN FRANCISCO, LONDON

Sponsoring Editor: George A. Middendorf
Project Editor: Alice Solomon
Designer: Michel Craig
Production Supervisor: Francis X. Giordano
Compositor: American Book–Stratford Press, Inc.
Printer: Halliday Lithographic Corporation
Binder: Halliday Lithographic Corporation
Art Studio: Danmark & Michaels, Inc.

**PRACTICAL PSYCHOLOGY**



Library of Congress Cataloging in Publication Data

Flanders, James P
Practical psychology.

Bibliography: p.
Includes indexes.
1. Interpersonal relations. 2. Self evaluation.
3. Intimacy (Psychology) I. Title. [DNLM: 1. Psychology, Clinical. 2. Mental health. WM100 F584p]
HM132.F586 301.11 75–43596
ISBN 0–06–042084–7

*To My Family*

# CONTENTS

# PREFACE FOR STUDENTS BY A STUDENT

People are what psychology is all about. The success of any contribution in psychology depends on whether it can be utilized by the individuals in our society. Work in psychology really centers around allowing people to live their lives fully, to attain and enjoy the goals they set for themselves.

Today is not easy for many people. More and more pressures accompany our advancing technology. Our very structures in society are undergoing great changes. The person having trouble with adjustment cannot count on his friends in a small town, or even a close-knit family, for help. Too often today's individual ends up in a psychoanalyst's office for the same problems that, in the past, his family unit could have helped him with.

It is common to hear people use terms describing mental illness in their everyday slang. "I think I'm going out of my mind" or "I'm so schizo today." We look at mental illness as an everyday occurrence. Mental institutions are filled with people who had trouble with adjustments or alternatives and could not find any help. The degree of acceptance concerning serious problems in living is reflective of the threat that such problems pose to the members of our society. Psychology must address problems in everyday living before lives are ruined.

Psychology has its work set out. It has a responsibility to do all it can to improve conditions for personal adjustment and satisfaction. Those in the field cannot let themselves off the hook by just pointing at society and blaming it.

I am familiar with some of the psychology literature, and I am disappointed in its contribution. In the introductory psychology course I took at another school, I discovered many new terms, but little knowledge that I could apply. The popular books on newsstands are "get well quick" works based on faulty or no research, and their eventual utility to the reader is suspect.

I believe that the single most important ability a person needs to attain what he or she can out of life is the talent to invent and use alternatives. When a person cannot come up with alternatives, his ability to adjust is zero. The key to adjustment is to be innovative in creating alternatives and to make the most out of each one. What do I mean? I will demonstrate through examples from my own experience.

Around five years ago, I had a close friend who became seriously involved with addictive drugs. My friend was not just fooling around; he was very quickly becoming an addict. I used all the strategies I could to try to alter the situation. I failed, our friendship dissolved, and I had a feeling of frustration. What should I have *done?* Recently I was dating one particular girl quite frequently. I was unsure of her feelings and, often, even more unsure of my own. My feelings began to fluctuate. Any attempt at verbalization became gradually more and more difficult. Our relationship still wavers in limbo. What should I have *done?*

These problems may be specific to me, but they are also universal. Everyone has difficulties in the social realm. Carl Jung said that the meeting of two personalities is like the contact of two chemical substances; if there is any transaction, both are transformed. What Dr. Flanders is trying to accomplish is to give his readers some amount of control over such transformations. With the applications I subsequently discovered in his book, I might have been able to gain enough insight into each transformation to have diverted my friend from drugs and told the girl exactly what I was thinking. This was the most important contribution of *Practical Psychology* for me. It spelled out definite alternatives.

**Michael Mattimore—**
*Undergraduate Student*
*Florida International University*

(This preface is printed with permission of Michael Mattimore, who used a prepublication draft of *Practical Psychology* in a course at Florida International University.)

# AUTHOR'S PREFACE

### GOAL

*Practical Psychology* aims at supplying the student with practical information for application in everyday social situations. This practical "user information" is also harmonious with research findings in psychology.

### USE

*Practical Psychology* will find potential use whenever the instructor deems interpersonal skill essential to course goals.

### LEVEL

*Practical Psychology* is suitable for use in undergraduate instruction at junior or community colleges, colleges, and universities—from the freshman through the senior levels.

### THEORETICAL APPROACH

*Practical Psychology* presents content in a manner that, hopefully, approaches theoretical neutrality. For example, Chapters 2 through 4 concern the topics of loneliness and intimacy. In these chapters the important topic of human intimacy, or attachment, is discussed in a manner independent of mediating processes. Thus the instructor and student can use their preferred theoretical orientations throughout, which is as it should be.

### ACKNOWLEDGMENTS

My beloved family gets most of my gratitude. My parents mustered the inexhaustible patience, skill, and love needed to endure the many trials I gave them. My wife, Juanita, and my children, Carl and Leah, continue to give me support and love.

Don Thistlethwaite became my mentor in graduate school at Vanderbilt University. He taught me how to write and how to think better. His personal style shows that it is indeed possible to do fine professional work and remain a beautiful person all at the same time. While at Vanderbilt, Professors Leland Thune, Jum Nunnally, Bob Liebert, and Bill Smith influenced and helped me. While doing postgraduate research at Walter Reed Army Institute of Research, Tom Frazier became my boss. His concern with practical matters coincided with mine at just the right time.

Any psychologist needs good colleagues, and I have been most fortunate in this respect. From graduate school days until now, Carl Young has been a source of encouragement and made suggestions leading to this book. (As if that were not enough, he introduced me to Juanita and later married us.)

A number of friends and colleagues have performed invaluable service by reviewing drafts of several chapters. H. Jim Owens, Irwin Silverman, Ryan Tweney, and Fred Frank plowed their way through early drafts of this text and offered suggestions. More recent drafts have benefited from comments by Bill Kurtines and Lloyd Bennett, who critically reviewed all the chapters. Dalmas Taylor, Hal Arkowitz, Vello Sermat, and Ralph Keyes generously provided excellent comments on Chapters 2 through 4, as Wally Wilkins and Hal Arkowitz did for Chapter 10. Dorothy Pincus kindly read Chapter 11. Don McCullough and John P. Robinson lent me research materials.

My department chairmen have helped make this book possible by actively contributing to the atmosphere of academic freedom, in which I have been surrounded by stimulating colleagues. Bob Guion and Hal Johnson at Bowling Green State University and Ron Tikofsky at Florida International University deserve credit in this respect.

So many students have given helpful suggestions over the years I have been developing these chapters that it is impossible to list all of them. Especially helpful were Lloyd Bennett, Mike Mattimore, Rodrigo Marulanda, Judy Schreibner, Jack Ortiz, Diane Paull, Brian Levi, Janet Schusheim, Joey O'Neill, Candy Hadler, Priscilla Schwartz, Lorelei Starkman, Ilene Graditor, L. D. Losada, Rick Briz, Carlos del Amo, Rosemary Connors, James H. Butler, Jeff Dorian, Marilyn Richman, Patricia Bryant, Maria Ana Alvarez, Stan Adelman, and Shelly Goodman.

A special tribute is due Chuck Blakey, who supplied many of the photographs for this book.

Editorially speaking, the professionals at Harper & Row have helped immensely. I owe Executive Editor George Middendorf a tremendous debt because he spotted potential in some early chapters despite the way I had written them. As fertilizer is to plants, Dr. Phil Zeigler's slashing editorial commentary was to my developing manuscript. Also, Mrs. Alice Solomon gave careful guidance to this book through the production process.

Finally, my thanks go to typists Beth Williams, Teresa Goicouria, Ronna Beckman, and Jeanne Sharp, who deciphered my scrawly printing into legible typed copy.

**J.P.F.**

# PRACTICAL PSYCHOLOGY

# RELATING TO OTHER PEOPLE

# A PSYCHOLOGY FOR RELATING TO OTHER PEOPLE

*Many everyday encounters are unpleasant, embarrassing, or fruitless, because of inept social behaviour. . . . Many of those difficulties and frustrations could be eliminated by a wider understanding, and better training in the skills of social interaction.*

MICHAEL ARGYLE

## SOCIAL RELATIONS

### The Hidden Curriculum

In his "Preface for Students by a Student," Michael Mattimore reflected on concerns common to everyone. We steer our course through life mostly by making decisions about such ordinary matters as how to express our feelings or how to help a friend. Our schooling provides magnificent instruction about many subjects, such as literature, mathematics, chemistry, farming, and fire prevention. In these areas and others, scientific information feeds into programs of instruction that often start before the first grade. By the time we graduate from high school, we are well equipped, for example, to arrange our *physical* surroundings so they will not burst into flames. But how are we equipped to arrange our *social* surroundings to avoid disaster and maintain health?

Social skills are picked up informally. Even though interpersonal skills are essential to social and occupational success in modern society, no widely adopted curriculum of human relations exists in elementary and secondary schools. The informal learning experiences that teach us about social relations with other people are often called the "hidden curriculum."

ACTIVITY 1.1.

Pause to reflect on the hidden curriculum of human relations you have experienced.[1] Write down the major social learning experiences that have influenced you the most. Were the learning situations in your school? In your home? Were there only a few individuals who taught you something new? In what ways has your education in human relations been fortunate? How might it have been improved? Respond in the space provided, emphasizing experiences whereby you learned something new about relating to other people.

________________________________________

________________________________________

________________________________________

________________________________________

________________________________________

________________________________________

________________________________________

________________________________________

________________________________________

________________________________________

Experiencing a fortunate hidden curriculum is important. Who among us has not wished to have succeeded in getting that quiet soul at the party to say a few words about herself? What salesman does not want to sell more? What parent does not want to take all possible steps to insure that the toddler stays away from the busy street when nobody else is around? The office manager wants to be rid of innumerable trivial problems. The nurse wants to calm those who are in pain. Practically all of us would pay dearly for the ability to meet new people with greater ease and poise. These and other highly personal concerns are the focus of this book.

As you read on, the purpose of this book should become clear. I wish to supply you with practical information for use in your everyday human relations. You will find information from psychology tailored to two main standards: practicality and fit with research. I envision a body of knowledge that is both practical for everyday living and embraced by researchers, who correctly demand that all knowledge fit with present and possible research findings. My approach is basically social, so practically all content concerns situations in which two or more people are interacting on a face-to-face basis. (See Figures 1.1 and 1.2.)

**Learning With and Without Psychology**

If one is looking for practical aids for improving social relations, there are two main sources of information. First, we have folk wisdom from parents, literature, religion, jobs, and other such sources. However, folk wisdom often contains vague and contradictory advice. For example, let us try a simple exercise. After I give you one proverb from folk wisdom, you try to give me a proverb that says exactly the opposite. Here are four proverbs from me to you:[2] Absence makes the heart grow fonder; opposites attract; familiarity breeds contempt; you're never too old to learn. In addition to offering vague and contradictory advice, folk wisdom often relies on authority that has little value to many of us, such as the pronouncements of a single person. The history of science shows that pronouncements about the state of nature are worthy of trust only when backed by evidence which can be shared between people. Thus we now consider the second source of information on improving social relations, the profession that is concerned with evidence and theory for studying behavior: psychology.

Psychology and related disciplines contain a growing body of information. What is the current state of psychology as a scientific enterprise? What does psychology offer to those of us who are concerned with user information? Psychology is a young, developing, scientific discipline. Although its findings and methods are undergoing vigorous growth and change, there is enough in current psychology to increase the interpersonal skill and social effectiveness of the user beyond that provided by folk wisdom. What's in psychology for you?

We can draw more specific *terms* and concepts from current psychology for describing our social environment than we can from folk wisdom. We will consult several *theories* about such topics as loneliness, intimacy, eliciting actions from others, and changing emotions. The research literature of psychology also offers *data* from empirical tests. Because such tests reflect the state of nature, they are of supreme importance over the long haul. A good collection of terms, theories, and data can sharpen our wits and increase our social skill. In this volume, I hope to provide such a collection, drawing from the information available from psychology in a selective way.

## INFORMATION IN PSYCHOLOGY

### Consumption of Information in Psychology

Psychology provides three kinds of information about human behavior; this information can be classified according to how it is used. First, there is *basic research information.* Scientists produce such information to be used or consumed by other scientists. Basic research information connotes high-powered, technical material. To get an idea of what this kind of information looks like, browse through one of the prominent psychology journals, such as *Journal of Personality and Social Psychology, Journal of Experimental Social Psychology, Psychological Bulletin,* and *Developmental Psychology.*

The second kind of information we can get from psychology is *professionally mediated information.* Such information is applied by a professional on behalf of a nonprofessional, such as yourself. For example, psychiatrists, clinical psychologists, school psychologists, and industrial psychologists apply such information to aid their clients.

The third and least available is *user information.* Such information can be applied by the individual nonprofessional person toward personal goals in everyday situations. Let me stress that in this instance the user is always one person, never a group or organization.

The current lack of user information came

**Figure 1.1.** This book stresses practical aspects of human contact. In modern society architectural barriers keep people apart. What features of the architecture in this prolograph might serve to inhibit meeting new people or interacting with acquaintances? (Photograph by Charles Blakey.)

**Figure 1.2.** In some older areas of modern cities, the architecture assists social interaction. What features of the architecture in this photograph might serve to facilitate meeting new people or interacting with acquaintances? (Photograph by Charles Blakey.)

about largely because of the historical development of psychology as a discipline. Academically based psychologists have typically been free to investigate any topic they chose. Unfortunately though, until recently journal editors have generally limited publication to basic research information in the form of theory-testing research using refined laboratorylike methods. Psychologists working for industry and other organizations have been restricted because they are paid to generate and apply professionally mediated information to serve their employers. Thus contemporary psychology can be characterized accurately as offering an abundance of basic research and professionally mediated information. A report entitled *Knowledge into Action: Improving the Nation's Use of the Social Sciences* supports my description of the information now available in psychology.[3]

The relative paucity of user information may be compared to the plight of the modern consumer. Until recently the consumer has had few champions or advocates. Similarly, until recently the user has had few champions or advocates in psychology. However, the need for practical, problem-oriented information has been recognized increasingly by the federal government, and research efforts are being channeled into social-action areas.

What will the future bring? Surely the professional journals will continue to report only technical information. The flow of user information will most likely surface in new journals and books, such as this one. But it must be recognized that all three kinds of information about behavior are essential. An overproduction of any one kind spells trouble, and that includes a possible obsession with user information in the near future as a reaction to the current state of affairs.

### Three Viewpoints in Psychology

There are three viewpoints in psychology, and each has something to contribute. We will build on the strengths of each. Because you will construct your own psychology of life from your own personal viewpoint, you should have a diversity of alternatives from which to select. In the sections that follow, each viewpoint is characterized briefly; then the pragmatic question "What's in this viewpoint for me?" is considered. The goal throughout remains practicality, so I did not attempt to survey each area comprehensively in this book. Rather, I selectively gleaned what is practical.

### Humanistic Psychology

The fundamental claim of humanistic psychology is the idea that human values do enter the scientific endeavor; therefore the role of human values must be recognized and dealt with out in the open. This fundamental claim is valid because the values of the individual scientist determine what research he or she does. My values comprise the filter through which material found its way into this text, and the same holds for selectivity in all other textbooks.

How do we reconcile the value-laden nature of science with its supposed neutrality in the ethical area? We deal with this matter more fully in Chapter 5, but here is a preview. We can distinguish between the value-laden activities of people who are scientists and the truly neutral structure and tools of the trade (terms, data, theories). As an example, a pair of pliers is morally neutral until it is used; we rightly speak about the values of the user or the use, but not of the pliers just lying there. My treatment of values in this book is to label them. Nevertheless, you should be aware that what I write for you and what you wrote to your grandmother once upon a time are both just teeming with values because of all the thoughts we choose *not* to write about.

Humanistic psychologists are concerned primarily with *self-actualization.* For you, self-actualization means realizing your own potential and capabilities. Two giant figures in humanistic psychology, Abraham Maslow and Carl Rogers, both contended that there is a tendency in each of us to self-actualize.[4] Humanistic psychologists are vitally concerned with exploring means to enhance personal self-actualization.

Most humanistic psychologists study man as a whole. When you greet a close friend at lunch, the emphasis would center on the whole of this luncheon meeting, not the position of your eyebrows during the greeting. Man is seen as a free agent having *free choice.* So you could read this sentence or skip it if you choose. It is not the environment, it is you who has control over your decisions. Humanistic psychologists emphasize experiencing your feelings and choices now, at this moment in time. Thus the past serves only to frame the present. And the future is determined by the present, not the other way around. Heavy emphasis is accorded to *expressing emotions* outwardly as well as feeling them inwardly. Emotions are roads on the map of living. *Honesty* and *authenticity* are central in our relationships to other people. Thus inside thoughts and outside actions should correspond. We men and women are seen as *creative.* When you can create, you can self-actualize. Finally, humanistic psychologists are deeply concerned about *intimacy* with a few close others. The opposite of rewarding intimacy is haunting loneliness. Intimacy comes from mutually sharing central aspects of self between two people. In short, humanistic psychologists are concerned first and foremost about that which is distinctly human.

What's in humanistic psychology for me? From the humanistic psychologists, we can learn to start where we ought to start: with where we are in life and with what we can gain from a consideration of human values. Accordingly, the following parts of this book concern where we are in life and values. In "Part Two: Human Contact Through Intimacy," our position in modern life is seen largely as seeking to fill the needs for human contact (intimacy, attachment) through interpersonal relations. In "Part Three: Values," values are seen as the allocation of scarce personal resources, such as time.

### Behavior Modification

Behavior modification psychology is dedicated to the practicality of stating and achieving goals. "Behavior mod" psychologists, as they call themselves, clearly emphasize outward behavior and the role of external forces in shaping that behavior. Imagine a coed who is terrified of all older men. From the behavior mod viewpoint, this is a contemporary learning problem involving the outward behavior of fear. Inner experience is there, but to actually help this girl, one engineers the *situation* so that new learning experiences counteract old ones. In the process of *behavior change,* emphasis is accorded to the *consequences* of her behavior. That is, think about what happens right after she says hello to the aging teacher or neighbor. Does he smile or rebuff her? In like manner, is it not the systematic influence of outside forces that molds a teenage gang member? How does a poor boy in a ghetto get status? What consequence follows doing as gang members do? Does the gang reward playing chess or rolling drunks? On the other hand, what consequences likely followed the daily events in the boyhood of a compassionate Pope John? In short, when examined in painful detail, outside forces of *reward* and *punishment* systematically determine whether a given bit of behavior occurs again or fades away. These little bits of behavior make up the puzzle of life. Returning to the case of the fearful coed, the behavior mod clinical psychologist might engineer a series of pleasant conversations with progressively older males to alleviate her fears.

At heart, behavior mod and humanistic psychologists have much in common. The persons subscribing to either viewpoint are concerned with human problems and human values. Both types of psychologists had to set up shop for themselves outside the giant factory of established laboratory psychology. Both recently set up formal associations with ringing cries for efforts relevant to human problems.[5] Both prefer to study the individual person rather than groups of persons. Besides having separate organizations, both work largely outside the laboratory and in the real world. Both are optimistic about change. As people, the advocates of behavior mod and humanistic traditions in psychology have a lot in common.

In their *theories,* these two schools differ regarding the control of behavior. Is control within or without?[6] Is responsibility within or without? The humanistic school says that you and only you will decide what you are going to do this Saturday night. The behavior mod school says outside forces will largely control your decision about Saturday night.

What's in behavior mod psychology for me? The behavior mod approach contains a wealth of specific procedures that we cover in "Part Four: Interpersonal Change." These procedures unquestionably make up the most powerful body of information in psychology today. The father of behavior mod, B. F. Skinner, has been voted the most influential living psychologist by his colleagues.[7] In fact Skinner was awarded the "Humanist of the Year" citation in 1972 by the American Humanist Association.

ACTIVITY 1.2.

With permission, silently follow a friend around for 15 to 30 minutes. Concentrate all of your attention on his public behavior and what follows. Report only public behavior, not your own inferences about motives. Do others smile after he or she speaks? What other consequences follow an utterance by your friend? Are some rewards perhaps off in the distant future? Are some supplied by inanimate objects? How about punishments? Write down mind joggers here from the detailed notes you take. Are you letting your inferences about motives and inner mental states creep in? It is natural to do so, but avoid it here at all costs.

______________________________

______________________________

______________________________

______________________________

______________________________

______________________________

______________________________

______________________________

______________________________

______________________________

### Social Psychology

Social psychologists break attitudes and actions into components to shed light on the magnificent complexity of normal everyday life. For example, a beautifully timed symphony of speech, glances, and other nonverbal actions happens each time you quit speaking and another person starts. How do you know when to quit speaking? How does the other know when to start? A lot more communication flows between two people face-to-face than just the words spoken.

What's in social psychology for me? From

the social psychology research tradition, we can tune in to the workings of complex elements of human relations. On the one hand, it is best to have a philosophy of whole people, not parts. On the other hand, what do we do when the complexity of life boggles our minds? Simplify, break down into parts, and build back up again. Social psychologists have also contributed a number of dimensions for describing interpersonal relationships, which we consider in Chapter 12.

ACTIVITY 1.3.

Observe two or more children. Look very, very closely at what they do with their eyes as they talk to one another. Who looks at whom or away, and when? If you have time, do the same with adults. Jot down key observations in the space provided. Include both observations of public behavior and your inferences about what the behavior means, but clearly separate the observations from your inferences.

## A Strategy for Self-Change

### Need for a Strategy

Suppose you want to alter some aspect of your daily life, such as eating 500 calories less per day. How should you attack the problem? This specific problem requires specific action, but many actions are possible. Any approach to specific problems such as this one requires us to confront the control-of-behavior issue head-on. If behavior is controlled mainly by internal forces as humanistic psychologists claim, efforts toward personal change should emphasize internal mental change, such as meditation for several hours. If behavior is controlled largely by external forces from the environment as behavior mod psychologists claim, efforts toward personal change logically should stress altering your surroundings, such as getting rid of all those snack foods.

Rather than adopt either of these extreme views, control from without or from within, we will adopt a compromise position. We will assume that our everyday actions are part of a system that includes both internal and external control. This assumption deserves some discussion because the source (internal, external, or both) of our everyday actions largely determines our efforts for personal change. I propose a simple model to describe the assumption that both internal and external forces influence our everyday actions.

### A Bicycle Model of Everyday Influence

Look at Figure 1.3 and you will see the Flanders bicycle model of everyday influence. There are two hubs of activity, namely, you and your surroundings. Each hub, or sprocket wheel, moves when the other one moves. There are both internal forces directed outward and external forces directed inward on the chain. You act on your surroundings with *internal forces* directed outward. For example, you have a strong internal desire to eat fewer calories. Your surroundings influence you with *external forces* directed inward. For example,

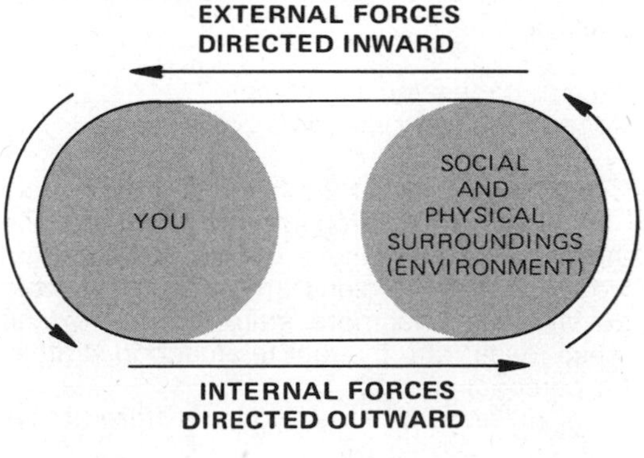


**Figure 1.3.** The bicycle model of everyday influence.

your friend removes all food from your reach. This is the key point! You and your surroundings move in constant interaction. Interaction here means something special: that social life is a system. It makes no sense at all to deal with social life without two elements and two relating forces:

Elements
1. You
2. Surroundings

Forces
1. Internal forces
2. External forces

By combining the emphases in humanistic and behavior mod viewpoints, the bicycle model builds on the strengths of both. It also reflects recent trends in both these traditions, which are moving toward a compromise position.[8] Take a look at how the bicycle model is distinctly social. Your thoughts and actions not only turn in relation to one another; your thoughts and actions are powerfully influenced by the thoughts and actions of others. A bicycle chain is strong and powerful. In fact if we press the idea of influence by others a bit, we arrive at a novel idea about how we use others in the process of looking at ourselves.

The behaviorist Bem claims we get our *self-perceptions* largely from our actions.[9] Bem's claim is exactly the opposite of the usual viewpoint. He claims that you and I derive our opinions by looking at our outward actions, not the other way around: Because I eat liver, I like liver. Actions determine attitudes, even in the case of attitudes toward ourselves. Going one step further, the sociologist Cooley suggests the famous looking-glass self:

*Each to each a looking glass*
*Reflects the other that doth pass.*[10]

Cooley's idea is that the faces of other people can be viewed as circular mirrors balanced on their shoulders. In these mirrors, we see what *we* think their opinions are of us. If you will go with me one more step, we can extend these ideas from thought to an action strategy for personal change.

In the bicycle model, you and I are always in motion. To reach the goals you set for yourself, you are wisest to enlist the powerful forces of the people and even the physical settings in your surroundings. The situation is much the same for others, whom you can (and perhaps must) assist. In this day and age, the means to virtually any goal involves both self and surroundings. Otherwise, it's a bicycle with no chain.

### The Strategy

In light of the preceding discussion, we will adopt a strategy for self-change that uses both internal and external influences whenever possible. A major aspect of using internal influences is to enlist the aid of influences in your surroundings. Going back to the goal of eating 500 calories less per day, you might take actions such as removing fattening foods from your dwelling and making sure your best friend lavishes praise on you for every day you meet your goal. This strategy forms a part of the more general practical approach discussed next.

## A PRACTICAL APPROACH

We take a practical approach on the basis of one possibly radical assumption: Personal adjustment is largely a function of the social world you and I experience as individual persons. While the causes for events that affect us everyday may lie partly at some level of society, say at the level of national government, your personal adjustment concerns the personal social world that centers about you! Improving personal adjustment therefore requires information that can affect your personal world in a practical way.

Assuming a reality basis of private experience, we do best to rearrange the reality in our personal social world because our private experience will eventually reflect that reality. Otherwise, the only recourse is to distort perception and experience so as to distort reality. Over the longer run, such distortion is dangerous and maladaptive in all senses of the term maladaptive (personally, culturally, biologically, etc.).

Another way to describe a practical approach to personal adjustment is to say what it is not. A practical approach does not emphasize sitting under a tree trying to juggle around the elements in one's mind to attain a state of momentary mental bliss. Rather, a practical approach concerns solving social problems, with emphasis on future actions in the face-to-face presence of other people. The practical approach should lead to greater mental bliss in the long run. And you can certainly sit under trees while contemplating these future actions (see Figure 1.4).

### Social Skill

At the beginning of this chapter, reference was made to a concept of social skill. It is now time to define that concept. My concept is essentially the same as that of Michael Argyle.[11] Each of us arrived at our own conceptions separately, without reading or communicating with each other.

In this concept, you are viewed as the central actor. You are relating to other persons. In dealing with another person, you hopefully enlist his or her aid for the benefit of both of you. To the degree that you are successful in eliciting certain actions from others (while minimizing their negative outcomes and maximizing their positive outcomes), you can be said to have a degree of social skill. For instance, take the case of the truly loving, socially skilled husband. In his human relations with his wife, by demonstrating loving actions himself he is socially skilled in bringing forth loving action from her. In another example, who is the world's most effective salesperson? Suppose we take the action of other persons' buying as the reflection of social skill. Is not the salesperson who sells the most therefore the most socially skilled salesperson? Likewise, does not the more skilled teacher elicit more learning actions from students? Note that the concept of social skill is specific to particular goals.

The concept of social skill just outlined has received strong support from research done by Julian Libet. Detailed analyses of moment-to-moment patterns in conversation revealed several social skill measures that were stable over time, valid, and differentiated between normal and depressed participants.[12] For example, persons who elicited a lot of positive remarks (and thus displayed higher social skill) generally tended to talk at a higher rate themselves and be less sensitive to any negative reactions they encountered. Dominating the structure of the patterns Libet found was a general dimension of social skill at eliciting positive responses from others.[13]

To the extent that mastery of the content in this book results in increased social skill, you should become more effective in eliciting the actions you desire from other persons. It would probably be useful to assess increases in your social skill as a result of mastering this text. But an ideal assessment would be out of the question because it would require specially trained detectives to follow you around and observe your every move. Nevertheless, it is possible to list some important

**Figure 1.4.** Meditating about personal change can be helpful, but a practical approach requires more. (Photograph by Charles Blakey.)

abilities and feelings that should reasonably accompany increases in your social skill:

1. *Describe social situations in detail.* When called on to describe interpersonal situations in your own life or someone else's, your description should display more precision and accuracy.
2. *Generate more response options.* When presented with a case example involving an interpersonal problem, you should be able to generate more response options for the central figure facing the problem.
3. *Order response options more rationally.* When given a list of response options generated by someone else, you should be able to order those you would try first, according to standards or criteria you can state openly.
4. *Experience increased social competence.* You should feel subjectively that you have more social skills at your command.
5. *Experience increased confidence in social situations.* Your feeling of greater social confidence at a higher level of social skill means that you should feel you have increased chances (probabilities) of social success and also decreased fears concerning future interpersonal situations.

The beauty of the items in this list is that increases can be measured objectively in all five cases. Actually, if even a modest increase occurs in only one case as a result of your taking this course, the course will have been well worthwhile.

### Openness

Remember our bicycle model of everyday influence. Just as the bicycle travels over the open road, I would like you to think of our approach to human relations as *open.* When you and a loved one speak openly, communication flows freely. "Open" here means "objective" or "communicating to another person freely and accurately." An open approach is necessary to communicate about human relations. If I am not open, what I try to communicate in these pages may not make it through to you—and that would be my fault. This openness means that in this book we will consider mainly those aspects of human relations that lend themselves to free and objective communication. (See Figures 1.5 and 1.6.)

At this point, I am afraid we have got about all the mileage we can out of our bicycle model. It is obvious that you and your surroundings are not rigid sprocket wheels, but ever changing. You as a sprocket wheel are linked to many other sprocket wheels, not just one. A valid picture of social life would require thousands of sprocket wheels, each linked to others in a maze of swirling action. So let us leave our bicycle with an appreciation of its simple beauty and utility.

### Practicality as a Two-Way Street

The ground we are about to cover will likely yield some measure of practical information. One can view the use of this information as we have thus far, namely, as an aid in shaping our own personal destiny. However, there is another viewpoint, one that emphasizes the larger social system. We can view user information as a catalog of ways in which the larger social systems of business, government, or other people can exert influence on us. Viewed in this way, the mastery of user information becomes a suit of armor for self-protection against being exploited.

## PERSONAL ADJUSTMENT AS PSYCHOLOGICAL WELL-BEING

### Defining Personal Adjustment

We can approach the idea of personal adjustment from different angles. The *normality* view defines "well-adjusted" as being normal relative to some society. The first obvious question is, then, "How do we define what is normal?" Here we consider two models for defining adjustment as normality, the medical model and a model described by Richard Warga.

The *medical,* or disease, view of adjustment concentrates on bad adjustment, or maladjustment. Maladjustment can be reflected legally or psychologically. Using a rough *legal* definition, we could define the maladjusted as those persons who are institutionalized for social reasons. Such a view is simplistic, and lawyers would certainly reject it. In relation to the legal definition, Clifford Swensen mentions a novel idea concerning the institutionalization of individuals in mental hospitals and prisons. He believes that "people are put in mental hospitals because they have upset

**Figure 1.5.** In most societies, social barriers exist against introducing oneself to a stranger. What would most likely happen if this man introduces himself to this young lady in this situation? (Photograph by Charles Blakey.)

somebody very much, having done so because they didn't follow the rules (social customs) for social interaction."[14] For every person inside the institution, several others who behaved in the same way are running around free on the outside because they learned and obeyed the unwritten rules in the hidden curriculum of everyday living.

Using a *psychological* definition within the medical view of adjustment, we could define adjustment as the lack of bothersome neurotic or psychotic symptoms. This definition particularly galls me because the emphasis is so sordidly on the negative. Surely there must be more to adjustment than a lack of problems! Nevertheless, the overwhelmingly dominant approach to mental health uses the disease view in both psychiatry and clinical psychology. When things get so painful they can no longer be tolerated, today's child or adult seeks help to put out the flames of pain, which is rather like seeking help from a fire department. But unlike fire department representatives, mental heath professionals do not make thousands of visits to kindergarten and grade school classrooms to spread information about how to prevent the flames from arising in the first place.

A more positive approach to defining adjustment based on normality is one given by Richard Warga. He says that the following characterizes a normal person: "(1) Behaves according to accepted social standards. (2) Controls his emotions. (3) Fulfills his human potential. (4) Conforms to social customs. (5) Is able to recognize consequences and thus guide his behavior. (6) Can postpone immediate gratification to achieve long-range goals. (7) Learns from experience. (8) Is usually happy."[15] Unfortunately, social standards are changing so quickly that a precise definition of normality might be obsolete by the time it appeared in print. In addition, social customs are incredibly numerous and specific to subcultures and situations within subcul-

**Figure 1.6.** What would most likely happen if this man introduces himself to this young lady in this situation? (Photograph by Charles Blakey.)

tures. Pity the young child who must master such myriad rules as the following:

Do not walk between two people who are talking to each other.
Peas are eaten with a fork (although it is easier to scoop them up in your spoon).
The moment saliva leaves your mouth, it is instantly changed from clean to filthy dirty. (Mud is a little dirty, but spit is filthy dirty!)

Swensen rightly points out "that most of what we call psychotic behavior is perfectly acceptable sometime, somewhere, in some situation."[16] Thus, to define what is normal would mean specifying with some precision those thousands of ever changing, unwritten rules, a task beyond the current capabilities of psychological science. In short, defining adjustment to mean normality is beyond the means of current psychology. (In fairness to Warga, the view of adjustment as normality is just one of several he presents.)

Leaving behind the view of adjustment as normality, let us briefly consider adjustment as *"a way of reacting to problems, not an absence of them."*[17] The importance of a sound way to approach problems cannot be denied. In fact we will adopt a problem-solving strategy in Chapter 6. But can we say that problem-solving *is* adjustment? Or is it just a means to adjustment? The fatal weakness with both the cultural normality and problem-solving views of adjustment is illustrated in Case 1.1.

**Case 1.1.** Bill Thompson has succeeded in every respect. He holds a high-paying job that fulfills his greatest talents. He has never received so much as a traffic ticket, let alone having been institutionalized. He controls his emotions superbly and maintains a wide circle of friends. His methodical approach to problems is the envy of all his acquaintances. We approach Bill and ask him, "Bill, taken altogether, how would you say things are these days?" His glance falls to the floor. He answers, "You know, some people think I am the ideal successful person in Mudville, but they're wrong. I don't show it, but inside I feel terrible. I'm worried about a lot of things and I'm just plain unhappy. I've got everything but happiness inside."

Yes, something is missing from adjustment as discussed thus far. Norman Bradburn tells us what it is.

In his massive study *The Structure of Psychological Well-Being,* Bradburn proceeds from an ancient truth.[18] "No man is happy who does not think himself so," wrote the Roman emperor-philosopher Marcus Aurelius. Despite being nearly 2000 years old, this argument devastates other approaches by pinpointing the crucial element of personal adjustment: self-report of psychological well-being. Regardless of whether one is inside or outside an institution, abnormal or normal by contemporary standards, *well-adjusted* means realistic psychological well-being or avowed happiness over time. Although an institutionalized person is unlikely to feel great psychological well-being, this definition curiously allows institutionalized persons manifesting strange behavior and even stranger defense mechanisms to be better adjusted than a perfectly normal but unhappy leader of society. Do you agree?

The definition of adjustment as reality-based psychological well-being is superior to the other definitions we considered. But it is not quite perfect either. Before we move on, two minor shortcomings of adjustment as psychological well-being will be discussed. To illustrate these two shortcomings, imagine two people who report happiness but would not seem very well adjusted. First, imagine a person who is evil but happy, perhaps a sadist. Second, imagine a blissful slave, who has happily resigned himself to his fate. Both these possibilities exist. However, they are unlikely to endure over time on a widespread basis. Before long, in either case, internal unhappiness will likely (but not surely) develop and lead to changes in external action and an adaptive fit with surroundings. Thus adjustment defined as realistic happiness over time fits with definitions that emphasize adjusting to our environment, such as Jahoda's.[19]

Curiously, a practical approach toward enhancing psychological well-being implies reaching a subjective, internal, reality-based happiness through improving external social reality over time. Even more curiously, this approach demands contributions from both internal mental and external behavior mod views of man. Traditionally, contributions of Laing's existential phenomenology and Skinnerian behavior mod have been treated as theoretically separate.[20] Here, the interplay between private experience and public action is emphasized. Practical (external) action paves the way toward enhancing reality-based (internal) happiness over time. In short, vocabularies to describe both internal experience and external action are required for our purposes.

### The Structure of Psychological Well-Being

Norman Bradburn did what a good psychologist should do: He plunged right into gathering evidence about his approach to psychological well-being. He views the whole topic as a forest and particular theories as trees.

On the basis of interviews with 2787 people throughout the United States, Bradburn provides rather solid evidence that overall psychological well-being is made up of two components: positive feelings and negative feelings. Using results from several studies of the National Opinion Research Center at the University of Chicago, Bradburn carefully documented the existence and reliability of three different dimensions of psychological well-being: overall psychological well-being, positive feelings, and negative feelings.

The two main conclusions from Bradburn's research are striking:

1. The degree of positive feelings is not related to the degree of negative feelings.
2. Overall psychological well-being = positive feelings − negative feelings.

Some factors in life can make us feel positive, negative, or both. Our overall happiness is predicted by the *difference* between positive and negative feelings. Thus you can report having lots of positive feelings and lots of negative feelings. Note here that Bradburn's concept of feelings does not mean just the restricted set of emotions present at the time of the interview, but rather feelings during "the past few weeks." All 2787 respondents were interviewed either two or four times.

At the time of this writing, Bradburn's findings represent psychology's best guess about the nature of psychological well-being. It is interesting indeed to see where such well-being is found nowadays and what factors seem likely to produce it.

### Where Is Psychological Well-Being Found?

#### Overall Psychological Well-being or Happiness

Bradburn found the usual socioeconomic indices to be strongly related to overall psychological well-being.[21] Having a higher income is associated with greater well-being at all ages, even with the effect of education level removed. If you have a higher level of education, you are likely to feel happier, but only if you are under 35 years of age. Being black means less happiness. Age has no relationship with reported happiness after we take out the effects of both income and education level. Amazingly, no sex differences appear. (It is unusual in psychology, or anywhere else for that matter, for the sex variable to have no effect.) Number of children has no effect on overall happiness, except for very low low-income adults, for whom more children means less happiness. Ability to pay off current debts has no effect. Bradburn summarizes nicely:

> *Thus we all know of individuals who are extremely successful and are yet wracked with psychological woes, and of individuals who have been plagued with misfortune and have few financial assets but manage to live happy lives. The existence of such cases should not, however, detract from the proposition that, on the average, those who have the better of it in life are also better off psychologically.*[22]

Do these results mean that the morally right thing to do to attain happiness is to go out and make a lot of money? Of course not; but money seems to bring happiness. Do the materialistic things in our materialistic society bring happiness? No, that explanation is a bit simplistic. A better explanation would rely on the specific opportunities available to people who have more money, such as mobility. And this consideration leads right into the more specific topics of negative and positive feelings.

#### Negative Feelings

To assess negative feelings, Bradburn asked his respondents to reply to questions to indicate if they felt

1. *bored*
2. *upset because someone criticized them*
3. *so restless that they couldn't sit long in a chair*
4. *very lonely or remote from other people*
5. *depressed or very unhappy*

during the past few weeks.[23] Responses to these five questions were consolidated into a single index of negative feelings. The pattern of factors associated with negative feelings is interesting.

Surprisingly, the socioeconomic indices of education level, age, and income level had a trivial association with negative feelings. Women reported more negative feelings than men, which may be because of occupational inferiority or better training in being socially sensitive as related to the female role. Also, men may report less discomfort to appear masculine. Especially high in unhappiness are all categories of people who are not married: separated, divorced, widowed (including widowers), and never married. Not being married has greater negative impact on men than women. When analyzed in detail, satisfactions and dissatisfactions in marriage showed a miniature pattern of the overall pattern, namely, two dimensions—one positive and one negative—unrelated to each other. And, of course, not having a job means unhappiness.

### Positive Feelings

To assess positive feelings, Bradburn asked respondents to answer if they felt

1. *pleased about having accomplished something*
2. *proud because someone complimented you on something you had done*
3. *particularly excited about or interested in something*
4. *on top of the world*
5. *that things were going your way*

during the past few weeks.[24] Responses to these five questions were consolidated into a single index of positive feelings.

Having a job means more positive feelings. Bradburn summarizes: "(1) Income is not the major source of satisfaction among high-prestige jobholders but is among low; and (2) income, rather than less tangible rewards, is the only work-related source of well-being among low-prestige jobholders."[25]

Perhaps the most important correlate of positive feelings is general social participation. Getting together with friends, traveling to meet them, chatting on the telephone, meeting new people, making new friends, keeping in touch with relatives, and taking part in organizations are used to index *social participation.*[26] Strange as it seems, social participation or lack of it is not related to negative feelings.

When we put together the findings about negative feelings and positive feelings just reviewed, it is almost as if there are two separate processes going on. Both are social processes. First, a satisfactory marriage parts the waters to deliver you from the oppressive land of dissatisfactions. Then, active social participation takes you into the promised land of positive feelings.

### Reservations about The Bradburn Findings

Monumental as they are, Bradburn's findings deserve some words of qualification. First, his results do not show cause and effect. He only found correlations or associations between various factors. Therefore we cannot distinguish between the explanations that "not having a job causes negative feelings" versus "having negative feelings causes one not to have a job." Second, his questionnaire certainly contained a limited set of questions. With more questions, future researchers might discover more than the two dimensions, positive and negative feelings. Third, he did not study extremely rich people, so we have no idea about the happiness associated with great wealth.

### Implications for Us

Taken together, all that we have considered previously has four implications for what you can do personally to attain overall happiness. The first is to prepare for a satisfying job that pays well. The second is to think seriously about the benefits of being married. The third is to hone your social skills to facilitate social participation. The fourth is to clarify your values. The first two are up to you. In this regard, I recommend taking full advantage of vocational counseling on your campus. Your tax dollars are paying for these

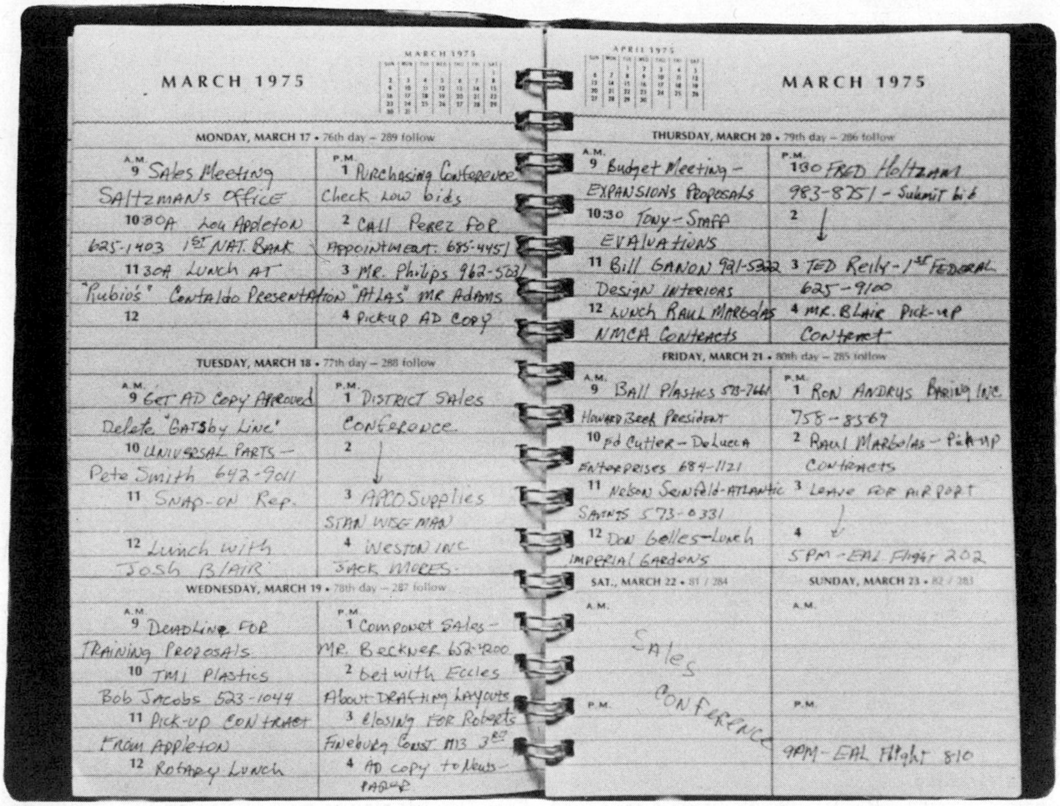


**Figure 1.7.** In modern society, time devoted to jobs and commercial consumption often squeezes social consumption and human contact into an inferior position, creating a time-scheduling barrier against human contact. (Photograph by Charles Blakey.)

services, so you might as well use them. The last two comprise the concern of this course.

## PREVIEW OF COMING CHAPTERS

One preview of coming chapters has already been accomplished by Figures 1.1, 1.2, 1.4, 1.5, and 1.6. These photographs and their captions are meant to play harmony to this chapter by introducing the central idea of human contact or intimacy.

Research on psychological well-being provides another link to the coming chapter. In all the research about what life experiences yield the good and positive fruits of psychological well-being, one rather specific kind of experience stands out in clear relief. Bradburn calls it social participation. In a broad-ranging review entitled "Correlates of Avowed Happiness," Warner Wilson says it all: "Perhaps the most impressive single finding lies in the relation between happiness and successful involvement with people."[27]

The assumption underlying Chapters 2 through 5 is stated nicely by Michael Argyle, the great English social psychologist: "Many people are lonely and unhappy, some are mentally ill, because they are unable to establish and sustain social relationships with others."[28] Because our physical and safety needs are mostly met, satisfying our needs for human contact through interpersonal relationships is what modern life is all about. However, imperfections in modern society tend to keep our social needs only minimally satisfied. Since more-than-minimal satisfaction is essential for adjustment, our attention will focus on identifying and attaining features of social relations that satisfy our social needs in these days of competition for our time (see Figure 1.7).

In Chapter 2, Bowlby's concepts of attachment and separation are used to parallel the concepts of human intimacy and loneliness. The importance of loneliness as a major problem in modern living, loneliness being viewed as the absence of human contact, is demonstrated. In Chapter 3, six features of emotional intimacy are described, along with arguments to support the importance of each. In Chapter 4, you will take a self-inventory on each of the six features of emotional intimacy in your own life; you will compare your current level of experience with your reasonable ideal. A number of opportunities for facilitating human contact are also discussed, such as encounter groups and volunteer work. In Chapter 5, we deal with personal values as the allocation of scarce personal resources, such as your time and affection. Many of the personal social problems we face daily are cast as results of commercial consumption outdoing social consumption for our time, largely because of the superior technology that underlies commercial consumption. The remainder of the book concerns specific procedures for eliciting desired actions in other persons and yourself.

**SUMMARY**

As an alternative to chance and folk wisdom, psychology offers some important aids for increasing social skill. In contrast to basic research information and professionally mediated information in psychology, user information can be applied by nonprofessional persons toward personal goals in everyday situations. This book comprises a collection of user information, building on the strengths of three viewpoints in psychology: (1) Humanistic psychology concerns itself with human values in the scientific enterprise and human intimacy. (2) Behavior mod psychology supplies specific procedures for personal change (Chapters 6 through 10). (3) Social psychology provides analyses of complicated social behaviors and dimensions of interpersonal relationships. Based on the bicycle model of everyday influence, the strategy for self-change involves enlisting the aid of both internal and external forces. The approach is practical and action oriented rather than contemplative because personal adjustment is assumed to reflect accurately the satisfactory or unsatisfactory state of one's personal social world. Mastery of the content in this text should lead to an increase in social skill, which is defined as the ability to successfully elicit desired action in your "other persons," or "meaningful others." Conceiving of adjustment as psychological well-being based on reality, we proceed on the research-backed assumption that involvement with people is crucially important. We now consider loneliness and intimacy in the modern world.

*The greatest single thing each of us can do in our quests for happiness and personal adjustment is probably to establish and maintain a meaningful, satisfying relationship with another person that will endure over time.*

THE AUTHOR

# HUMAN CONTACT THROUGH INTIMACY

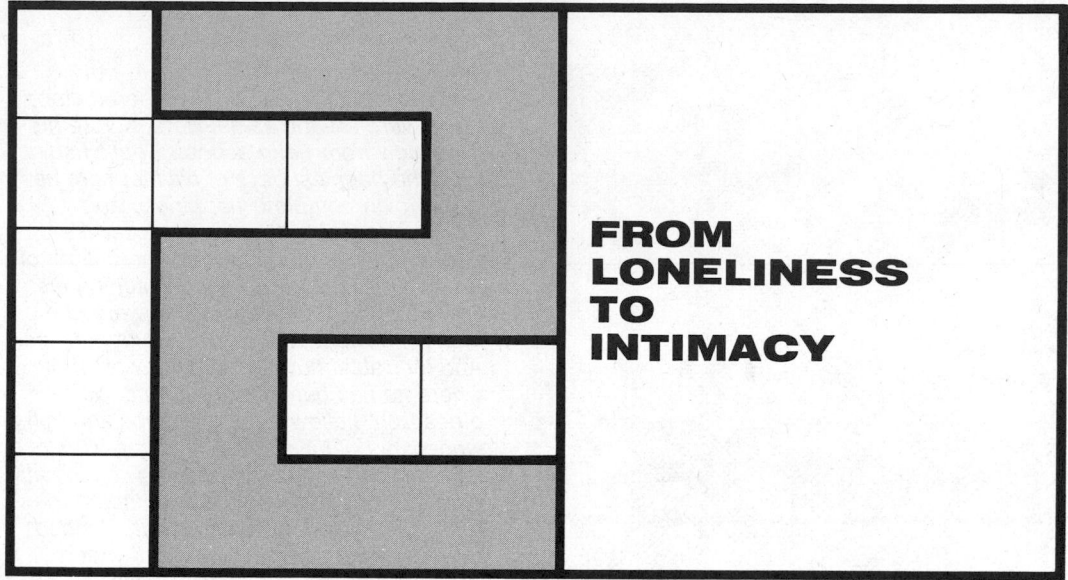

# 2 FROM LONELINESS TO INTIMACY

Seeking human contact and intimacy probably ranks as the most widespread social pattern of action across all humanity. Attempts to avoid separation from people and loneliness also seem nearly universal. The topics of loneliness and intimacy touch each one of us deeply. The next three chapters are therefore devoted to them.

Our goal will be to paint a realistic picture of loneliness and intimacy that is relatively independent of theory. The resulting portrait should lend itself to interpretation by whatever mode of explanation you choose to apply. You may embrace biological, mental, behavioral, humanistic, psychoanalytic, religious, or environmental concerns as your personal preference. Any or all can be brought to bear on the topics of loneliness and intimacy.

## THE CONCEPT OF LONELINESS

### An Example

As the backdrop for our discussion of loneliness, we begin with an example from literature. As you read this case, try to discover two fundamental experiences in the life of the central figure; try to guess what they are. We will return to them (p. 26) because they illustrate our concerns here.

**Case 2.1.** Knulp, created by the novelist Hesse in his book *Knulp,* lived the life of a delightful vagabond. He charmed all he met. A bit of Knulp lives in each of us, especially that part longing for human contact. Let us approach the aging wanderer to probe his mind. We catch up to him as an old man making a pilgrimage to his boyhood hometown. Perhaps he wants to take one last look at this village nestled deep in the Alps.

*He stopped outside the little house where his father had lived long ago and for a time, leaned his back against the old door. He went to the garden and looked over a loveless*

*new wire fence into a newly laid-out vegetable patch—but the weathered stone steps were still the same. Here, before his expulsion from Latin school, Knulp had lived the happiest days of his life; here he had known complete happiness and fulfillment, joys without bitterness, the sweetness of stolen cherries, the delight of tending his little garden and watching his flowers grow, the lovely gilly flowers, the merry bindweed, the tender velvet pansies. And the rabbit hutches and the workshop where he had built kites and made water pipes from hollow elder branches and mill wheels out of balls of string with pieces of shingle for paddles. He had known the cats on every one of these roofs, sampled the fruit in every garden roundabout, climbed in every tree, and made himself green dream nests in their crowns. This bit of world belonged to him, he had known every inch of it and loved it; every bush and every slope had held meaning for him, had had its tales to tell; every rain or snowfall had spoken to him; the air and earth had lived in response to his dreams and desires. And even today, it seemed to Knulp, this world belonged to him as much as to any of the owners of these houses and gardens. Which of them could claim to prize it more highly or to find more memories in it? . . . He saw his father's garden and his own little flower bed . . . and little mounds of pebbles where he had deposited the lizards that he caught over and over again, inconsolable that none would stay and become his pet, but always eager and full of hope when he had captured a new one. Today he would have given all the houses and gardens, all the flowers and lizards and birds in the world for a single one of the summer flowers that had put forth their precious petals—ever so slowly—in his little garden.*[1]

*[Having been crushed by an early love, Knulp reminisces,] ". . . and, well, it was horrible. All my trouble had been for nothing. . . . I'd still give my right hand for it to have turned out differently . . . she wasn't to blame . . . since then I've had good friends and casual friends; but I've*

**Figure 2.1.** The later years, a time of loneliness for many. (Photograph by Charles Blakey.)

*never relied on anyone's word and I've never given my own. Never again. I've lived my life as I saw fit, I've had my share of freedom and good things, but I've always been alone."*[2]

*"Every human being has his soul, he can't mix it with any other. Two people can meet, they can talk with one another, they can be close together. But their souls are like flowers, each rooted to its place. One can't go to another, because it would have to break away from its roots and that it can't do. Flowers send out their scent and their seeds, because they would like to go to each other; but a flower can't do anything to make a seed go to its right place; the wind does that and the wind comes and goes where it pleases."*[3]

*"I didn't wrong Henriette or Lisabeth knowingly. But because I once loved them both and wanted to make them my own, they became for me a kind of dream figure, which looks like both of them and is neither. That figure belongs to me, but it no longer has life. And I've often had such thoughts about my parents. They think I'm their child and that I'm like them. But though I love them, I'm a stranger to them, a stranger they can't understand."*[4]

After touring the village, Knulp begins to leave. A blinding but silent snowstorm numbs all his senses, but not his emotions and his mind. Our loveable wanderer passes his final hours stumbling toward an unknown destination and speaking with God.

*"That was the time," Knulp repeated over and over again. "When I was fourteen and [my love] Franziska failed me. Everything was still possible. And then something went to pieces inside me; from then on, I was no good—You should have let me die when I was fourteen. That was the big mistake. Then my life would have been as beautiful and perfect as a ripe apple."*

*But God smiled all the while, and sometimes his face disappeared in the driving snow.*

*"Come along, Knulp," he said reprovingly. "Think of your youth, that summer in the Odenwald and the times in Lachstetten. Didn't you dance like a deer, didn't you feel the joy of life in every bone? Didn't you sing and play the accordion till all the girls had tears in their eyes? Do you remember . . . Henriette, your first sweetheart? Was all that for nothing? Enough of that, Knulp. . . . Can't you see what it all means? Can't you see that you had to be a gadabout and a vagabond to bring people a bit of child's folly and child's laughter wherever you went? . . . Don't you see that whatever happened was good and right, that nothing should have been any different? . . . I wanted you the way you are and no different. You were a wanderer and in my name and wherever you went, you brought the settled folk a little home sickness for freedom. In my name, you did silly things and people scoffed at you; I myself was scoffed at and loved in you. You are my child and my brother and a part of me. There is nothing you have enjoyed and suffered that I have not enjoyed and suffered with you."*

*"Yes," said Knulp, nodding heavily. "Yes, that's true, and deep down I've always known it."*

*He lay resting in the snow. His weary limbs had grown light and his inflamed eyes smiled.*

*When he closed them to sleep a little, he still heard God's voice speaking and still looked into His bright eyes.*

*"So you've nothing more to complain about?" God's voice asked.*

*"Nothing more," Knulp nodded with a shy laugh.*

*"And everything's all right? Everything is as it should be?"*

*"Yes," he nodded. "Everything is as it should be."*

*God's voice became softer. Now it sounded like his mother's voice; now like Henriette's, and now like the good, gentle voice of Lisabeth.*

*When Knulp opened his eyes again, the sun was shining. It dazzled him so that he quickly lowered his lids. He felt the snow lying heavy on his hands and wanted to shake it off, but the desire to sleep had grown stronger than any other desire.*[5]

(From *Knulp*, by Hermann Hesse. Copyright 1971 by Farrar, Straus & Giroux. Reprinted by permission.)

## Defining Solitude and Loneliness

### Solitude

Suppose you have made your way to the edge of Crater Lake in Oregon at sundown. Long ago a volcano thundered up its anger at the sky, but the scene is placid now. Perched there on the brink of this immense natural bowl of water, you gaze westward upon the majestic panorama of sunset. The lake lies perfectly still. As the night chill sets in, you begin to think how insignificant you are in the scheme of nature. You are alone, drinking in the beauty of the solitude, feeling at one with nature. Close your eyes and picture the scene. Is this loneliness?

The scene portrayed is helpful because it contains heavy doses of two components that are *not* essential for loneliness. First, being physically separated from other people is not necessary for loneliness; you can be lonely while surrounded by a crowd. Second, intellectually concentrating on the solitude of being apart from other people and united with nature is not necessary for loneliness. In his book *Loneliness and Solitude,* Moustakas conceives of psychological *solitude* as feeling alone, silent, and in communion with nature or art.[6] We will adopt this definition. In the scene at Crater Lake, you experience solitude.

Poets have always captured the essence of emotions in a special way. While scientists and poets both possess the ability to transmit a description of emotional experiences, poets and other artists allow the reader to share the experience. The following is a poem about solitude by May Sarton.

*COLORADO MOUNTAINS*

*Plain grandeur escapes definition. You*
*Cannot speak about the mountains well.*
*About the clear plane, the sharp shadow*
*You cannot tell.*

*Mountains define you. You cannot define*
*Them. And all your looking serves to set*
*What you have learned of the stern line*
*Against an absolute.*

*The frail taut structure of a human face*
*Beside the sheer cliff drawn, all that you loved,*
*All that can stand in such a bare clear place*
*Is to be proved.*

*And love that is a landscape in the past*
*Becomes, like mountains, changeless. It is there.*
*It is standing against its own image at last*
*In a high air.*



### Loneliness

In contrast to physical separation and solitude, we conceive of psychological loneliness as a painful wish for meaningful human contact. We will adopt Helena Lopata's conception of loneliness from her paper "Loneliness: Forms and Components."[7] *Loneliness* means a wish for a form or level of social interaction different from the one presently experienced; the form or level can include changes in the number of people, changes in action, or changes in expressions of sentiments. An equivalent definition (by your author) views loneliness as a painful feeling of being separated or apart, usually from other persons, coupled with a wish for improved human contact or intimacy.

Robert Weiss describes some unique characteristics of loneliness in his book *Loneliness: The Experience of Emotional and Social Isolation:*

> *Loneliness is not simply a desire for company, any company; rather it yields only to very specific forms of relationship. Loneliness is often uninterrupted by social activity; the social activity may feel "out there," in no way engaging the individual's emotions. It can even make matters worse. However, the responsiveness of loneliness to just the right sort of relationship with others is absolutely remarkable. Given the establishment of these relationships, loneliness will vanish abruptly and without trace, as though it never had existed. There is no gradual recovery, no getting over it bit by bit. When it ends, it ends suddenly; one was lonely, one is not any more.*[8]

Weiss summons his clinical experience to propose two different types of loneliness, which we shall call "social loneliness" and "emotional loneliness." Weiss's distinction is modest and in line with the research literature on loneliness, which is also modest. But most important, Weiss gives us the means to link his theory to events we can observe.[9]

*Emotional loneliness* stems from "the absence of a close emotional attachment."[10] Merely joining a group or having friends does not ward off emotional loneliness. Only a new or recaptured emotional relationship can do that. Specific reactions in emotional loneliness can be called "symptoms." Symptoms of emotional loneliness include a nameless fear that resembles a childhood terror of being abandoned, restlessness that prevents concentration and keeps one physically moving about, increased sensitivity to threat, an acutely painful feeling of apartness, and a continuous searching for a satisfactorily deep emotional relationship. The search process leads the emotionally lonely individual to be "forever appraising others for their potential as providers of the needed relationship, and forever appraising situations in terms of their potential for making the needed relationships available."[11] We shall call the antidote to emotional loneliness "emotional intimacy," the kind of human contact that provides a close emotional attachment.

*Social loneliness* is caused by "the absence of an engaging social network."[12] Symptoms of social loneliness are somewhat different from those of emotional loneliness. Both kinds of loneliness share the same driving restlessness and search for satisfactory relationships. However, in the case of social loneliness, the dominant feeling is one of boredom or aimlessness or exclusion. The antidote to social loneliness is "social intimacy," which means being included in a kin or friendship network of social interaction. Examples follow.

**Case 2.2.** Ray has just been sent overseas by his corporation as a part of a crisis-solving team. The other experts are all friendly enough, but he doesn't feel close to any of them. The crisis stretches into several weeks, and Ray begins to feel the pangs of emotional loneliness. These feelings are reminiscent of a haunting experience from childhood, when his parents actually lost him for an afternoon.

**Case 2.3.** Missy has come to live in Miami because her husband got transferred and the move was necessary. But all of Missy's relatives and friends are in the North. Her husband works long hours, and she has the "newcomer blues."

The example in Case 2.3 illustrates social loneliness. Weiss contends that feelings of social loneliness are reminiscent of "the small child whose friends are all away."[13]

ACTIVITY 2.1.

Recall the occasion of your own greatest loneliness. Describe it in the space provided, including when, where, the cause(s), and your resolution of it (if you did resolve the loneliness).

______________________________

______________________________

______________________________

______________________________

______________________________

______________________________

______________________________

______________________________

______________________________

______________________________

## ORIGINS OF LONELINESS: ATTACHMENT AND SEPARATION

Let us pose a basic question. Why should loneliness exist at all? Why should almost no one be satisfied to go home from work to an empty residence and stay there alone during all nonworking hours? Is there some common origin to our feelings of loneliness and our seeking of human contact? Yes, there is. The best guess about the genesis of these phenomena lies in the study of "attachment" and "separation," childhood processes that develop into more complex adult kinds of intimacy and loneliness.

### Attachment to People: The Invisible Rubber Band

One day in a London park, an observer watched some 2-year-old children playing near their mothers.[14] A child would typically toddle a short way, halting quite often to look back at mother. After a longer halt, he would rush back to her, only to embark on a new foray from the home base of exploration. It looked as if the child were tied to mother by an invisible rubber band.

From earliest infancy, when attachment to other people begins, an invisible rubber band tends to develop that links virtually every human to someone else. The disposition to seek the closeness and proximity of a specific other person is called *attachment.* Disruption of attachment, or *separation,* is the other side of the coin. Knulp exhibited both.

Remember the two "fundamental experiences" to look for in Knulp's life? By now you have probably guessed them to be attachment and separation. In the beginning of the passage about Knulp, he reminisced about his idyllic childhood. Early in his life, he had formed close attachments. Later in life, when he tried to form new emotional attachments, he failed. Then he withdrew. His mental life became filled with longings for lost days of childhood joy and lost opportunities for emotional intimacy.

Poor Knulp gained and lost paradise, although God rectified his life at death's hour. Franziska's rejection had planted a lingering fear of close human contact that robbed Knulp of the intimacy he so desperately needed. Separation became permanent. Never again would he dare to reveal and express himself so fully. He kept his distance. He felt emotional loneliness and restless. In a literal way, that loneliness kept him on the move. Hopefully, most of us have a happier tale to tell than Knulp. In fact the attachment process in humans often develops smoothly. Now let us trace that development.

Attachment in the child is directed at maintaining his tie to his mother. Occasionally another "object of attachment" exists, but usually it is the mother. The attachment usually focuses on a *specific* relationship with the *specific* other person. At about age 3, some changes begin. Curiosity leads to much more exploration away from mother, and the attachment becomes less focused on mother and more diffused. By adolescence, the child has begun to focus on peers as objects of attachment. Most adolescents are still attached to their parents; but some cut themselves off completely from parents, and some remain totally attached to mother. In later life, attachment shifts to one's spouse. Upon the death of an elderly person's spouse, attachment shifts to elderly peers and younger people.[15]

Note that all the developments of attachment discussed in the paragraph above have not been disrupted by separation. That is, there is an available object of attachment in each instance.

Most students of attachment, including John Bowlby, picture the role of the mother and family as essential for healthy attachment. They most certainly do not favor tearing the child away from mother at a tender age to foster self-reliance. To the contrary, the mother (or other stable object of attachment) provides a base from which the child's normal explorations grow at a gradual pace. The family later provides a stable base for the similar explorations by adolescents. Such a pattern seems to characterize psychologically healthy offspring, as indicated by Bowlby's research.[16] In short, "far from sapping a child's self-reliance, then, a secure base and strong family support greatly encourage it."[17]

Of course the smooth development of attachment throughout the life span can and does get disrupted. Bowlby and others see many problems in living as effects of attachments that never developed or somehow got sidetracked. The lawbreaker or dropout from society trying to prove that he counts for something *for someone* is another example. In this latter case, the lawbreaker or dropout experiences too little rather than too much intimacy, a condition often associated with separation from other people.

### Separation

In the present context, separation means disruption of attachment whereby proximity to the object of attachment is no longer available. A 1-year-old usually becomes upset when he loses sight, sound, or touch of mother. Usually becoming upset prompts the child to try to maintain closeness with mother. Prolonged separation is a difficult experience. In a number of studies, observers have looked at children's reactions to separation from mother because of hospitalization. For example, James Robertson studied children aged

2 to 3 in residential nurseries and hospital wards.[18] Upon prolonged separation, the child goes through three clear reaction phases: protest, despair, detachment. The severity of the reaction in the children Robertson studied was effectively reduced by the presence of a brother or sister (even a very young one) or a mother-substitute. A problem related to separation concerns the case when no object of attachment is available and thus no attachment develops in the first place. Let us look at some specific reactions to childhood separations, the probable forerunners of adult loneliness.

In a variety of experiments in which children have been separated briefly from mother, several common reactions were found to occur.[19]

1. *When mother leaves, children aged 11–36 months stop playing, express distress, and often search.*
2. *Children of age 2 do not exhibit noticeably less reaction to separation than do 1-year-olds, but children of age 3 do.*
3. *Children use vision and verbal communication with mother rather than touching her as they get older.*

Adults are well aware of these reactions. In one study of 700 children and their parents in Nottingham, England, researchers Newson and Newson found that 27 percent of the parents used threats of abandonment as a means of discipline.[20]

### Bowlby's Theory of Attachment

Bowlby believes that attachment is instinctive in its origins. Aside from the common observation that attachment and separation reactions occur in animals, there is some hard evidence for support of Bowlby's position as it applies to animals. The key is to show that attachment is not learned. In fact, "rigorous evidence that attachment behaviour can develop and be directed towards an object that supplies none of the traditional rewards of food, warmth, or sex is available only for guinea pig, dog, sheep and rhesus monkey."[21] For example, in the famous research of Harry Harlow, infant monkeys were raised in the presence of two artificial mother-objects—one made of cloth and the other of wire. Regardless of which mother-object had the bottle and nipple sticking out, the baby monkeys formed an unmistakable attachment to the soft mother-object. They clung to it for 15 hours daily, versus one or two hours for the the wire mother-object.[22] When frightened, they clung to the cloth mother-object in terror.[23] Harlow's work shows that attachment in infant monkeys (1) occurs without prior learning and (2) is directed toward an object mainly on the basis of softness of touch. In brief, Bowlby's theory seems to hold for some animals. Does it hold for man?

So far, no one has been sadistic enough to repeat the many animal studies on humans. For this fact, we can be thankful. However, it also forces Bowlby to admit that "inevitably, the evidence for man is inconclusive."[24] A similar case exists for the origin of the fear of separation, whose genesis as yet remains undetermined.[25] Therefore the theoretical issue of nature versus nurture is a matter for the scientists. Of more relevance are the processes of attachment and separation for us as users.

### Attachment as Adaptive

There seems to be agreement on the biological adaptiveness of attachment, regardless of how it comes to be. The young animal without a predisposition to attach itself to mother will make a juicy meal for predators. The same is true for the human infant, a creature more helpless than most animal infants. Presumably those animals and humans having predispositions to form attachments wired into them have been selected to survive by the evolutionary process. Thus attachment seems highly adaptive for the survival of the young human infant.[26]

### Attachment in Adults

All this information on attachment bears directly on the emotional processes of the developing person. The natural process of separation leads to a fear of signals associated with separation. From research, we know that, for children, such signals include sudden noise, strange people, animals, and darkness.[27] Certainly, the individual child associates the fear of separation with a personal and unique set of signals that eventually come to elicit fear in and of themselves.

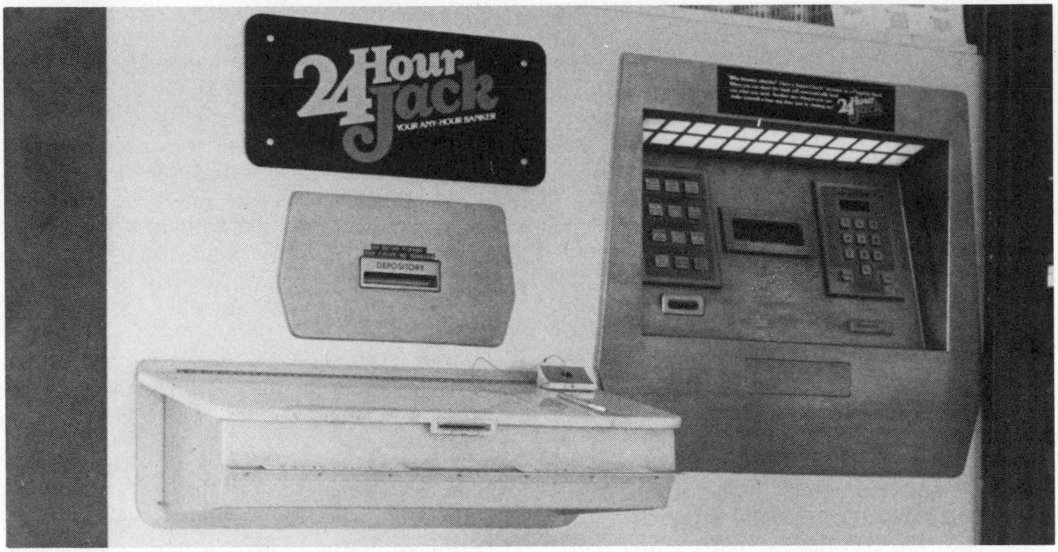


**Figure 2.2.** Example of technology that induces one to spend less time at home: a 24-hour machine banking service. (Photograph by Charles Blakey.)

The process by which attachment becomes elaborated into the vastly more complex patterns of intimacy seeking in adulthood remains cloaked in mystery. Until research can shed light on this matter, it is reasonable to speculate that the maturing mind learns to distinguish between "access to" and "presence of" objects of attachment; that is, most of the time adults need access to others rather than their immediate presence in order to avoid distress. When access is blocked to social participation that leads to emotional intimacy or social intimacy, we feel loneliness.

## Attachment in Modern Society

What happens to our predisposition for attachment when it exists in the modern, manmade world? There are a number of indications that all is not well. "Only in the more economically developed human societies, especially in the Western ones, are infants commonly out of contact with mother for many hours a day and often during the night as well," asserts Bowlby.[28] He then goes on to propose that too little mothering is the main problem, although smothering a child with attention can stunt the child's exploration activities, leading to an unhealthy, anxious kind of attachment.[29]

As a summary, Bowlby states, "It is unfortunate that the modern technological world works against us. Prodigal in the material wealth it yields, it must be recognized that, by its emphasis on mobility and its contempt for the stay-at-home, it is no friend of mental health."[30] The rest of this chapter and Chapter 5 further explore this theme.

## INDICATIONS OF LONELINESS TODAY

### Snapshots of the Golden Age of Loneliness

Before jumping into empirical evidence that associates reported loneliness with problems in modern living, let us pause to reflect anecdotally on modern life in the Western world. To the astute observer, there are indications everywhere that a lot of people are lonely. One observer, Ralph Keyes, gives us verbal snapshots in his book *We the Lonely People: Searching for Community*.[31] In this section, I summarize a few of the many vivid indications Keyes presents as indications of inadequate human contact. For our purposes, these verbal snapshots can be considered a potpourri of the modern loneliness problem. The events pictured are neither cause nor effect but rather elements in a web of mutual cause-and-effect.

Modern-day shopping involves patronizing stores such as supermarkets that are engi-

**Figure 2.3.** Automobiles bring people together, but roads slice up neighborhoods and travel by car occupies much of our time. What is the overall result? (Photograph by Charles Blakey.)

neered to minimize human contact, maximize buying, and get us out as quickly as possible. Unlike some modern European supermarkets, there are no special places to linger in them; and we are ushered out through checkout lines as quickly as the store manager can arrange it. Psychologists who cooperate with this trend have even done research to determine what kind of music keeps our feet moving most quickly as we shop. We do not resist. We believe that "supermarkets are a great advance over the corner store."[32] In short, we *want* to be rushed out; we don't want to linger.

Personal billing messages are typed by computers and delivered by unknown mailmen. Anonymity brings relief from urban stress. We purchase unlisted telephone numbers. We may remove our name from the apartment directory or abbreviate it.

If you encounter problems in relating to people, a new escape exists: Just move away. If you are married, get a no-fault divorce. You can light out down the interstate and change your place of residence just like 40 million Americans do every year.[33]

We vote down bond issues for parks. Who needs parks in suburbia when everyone has his own backyard? Besides, parks bring in a less desirable type of people.

A survey of 75 white, middle-class male suburbanites in Michigan showed that most of their relations with other men on the block took place standing up. These men defined a good neighbor as "one who 'is available for emergency aid; can be called on to trade mutual aid; lends and can be loaned to; respects privacy; friendly, but not friends.' Only four of the men said they had neighbors they also considered friends."[34]

Technology often comes to the rescue. In ancient times, the dishes were washed and dried in a ritual of family cooperation, as in the home of one Jimmy Flanders, age 6. Now one person loads the dishwasher. Superior technology, is it not?

Much if not most family interaction used to occur during regular mealtimes. Individually portioned foods, frozen dinners, fast foods, and other technological advances now allow family members to organize their daily time schedule around their own desires, not around three regular meals. The accomplishments of food-service technology are truly impressive. Also, you can withdraw money for a shopping excursion at any hour your heart desires. This opportunity is made possible by automated banking machines, as shown in Figure 2.2.

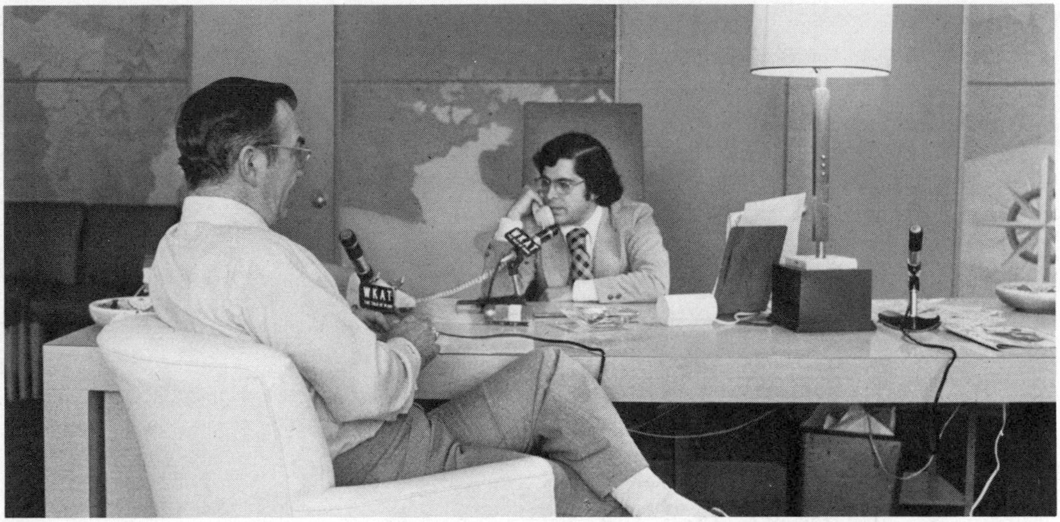


**Figure 2.4.** A call-in talk show in progress: a vicarious substitute for intimacy. (Photograph by Charles Blakey.)

ACTIVITY 2.2.

Keyes states, "Cars are at once our greatest convenience, our most certain place of privacy, and our major source of mobility."[35] Have cars contributed to human contact? If so, why? If not, what might be done to change the role of cars in facilitating human contact? (See Figure 2.3.)

______________________________________

______________________________________

______________________________________

______________________________________

______________________________________

______________________________________

______________________________________

______________________________________

______________________________________

______________________________________

Once inside the castle of one's home, a variety of media are available for the PASSIVE person. We can sit there and soak up television, stereo with or without headphones, radio, excellent news publications, and a dazzling variety of magazines carefully tailored to our own special interests.

Certain media offer substitutes for face-to-face intimacy. The faultless Johnny Carson can engage anyone in witty conversation. Call-in talk shows have grown by leaps and bounds to the point of specialization, such as call-in talk shows about sports or sex (Figure 2.4 shows one in progress).

According to Keyes, true intimacy requires "a time to cry, to reveal, to take off one's shoes and relax. . . . To do so with friends, even with family (maybe especially with family) is scary and risky. It might lead to rejection, even worse—to commitment. The safest, most convenient alternative is to seek a few day's intimacy with strangers, love and let loose."[36] We see the fear of intimacy illustrated in a cover story in the January 1974 issue of *McCall's;* it's about Elizabeth Taylor and is entitled "I Don't Ever Want to Be That Much in Love Again."[37] The famous actress provides millions with a clear display of vicarious punishment. The model to be imitated is Elizabeth Taylor; the punished action is human contact, commitment, and giving; and the punishment is separation from Richard Burton, with ensuing grief. Ms. Taylor says, "I don't want to give as much of myself. It hurts. I didn't reserve anything. I gave everything away . . . my soul, everything . . . and it got bruised and hurt. Like a snail, I guess I'm retreating. . . ."[38]

Take a look at the weekend movie section

**Figure 2.5.** A modern singles bar: loneliness today and the search for contact. (Photograph by Charles Blakey.)

and classified ads in any metropolitan paper. Singles dances, cruises for divorced people, clubs for tall people, and direct advertisements for companionship are the order of the day. Singles clubs and publications flourish, reflecting an intense need for human contact, as illustrated in Figures 2.5, 2.6, and 2.7.

Gaze about the local newsstand or porno place in almost any big city in the United States and you will find another kind of magazine, the swingers' magazines. These carry thousands of ads and have circulations in the hundreds of thousands. Just send in a dollar, and your letter will be forwarded to someone advertising for sex with "discretion assured." (See Figure 2.8.)

Keyes believes that the moving force behind withdrawal is raw fear. We fear intimacy. We fear being known.[39] The alternative to fear is intimacy, or community, which Keyes defines uniquely. For Keyes, *community* means that your presence is recognized as unique and your absence will be noticed. In times of yesteryear, "we lived on a smaller scale and we were stuck with each other, there was no choice but to accept and forgive. Being known wasn't so scary because there wasn't much alternative."[40] In the old days, home and homey kinds of hangouts served as locations for community. Today our job is reestablishing community somehow. The solutions cannot involve turning back the technological clock. Rather, truly modern solutions will involve structuring time and space.

ACTIVITY 2.3.

List in the space provided the places in your life where you would be missed if you were gone; that is, list the names of specific persons or groups who would make a real effort to trace your whereabouts if you were to suddenly vanish.

______________________________
______________________________
______________________________
______________________________
______________________________
______________________________
______________________________
______________________________
______________________________
______________________________

To create community again, Keyes suggests three main routes. First is to somehow create hangouts again, such as the neighborhood drugstore, grocery store, or bar that serves a definable community. Second is to create towns or family clans that number no more than 500. Unfortunately, he offers no suggestions for creating these. Third, Keyes suggests that people join common-interest groups and clubs. Keyes has given us an artful snapshot album picturing the current golden age of loneliness; it is perhaps too much to ask that he give us the answers as well. At the end of his book, he finally admits, "So, like most, I'm reduced to grabbing for community where I can find it."[41] But he does give us a couple of ideas that may help pave the road toward possible solutions: (1) Places where community is found, including hangouts, welcome a diversity of generations.[42] (2) Regular meetings for airing issues of hostility and love seem essential for the relief of stress.

ACTIVITY 2.4.

Suppose you were to take Keyes at his word and see to it that your household has a diversity of generations living in it. What gains and losses would you incur if one elderly in-law and one small child were both adopted and came to live in your household right now? Try to be specific in listing both gains and losses.

**THE SINGLE FLORIDIAN®**

Published by:
D. Pincus
P. O. Box 414675
Normandy Branch
Miami Beach, Florida 33141
EDITOR - Dorothy Pincus
Activities Editor - Lorraine Silver
Assistants to the Editor:
Stephanie Pincus, Wendy Pincus
Secretary - Lillian Blaik

**Subscription Rates:**
$ 5.50 for 6 months
$10.00 per year

We assume no responsibility for listings, events, or changes in programs.
© 1973 Dorothy Pincus

**September, 1974**
**Vol. 2, No. 5**

**SINGLES DANCE**
Every Tues., Fri., Sat. and Sun., 8-11 p.m.
Couples Welcome Also
STARDUST BALLROOM
Refreshments, Door Prizes, Mixers
1855 Hollywood Blvd.
at 105 N. 19th Ave.
Phone 920-3957

**Age Group Code:**
(A) Under 30
(B) Thirties
(C) Forties
(D) Fifties
(E) Sixty and Over
(F) Mixed

**Hi Fellow Singles:**

Well Summer is over and all the single clubs are starting to swing again.

There are lots of interesting things brewing for singles (like a Weekend Club for Singles) etc., but the plans were not ready in time for this issue. We also couldn't hold the September issue for the Singles Fiesta, so all the news on that will be in our October issue.

Have a good Labor Day Weekend, and a Happy New Year to our Jewish Readers.

Have a good month.

D.P.

**FEATURES**

| | Page |
|---|---|
| Regularly Scheduled Events | 1 |
| Kudos | 3 |
| The Crystal Ball | 3 |
| Rocky Mountain High | 3 |
| Profiles of the Month | 4 |
| Subscription Blank | 5 |
| Julian's Cooking Gems | 6 |
| Travel With Carol | 6 |
| New Clubs Forming | 7 |
| Help Wanted | 7 |
| Rachel Copelan | 7 |
| I'm Single and I Love It | 8 |
| When a Mrs. Becomes a Miss | 8 |
| Calendar | 9 |
| Special Events | 10 |
| Reflections on an August Afternoon | 13 |
| Singles Eye View | 13 |
| Help for Single Parents | 14 |
| Singles Bowling Listing | 14 |
| Dating Menu | 15 |
| Astrological Sign of the Month | 15 |
| Chit Chat Chatter | 15 |
| Dating Ad Section | 16 |
| Special Interest Groups | 19 |
| Dating Services Listing | 19 |
| Swinging Singles Lounges | 19 |
| Key Clubs | 20 |
| Discount Coupons | Inside Back Cover |

Single Floridian September, 1974

**Figure 2.6.** A singles magazine: contents of one issue of *The Single Floridian.* (Copyright 1974 by *The Single Floridian.* Reprinted by permission.)

## Loneliness in the City

A most perceptive theory about loneliness in the city today comes from architect Christopher Alexander. In "The City as a Mechanism for Sustaining Human Contact," he begins with these startling words:

> *People come to cities for contact. That's what cities are: meeting places. Yet the people who live in cities are often contactless and alienated. A few of them are physically isolated . . . almost all of them live in a state of endless inner loneliness. They have thousands of contacts, but the contacts are empty and unsatisfying.*[43]

Alexander goes on to trace the history of loneliness in cities, integrating a variety of sociological arguments. In the remainder of this section, his central arguments are described and evaluated.

Increased technology, mobility, and communication has led to the rise of modern cities. In these cities, there are obviously more contacts per person per day than elsewhere; but the contacts also become more superficial. To overcome the largely trivial human contact available in modern cities, it is necessary for city dwellers to meet other persons *informally on a daily basis.* Unfortunately, the physical arrangements of modern cities and the arrangement of time in our daily lives combine to form an effective barrier against intimate human contact.

Alexander claims that "primary groups" maintained effective human contact in preindustrial society. By *primary group* is meant a small group of people characterized by face-to-face association and cooperation. Three kinds of primary groups once provided interpersonal support and human contact: the extended family (which includes relatives), the neighborhood group of adults, and the children's play group.[44] Unfortunately, the neighborhood group of adults has mostly vanished because today people associate mainly for some specific purpose or function. In days gone by, the preschool child usually had immediate access to a stable cluster of peers. In modern suburbia, the child has access to a changing, unstable peer group at nursery school for perhaps 15 hours a week. However, to a child, the week is 100 waking hours long. For the other 85 hours, the child can go to other children's houses. But seeking out other children in their houses is often difficult before age 4 because streets are unsafe for toddlers, fences are common, and sidewalks do not exist in many areas. At home, there are not likely to be many children because families today are small. Finally, Alexander says that the extended family has been largely replaced by the nuclear family.

In short, the effectiveness of all three primary groups has been seriously reduced, if not destroyed, in the transition to modern city life and suburbia. The primary groups of days gone by have been stripped down to the nuclear family for most of us. And even the nuclear family seems under heavy attack by the stresses of modern life, as divorce statistics show. The loss of a member of the nuclear family can be shattering because fewer kinfolk are around to help survivors, including children, bear the grief. We behold the result of all these factors as haunting loneliness on an epidemic scale throughout the land.

ACTIVITY 2.5.

Alexander implies that financially poor, inner-city youngsters may be better off than their comfortable counterparts in suburbia. Would you agree? What factors other than the role of primary groups might affect the quantity and quality of human contact available to ghetto youngsters?

More specifically, Alexander describes the rise of *the autonomy-withdrawal syndrome* in modern urbanites and suburbanites. He claims that individualism began as a healthy, democratic respect for the individual's rights. Under modern stress, however, this original individualism has become warped into an unrealistic belief in the self-sufficiency of the individual person, or *autonomy.* Tots can be cared for at the day care center; teenagers can hang out with their crowd most of the time; women can make it on their own; men can catch a meal from the Automat; and old people can fend for themselves. In all these cases, real human needs can be "satisfied" with transient human contact or none at all. The unhealthy belief in autonomy is manifested in overt actions of withdrawal.

*Withdrawal* means physical and/or mental retreat from other people. Physical retreat is illustrated, for example, by locking doors; mental retreat is illustrated, for example, by a lady walking down the city sidewalk in curlers, past people who do not exist for her. The withdrawal pattern is common; it is caused by modern stress. Such stresses include pressure to succeed, danger, physical noise, information overload, absence of clear moral guidelines to assist in decision making, and the temptation to take on too many roles at once. The stress can be relieved in several ways, one of which is to seek privacy.[45] Hence the modern worker breathes a sigh of relief upon entering the household at day's end. He and she shut out the stressful world with a blessed close of the door. Privacy reigns supreme, and the backyard takes on added importance, as shown in Figure 2.9. The action of withdrawal is sustained by the relief from daily stresses afforded by privacy.

**SINGLE FLORIDIAN DATING AD SECTION**

An exciting new concept in meeting people, a supplement to the lounge, dance, singles organization scene.

Write about YOU! Your interests, sense of life, your likes and dislikes, whatever you feel gives a sense of you.
Reading the ads will help you get ideas.
You are completely anonymous. Ads are listed by box number.

ADS are 10¢ per word. Replies are 50¢ each.

Place in a sealed, stamped envelope with your return address. In pencil write the box number you are replying to. Place this envelope in an envelope addressed to The Single Floridian Magazine and enclose 50c for each reply. We will forward your letter.

**MALE ADS**

M 107 (MB) - Single young man, 40ish, seeking young female mate. Loves dancing, swimming, ice skating, boating, concerts, ballet, music, movies, nature hikes, theatre, and outdoor barbecues.

M 117 (NM) Tall businessman, 43, wide varied interests from sports to heavy discussion, would like to meet a slim, confident woman to share these interests.

M 125 (SW) Considerate male, private pilot, physical education teacher is interested in meeting a slim 25-32 year old female who is in love with love, and feels that loving someone special and being loved in return, is the most important thing in her life.

M 135 (SW) - Nice looking, intelligent man, 5'9", is looking for swinging woman under 35 who enjoys parties, movies and intellectual pursuits. Being together can be beautiful!

M 139 - (Ft.L.) Male, mid 40's, 5'8", young at heart! Would like to meet girl in 30's, also young at heart! Likes dancing, theatre, movies, and fun.

M 145 (MIA) Good looking, tall, professional guy, 35, recently divorced, can't handle bar scene. Seeks attractive, modern thinking, sophisticated, unencumbered partner 23-33 for boating, tennis, etc.

12

**MALE ADS**

M147 (Hol.) College professor, tall, trim, nice appearing. I'm in my late 40's, mod, fun-loving. Beach pad. I wish to meet a slender, witty, attractive lady, unencumbered, good sense of humor: for beach, dancing, weekend camping, great conversations. Hollywood area.

M 149 (PP) Single man, 5'3", 30 years old, looking for short female who plays tennis and swims.

**FEMALE ADS**

F 124 - (Hia) Sincere Aquarius, 5'3", brunette with a zest for loving and living, desires to meet gentleman over 40 years; for dining, fishing, boating. Sincere only need reply.

F 132 - (SM) Female, attractive, 5'9", 25, totally enjoys life, has a wide range of interests and will try almost anything; loves dancing, seeks tall male, 28-35 with intelligence, personality and good sense of humor..

F 134 - (MB) Short, blonde, conservative, Cancer, 25, new to Miami. Wishes to meet fun loving, ambitious, established, Jewish males 25+. Enjoys shows, dinner, talk. No hassles!

F 136 - (MB) I am warm, compassionate, and love laughter. I'm also serious, quiet and poetic. I enjoy people, life, ideas, good conversation, reading and children. Particularly my own two beautiful little girls. I am 34, 5'7", pretty and ALIVE.

Single Floridian March 1974

**Figure 2.7.** The dating ad section of *The Single Floridian.* (Copyright 1974 by *The Single Floridian.* Reprinted by permission.)

ACTIVITY 2.6.

Buy a copy of your local newspaper, and bring the newspaper to class. Begin on page 1 and go through the paper, marking items that reflect modern trends toward or away from human contact. All items are fair game, from the story in which a president advises us to ask not what our country can do for us, but ask what we can do for ourselves, to the want-ad publicizing a high-rise with better security than Alcatraz had. Using your one-day slice of local life as the sole basis for judgment, is the overall trend toward or away from human contact?

ACTIVITY 2.7.

Suppose we view various means of withdrawing as part of a larger vicious cycle wherein stress causes withdrawal, which causes more stress by reducing intimate human contact, which causes more stress, which causes more withdrawal, and so on. From your own experience, identify a person you know well and trace the specific actions that might be involved in such a vicious cycle of withdrawal stress withdrawal stress. The individual need not be lonely or disturbed, and you need not name him or her. Rather, the individual should be someone whom you know well, even yourself.

______________________________

______________________________

______________________________

______________________________

______________________________

______________________________

______________________________

______________________________

______________________________

______________________________

**Figure 2.8.** A pornography store: loneliness today and a substitute for intimacy. (Photograph by Charles Blakey.)

Let us summarize Alexander's basic claim: Individuals in modern society face a loneliness problem greater than that faced by their parents and grandparents. To establish that loneliness plagues us more than our ancestors, Alexander uses two main lines of argument. The sociological argument that the main primary groups have vanished presumes that those primary groups were functioning well in the good ole days. Unfortunately, virtually no direct data are available to reflect just how interpersonally good the good ole days really were, apart from nostalgic speculation. However, photographs and newspaper articles supply some evidence. Two recent books document the hardships of days gone by: *Wisconsin Death Trip*[46] and *The Good Old Days—They Were Terrible!*[47] Figure 2.10 gives you a sample from the former book. (Incidentally, memorial photography of infants was an accepted art form at the time Van Schaick took his pictures, George Talbot tells me.[48])

A more promising line of argument would tie loneliness directly to indicators of modern social problems, such as mental illness and suicide. For this argument, Alexander marshals convincing evidence and we shall do likewise. In the following section, support will be provided for the claim that loneliness is associated with indicators of modern-day problems in living.

## EVIDENCE CONCERNING LONELINESS TODAY

### The Nature of Correlational Evidence

In this section, we review evidence showing that loneliness is related to indicators of problems in modern living. The evidence is correlational, which means only that two variables are "related." In *positive correlation,* when one variable goes up, the other also goes up. For instance, IQ scores and grades in high school are positively correlated because people who score higher on IQ tests tend to have higher grades in high school. In *negative correlation,* when one variable goes up, the other goes down. For example, athletic ability and grades in high school might be negatively correlated if those with athletic ability stay away from their studies.

Our aim is to show that indicators of problems in living go up when reported loneliness goes up, and vice versa. Merely to show such

**Figure 2.9.** Loneliness today and the withdrawal-autonomy syndrome, whereby privacy reigns supreme and the backyard becomes sacred. (Photograph by Charles Blakey.)

a relationship by no means demonstrates that one variable causes the other. Rather, correlational evidence allows us to conclude only that reported loneliness and problems in modern living somehow "go together." This conclusion is important enough.

### Widespread Loneliness

In the nationwide survey conducted by Norman Bradburn (see Chapter 1), participants were asked, "During the past few weeks, did you ever feel *very* lonely or remote from other people?" Of a national sample that matched the United States population as a whole, 26 percent replied yes to this question.[49] Note that the question asked if they were "very" lonely.

For several years, Vello Sermat has been taking surveys concerning felt loneliness. In one report, his assistants content-analyzed 401 autobiographical essays written by students at four universities. Results showed that 79 percent of the individuals had experienced "quite upsetting" loneliness at some time in their lives.[50] These reports came from college students, so Sermat then gathered data from a noncollege population as well. He requested volunteers to fill out a survey using an appeal in the Canadian national magazine, *Homemaker's Digest.* Of these respondents, 90 percent indicated having felt quite upsetting loneliness at some time.[51] In conclusion, there is good reason to believe that the experience of loneliness is widespread.

### Loneliness and Social Isolation

Researchers of loneliness distinguish between loneliness and social isolation. Recall that we defined *loneliness* earlier as a feeling. In contrast to the inner feeling of loneliness, *social isolation* means absence of outward actions that characterize interpersonal interaction or social participation. You measure loneliness by asking someone how lonely he or she feels. You can measure social isolation by asking someone *how often* he or she associates with friends or *how many* friends he or she has. In our discussions to follow, we will use these terms consistently as defined here.

Common sense tells us that loneliness and the number of social contacts would be negatively correlated with each other, but not perfectly. After all, you *can* have a great deal of contact with people but still remain emotionally distant. On the other hand, your social needs could hardly be met if you had no contact with others. There is some evidence to show that the relationship between loneliness and number of social contacts is one of negative correlation (i.e., as the number of social contacts goes down, loneliness goes up). Joep Munnichs surveyed 410 persons over age 65 from communities of various sizes to discover just such a negative correlation.[52] As number of contacts went down, felt loneliness went up. In 1945, at the end of World War II, Duvall studied "Loneliness and the Serviceman's Wife" by interviewing 10 fiancées and 67 wives of servicemen.[53] Those women mentioned loneliness most often as their greatest problem, and "the extent of the wife's social participation was closely related to the degree of her loneliness, the more active wives feeling the less lonely."[54]

### Loneliness, Social Isolation, and Suicide

The tragedy of suicide seems to occur most often when the victim needs contact with other people the most. In a study of 26,000 files accumulated by the Los Angeles Suicide Prevention Center, Carl Wold found that emotional depression characterized 85 percent of the callers.[55] And Bradburn found loneliness to correlate 0.72 (out of a possible 1.0) with feelings of depression for men and 0.71 for women.[56] So the feelings of depression and loneliness are positively related.

An extremely detailed study entitled *Adolescent Suicide* was carried out by Jerry Jacobs.[57] Working as a researcher in UCLA's School of Medicine, Jacobs set out to study adolescent suicide attempters immediately following the suicide attempt. Over a 9-month period, he easily acquired a sample of 50 young people who had attempted to kill themselves. Then he found a matched group on nonattempters. Jacobs's final sample consisted of 31 closely matched pairs of attempters and nonattempters. He gleaned an incredibly detailed case history for each teenager. Sometimes suicide notes were available. The following is the third note from a 19-year-old student, who actually did commit suicide at a Los Angeles college.

> *Dad,*
>
> *Im am (sorry) I tried everything but nothing seemed to help. I was afryed to live because I was alone. I asked Margaret for help but I didn't get any. I beegged and prayed with all my heart but she couldn't come back when I needed her most. I love her dad and I love you and Mom. I am sorry I couldn't find help but thats the way it goes. Sorry your son, Gary. P.S. "over"*
>
> *To Margaret, I love you and I no it now. Im sorry it was to late. There is nothing I could say that would make you see what was happening to me. I am sorry.*
>
> *Evens in heavens. Ill love Margaret and Ill wate for you there. Gary.*

Below is the final portion of a letter written by a 17-year-old black male named William to his father the day before his suicide attempt (his second). Reeling from a chaotic upbringing, this boy tried desperately to reunite his parents, but he could not. He lacked intimacy and he knew it.

> *Daddy I am up by myself I been up all night trying to write you something to cheer you up because I could your heart breaking when you first asked Stan's wife if they would have room and that Sunday dad it hard but I fought the tears that burned my eyes as we drove off and daddy part of my sickness when I had taken an overdose I did just want to sleep myself away because I missed you dad you made me feel like I just found where I belong just like a lost piece of puzzle.*
>
> *But when I left I felt like I had killed something inside of an I knew you hated to see me go and I hated to go to but daddy well I knd of missed mother and after I had see her I miss you and I remembered what you said I settle down but daddy I tried hard so I went and bought some sleeping pill and took so both of you could feel the same thing.*

From numerical analyses of events prior to suicide attempts and the case histories themselves, Jacobs's data strongly support his

The naked body of the wife of Fritz Armbruster, a woman who had worked in Best's Butcher Shop, was found frozen by the roadside near Albion, 6 miles from Black River Falls. She and her husband had separated, he living in town, she living alone in the house. Although no one had noticed that she had been suffering from any physical or mental disorder, "2 years ago, the loss of a child is said to have affected her very deeply and may have led to her becoming partially demented. The probability is that she rose in a fit of delirium and wandered away."

[12/4, Town]

"The little child of Newton and Etta Riggs Loomis was removed to the home of its grandparents, Mr. and Mrs. J. C. Loomis, after diphtheria was pronounced to be in the home of Mrs. Ann Riggs, in the hopes that it might escape the dread disease. But the monster followed it and the child died Monday, aged 2 years."

[1/15, County, from Alma]

"Mrs. James Baty of Merrillan, while visiting the family of John Baty at La Crosse, died suddenly of a hemorrhage of the lungs. She leaves a husband, her family of 6 children having died of diphtheria last summer."

[5/8, County]

"Searchers from Glidden, Ashland County, have thoroughly gone over the premises of James Beckey, the hermit, who was found dead in his hut . . . but no money has been found excepting 15 cents. It is generally understood that Beckey had hidden about $50,000 in government bonds. . . . He was a formerly wealthy man, living near Eau Claire. His wife left him 10 years ago and after that time Beckey became morose and solitary. He built a hut near Glidden and had lived the life of a hermit up to the time of his death."

[12/21, State]

Mrs. Friedel had a picture taken of her little baby in its coffin. Then when a fellow came up the road who did enlargements, she had just the baby's face blown up to a two foot picture. But, since the baby's eyes were closed, she had an artist paint them open so she could hang it in the parlor.

[Town Gossip]

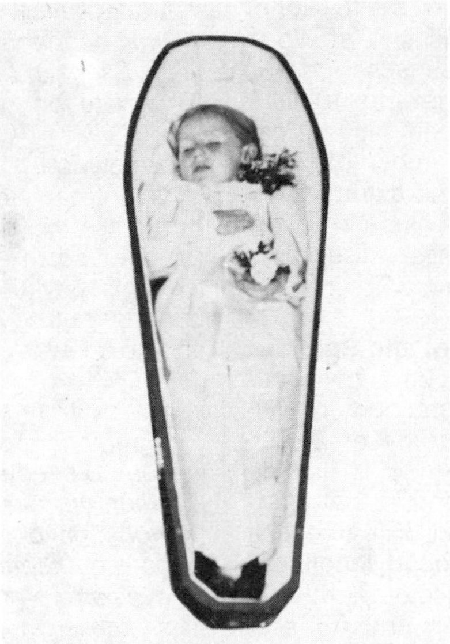

*Figure 2.10. Hardship yesterday, when times were hard and the tragedy of childhood death was common. (Photo is "Small Girl in Casket Standing Upright" by Charles Van Schaick, reproduced by permission of State Historical Society of Wisconsin; text from WISCONSIN DEATH TRIP, by Michael Lesy, Copyright © 1973 by Michael Lesy. Reprinted by permission of Pantheon Books, a Division of Random House, Inc.)*

"A woman was recently found wandering about the streets of Eau Claire with a dead baby in her arms. She was from Chippewa County and had lost her husband and was destitute."

[7/5, State]

"Mrs. Otto Olson, of Hinckley, Minnesota, is wandering about Northern Wisconsin and Minnesota looking for little ones who are supposed to have been burned to death in the great fire at Hinckley last summer. The woman is nearly crazed with grief and clings to the belief that her children are alive."

[11/29, State]

"Admitted March 8th, 1901. Town of Garfield. Norwegian, aged 45. Married. Five children. Youngest 8 months old. Farmer in poor circumstances. . . . Deranged mostly on money matters. Constantly worrying and thinks he owes different parties. . . ."

[Mendota State, 1899 Record Book (Male, J), p. 377, patient # 8756]

"A farmer owning land at Red Cedar Lake claims to have seen a reptile about 40 ft. long in the water, carrying off one of his hogs, which was squealing vigorously."

[8/21, State]

"The dead body of an unknown suicide was found hanging a few days ago to a tree near Potsoi, Grant County. That body was supposed to have been that of a railway workman."

[5/7, State]

"The funeral services of the little child of Jimmie McWilliams that died last Friday was held at his house last Sunday. . . . The whole community deeply sympathize with Mr. McWilliams and wife in this doubly deep-pained affliction, this being their only boy, and the fourth one that death had taken from them during the past few years. Surely this is the point where faith must take the place of reason."

[8/27, State]

theory that a *sequence* of events comes before adolescents' suicide attempts:

> *The process that led to the adolescent suicide attempters' progressive isolation from significant others and, finally, to the suicide attempts, is described below.*
>
> 1. *A long-standing history of problems (from childhood to the onset of adolescence).*
> 2. *A period of "escalation of problems" (since the onset of adolescence and in excess of those "normally" associated with adolescence).*
> 3. *The progressive failure of available adaptive techniques for coping with old and increasing new problems which leads the adolescent to a progressive social isolation from meaningful social relationships.*
> 4. *The final phase, characterized by the chain reaction dissolution of any remaining meaningful social relationships in the weeks and days preceding the suicide attempt.*

(The two suicide notes and the list of four points are from *Adolescent Suicide,* by Jerry Jacobs; the first note is from p. 93, the second is from p. 98, and the list is from p. 64. Copyright © 1971 by John Wiley & Sons, Inc. Reprinted by permission of John Wiley & Sons, Inc.)

Other research on adolescent suicide echoes Jacobs's theory. For example, after compiling detailed case histories of 41 New Jersey schoolchildren, James Jan-Tausch concluded that "in every case of suicide, the child was described as having no close friends with whom he might share confidences or from whom he received psychological support."[58]

What trend is suicide among young people taking? Jacobs reports that suicide is the fifth leading cause of death among adolescents from 15 to 19 years old.[59] Suicide rates for adolescents in that age range rose by 67 percent from 1954 to 1964.

Moving now to suicide among older age groups, we note that Blanc, Bourgeois, and Henry studied 500 cases of young adult suicides in Europe from 1960 to 1964. They concluded, "Statistical treatment of suicidal behavior emphasizes the importance of social isolation and confirms, in the majority of cases, a direct relationship to a socio-affective situation considered intolerable."[60]

E. Wilbur Bock is a sociologist at the University of Florida who has studied suicide in Pinellas County, a retirement area on Florida's West Coast that includes St. Petersburg. In a massive survey project, persons over 65 who committed suicide between 1955 and 1963 were compared with a sample of 2544 elderly respondents who represented the general elderly population of the area in 1959. Bock's extensive findings are summarized here: "Marriage, kin networks, and organizational membership were each independently and significantly associated with suicide. Thus, these were various kinds of social involvement that could provide meaningful interaction and help prevent suicide."[61]

Repeating the findings of numerous studies, Bock found that the widowed, especially men who had lost their wives, were more likely to commit suicide than were the married. Since the male sex role in America stresses achievement and the wife is cast as household social chairman, married men are probably more at a social loss when they lose a spouse than are their wives. As we might expect, elderly widowers were also more socially isolated than were married males, married females, or widows. Curiously, one of the highest suicide rates was displayed by *married* males who had no organizational memberships or kin in the county.

In Bock's research, a nuclear family alone did not suffice to fill all needs for social contact. In fact whether a person belonged to a voluntary organization was a better predictor of suicide than marriage or presence of relatives. In Bock's research, we have data that indirectly support the claim by Weiss that different kinds of loneliness exist and go away in response to different kinds of social interaction.

In conclusion, the evidence to date indicates that loneliness and social isolation are positively correlated with suicide attempts and suicide. The overall amount of empirical data is limited, but it is dramatic and rather consistent.

### Loneliness, Social Isolation, and Various Problems in Living

Telephone crisis centers have spread like wildfire in the last several years. These service

**Figure 2.11.** Telephone crisis center in operation. (Photograph by Charles Blakey.)

centers offer the opportunity for individuals in a crisis to talk to someone immediately, while the crisis still exists. Figure 2.11 shows such a center in operation. The crisis centers also offer researchers a priceless opportunity to collect information about what kinds of problems affect wide segments of the population. Do those who call in feel lonely? Sermat reported in 1973 that "the staff of the Toronto Distress Center, which maintains a 24-hour telephone service for people who want to contact someone during a crisis, report a very high proportion of the nearly 20,000 calls they receive per year bring up the topic of loneliness."[62] In 1974, he reports, "This number is increasing every year."[63]

Ruby Abrahams tabulated the first 560 calls received by the Widowed Service Line, a telephone crisis center serving metropolitan Boston. "Loneliness and isolation were the main problems for approximately 73 per cent of the callers."[64] While most of these callers were female, they were not all elderly; of the 511 who gave their age, exactly one-third were under 50. Thus loneliness is by no means limited to the elderly, even in the use made of a phone crisis center for widows—whom we might expect to be older.

Another place where citizens having problems in living can seek aid is the community service center. Kenneth Kammeyer and Charles Bolton compared clients at two California community service centers (one in the Davis community, the other in the Woodland community) with samples reflecting the whole community.[65] Being a "client" in this study means that, for whatever reason, the person availed herself (himself) of the service center's aid. For our purposes, the critical data involve responses to the researchers' question, "About how often do you get together with friends?"[66] In the Davis community, 72 percent of the clients answered "occasionally" or "never," while only 33 percent of the whole community sample gave these answers. In the Woodland community, comparable figures of 56 percent for clients and 36 percent for the community in general were found. In short it appears that social isolation relates to a variety of problems in living.

In a related study, Marjorie Lowenthal and Clayton Haven sent questionnaires to 112 older people in San Francisco.[67] These researchers defined social isolation as reports of visits only by relatives, reports of having contacts only with persons in the same dwelling, or reports of having contacts only to obtain the necessities of life. Psychiatrists rated the questionnaires independently to render a psychiatric (subjective) judgment—either "impaired" or "unimpaired." Of those respondents having low social interaction, 58 percent were rated as "impaired," or unhealthy, compared with only 27 percent having high social interaction. Again the relation between problems in living and social isolation emerged.

Finally, in a large study of 1000 men diagnosed at an army mental hygiene clinic, Herman Lantz asked the subjects how many childhood friends they had had when they were between 4 and 10 years of age. The results are dramatic. Forty percent of those diagnosed as "normal" reported five or more friends, and none of the normals reported no friends. On the other hand, only 1 percent of those diagnosed as "psychotic" reported five or more friends, and 38 percent reported having no friends.[68]

### Conclusions

From the research reviewed, we can safely conclude that loneliness and social isolation are related to indicators of a variety of problems in modern living, including attempted and successful suicide. However, the research is scarce indeed. Also remember that the problems in living to which loneliness and social isolation have been empirically related are mostly *extreme* problems in living.

There is also some evidence from Bock to show that different kinds of social relationships function independently with respect to one problem in living (suicide). This finding reminds me of the Bradburn results discussed in the last chapter: He found that a successful marriage relationship (emotional intimacy) was associated with a lack of negative feelings. He also found that successful participation in a social network outside marriage (social intimacy) correlates positively with positive feelings. Not only that, but the two relationships were independent of each other. Therefore, indirect as the Bock-Bradburn-Wilson findings are, I will tentatively conclude that the Weiss proposal for two *independently functioning* systems of intimacy has received a measure of support.[69]

### Personal Implications

At this point you may be thinking, "In fact, I have felt loneliness at times and I wish I had more friends. With all that research relating loneliness and isolation to serious problems in living, am I sick? Worse yet, am I mentally ill?" Rest easy, because the answer to this question is no.

It is perfectly normal to feel lonely and wish for more friends. At some time, who doesn't? In addition, the evidence we have reviewed focused on the extremes. At the extremes, deeply disturbing loneliness and social isolation are clearly related to suicide, so I emphasized those results. Also, the research findings offer little specific data about the low and moderate ranges of loneliness, which most of us feel.

Since low and moderate degrees of loneliness are normal, the appropriate course of action is how to minimize it in our own lives. But to minimize any problem, we must be able to get a handle on it by identifying its components. Nobody has ever done that for a loneliness-intimacy dimension.

## ESTABLISHING A DIMENSION FROM LONELINESS TO INTIMACY

I propose the existence of an important interpersonal dimension of human contact that runs from emotional loneliness to emotional intimacy. Although there is no single ideal degree of human contact, for each of us there is an optimal range of human contact. The question relevant for users is, "Specifically what adult modes of action characterize human contact within my optimal range of intimacy?"

Identifying modes of adult action that characterize satisfying emotional-intimacy relationships will be our task in the next chapter. In the process, we will draw on many areas of psychology. If we were to stick with the attachment literature, we would stop at childhood. Even though a lot of attachment research is being done and the methods are being improved, the transition to adulthood is a research vacuum.[70] If we rely on the loneliness literature, we get a view of the problem but no answers. Therefore it is time to shift from the negative emotion of loneliness to the practical attainment of intimacy.

Before proceeding, there are some difficulties with the concept of intimacy. We consider them briefly here because I want you to know what we are up against. In the process, we will focus on adult *emotional* intimacy; so "intimacy" or "loneliness" means emotional intimacy or emotional loneliness from here on out (unless otherwise stated).

A story called "The Tail of a Lonely Elephant" will be used to illustrate some of the difficulties with the concepts of loneliness and intimacy.

**Case 2.4.** Once upon a time, some psychological researchers decided that the findings from rat research were too small. Therefore they did the logical thing and brought an elephant into their experimental chamber. Little did they know that Herbie the elephant had become very lonely during the long voyage from his homeland. Nevertheless the compassionate scientists did the best they could to attend to Herbie's physical needs. After being fed well and cared for, Herbie was ushered into a large glistening white chamber to be researched. Since psychology has developed mainly along the lines of the physical sciences, the scientists decided to analyze components of Herbie's behavior in microscopic fashion. They could integrate the pieces of the puzzle afterward. In the true spirit of this research tradition, two teams of four psychologists each were formed. To avoid any bias, they knew nothing of the study beforehand. They were to be blindfolded, and each one's left hand was to be tied behind each of their backs. One by one, they would enter the chamber to have 5 minutes alone with Herbie. After feeling about with their unrestrained right hands, each would later write a report. The first psychologist grabbed Herbie's tail and felt it move up and down in rhythm. So he reported that a snakelike creature was writhing up and down in rhythm. The second psychologist felt Herbie's huge flat side, so his report told of a gently convulsing flat mass of protoplasm. The third psychologist happened upon the end of Herbie's ivory tusk, and he reported a smooth inanimate object with water running down it. The fourth psychologist felt Herbie's leg and reported that a tree seemed to be growing right out of the floor. In fact all were wrong. In fact the lonely Herbie was crying for some elephant company. The next day four more psychologists had the misfortune to study Herbie, who was mad by then. I'll leave the description of their reports up to you and your imagination. Actually the only person who knew what was happening with Herbie was an undergraduate student hired to be Herbie's keeper. By staying with Herbie many hours each day, the student knew what Herbie looked like and that Herbie was lonely. The student wrote a term paper on his own impressions of Herbie. One of the psychologists gave it a C— because it wasn't typed and no numerical data were presented. The tale has a happy ending because Herbie was able to disguise himself as a race car and earn enough money for his trip home.

Human contact in adulthood has much in common with Herbie.

1. Touching one place on Herbie will not tell us his shape. Similarly, looking at any one specific behavior in the adult human will not tell us much about human contact for that individual. Even in children, a number of separate "control systems" (as Bowlby calls them) function toward a common goal of maintaining closeness to mother. A child may cry, run, search, maintain eye contact, and so on, all with that goal. Not only do adults have multiple means to attain emotional closeness with other people, but we very likely pursue several qualitatively different kinds of closeness as well (e.g., physical proximity, disclosure of personal information). At any given time, one or many control systems may be working.
2. Observing Herbie for 5 minutes or even a couple of hours will not tell us much about him or his goals. Unfortunately, most laboratory experiments last only a brief while. The same is true for the study of intimacy in adults. Only over time do some

of the most significant patterns of adult action appear (e.g., attachment, mating, mothering).

3. Observing Herbie in a sterile experimental chamber will not tell us what he is like in his natural environment. The same holds for the study of intimacy.

The next chapter will present six features of the loneliness-intimacy dimension. The six features do not guarantee intimacy; they merely characterize it. The practicality comes from likely personal betterment if we can at least identify the features that characterize adult intimacy.

## SUMMARY

In this chapter, we addressed the main concepts bearing on close relations to other people. Loneliness was viewed as a painful feeling of being separated or apart, coupled with a wish for improved human contact or intimacy. Weiss distinguished two kinds of loneliness: (1) emotional loneliness, stemming from the absence of close emotional attachments, and (2) social loneliness, caused by lack of an engaging friendship or kin network. Bowlby's concept of attachment was seen as the childhood antecedent of adult dispositions toward emotional intimacy. In both childhood attachment and adult intimacy, separation from the object of attachment leads to eventual distress and a variety of strategies to restore closeness. Unfortunately, certain aspects of modern life work against establishing and maintaining close emotional relationships, as evidenced by widespread loneliness in contemporary society. Not only is reported loneliness widespread, but it is positively related to indicators of a wide variety of problems in living. Although the research on loneliness tends to highlight extreme loneliness and dramatic behavior such as suicide, the concern in this book lies with the low and moderate ranges of loneliness, which most of us feel. I proposed a dimension of interpersonal contact that runs from emotional loneliness to emotional intimacy. Each of us is presumed to have an optimal range of intimacy on this dimension, where we will be most comfortable. In the following chapter, we consider six features of emotional intimacy in human adults.

*PANIC*

*And is there anyone at all?*
*And is*
*There anyone at all?*
*I am knocking at the oaken door . . .*
*And will it open*
*Never now no more?*
*I am calling, calling to you—*
*Don't you hear?*
*And is there anyone*
*Near?*
*And does this empty silence have to be?*

*And is there no-one there at all*
*To answer me?*
*I do not know the road—*
*I fear to fall.*
*And is there anyone*
*At all?*

(From Eithene Tabor, *The Cliff's Edge: Songs of a Psychotic*, p. 36. Copyright 1950 by Sheed and Ward, Inc. Paperback Edition, 1959. Reprinted by permission of Sheed and Ward.)

# FEATURES OF EMOTIONAL INTIMACY

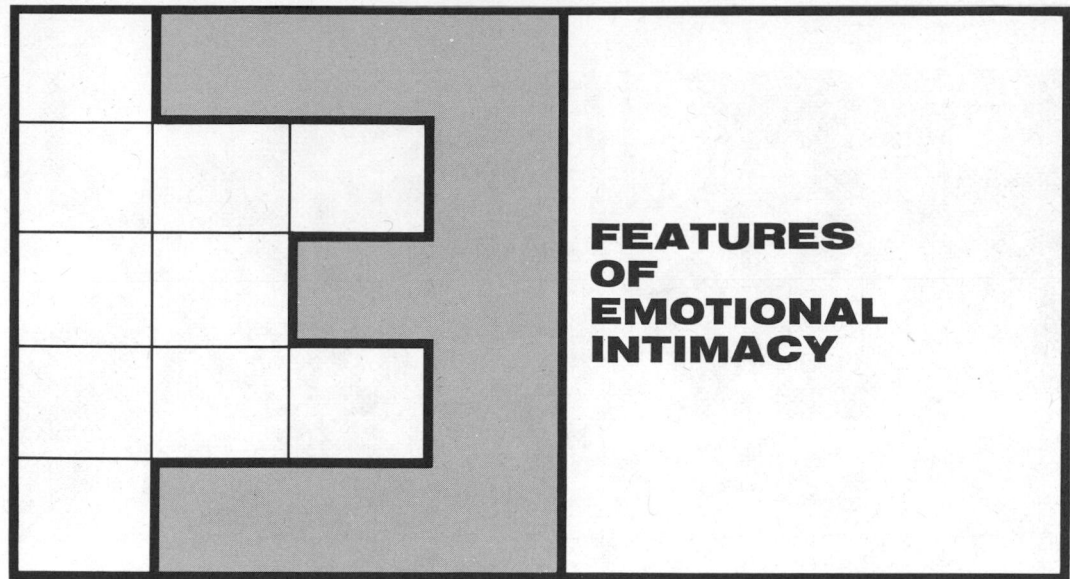

There are six features of emotional intimacy: (1) time for frequent interactions with one other person, (2) informal interactions, (3) self-disclosure, (4) touching, (5) a favorable accumulation of rewards over time, and (6) a fair relationship. The first two are features necessary for emotional intimacy to exist; the second two are necessary for emotional intimacy to develop; and the last two are necessary for emotional intimacy to endure over time. As we consider the six features remember that they do not guarantee emotional intimacy; rather, they characterize it. To put it another way, it seems difficult to conceive of emotional intimacy without the presence of all six *over time.* On any given day or in any given interaction, however, it is unlikely that all features will be present. As in the cases of mating and mothering patterns, a span of months is needed before the full range of features becomes evident. In all except the sixth, the forerunners of each feature can easily be found in childhood patterns of attachment.

## FEATURES NECESSARY FOR EMOTIONAL INTIMACY TO EXIST

### Time for Frequent Interactions with One Other Person

Time to spend with a person is absolutely necessary for emotional intimacy to blossom. In a pioneering statement, Christopher Alexander proposed two necessary conditions for intimate contacts. "These conditions are: (1) The people concerned must see each other very often, almost every day, though not necessarily for very long at a time. (2) They must see each other under informal conditions, without the special overlay of role or situation which they usually wear in public."[1] Alexander claims that if meetings cannot take place with reasonable frequency, establishing an intimate relationship becomes extremely difficult. If two people meet but once a week, conversation about current events and other fascinating but superficial events tends to fill up the time. Without frequent meetings, it is natural to perceive that a relationship has a scattered past and

**Figure 3.1.** Intimates are drawn from friends, friends from acquaintances, and acquaintances from groups such as this. (Photograph by Charles Blakey.)

an uncertain future. Time is certainly a logical necessity for human activity devoted to any purpose, and intimacy is no exception.

The importance of maintaining a stable relationship with one person over time cannot be overemphasized, because emotional intimacy is a deep relationship between two people. You can maintain such relationships with more than one other person, of course; but in each instance the relationship is unique. If the literature on attachment tells us anything, it is that growing humans become attached to a *stable, permanent* figure of attachment. The absence of a permanent mother or a succession of caretakers leads to protest, despair, withdrawal, anxious attachment, and other harmful reactions to separation.

At first blush, the importance of frequent meetings with one other person would seem simple enough to arrange. Unfortunately, modern life favors frequent meetings but not with one person. In *Future Shock,* Toffler claims that one offshoot of rapid technological change is the pressure to move from one human relationship to another.[2] It seems that mobility figures support his claim, at least for the United States. As Vance Packard tells us in *A Nation of Strangers,* 40 million Americans move every year; this is 20 percent of the population. The average American moves 14 times in a lifetime.[3] Similar trends are emerging in other nations according to the extent of their industrialization. Practical measures for dealing with these trends are discussed in the next two chapters.

Finally, note that this first feature of emotional intimacy speaks of frequent interactions that actually occur over time. Frequent meetings are not required during any particular week. The important thing is having frequent meetings over months and years.

### Informal Interactions

As already mentioned, intimate contact requires not only regular meetings, but also informal meetings. Unless the roles of work and public occasions are stripped away, the inherent role expectations spell out rules that define actions in advance and thus inhibit participants from expressing themselves. To attain intimacy requires one to make provision for regular, informal meetings, which may be difficult indeed. Informal interactions means meetings not characterized by the predominance of a commercial transaction or any other set of role requirements that prescribe what one is to do during the course of the interaction.

Both the features of time for frequent interactions and time for informal interactions cause me to think about the time we often grudgingly give to the elderly. As for myself, I am already looking toward old age with some uneasiness about the time my family and friends will spend with me then. This concern about time allocation and the elderly is explored further in an addendum to this chapter.

ACTIVITY 3.1.

How much informal time do you have during the week? On weekends? Can you interact informally while eating? Driving? Watching TV? Shopping?

________________________________________

________________________________________

________________________________________

________________________________________

________________________________________

## FEATURES NECESSARY FOR EMOTIONAL INTIMACY TO DEVELOP

### Self-Disclosure

Given that there is time available for frequent and informal meetings with one other person, increased intimate contact seems to be virtually defined by self-disclosure of personal information. Since 1960 the investigation of self-disclosure has been spearheaded by Sidney Jourard almost singlehandedly. An interesting personality himself, Jourard became convinced early in his clinical practice that good therapy requires self-disclosure, especially self-disclosure by the therapist. He summarizes his views in this way:

> *Self-disclosure is a symptom of personal health and a means of ultimately achieving a healthy personality. When I say that self-disclosure is a symptom of personal health, I mean that a person who displays many of the other characteristics that betoken healthy personality will also display the ability to make himself fully known to at least one other significant human being.*[4]

Alexander equates intimacy and self-disclosure for all practical purposes: "Intimate contact is that close contact between two individuals in which they reveal themselves in all their weakness, without fear."[5] As for the importance of intimate contact, Alexander claims it is crucial: "An individual can be healthy and happy only when his life contains three or four intimate contacts. A society can be a healthy one only if each of its members has three or four intimate contacts at every stage of his existence."[6]

Why should disclosing ourselves (to some optimum degree) make us feel better? We scientists cannot give you the answer now. The best we have to offer is the recent "opponent-process theory of motivation" of Richard Solomon and John Corbit.[7] These authors claim that our emotions are not single states but *dual cycles.* For example, they say that positive feelings of love and intimacy must be followed by negative feelings of loneliness. Somehow, perhaps with the evolution of the human brain through the eons of time, our nervous systems developed a balancing mechanism to assure stability of emotions to aid in survival. Possibly making love all the time could be hazardous to your health!

ACTIVITY 3.2.

Answer this question: Why should self-disclosure (to some optimum degree) make us feel better? Ralph Keyes's observation may assist you: "Problems discussed openly in a meeting are so much less threatening than those muttered in hallways."[8]

________________________________________

________________________________________

________________________________________

________________________________________

________________________________________

________________________________________

*Love and friendship are there for the purpose of continually providing the opportunity for solitude.*

RANIER MARIA RILKE

*Love has no meaning without loneliness; loneliness becomes real only as a response to love.*

CLARK MOUSTAKAS

### Evidence Concerning Self-Disclosure

Sensible as the claims by Jourard and Alexander may sound to us, they need support by evidence. A modest body of evidence exists. In a survey of elderly people in the San Francisco area, Lowenthal and Haven inquired about the presence of at least one confidant in whom each respondent could confide.[9] Oldsters who lacked a confidant were also likely to feel depressed about life. Those having at least one confidant felt more positive life satisfactions than those lacking a confidant, regardless of whether the level of social interaction had increased or decreased over the last year. This finding repeats, or replicates, the Bradburn results.[10]

In other research, Jourard found that self-disclosure and liking are positively correlated; so, in general, we like persons more who disclose more.[11] Does this relationship hold up in marriage? Apparently it does, since Levinger and Senn found that marital satisfaction is correlated with self-disclosure to one's partner.[12] However, these results show clearly the weakness of correlational studies: Does liking cause disclosure or does disclosure cause liking? Clearly, it would be comforting to have some studies in which one factor came first and therefore *produced* the other.

In one such study, Taylor, Altman, and Sorrentino arranged for liking to come before and therefore cause disclosure.[13] They exposed U.S. Navy recruits to actors, who acted so as to appear more and less likable. As we would expect, the recruits disclosed more to the more likable, more positive partners. Therefore liking can cause disclosure. On the other hand, it also seems true that disclosure *may* cause liking: Worthy, Gary, and Kahn found that individuals liked others more who had disclosed more in a laboratory experiment.[14] Thus there is some laboratory evidence for both the liking ⟶ disclosure idea and for the disclosure ⟶ liking idea. Both processes probably operate in real life.

The conclusion that self-disclosure *can* cause liking is important because you can change your own self-disclosure patterns more easily than how another person likes you. However, common sense would clearly suggest that the disclosure ⟶ liking process operates only under conditions of selective disclosure. Telling strangers all our faults will not lead them to like us!

ACTIVITY 3.3.

Think about the people in your immediate family as you were growing up. Who disclosed the most? Who disclosed the least? Why? Were cultural roles involved? If you had the power, how would you have changed the patterns of disclosure in your family at that time? Can one disclose too much?

________________________________________

________________________________________

________________________________________

________________________________________

Reviewing Jourard's pioneering research provides a fascinating potpourri of findings about self-disclosure.[15] For example, does the "rugged manliness" cultural role for men predict that man disclose less than women? Indeed, men do disclose less about themselves than women.[16] Jourard believes that living up to the "tough guy," or machismo, image produces incompetence at loving through lack of insight and empathy because tough guys settle disputes in their own characteristic way. Not only do women disclose more, but they receive more personal communications than men.[17] Jourard also believes that disclosing less makes men more difficult to love than women. Do you agree? Jourard has found that when we marry, our self-disclosure becomes concentrated toward our spouse, although the total amount of information disclosed remains unchanged by marriage.[18] As we might predict, people who like their parents more also tend to be high disclosers to others in general.[19]

In a study of person perception, Dalmas Taylor and Leonard Oberlander showed pictures that contained human versus nonhuman figures to Navy men. Men who reported disclosing more about themselves to others were also more skillful at detecting if a given picture contained a human figure imbedded in it. This result held only for detecting human figures, not nonhuman figures. Thus high disclosers may be more sensitive to certain human cues in their perception of the environment.

In laboratory experiments, the length of interaction is usually short, lasting only a few minutes or hours. However, the results of such experiments may tell us something important about self-disclosure in short interactions. Specifically, several researchers have found that a lot of personal disclosure crammed into a short time leads to *less* liking from the other person. Jourard found self-disclosure by student nurses to parents and female friends to correlate highly with grades in nursing courses.[20] More disclosure was associated with better grades in nursing courses, but not in nonnursing courses. In an experiment by Kaplan, Firestone, Degnore, and Moore, participants role-played interviewees in three different interview settings: business, psychotherapy, and sexual.[21] The interviewer was played by an experimenter. "In all settings, interviewer attractiveness decreased with intimacy of question [asked by the interviewer], this effect being especially pronounced under the high-formality business setting."[22] These results are important because they support the claim that *developing emotional intimacy is a gradual process that cannot be hurried.*

ACTIVITY 3.4.

Think about your present or anticipated job. Would self-disclosure on or off the job assist you in your work? Might the same apply to you in training or on the job? Why or why not?

______________________________

______________________________

______________________________

______________________________

______________________________

### Social Penetration Theory

Irwin Altman and Dalmas Taylor's theory of social penetration is a theory about intimacy.[23] They propose a "social penetration" dimension similar to our loneliness-intimacy dimension, but they do not discuss loneliness. According to their theory, as you get to know someone more deeply, it is like peeling away the layers of an onion. With continued interaction under conditions favorable for intimate contact, you move from outer toward inner layers of the self.

Figure 3.2 shows the movement toward intimacy at a variety of stages. Persons A and B, say yourself and your other person, are in the process of coming closer together. The arrows represent penetrations, which have two aspects. These two aspects characterize ways of theorizing about the dual nature of self-disclosure. We will consider each of these in turn.

The *category depth* aspect concerns how deep, personal, or private are the topics of conversation. As you move from outer skin to inner core, you uncover more vulnerable and unique aspects of your other person. Altman and Taylor list several key properties to category depth.[24] As you proceed from outer skin to inner core, you go in the direction suggested by the following statements:

1. From biographical information (e.g., age, sex, personal history) to central fears, self-concepts, and values.
2. From specific fragments of the other person to general, basic structures. From these basic structures, you should be able to predict your other person's actions and feelings in many situations. Such basic structures might include one's basic trust of other people.[25]
3. From high visible to low visible facts about your other person. Blond hair is high visible; a secret love affair is low visible.
4. From common to unique traits of personality. A southern accent may be common, while membership in a snake-handling religious sect is unique.
5. From safe to vulnerable information (if the information disclosed were headlined on page 1!).
6. From socially desirable to socially undesirable characteristics.
7. From momentary emotions to long-standing emotional commitments.

The *category breadth* aspect concerns the range of topics of conversation, such as fam-

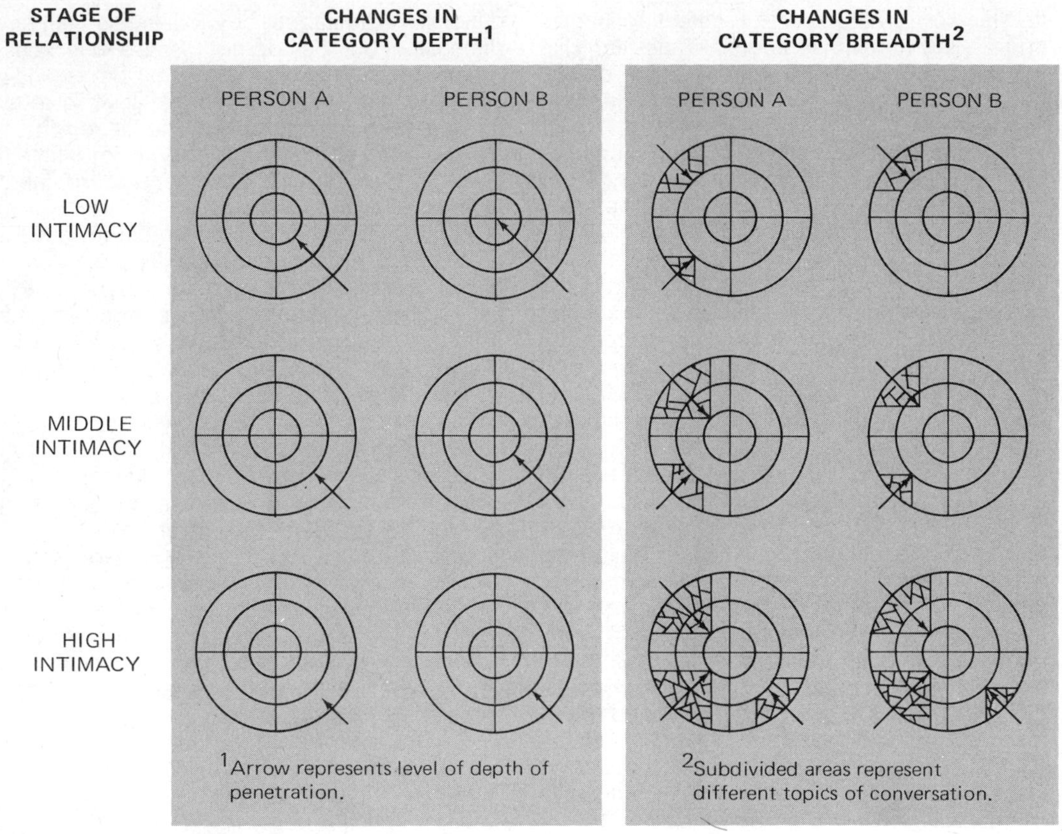


**Figure 3.2.** The social penetration process. (Closely adapted from SOCIAL PENETRATION: THE DEVELOPMENT OF INTERPERSONAL RELATIONSHIPS by Irwin Altman and Dalmas A. Taylor. Copyright © 1973 by Holt, Rinehart and Winston, Inc. Reprinted by permission of Holt, Rinehart and Winston, Inc.)

ily or school. If you refer to the right box in Figure 3.2, you will see social penetration, category depth, and category breadth all illustrated. As you penetrate deeper, the arrow of penetration cuts a swath in a given topic area. Depth is how deep toward the center the arrow goes. Breadth is indicated by the number of arrows (different topics of conversation) and subdivisions within each topic. In their book *Social Penetration: The Development of Interpersonal Relationships,* Altman and Taylor have collected a body of evidence convincing enough to indicate that their theory is on the right track.

One of Altman and Taylor's claims is that emotional intimacy is accompanied by a specific pattern of information exchange. Altman and Taylor predict two events as you develop emotional intimacy with another person:

1. You will have a rapid increase in the exchange of more superficial information, which soon levels out.
2. You will have a slow increase in highly personal information exchanges. This rise will be marked by occasional plateaus, where you stay at the same level of intimacy (or category depth) while exploring the other person's personality in a variety of areas.

Their research bears out the likelihood that these two processes do accompany social penetration. Both specific processes were found to occur in the friendship development of college roommates,[26] of Navy recruits paired off and confined with each other in a room for 10 days,[27] and in two laboratory studies of short duration.[28]

In short, self-disclosure has two aspects, both of which agree with common sense. Category depth means how deeply you get to know your other person, and category breadth reflects the range of your acquaintanceship. Some degree of both depth and breadth are required for intimacy. Without depth, a relationship is shallow. Without some breadth, you do not have an intimate, but rather a colleague or acquaintance who touches on a narrow base (e.g., engineering, accounting, physical sex).

### Self-Disclosure in the Hospital

Sidney Jourard wrote his popular text *The Transparent Self* especially for nurses taking college courses. In "Part Six: A Human Way of Being for Nurses (and Other Helping Professionals)," he preaches the gospel of mental health through self-disclosure. His occasional references to the need for privacy are generally overwhelmed by a flood of information about the blessings of making yourself transparent. In response, Paul Cozby finishes his review of the self-disclosure research with the warning that "value-laden speculations that close off areas of investigation can only be seen as a hindrance to our understanding of self-disclosure."[29] The speculations were unmistakably those of Jourard, and the area closed off was the need for privacy. The hospital represents one job situation, and the same issue is present in other job settings, where everyone encounters acquaintances and friends. "How much should I disclose?" That is the question.

A simple resolution of this matter would make the distinction between work and play. We could disclose only slightly on the job so we can develop emotional intimacy—and really do it right—while off the job. However, the case is not that simple. As Jourard points out in condemning his favorite topic, the standoffish "bedside manner" used by some nurses to insulate themselves from patients, the job itself may demand a considerable amount of self-disclosure.[30] OK, so the nurse has got to be able to elicit enough self-disclosure to help diagnose initially and to console the patient later. But where does it end? Is the poor nurse not in role conflict between the demands of her (his) role as human being versus her role as professional having scarce time? Does a similar situation apply to you in your current or anticipated job?

To aid in resolving this issue, I can offer some shamefully general suggestions. First, there exists a purely social aspect to almost all jobs today. For most of us, a reservoir of potential friends and intimates is to be found on the job. The same holds true for all the other people at our job. Therefore it is not wise to refrain so much from self-disclosure as to alienate acquaintances on the job. (The unique value of acquaintances is discussed more fully in Chapter 11 on Meeting New People.) Second, certain tasks at work require self-disclosure by at least one party (e.g., the incoming patient in a hospital). I predict happiness on the job to be greater for those who are at least willing to disclose as much about themselves to clients as clients are expected to disclose.[31] Third, each person's privacy should be respected.

## Touching

### The Importance of Touching in Adulthood

Must you touch your other person in the process of being emotionally intimate? Do we not touch good friends more, including those of the same sex? Is not "physical distance away from" a general gauge of intimacy? Distance away from can be far apart. Distance apart can be very small, as when two bodies unite in sexual intercourse. Logically, touching is not necessary for intimacy because two people might fall deeply in love over the years but never touch each other. However, despite this extreme possibility and logical disclaimer about the absolute necessity of touching for intimacy, we are going to assume that at least some touching is necessary for intimacy with either sex for all practical and realistic purposes.

In recent popular books, such as Desmond Morris's *Intimate Behavior*[32] and Ashley Montagu's *Touching,*[33] the innate need for human touching has been eloquently voiced. The same argument is voiced by developmental neuropsychologist James Prescott.[34] The argument goes like this: Before birth,

you were touched on all sides and joggled around so that your senses bathed in the richness of superstimulated body contact. After birth, your senses were deprived of such stimulation. If you were lucky, you got enough cuddling to adapt and keep you going through adulthood. If you were unlucky, you wound up in a residential institution that could not provide much body contact due to limited staff. Evidence concerning the important role of body contact is beginning to accumulate. (See Figure 3.3.)

### Evidence Concerning Lifelong Effects of Early Touching

In extreme cases, infants raised in institutions and deprived of body contact sit and rock back and forth for hours during childhood, and, at puberty, become aggressive. They suffer emotional disturbances throughout life.[35] In such cases, brain cells actually develop fewer connections with other brain cells than is the case for children who experience a lot of early body contact. The brighter side of the picture is found in evidence that the growing person can overcome such deficits in stimulation. But "critical stage" theorists hold that such early damage is forever irreversible.

In contrast to the critical stage theorists, researchers James Prescott and Jerome Kagan recently found that stimulation in *later* childhood and adolescence produces seemingly normal adults out of children deprived of stimulation during a supposedly "critical period."[36] The implication for us is that *some* touching at *some* point in development (early or late) seems necessary for producing normal adults. For example, in a careful cross-cultural study of 49 societies, Prescott found that either high infant physical affection or later permissiveness toward sexual body contact produced nonaggressive adults.[37] Discovery of this rule allowed him to correctly predict adult aggressiveness in an amazing 48 of 49 cultures he studied!

Impressive as these results are, they are correlational in nature. Thus it is possible to attribute both early lack of touching and later aggressiveness to some third unknown factor. Such a factor could be poverty or lack of

**Figure 3.3.** Touching, a feature of emotional intimacy. (Photograph by Charles Blakey.)

social skills. This "third-factor argument" is a bit weak when we apply it to the extremely diverse set of societies studied by Prescott, but it is nevertheless valid theoretically. To rule out the third-factor argument, we need experiments. In an experiment, the researcher can demonstrate changes at will and use experimental control to rule out third-factor arguments. (Herbie the elephant's satire aside, laboratory experimentation has many virtues.) Fortunately, enough laboratory evidence exists to indicate that early body stimulation produces substantial and lasting changes in later life.

In an interesting simulation of humans entering a world of stress, Seymour Levine provided infant rats with various degrees of body contact through handling by human caretakers.[38] He later subjected the animals to stressors, such as electric shock and cold temperatures. Levine found that handling reduced the ill effects of stress and increased secretion of body hormones which were helpful in preserving the integrity of body tissues under stress. The results showed that animals who experienced more touching in infancy were better able to cope with stress in later life.

In Harlow's classic research on monkeys, sensory deprivation in infancy ruined social development later on.[39] However, in research by Manson, baby monkeys were given a "swinging mother" made out of a Clorox bottle wrapped in fur and having a pie pan bolted onto the bottom of the bottle.[40] These monkeys did not develop incessant rocking, depression, withdrawal, and autistic behaviors, as did monkeys reared with an immovable substitute mother.[41] Also, Berkson showed that blind infant monkeys reared with their mothers developed normal social behaviors later on.[42]

In summary, the research provides support for the ideas that depriving the very young of touching (1) is *correlated* with adult aggressiveness in humans and (2) *causes* emotional problems in animals. Physiological research indicates that different patterns in brain functioning follow from different body contact experiences in infancy.[43] With the importance of early touching firmly established, we will assume that some touching is needed for intimacy in adulthood as well.[44]

## FEATURES NECESSARY FOR EMOTIONAL INTIMACY TO ENDURE OVER TIME

### Favorable Accumulation of Rewards Over Time

"What is the 'stranger-on-the-train phenomenon?' " I asked my students, and a variety of interesting replies comes back. John Thibaut and Harold Kelley, two sharp-eyed researchers, noticed that strangers sometimes pour out their innermost secrets to other strangers.[45] For example, when doing a survey on intimacy, Zick Rubin had students collecting handwriting samples at the Boston airport.[46] One lady wrote, "I'm supposed to be a respectable housewife, but guess what? I am at the Logan Airport now going back to Cleveland to my impotent husband. I just left my lover in Boston."[47] Rubin also found that non-Bostonians disclosed more than Bostonians. Intuitively, we can say that "they will never see one another again and their secrets will not be revealed."[48] Are the strangers on the train or, as the song goes, "Strangers in the Night" intimates? Of course not; but why not? Such persons cannot be called intimates precisely because they lack an emotional commitment to each other. Or, in other words, there has been no accumulation of rewards in their relationship.

#### Accumulating the Rewards

Continuing with social penetration theory, Altman and Taylor tell us that long-standing intimate relationships are characterized by a storehouse of accumulated rewards. The *rate* at which social penetration proceeds depends on the relative ratio of rewards to costs in the relationship.

**Case 3.1.** George and Edie have been dating for about a month. They usually squeeze in two dates per week, and the dates are packed with fun. If we asked, each one would say, "I'm getting a lot out of this relationship and the negatives just aren't there."

Social penetration theory would predict a rapid rate of penetration, because the ratio of rewards to costs is high. Note that a gigantic mountain of rewards has not been accumulated—but so far, so good. As the relationship deepens, the rate of penetration slows down dramatically. Penetration from outer to middle layers can proceed quickly. However, beyond a moderate level of intimacy, according to social penetration theory, the penetration tends to slow because people become cautious.

After seven months of dating, George and Edie feel they have reached a plateau. Social penetration theory would say that such a plateau is characteristic in deepening an already established relationship. They are intimate physically. They are disclosing hopes and plans about the future, but not their deepest thoughts. Each still expresses a high reward-to-cost ratio. On the basis of the favorable ratio, we predict forward penetration but at a slow pace.

### Easy In, Easy Out

Breaking off a relationship is called depenetration. Not much is known about how a relationship disintegrates, but we do know that it happens all the time. We can easily speculate as to why it happens, such as conflict or a more attractive alternative relationship. But how does it happen, and when does it fail to happen?

According to Altman and Taylor, building up an intimate relationship with your other person involves accumulating a lot of rewards over time. It is simply impossible to accumulate much in the way of rewards in a brief time span. They say, "In terms of our framework, relationships that have accumulated a broad reservoir of positive reward/cost experiences will be better able to absorb conflict than those based on a more limited pool of experiences. Thus, the summer romance or quickie marriage are particularly susceptible to upheaval, since such bonds typically develop quite quickly, often more rapidly to intimate, central areas of personality, but normally have a narrow experiential base."[49] It is this "easy in, easy out" idea that probably prompted Alexander and certainly your author to emphasize that we need to have time available to develop intimate relationships.

### Fair Relationship

J. Stacy Adams, Elaine Walster, Ellen Berscheid, and G. William Walster call it "equity."[50] Homans calls it "distributive justice."[51] Jourard, Altman and Taylor, and Rubin call it "reciprocity."[52] You or I might call it "fairness." In all these cases, there is one common idea: We expect to get out of a relationship roughly what we put into it. Lurking behind this general expectation lies a shadowy parallel: Relationships that do not conform to this idea of fairness will not endure unless held together by an outside force.

ACTIVITY 3.5.

Write a brief description of an unfair romantic relationship, perhaps one you have observed or experienced. Try to be specific in discussing the inputs of each party and the resulting experiences. Remember the relationship is to be *unfair.*

________________________________________

________________________________________

________________________________________

________________________________________

________________________________________

________________________________________

________________________________________

________________________________________

________________________________________

________________________________________

The fairness idea has been researched with some success, and we will save the details for the next chapter.[53] Now we will be content with three implications: (1) in selecting other persons as friends and possible intimates, we tend to choose those at approximately our own level of social desirability. (2) Once in a relationship, we should keep a rough balance between our own inputs and outcomes compared to those of the other person, or someone will soon perceive the relationship as unfair. (3) Our self-disclosure begets self-disclosure from our other person.

Strong empirical support stands behind the third implication.[54] For example, in Rubin's research at Logan Airport, his students were supposedly collecting samples of handwriting. The student would introduce himself to a departing airline patron. After requesting a sample of handwriting, the student would first write out a sample himself. In fact the so-called sample was a message of low, medium, or high intimacy. For low intimacy, the student wrote, "Right now, I'm in the process of collecting handwriting samples for a school project. I think I will stay here for a while longer, and then call it a day."[55] For medium intimacy, the student wrote, "Lately I've been thinking about my relationships with other people. I've made several good friends during the past couple of years, but I still feel lonely a lot of the time."[56] For high intimacy, the student penned the words, "Lately I've been thinking about how I really feel about myself. I think that I'm pretty well adjusted, but occasionally I have some questions about my sexual adequacy."[57] The central question was, Would the patrons imitate the student? Upon judging patrons' written statements for intimacy, Rubin revealed some puzzling results. As students' statements went from low to moderate intimacy, the patrons also increased the intimacy level of their disclosures. But when exposed to high rather than medium intimacy samples, the patrons showed a dramatic drop in the personal value of material they disclosed. Thus disclosing more of oneself elicited more disclosure from other persons, but only up to a point. After that point, the other person appeared to get scared off by the blast of premature personal disclosure.

Intuitively compelling as the fairness idea is, it has been attacked by Erich Fromm as an evil side effect of modern capitalistic society. Having adopted the notion of fairness, I must either cave in to Fromm's arguments and admit defeat or respond to them. Since the list of the six features of emotional intimacy is now complete, we therefore turn our attention to Fromm's criticism and love in general.

## EMOTIONAL INTIMACY AND LOVE

As you read these pages, you are probably trying to relate intimacy and love. Love is such a broad concept that I cannot give you *the* definition. Rather, I owe it to you to relate my conception of intimacy to a reasonable concept of love.

As used here, *intimacy* means the kind of human contact characterized by the six features discussed in this chapter; nearly all of us need intimacy, as discussed in this and the last chapter. As such, the intimacy concept includes both the open, objective features emphasized in the six features and the accompanying feelings.

On the other hand, *love* means a private experience. Love is inside people's heads. There are many theoretical systems to describe it, but the concept of love properly belongs in the public domain;[58] that is, to find out what love in general means requires trying to find out common threads from inside many people's heads. Our best guess here comes from the research of Clifford Swensen.

### Swensen's Six Components of Love

Of all the researchers who study love, Swensen has been gathering and refining his data the longest. His program of research began with early attempts to discover how college students view love relationships.[59] Swensen has been refining his "Scale of Feelings and Behavior of Love" questionnaire with nonstudent populations. The product of his efforts is found in research reports about his questionnaire, which lists six components of love. These dimensions are derived using factor analysis, a complex mathematical procedure for identifying common threads, or dimensions, in otherwise confusing masses of data. In this case, the dimensions reflect common modes of rating one's own feelings and behaviors about love relationships on a questionnaire, that is, what is in people's heads concerning love.

Swensen's six dimensions are (1) verbal expression of feeling, (2) self-disclosure, (3) toleration of the less pleasant aspects of the loved one, (4) nonmaterial encouragement, (5) unexpressed feelings, and (6) material services performed for the loved one. These six dimensions can be easily related to the theory of intimacy I present. In the following paragraph, Swensen's dimensions are related to features of the loneliness-intimacy dimension.

Swenson's self-disclosure is identical to self-disclosure as described in this chapter. Excepting unexpressed feelings, all Swensen's other dimensions come under the "accumulation of rewards over time" feature we have discussed. Specifically, verbal expression of feeling, toleration of the less pleasant aspects of the loved one, nonmaterial encouragement, and material services performed for the loved one are all deposited in a storehouse of rewards and costs over time; the storehouse is specific to the relationship between you and your other person. Tolerance for your other person's shortcomings clearly concerns the negative, or cost, aspect of human contact, and the costs of human relations accumulate just as the rewards do.

### Fromm's Criticism of Modern Love and a Rebuttal

#### Fromm's Criticism

In the last few pages of his widely read book *The Art of Loving,* Erich Fromm levels a furious broadside attack toward the legitimacy of "fairness" in love relationships.[60] By fairness, he means the same concept we have discussed, where both parties receive from a relationship according to how much they put into it.

Here is Fromm's argument in detail: "Capitalistic society is based on the principle of political freedom on the one hand, and of the market as the regulator of all economic, hence social relations, on the other."[61] The all-important rule of the commercial marketplace is fair exchange, pure and simple. Interpersonal exchange and love relationships are governed by the same rule. "While a great deal of lip service is paid to the religious ideal of love of one's neighbor, our relations are actually determined, at their best, by the principle of *fairness.*"[62] Unhappily, "modern man has transformed himself into a commodity; he experiences his life as an investment with which he should make the highest profit. . . . His main aim is profitable exchange of his skills, knowledge, and of himself, his 'personality package.' . . . Life has no goal except the one to move, no principle except the one of fair exchange, no satisfaction except the one to consume."[63] In contrast, "to love means to commit oneself without guarantee, to give oneself completely in the hope that our love will produce love in the loved person."[64] In love, says Fromm, we throw away the balance sheet and proceed on the basis of faith and trust.

Noble as these compassionately intended words about love ring in our ears, I believe Fromm's criticism of fairness is dead wrong. In the next section, I argue that a realistic look at the way love blossoms and withers in the real world compels us to include fairness as a feature of intimacy and of love. However, the silver lining in Fromm's cloudy argument is the basic insight that the larger economic system exerts a powerful influence over our most intimate interpersonal relationships in unseen ways; that idea is probably the most important one in his book.

#### Rebuttal of Fromm's Criticism

A careful look at the rise and fall of friendships and loves in real life should convince any observer that both social penetration and social depenetration are part and parcel of life itself. You meet countless acquaintances you never see again. Friendships dissolve. Engagements to marry are often broken. And marriages end, as divorce statistics show. However, the widespread existence of social depenetration does not make it right. In other words, to defeat Fromm's argument (that fairness should not be a part of love or intimacy) requires a counterargument to show that social depenetration is the right course of action on occasion.

In their preoccupation with the joys of life, I am afraid that professional students of love have neglected two fundamental facts of life. First, sharing love and intimacy takes time. Because there are only 24 hours in a day, your love and intimacy relationships must be either few in number or superficial in nature. Because sharing love is not superficial by definition, you can actually share love with only a very few people. The most love-giving saints in history had only 24 hours a day, and they actually shared love with very few people and God. To be sure, they may have harbored intellectual and emotional feelings of love toward every living creature. Nevertheless, their daily ration of 24 hours of time allowed them to actually share a love relationship with only a few parties. The same is true for each of us. Only a time machine could change this fundamental fact of life.

Another fact of life is that social depenetration often occurs for good reason. To be sure, some relationships do not deserve to end. But sometimes they *do* deserve to end, and this is the claim needed to refute Fromm's main thesis. Consider these examples of two friends.

**Case 3.2.** You have struck up a friendship with John. He's an OK guy and you two spend a couple hours together each day. However, last week each of you separately met a new friend. In both your case and John's, the new friend offered each of you far more. Your relationship with John ends with no hard feelings.

**Case 3.3.** You have struck up a friendship with John. You two are living together and are the best of friends. However, for some unknown reason, he starts running around with an extremely undesirable crowd. He has started drinking heavily and, before long, he shifts to hard drugs. Nothing you do affects him in any way. Still later, he obtains night employment as a hired killer. After a few jobs, he tells you how much he enjoys killing. He starts to take your money. He starts to yell at you. You can stand it no more. You have a long talk in which you pour out your feelings and ask if you can do anything to help. John replies that you should keep your mouth shut and stop bothering him. If you don't, he's going to bring his work home, and you know what that means.

In both Case 3.2 and Case 3.3, social depenetration is clearly warranted. In fact, social depenetration is warranted and *right* when a mistake has been made in striking up the relationship in the first place or when one party (or both) becomes exploitive. Given that all love and intimacy relationships begin with largely uninformed optimism about the other person, it is only human to allow for mistakes and therefore depenetration.

My argument makes a compelling case for the legitimacy of social depenetration in certain cases, when one party exploits the other. *Exploitation* here means precisely a significant departure from fairness; so fairness is a characteristic of love and intimacy relations. These arguments notwithstanding, Fromm still gives us a couple of real pearls we can use.

### Fromm's Contributions

***Tolerance in Love.*** Fromm's main argument that fairness should not be a part of love contains a grain of truth. But instead of arguing for exclusion of fairness altogether, we should argue for tolerance in love. Most theories of love include tolerance as a component, as did Swensen's research. What, then, is tolerance?

*Tolerance* in love and intimacy means looking at the fairness feature over months and years. At the end of each day or week (perhaps even month), intimates should not whip out their ledger of rewards and costs to tally up an overall balance. No, love and deep emotional intimacy require flexibility in looking at the fairness of the relationship. The time span over which fairness in a relationship is determined in your mind thus increases with the deepening emotional intimacy of the relationship. Fromm was incorrectly arguing that the time span for looking at fairness in a love relationship is infinite. The time span is not infinite, but it should be very long. It was not always this way; at one time exploitation such as wife-beating was acceptable. Now things are different. Ultimately, we are well advised to take account of fairness in all of our relationships *with all due tolerance*. If intolerable departure from fairness (exploitation) is found over years' time, those who tolerate it are properly known as saints, masochists, fools, or trapped victims.

The thoughts about fairness here apply to voluntary intimacy relationships and hence not to relationships between parents and young children. However, as you matured to become an adult, your relationship with your parents most likely became a voluntary one. As the relationship with parents becomes voluntary, the fairness idea becomes applicable. Because many adults have much to thank their parents for, the fairness idea implies *extremely* great tolerance in love and intimacy toward our parents when we are adults.

Fromm's contribution here is substantial. He reminds us that tolerance is a part of love and intimacy, and this involves fairness.

***Economic System's Influence on Interpersonal Affairs.*** Fromm began his attack on fairness with the claim that social rules mirror the rules in the larger economic system. He then argues, "The *principle* underlying capitalistic society and the *principle* underlying love are incompatible."[65] I agree with his initial claim, but not his latter argument. The problem lies in trying to pinpoint just what aspects of the modern capitalistic system do damage interpersonal relationships. I claim that the harmful aspect is the particular direction taken by commercial technology, not capitalism or business per se. This argument will be extended at length in Chapter 5 on values. The argument will be that specific technology (*not* capitalism) has subtly affected how we as individuals spend our time.

**CHAPTER SUMMARY**

In this chapter, six features that characterize emotional intimacy are identified. They are:

A. Features necessary for emotional intimacy to exist
   1. Time for frequent interactions with one other person
   2. Informal interactions

B. Features necessary for emotional intimacy to develop
   3. Self-disclosure
      a. Category depth
      b. Category breadth
   4. Touching

C. Features necessary for emotional intimacy to endure over time
   5. Favorable accumulation of rewards over time
   6. Fair relationship

These features do not guarantee intimacy. Rather, they characterize it.

**PREVIEW**

The practical importance of the six features of emotional intimacy is that they are visible. They are out in the open. You can get a handle on them in your own life. You can affect your own destiny by arranging your life to attain optimal intimacy for you.

From this point onward, we assume that for every person there exists an *optimal* range of emotional intimacy. Inside the optimal range, you feel neither the painful loneliness of too little intimacy nor the overload of too much. In the next chapter, you will take self-inventory on each of the six features as they apply to your own life. Throughout that chapter the emphasis is on options you might realistically take to change your current level of emotional intimacy if you choose. Nowhere is it assumed that you fall either above or below the optimal range, or even that you now want to change. Rather, the more options you have is seen as beneficial in all cases.

# addendum to chapter three: The Ghost of Loneliness Future

I am afraid of growing older. The passage of time does not bother me, but the end of the road looms dark and shadowy. With modern social trends emphasizing superautonomy for the individual person and mobility away from home, we children are seduced into neglecting our aging family, especially our parents. Loneliness in old age shows no respect for social class. The wealthy achievers of today can easily become the throw-away old folks of tomorrow. The specter of rattling around in either a dingy or a deluxe nursing home, eagerly awaiting bimonthly letters from distant children, clouds the future for most of us. Will making a million dollars save you? No, because human contact, not money, is needed to ward off loneliness. When Butler asks in his book *Why Survive? Being Old in America,* he has a point.[66] Frankly, I am scared stiff. I'll demonstrate what I mean with two real cases.

While Miami Beach conjures up images of glistening hotels and gentle surf, there is another Miami Beach: The so-called South Beach portion houses a large concentration of elderly people, many of them Jewish and poor. A glance at the *Miami Herald* reveals their plights, as in the following two stories, printed in 1974 near Mother's Day.

**The Case of Rose Goldberg.**

*Rose Goldberg sat sobbing on a hard wooden chair at Miami Beach Police headquarters Saturday (see Figure 3.4).*

*"I have no home! Where can I go?" asked Mrs. Goldberg, 74. Wearing a torn white sweater with two $1 bills, all she has, folded neatly in the pocket, she was homeless—evicted from her South Beach hotel room because she was 10 days late with her $150-a-month rent.*

*Trembling hands clutched her cane and a crumpled green paper sack containing her heart medicine and hairpins, all she'd been able to salvage when a Metro deputy summoned by the owner of the Regal Hotel, 615 Fifth St., locked her out of her room Friday.*

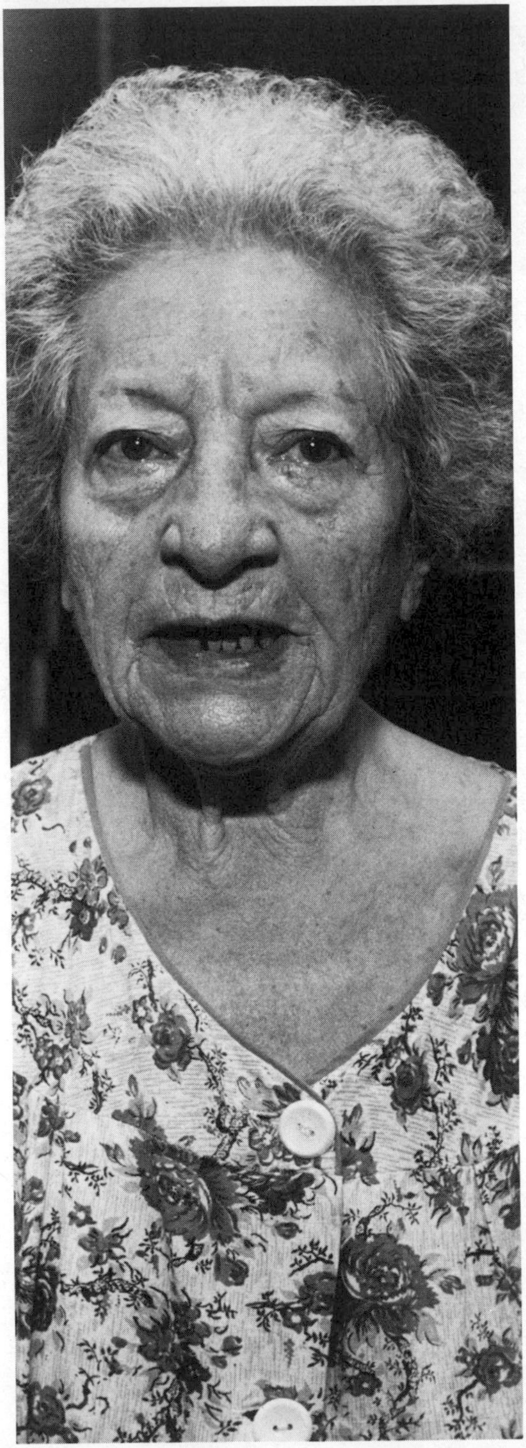

*Once she was a wife and mother. Now she is alone. European born, she has no brothers and sisters. "Hitler killed them," she says.*

*She came to this country and married.*

*Her only son counted the days until he could join the Navy. He was killed in 1945.*

*Her husband, a Brooklyn carpenter, died a year later, in 1946.*

*Regal manager-owner, Jaime Schuster, 41, acknowledged summoning the Metro deputy to evict Mrs. Goldberg.*

*"I don't want this kind of customer in my hotel," he said. "She doesn't want to pay the rent."*

*On Saturday, May 4, he says, she told him she would pay the rent Monday.*

*She didn't. She says her Social Security check failed to arrive.*

*Miami Beach Police Lt. George Morgan tried to help Mrs. Goldberg. He said Schuster told him he would not permit her to live out her $150 month's security deposit because she violated her lease when she failed to pay her rent on time.*

*"Talk to my lawyers," Schuster replied, when a reporter asked if he plans to return her deposit.*

*Sympathetic Miami Beach police officers took Mrs. Goldberg to another South Beach hotel, where she spent Friday night. But she left there Saturday, refusing to go back, because kosher dietary rules, which she has adhered to all her life, are not observed there.*

*At the Regal, she fixed her own meals in her room. . . .*

*Jeffrey Solomon, of the Jewish Family and Children's Service, said the organization would pay Mrs. Goldberg's bill for the weekend at a kosher hotel and send a case worker to see her Monday. Granada Hotel owner, Annie Lefkowitz, agreed, saying she would be welcome.*

*Mrs. Goldberg still wept.*

*"You'll have a nice bed and a room. You can take a nap. And you'll have three Kosher meals a day," promised Ward, a husky rookie whose father and uncle are also policemen.*

**Figure 3.4.** Rose Goldberg, 74, after eviction . . . her husband, son, family, all dead. (Photograph by Albert Coya. Copyright 1974 by *The Miami Herald*. Reprinted by permission.)

*"I'm ashamed to go like this," Mrs. Goldberg said, looking down at her red slippers. "I gave away my best clothes because I never go anywhere."*

*"You look fine," Evans said, taking her hand.*

"We have this every day," *a police captain said angrily.*

*By Saturday evening, Mrs. Goldberg was in a room at the Granada, 1017 Meridian Ave., looking forward to spending Mother's Day there.*

*"She's fine," Mrs. Lefkowitz said. "We would have taken her in even without the money."*

**The Case of Sylvia Goldman.**

*Sylvia Goldman felt alone enough to cry Sunday, though she was surrounded by 300 other older people at a Mother's Day party in the South Beach Activities Center.*

*"I am lonely, and I miss my children," said Mrs. Goldman, 69, as she swabbed a tissue across her eyes in a vain effort to keep pace with her tears. "I know that I should be happy, but I am not."*

*While others around her clapped hands and sang along with the accordion player squeezing out old Jewish folk songs, Mrs. Goldman sobbed.*

*"I still haven't gotten used to it—being alone," she said. "I just like to know that my children still care about me, and I wish that I could have seen them today."*

*The party for South Beach's elderly, sponsored by the Jewish Community Centers of South Florida, honored people over 90 years old, mothers and couples who have been married more than 60 years. For most, it was a festive occasion.*

*"I'm the oldest person in the room—how about that?" beamed Julius Levey, 98, of 7143 Bonita Ave. "I look good, too, don't I? I don't feel too good, everything's the matter—can't hear well, see well or walk well—but I'm here and that's something."*

*Earlier in the day, social worker Sylvia Josephson received a telephone call from Montreal from Sylvia Goldman's daughter, who was worried about her mother.*

*"She had called her mother to wish her a happy day and she said her mother was very depressed about being alone," Mrs. Josephson said. "I went over to see Mrs. Goldman and brought her back here to the party—if she knows someone cares enough to do that, maybe she will feel a little better."*

*Off in a corner, David and Elsie Galantiere were holding hands and were all smiles as they were honored for being married 70 years.*

*"The ceremony was in Chicago in 1904," said Mrs. Galantiere, 87. "We've enjoyed it—that's the way marriage should be."*

*Back at her table, Mrs. Goldman was smiling at last. "When you're a mother and it's Mother's Day, you can't be alone," she said. "If you can't be with your children, the next best thing is to be with other mothers and fathers."*

(Rose Goldberg's story, entitled "Alone and Evicted, Rose Finds Haven for Mother's Day" and written by Edna Buchanan, appeared in *The Miami Herald* on May 12, 1974, pp. 1A, 2A. Sylvia Goldman's story, entitled "Mother Feels Lonely amid 300 Partygoers" and written by Ron Sachs, appeared in the May 13, 1974, edition, p. 1B. 

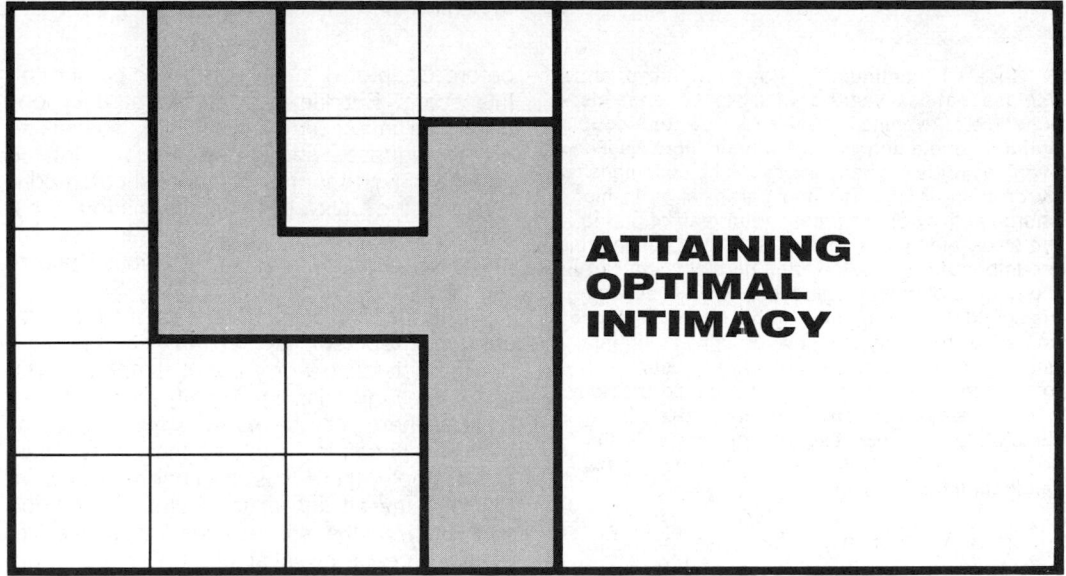

# ATTAINING OPTIMAL INTIMACY

*As there is both good and bad society, there is also both good and bad solitude.*

ST. FRANCIS DE SALES

*Solitude is to the mind what fasting is to the body, fatal if too prolonged, and yet necessary.*

VAUVENARGUES

*Solitude is a good place to visit but a poor place to stay.*

JOSH BILLINGS

## EXPECTATIONS FOR THIS CHAPTER

What can I expect from this chapter? Two things cannot be expected: a cure-all or a sex manual. You can realistically expect the same three results from this chapter as from the book in general.

First, you can expect to sharpen your perception of your own social world, especially the loneliness-intimacy aspect of it.

**Case 4.1.** Roy reads Chapter 2 through 4 of *Practical Psychology.* Beforehand, he had no pressing social problems except for occasional loneliness, which is common. Afterward, he feels the same way, but now he is able to describe his social world with somewhat more precision. Specifically, he can describe the time feature in his desire for human contact as potentially troublesome over the long run. His current schedule allows no really informal times for socializing with his wife except on weekends.

Second, you can expect to be able to generate more options for your efforts at change.

**Case 4.1 (continued).** Roy thinks it over and decides that next year he will try to rearrange his schedule of evening activities to allow for a couple hours of time alone with his wife on three weekday evenings. This rearrangement will be accomplished by dropping two clubs and participating in his church activity on the weekend instead of during the week. He makes this decision after considering a number of options: lowering his sights concerning the degree of human contact he wishes, changing his schedule at work, moving his family residence across town, taking that new job in West Virginia, and so on. In this case, exposure to user information helped Roy spot a possible problem before it arose. The exposure also aided him in generating personal response options by listing some general response options to managing his personal time.

Third, you can expect to raise the odds for self-change because the several features of intimacy described earlier lend themselves to specific means for change.

**Case 4.1 (continued).** Roy feels he has a good marriage, but it is not all it could be. A particular activity in this chapter causes him to think about his self-disclosure to his wife. He realizes that it has been months since he has clearly let her know how deeply and sincerely he loves her. In fact he does love her truly and would give his life for her. But he has not been expressing this innermost feeling. Starting today, he will indeed raise the odds for making more of his marriage. If we pursued the matter, we could list a hundred desirable actions his wife would be more likely to exhibit as a result of Roy's new expressions of love and respect, as well as the more satisfying emotions she would begin to feel.

## SELF-INVENTORY

### Orientation

What is a self-inventory? Quite literally, *self-inventory* means taking stock of ourselves. We are going to survey ourselves on individual features of the loneliness-intimacy dimension to see where we stand. Basically, the goal is to compare where you are at with where you realistically want to be in regard to human contact. But before we start on this novel undertaking, several problems confront us.

Here are the problems. Each is first posed in quotation marks and then answered immediately. "How can I be sure the features of intimacy discussed in this book are the real ones? After all, I have never seen such a list before Chapter 3." You can never be sure on this score. But life is a series of decisions based on incomplete information, so making a "best guess" should be nothing new to anyone. Given the importance of human contact and the utility of user information about loneliness and intimacy, the present user information is superior to the previous state of affairs.

"But the list of six features may not be complete. Something vital may be missing." Let the scientists worry about that. Or, if you see something missing, fill it in yourself.

"But there may be *many* ways to take inventory concerning each of the six features. For example, there must be hundreds of ways to make myself known to others." It is good that each of the six features lends itself to multiple means of satisfaction. For one thing, the professionals can investigate each more fully. For another, you will often be able to create personalized means of satisfaction regarding each feature. As an example, one specific kind of reward we shall discuss is status. When you wish to confer status upon your other person, there are many ways to do it. One of your most rewarding features may be that you are a great listener who can confer status by listening. Or, you might have a talent at giving compliments. In each case you are conferring status in different ways. One purpose of the self-inventory here is to spotlight the many ways of getting where you want to be with respect to all the features of intimacy.

"But where will I end up after I'm all done? If I know you, Flanders, by now, I would guess that you are not apt to prescribe any universal ideal levels concerning, say, how much I ought to self-disclose or touch." The end point here is a comparison by yourself between present position and realistic ideal position. There is only one superexpert on your social world, and that is you. I hope that ideal levels will never be published, although research-backed guidelines about danger zones would probably be useful.

With the problems out of the way, we can proceed to take self-inventory. We now consider each of the six features of the loneliness-intimacy dimension individually. Remember that each feature is considered necessary over time; but the relative importance of each is for you to decide.

**Inventory of My Time**

In taking inventory of your time, the goal is to see what time is available for informal socializing. In taking a time inventory, we will consider together both of the features necessary for intimacy to exist, namely time for frequent and informal interactions.

ACTIVITY 4.1.

In your mind, run through your daily activities for a whole week. Your task is to create your own, personal *categories concerning how you spend your time.* In the space provided, list the things you do regularly. For standing commitments or regular appointments, try to be specific. Start with Monday morning and go from there.

______________________________

______________________________

______________________________

______________________________

______________________________

______________________________

______________________________

______________________________

______________________________

______________________________

ACTIVITY 4.2.

In the chart labeled Table 4.1, fill in every hour of every day with some category from Activity 4.1. If weekday bedtimes vary somewhat, take an average and define it as your nightly bedtime on weekdays. Do likewise for weekend sleeping hours.

ACTIVITY 4.3.

Now that you have the chart all cluttered up with labels, we simplify. With a pencil, lightly shade in all the time that is *not* available for informal interactions. Such time includes hours for sleep, most job-related activities, and some mealtimes. If in doubt, shade it in. If only a portion of a given time block (e.g., 15 minutes) is available for informal interaction but you cannot tell in advance exactly when that portion occurs, arbitrarily leave that portion unshaded (i.e., one-fourth of the block) at the beginning of the time block. For the assembly-line worker, a 15-minute afternoon break is informal if he can talk about a wide range of topics. But the break would not be informal if he had to remain in a certain location and stay largely in his role of assembly-line worker by talking shop with the foreman. On the other hand, the same worker might regularly put in 2 hours of lawn work on Saturdays. Suppose about 30 minutes' worth of visiting with neighbors unpredictably but generally occurs while he is doing the lawn work. The first 30 minutes of the 2-hour lawn-work block of time is informal time and should not be shaded.

ACTIVITY 4.4.

How many hours do you have available weekly for informal interactions?

______________________________

Over how many days are these times spread?

______________________________

ACTIVITY 4.5.

How many hours would you *realistically* like to have available for informal socializing?

______________________________

Over how many days would these times be spread?

______________________________

ACTIVITY 4.6.

Subtract the corresponding numbers you have entered in Activity 4.4 from your realistic ideal numbers in Activity 4.5 and enter the difference in the following two blanks:

______________________________

______________________________

| | MON. | TUES. | WED. | THURS. | FRI. | SAT. | SUN. |
|---|---|---|---|---|---|---|---|
| MIDNIGHT | | | | | | | |
| 1 A.M. | | | | | | | |
| 2 A.M. | | | | | | | |
| 3 A.M. | | | | | | | |
| 4 A.M. | | | | | | | |
| 5 A.M. | | | | | | | |
| 6 A.M. | | | | | | | |
| 7 A.M. | | | | | | | |
| 8 A.M. | | | | | | | |
| 9 A.M. | | | | | | | |
| 10 A.M. | | | | | | | |
| 11 A.M. | | | | | | | |
| NOON | | | | | | | |
| 1 P.M. | | | | | | | |
| 2 P.M. | | | | | | | |
| 3 P.M. | | | | | | | |
| 4 P.M. | | | | | | | |
| 5 P.M. | | | | | | | |
| 6 P.M. | | | | | | | |
| 7 P.M. | | | | | | | |
| 8 P.M. | | | | | | | |
| 9 P.M. | | | | | | | |
| 10 P.M. | | | | | | | |
| 11 P.M. | | | | | | | |

ACTIVITY 4.7.

In *We, The Lonely People: Searching for Community,* Ralph Keyes notes the importance of common rituals, such as Thanksgiving dinner or religious ceremonies. He writes about a Catholic communion service that "the feelings were of *that* group of people, for each other. There were people in that group I had never come to understand and care for—until that moment. And that to me is what's important about ritual: having times to celebrate what's in common. Communities of people need that time as much as they need time to air what divides."[1] List in the space provided the rituals in which you can predict you will participate over the next several years. *Rituals* are any formal and customarily repeated acts or series of acts. These answers should reveal some interesting life-styles to share in class.

Daily rituals

______________________________

Weekly rituals

______________________________

Monthly rituals

______________________________

Yearly rituals

______________________________

Other rituals

______________________________

Our self-inventories of weekly time patterns should give us a helpful perspective on what each of us is doing with our life. While time itself does not constitute the activities of major concern in our lives, time is *the* dimension along which our activities are ordered in linear fashion. As such, use of time would seem to be the most important dimension in all of psychology for researchers and users alike.

> *That is the only time, which a man can call his own—that which he has all to himself; the rest, though in some sense he may be said to live in it, is other people's time, not his.*
>
> CHARLES LAMB

> *I despise making the most of one's time. Half of the pleasures in life consist of opportunities one has neglected.*
>
> OLIVER WENDELL HOLMES, JR.

> *There are optical illusions in time as well as in space.*
>
> MARCEL PROUST

## Inventory of My Self-Disclosure

### Category Depth

We are indeed fortunate that several self-disclosure measures have already been developed. While Jourard clearly looms as the pioneering researcher in this area, Altman, Taylor, and their students have completed the most extensive scaling of self-disclosure topics to date. In a technical report, Taylor and Altman asked college students to rate for intimacy 671 statements in 13 topic areas of conversation.[2] Before completing Activity 4.8, be sure to check with your instructor first.

ACTIVITY 4.8.

In the boxes along the top of Table 4.2, place the initials of (1) your spouse, (2) your mother, (3) your father, (4) a relative, other than a parent, to whom you feel closest (e.g., brother, sister, uncle, cousin), (5) your closest same-sex friend, and (6) your closest opposite-sex friend. If no one person clearly fits in a given category, leave the box for that category blank. If a person fits the description in any category according to your feelings, use that person. For example, if your stepfather filled the role of father according to your feelings, fill in his initials in the box for father. If no one filled that role, leave it blank. If you are not getting married until next year but feel married already, fill in the initials of your future spouse. In short, you and you alone are the final judge of who fills each role in your life. If I have left out a role that you

| Item | | Fill-in Number | Spouse | Mother | Father | Closest Relative | Closest Same-Sex Friend | Closest Opposite-Sex Friend |
|---|---|---|---|---|---|---|---|---|
| **0-1.** | My feelings about the place of religion in everyday life. | ◯ | | | | | | |
| **0-2.** | The reasons why I am or am not religious. | ◯ | | | | | | |
| **0-3.** | Whether or not I have ever asked for advice from a minister, priest, or rabbi. | ◯ | | | | | | |
| **1-1.** | The age at which I would like (ideally) to marry. | ◯ | | | | | | |
| **1-2.** | The way in which I (would) want to raise my children. | ◯ | | | | | | |
| **1-3.** | What I would do if it seemed that my marriage was not a success. | ◯ | | | | | | |
| **2-1.** | My feelings about standards of sexual behavior before marriage. | ◯ | | | | | | |
| **2-2.** | What I do to attract a member of the opposite sex whom I like. | ◯ | | | | | | |
| **2-3.** | My love life. | ◯ | | | | | | |
| **3-1.** | Whether or not my parents spanked me as a child. | ◯ | | | | | | |
| **3-2.** | The way I behave when I am around my parents. | ◯ | | | | | | |
| **3-3.** | How well the members of my family and close relatives get along. | ◯ | | | | | | |
| **4-1.** | My general health at this time. | ◯ | | | | | | |
| **4-2.** | What special effort, if any, I make to keep fit, healthy, and attractive, e.g., calisthenics, diet. | ◯ | | | | | | |
| **4-3.** | How satisfied I am with different parts of my body—legs, waist, weight, chest, etc. | ◯ | | | | | | |
| **5-1.** | Things I'd really like to have if I could afford them. | ◯ | | | | | | |
| **5-2.** | How important money is for my happiness. | ◯ | | | | | | |
| **5-3.** | My total financial worth, including property, savings bonds, insurance, etc. | ◯ | | | | | | |
| **6-1.** | What I think about politics in my hometown. | ◯ | | | | | | |
| **6-2.** | Political policies that I disagree with. | ◯ | | | | | | |

| Item | | Fill-in Number ↓ | Spouse | Mother | Father | Closest Relative | Closest Same-Sex Friend | Closest Opposite-Sex Friend |
|---|---|---|---|---|---|---|---|---|
| **6-3.** | What I believe should be the laws concerning marriage between blacks and whites. | ○ | | | | | | |
| **7-1.** | What animals make me nervous. | ○ | | | | | | |
| **7-2.** | My ups and downs in moods. | ○ | | | | | | |
| **7-3.** | What feelings, if any, I have trouble expressing or controlling. | ○ | | | | | | |
| **8-1.** | My favorite hobbies. | ○ | | | | | | |
| **8-2.** | Whether or not I like to do new and different things. | ○ | | | | | | |
| **8-3.** | Whether or not I enjoy reading love and romance stories. | ○ | | | | | | |
| **9-1.** | How much I enjoy talking with other people. | ○ | | | | | | |
| **9-2.** | The kind of person I like to have as a friend. | ○ | | | | | | |
| **9-3.** | Whether or not I need people in order to be happy. | ○ | | | | | | |
| **10-1.** | How I feel about people who are careless in picking up clothing, personal effects, etc. | ○ | | | | | | |
| **10-2.** | Whether or not I think there are situations in which I think lying is OK. | ○ | | | | | | |
| **10-3.** | My opinion about how capable and smart I am compared to others around me. | ○ | | | | | | |
| **11-1.** | How many different jobs I have had. | ○ | | | | | | |
| **11-2.** | My ambitions and goals in my work. | ○ | | | | | | |
| **11-3.** | Whether or not I ever lied to my boss. | ○ | | | | | | |
| **12-1.** | My date of birth. | ○ | | | | | | |
| **12-2.** | The name of the place or places where I grew up. | ○ | | | | | | |
| **12-3.** | My weight. | ○ | | | | | | |

feel is important to you personally, fill it in with description and initials in the margin.

Filling in the table is a three-step process. The steps are as follows:

Step 1. Rate each item on how intimate or personal it is for you.
Step 2. Fill in the table to indicate your own self-disclosure at the present time.
Step 3. Fill in the table to indicate your realistic ideal.

Let us take these three steps one at a time.

*Step 1.* To assign an intimacy value to each item, turn to Table 4.2.[3] Down the left-hand side you see a number of items. Each item stands for a given topic of conversation. Look at the first item, numbered 0–1, "My feelings about the place of religion in everyday life." To the right of this item and just under the arrow, there is a circle. To assign your personal intimacy value to item 0–1, you simply put a number in that circle. Use the following scale:

1 = low intimacy-value
2
3 = middle intimacy-value
4
5 = high intimacy-value

For example, if you feel that "My feeling about the place of religion in everyday life" has low intimacy-value for you, you would place a "1" in the circled blank space. This number we will call the *fill-in-number.* (As an example, I have assigned the fill-in-number "1" to item 4–1.) The fill-in-number that I have marked after item 4–1 is purely to show how the assignment of fill-in-numbers is done. At this time, go through all items from 0–1 through 12–3 and enter your own fill-in-number for each one. Do this quickly and please do not think about the rest of the table while doing it. Remember that the fill-in number will be *1* or *2* or *3* or *4* or *5* in all cases. Go ahead. Finished? By now, you should have assigned a fill-in-number to all items in Table 4.2. Now you are ready to enter these numbers in the rest of the table.

*Step 2.* Before proceeding, let us get clear on what these fill-in-numbers mean and how we will use them. We are about to go down the table, row by row. For each row, we will go from left to right, box by box, starting with spouse first, mother second, and so on. Within each individual box, the question is, of course, whether the other person in question (e.g., mother) knows the information in question (e.g., item 4–1 about "My general health at this time"). For every box, either the person knows it or does not. If he or she knows it, we enter the fill-in-number for that row. If he or she does not know it, we enter nothing. In other words, the fill-in-number does *not* indicate the degree of knowledge the other person has about a given item. Either the other person knows or doesn't. Rather, the fill-in-number means what you assigned it to mean in Step 1 previously, namely how intimate **you** rated each item to be.

In Step 2 there is one important rule: The *only* entry you can make in the row for each item is the circled fill-in-number for that item. Thus, the only number I could put in any given box to the right of item 4–1 is a "1" because that is the fill-in-number I gave to item 4–1. You may ask, "Couldn't we save a lot of trouble just by putting an "X" in each box or leaving it blank rather than using different fill-in-numbers for each item?" This seems true, but it would rob us of some important analyses we can do later.

In short, when we finish with Step 2, each box in Table 4.2 either is going to have the fill-in-number at the left of its row inside of it or is going to have nothing inside of it. The only number you can enter in the first row (for item 0–1) is the fill-in-number you put in the circle for item 0–1. The same rule holds for all rows: The only entry you can make in a given row is the fill-in-number for that given row.

*Step 3.* Now that you have finished your second task, we are going to add one more operation to the completing of each box. Recall that you have just entered the fill-in-number for each person in the upper left of each box or you left it blank. By doing so, you also marked the status quo, that is, the state of affairs that actually exists now. Now think about your *ideal* state of affairs. If you ideally want the person in question to know the information in each row, then once again place the fill-in-number in the boxes for that row. If you ideally wish the person in question did *not* know the information denoted by the given item, then do not insert any number. This time, we place the fill-in-number lightly in the lower *right* corner of each box and circle it (as I have done for item 4–1). The circled number for item 4–1 in the first box means your author ideally *wants* his spouse to know about his health. Remember, you are to place a fill-in-number in, or leave blank, the lower *right-hand* corner of each box. Again obey the same rule: The only entry you can make in a given row is the fill-in-number for that given row. Now go ahead and fill in your ideal state of affairs for each box in Table 4.2.

Before we go on to make some sense of Table 4.2, some warnings are in order:

1. Do not try to calculate totals. Totals or sum scores are meaningless because there are no national norms. Even if there were norms, your concern should be with your own ideals, not with what is happening in society at large.
2. Do not worry if you have a lot of blank boxes. In the first place, who would want to be exposing their innermost self to all their intimates? In the second place, many of the items ask about specific topics. The specific topics may or may not have come up in your conversations with, say, your spouse. If they have not come up, don't worry about it.
3. Do not take comparisons with your classmates too seriously. We expect huge individual differences in self-disclosure.
4. Do not become alarmed on the basis of what anyone else tells you about your responses to Table 4.2, including professional psychologists. The items I have chosen were selected for users and *not* professionals, so Table 4.2 is most definitely not a clinical instrument. Rather, it is to assist you in taking self-inventory.

To continue our consideration of category depth, you may have noticed that the items in Table 4.2 come in groups of three (e.g., the first three items relate to religion). In each group, I chose items to be different according to how intimately they were rated in the original Taylor and Altman research.[4] Now we will look back over Table 4.2 and do an eyeball analysis of the uncircled numbers (e.g., number in the upper left of boxes). Remember, it is of no value and perhaps even harmful for you to do a calculated, numerical analysis. Any conclusion you draw from Table 4.2 should reflect a comparison between self-disclosure now versus your own personal ideals, not the self-disclosure or ideals of anyone else.

Looking back over Table 4.2, we are looking at category depth (represented by the uncircled numbers), which means depth of social penetration. A lot of 1s means a lot of self-disclosure at a superficial level. A lot of 5s means a lot of self-disclosure at high levels of intimacy. If Altman and Taylor's theory is correct, there should be a wedge-shaped penetration by your other persons into you, reflected by more 5s than 3s and more 3s than 1s. In the absence of norms, I speculate that the *average* pattern in Table 4.2 consists of several 1s, some 2s and 3s, and a scattering of 4s and 5s. In the total absence of research data, I speculate that a virtual absense of uncircled numbers reflects social isolation and the need for more human contact. Realistically, I expect the range, or spread, of patterns that clinicians would classify as "normal" or "healthy" to be enormous.

### Category Breadth

As you were going through Table 4.2, you probably also noticed that there were 13 different topic areas. These 13 topic areas came from Taylor and Altman's research and are indicated by the first number in front of each item; these arbitrary numbers ran from 0 through 12.[5] Here are the topic areas by number, which correspond to the topics of conversation: 0 = religion, 1 = marriage, 2 = sex, 3 = parental family, 4 = own body, 5 = money and property, 6 = social issues, 7 = emotions and feelings, 8 = own interests, 9 = social relations, 10 = values and self-concept, 11 = work, and 12 = biographical and personal facts. Thus, 0–1, 0–2, and 0–3 all involved religion; items 1–1, 1–2, and 1–3 all involved "own marriage"; and so on down through items 12–1, 12–2, and 12–3, which all involved "biographical and personal facts."[6]

By including three items from each topic area (see footnote 3), you will notice that I have implicitly weighted each of the 13 topic areas equally in importance. Such equal weighting is appropriate for use by multitudes of readers, but for *your* personal purposes, certain areas should obviously be weighted more heavily. To have a truly customized idea of your own self-disclosure, you might want to apply your *own* personalized weightings of importance and also use more than three items per area!

To do an eyeball analysis of Table 4.2 regarding category breadth, recall that category breadth means the *variety of topic areas disclosed.* Since I have grouped items in each topic area together, the dispersion versus clustering of numbers in the table reflects category breadth. Remember, we are still dealing with only the heavy, uncircled numbers that reflect your status quo.

To compare status quo with realistic ideal, merely compare the two. There is a difference between current status quo and ideal whenever a box has only one number in it. Thus, scanning Table 4.2 for such boxes gives you an idea of (1) the degree of such differences and (2) just where they are located.

**Case 4.2.** Jill looks over Table 4.2 and sees an evenly distributed pattern of actual (uncircled) disclosure over topic areas. She concludes correctly that she scores high on category breadth.

**Case 4.3.** Willie skims over Table 4.2 and sees clusters of actual disclosure, not an evenly distributed pattern. Confused, he asks his instructor, "What does it mean if I have clusters of self-disclosure? I know it means I disclose only in a few areas, but what does *that* mean?" Laura, his instructor, replies, "Willie, there is no evidence I can give you at this time that relates category breadth to adjustment. I can tell you that you score moderately low on category breadth, but the meaning of that fact is as yet undiscovered. All we have at present is Altman and Taylor's *theoretical prediction* in social penetration theory that broadly based relationships with high category breadth should be less likely to break under stress. On the other hand, they also say that with a great accumulation of rewards over time, a relationship can be strong. So, even if you clustered a great deal, you can still have a solid relationship. That's all I can say now. In a few years, I hope there will be more evidence to relate to the dimension of loneliness-intimacy in general and social penetration in particular." Laura echoes your author's thoughts precisely.

**Target Person**

You are the discloser. Across the top of Table 4.2 you listed target persons to whom you disclose. To assess disclosure to any given target person, just glance down the column for that particular person. To compare your disclosure across target persons, compare columns.

So little is now known about target disclosure that I can give you no definite guidelines. Rather, from glancing over your disclosure across target persons, you may detect the image of a pattern. What does it mean if your disclosure is varied, so that different target persons get differing category depths and breadths? Such varied disclosure is to be expected.

One possible worrisome pattern might be disclosure of far greater depth and/or breadth to other persons outside the immediate family than to a spouse. On the one hand, it is possible that having a confidant other than, say your spouse, is healthy, although I know of no evidence directly on this topic. On the other hand, extremely low disclosure to spouse together with far more depth and/or breadth to an other person may reflect a need to improve communications in the marriage. Again, be warned that I am pointing out only possible danger from an extreme pattern of self-disclosure—and I do mean e-x-t-r-e-m-e.

**Case 4.4.** Lorelei looks over Table 4.2 and notices that virtually all of her disclosure, some of it quite intimate, goes to two persons, her husband and a friend from work. She sees both nearly everyday. Her marriage is a happy one. She has some informal time nearly everyday, although this time averages out to only about one hour on weekdays. She sees no cause for alarm.

**Case 4.5.** Nina gazes over Table 4.2 and notices that virtually all her disclosure, some of it quite intimate, goes to one confidant from work, Shari. Nina now has half an hour of informal time each day during the week, but her husband's job requires traveling during the week. So, she and Shari spend time together. Her marriage is acceptable. Upon thinking about it, Nina asks her husband to fill out Table 4.1 and Table 4.2 as well. His pattern of time and disclosure comes out much the same as hers. They both feel that their marriage is declining in quality, but only gradually. They sit down to discuss the possibility that they may be gradually drifting apart. Their discussion wisely focuses on identifying all the possible options for improvement they can. They begin to see that commitment to differing personal values, such as "advancement on the job" and "seeking human contact," involves spending their time in different ways. They had always known this but had never confronted it until now. Whenever they finally make their decisions, we can hope they will have the most complete set of possible options at their fingertips.

### Summary

After taking inventory, we discussed three aspects of your self-disclosure: category depth, category breadth, and target person. Sheer repetition should have drummed in my many warnings and cautions regarding the absence of evidence about *specific* patterns of self-disclosure. From the previous chapter, we can conclude that self-disclosure is important for each of us. From the inventory of self-disclosure, you must draw your own conclusions. Whatever you conclude, do not conclude prematurely that you are in trouble now, or even potential trouble. By "prematurely," I mean before completing this chapter and/or relying heavily on the views of other people. In short, don't jump off the deep end just because you fall somewhat shy of your ideals. Who doesn't?

### Inventory of My Touching

As with self-disclosure, little evidence is available about *specific* implications of body contact patterns—beyond the general fact that touching is important. Therefore we will simply take inventory as before.

ACTIVITY 4.9.

This inventory concerns the role of touching in your relationships, with primary concern for *your* welfare. Therefore the inventory concerns you being touched by other persons. Figure 4.1 shows the front and back views of one human body, which represents yours. For this activity, the information is confidential and possibly X-rated, so use a separate sheet of paper. Across the top put the initials of the same other persons whose initials you put across the top of Table 4.2. Down the left margin put numbers corresponding to the body regions in Figure 4.1. Then draw boxes as in Table 4.2. To take inventory, enter one number into each box as follows:

1. Enter "1" if *they touch you* only rarely, not as a regular part of your relationship.
2. Enter "2" if they touch you as a regular part of your relationship.
3. Leave the box blank if touching never occurs.

If you like, complete this table again with circled entries showing how you touch these other persons rather than how they touch you.

After completing activity 4.9, you are on your own to draw conclusions. Evidence to guide you will be available someday. Until then, I can only (1) identify the touching feature of intimacy as important and (2) refer you back to the warnings and cautions already given regarding self-disclosure.

### Inventory of My Accumulation of Rewards Over Time

*Time is money—says the vulgarest saw known to any age of people. Turn it around*

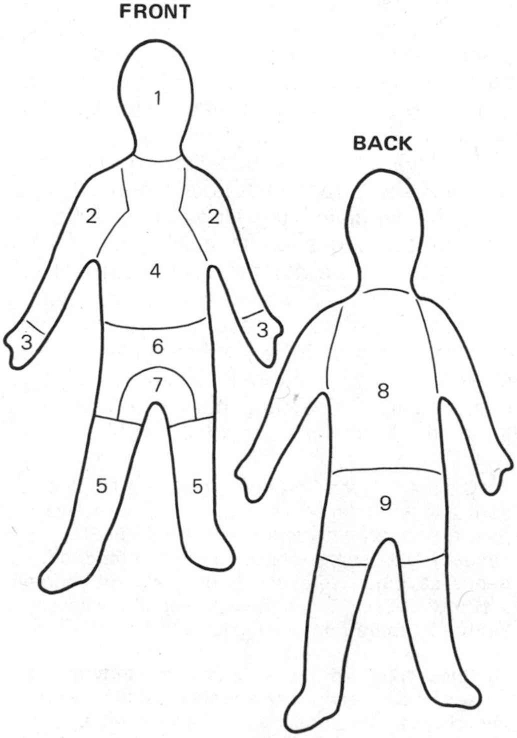


**Figure 4.1.** Human figure for inventory of my touching.

*and you get a precious truth—money is time.*

GEORGE GISSING

As any good relationship deepens, a lot of rewards and some costs are exchanged and accumulated in the persons' minds. Whenever we get right down to the nitty-gritty of discussing just what the rewards might be, a few of my students usually object to pursuing this topic further. It is not fruitful to analyze a beautiful and intimate relationship bit by bit, they say. The claim is that intimate relationships are made up of personal, intangible, mystical things, and we had better not mess around with such things. I agree with the personal and intangible part, but not the mystical. A shroud of mystery has always surrounded the unknown processes of body and behavior. But it is precisely the attempt to discover just what goes into the making of a good thing (i.e., beautiful human relationship) that is worth the effort. If we can discover what makes up a good interpersonal relationship, then maybe we can have more of it. Moving toward such discovery does not mean that we psychologists will capture an area such as love or intimacy and wrest it away from philosophy and literature. No, the discovery process means that authors and philosophers will come to share such areas with psychologists, which is all to the good.

Despite all this justification and good intentions, there remain serious technical problems in identifying the kinds of rewards that go into building and maintaining an intimate relationship. The knottiest problem can be stated simply: To count toward an intimate relationship, rewards have to have something personal about them. Whatever it is that makes them personal must be something special, and it is clear that not all rewards have it—as the following cases illustrate.

**Case 4.6.** Mr. Scrooge McTightwad is known as the town miser. On his way to work, he walks past a beggar, who requests a handout. He casually flips some money to the outstretched hands saying, "Here, my good man, get yourself a cup of coffee." Does the coin count toward any kind of intimate relationship?

**Case 4.7.** An anonymous young lady avails herself of the services of a male prostitute. After intercourse, the prostitute remarks what a wonderful sex partner she has been. Do the prostitute's sex actions and remark count toward any kind of intimate relationship?

**Case 4.8.** Bill invites Carol over to his place for a Friday evening meal. He serves a TV dinner and a superbly crafted cake purchased from the bakery. Does this dinner count toward any kind of intimate relationship?

Before rendering final judgments about these three cases, let us reconsider each in turn, but with a few critical elements changed.

**Case 4.9.** Mr. Scrooge McTightwad is rumored to have a girlfriend. Indeed, we see him on the way to her house, and he is carrying a mysterious package. He can barely heft this square but thin object covered with brown paper. Upon arriving, he presents her with a painting. It may not overwhelm the art critics in New York or Paris, but he spent all last weekend painting it. Does the painting count toward any kind of intimate relationship?

**Case 4.10.** The anonymous young lady moves to a nearby town and falls in love with the local pharmacist. They see each other constantly. Upon having had intercourse with her the first time, he gasps at what a wonderful sex partner she has been. Do his sex actions and remark count toward any kind of intimate relationship?

**Case 4.11.** Bill invites Carol to his place for a Friday evening meal. He serves a delicious gourmet feast, complete with home-grown herbs, his own French bread, and even liqueur after dinner. Does this dinner count toward any kind of intimate relationship?

I am sure almost everyone has answered no to the first three cases and yes to the last three. In both sets of cases, there were exchanges of rewards that had equal value (we assume perfectly equal dollar value or dollar estimate of worth by the recipient here for sake of argument). Yet, in the last three cases, there was something special about the exchange that made it count toward an intimate relationship. What was that something special? Does adding that special something guarantee intimacy? In the following paragraphs, I believe we can isolate the special something; but, alas, I know of nothing that guarantees intimacy.

The special personal something that counts toward an intimate relationship is a *scarce personal resource.* In other words, I claim that the key ingredient of personal rewards that makes them eligible for deepening social penetration is *scarcity.* In the cases about Mr. Scrooge McTightwad, his time was scarce but his money was not. He had a lot of money, but he was issued only 24 hours of time per day, just like all the rest of us. In the cases of the anonymous young lady, the sex actions and the remark of her pharmacist were reserved just for her and therefore were scarce. In contrast, the prostitute sold the same sex actions and gave the same remark to all his customers. In the cases of Bill and Carol, Bill spent the same amount of money on both occasions. However, in the second instance, he poured his own precious time into preparing the dinner. Is it not the investment of a scarce resource, usually time, that makes homemade goodies special compared to bought goods? In all these cases, the special something consisted of scarce personal resources. Such resources are usually (but not always) a direct function of the personal *time* invested in those resources.

For a comprehensive system of rewards, we turn to the work of Uriel and Edna Foa. These researchers developed a system of interpersonal "resources," as they call them, based on research.[7] Since we cover their system more fully in Chapter 8, here we will go directly to applying their system. The system consists of six categories of resources; these resources are categories of meaning. Let us first list the six kinds of resources and then apply them.

1. *Love.* Love means affection. Love here incorporates at least Swensen's six components discussed in the previous chapter. In the Foa and Foa system, love means a category of meaning inside the head of a person, that is, the same meaning we used in discussing love in the previous chapter. Thus, you could convey love by baking a cake, kissing, spending time, and so on.
2. *Status.* Status means respect. Saying "I admire your work" conveys respect.
3. *Information.* Information means factual content.
4. *Money.* Money is any token that has a standard unit of exchange.
5. *Goods.* Goods are tangible objects.
6. *Services.* Services are labor for another person. A barber performs a service. So do you when you do a favor for a friend gratis (free).

ACTIVITY 4.10.

Six kinds of rewards or resources in the Foa and Foa system are listed. After each one, list two specific rewards you could offer to another person. Make one a scarce personal resource and the other not so scarce for you to supply. It may help to think in terms of a real relationship you have (or had) with a specific other person. If the meanings of the six kinds of rewards are not clear, turn to Figure 8.1 in Chapter 8 and read the accompanying section. Read "Kinds of Rewards," where each is treated in more detail.

*1. Love. Scarce*

____________________________________

*Not Scarce*

____________________________________

*2. Status. Scarce*

____________________________________

*Not Scarce*

____________________________________

*3. Information. Scarce*

____________________________________

*Not Scarce*

____________________________________

*4. Money. Scarce*

____________________________________

*Not Scarce*

____________________________________

*5. Goods. Scarce*

______________________________

*Not Scarce*

______________________________

*6. Services. Scarce*

______________________________

*Not Scarce*

______________________________

### Intriguing Afterthought

It may well be the case that all scarce personal resources (not commercial resources) derive ultimately from the investment of personal time. For example, picture a row of raw wood shanties turning gray, lining a mining-town street in Appalachia somewhere. A miner toils endless hours to barely support his family, and each child gets a tiny allowance each week. Suppose the oldest boy saves up his allowances and buys his best girl a piece of jewelry. Although the jewelry is an object, it is certainly scarce. In this example, we can trace the scarcity of gifts back to the scarcity of money in the boy's family. Going one step further, the scarcity of the money derived from the father's scarce time invested in getting the money. As an intriguing afterthought on scarce personal resources, can they *all* be traced ultimately back to the investment of personal time?

### Inventory of My Fairness

Have you ever heard the old saying, "You only get out of a relationship what you put into it?" Psychologists have elaborated this saying into a clever theory of fairness, or "equity." The theory draws heavily on the idea we considered in the last section: human relationships involve the exchange of social and other resources. In all human relationships, be they business or love, various conceptions of fair play exist. Equity theory tries to spell out the concept of fairness in useful terms.

In a remarkably clear and broad statement, Elaine Walster, Ellen Berscheid, and G. William Walster provide a handy introduction to equity theory.[8] They begin with a few basic propositions: "*Proposition I:* Individuals will try to maximize their outcomes (where outcomes equal rewards minus costs). . . . *Proposition II A:* Groups can maximize collective reward by evolving accepted systems for 'equitably' [fairly] apportioning rewards and costs among members."[9] As a result of such cultural systems to insure fair play, "*Proposition III:* Individuals who discover they are in an inequitable relationship attempt to eliminate their distress by restoring equity. The greater the inequity that exists, the more distress they feel and the harder they try to restore equity."[10] Finally, restoring equity can take two basic forms: either actual or psychological equity can be restored. Now let us apply these propositions to human relationships of varying intimacy.

**Case 4.12.** Ron and Rhonda have been engaged for about two months, but their relationship is beginning to turn sour. Even though Ron puts all the time, money, affection, and effort he can into the relationship, Rhonda plays it cooler and cooler as the days go by. She makes herself unavailable half the time he calls, does not respond to his financial sacrifices, and refuses to give any affection other than an occasional smile and a ritual good-night kiss. She is stringing him along and enjoying every minute of it.

According to the theory, a fair relationship *requires* that you and your other person both get out of the relationship according to what you put into it. Schematically, the theory says:

$$\frac{\text{Your outcomes}}{\text{Your inputs}} \quad \text{must equal} \quad \frac{\text{other person's outcomes.}}{\text{other person's inputs.}}$$

You "inputs" consist of all resources (rewards and costs) you put into the relationship; your "outcomes" consist of all resources (rewards and costs) you get out of the relationship. In this case, a fair relationship would clearly require:

$$\frac{\text{Ron's outcomes}}{\text{Ron's inputs}} \quad \text{must equal} \quad \frac{\text{Rhonda's outcomes.}}{\text{Rhonda's inputs.}}$$

There are any number of fair relationships between Ron and Rhonda that might occur. Below are three fair patterns for Ron and Rhonda.

Fair:

| Ron's outcomes are LARGE |
|---|
| Ron's inputs are LARGE |

and

| Rhonda's outcomes are LARGE. |
|---|
| Rhonda's inputs are LARGE. |

Fair:

| Ron's outcomes are LARGE |
|---|
| Ron's inputs are MEDIUM |

and

| Rhonda's outcomes are LARGE. |
|---|
| Rhonda's inputs are MEDIUM. |

Fair:

| Ron's outcomes are LARGE |
|---|
| Ron's inputs are MEDIUM |

and

| Rhonda's outcomes are MEDIUM. |
|---|
| Rhonda's inputs are SMALL. |

In these three cases, each gets out according to what they put in, so fairness obtains. However, in Case 4.12 I actually described a horribly unfair relationship, which we can picture in this way:

Unfair:

| Ron's SMALL outcomes |
|---|
| Ron's LARGE inputs |

do not equal

| Rhonda's LARGE outcomes. |
|---|
| Rhonda's SMALL inputs. |

In a real-life romance, there are surely all sorts of resources being exchanged, focusing around love. At this stage of the art, it is surely premature for us to attempt to assign numbers to resources exchanged in our everyday lives in intimate relationships to calculate fairness. Nevertheless, a picture of the resources invested in Ron and Rhonda's relationship is easily seen to be unfair. (The term *invested* is used instead of *exchanged* because of the possible importance of solitary activities to the relationship. For example, Ron may spend two sleepless nights per week and worry for 20 daytime hours weekly. While these resources [time, emotion] are not exchanged, they are surely invested in the relationship.) Some of the resources invested by Ron and Rhonda are listed in Figure 4.2. Notice that the outcomes are personal for each party, so that Figure 4.2 is unique to the relationship between these two people.

ACTIVITY 4.11.

In this activity, try your hand at filling in Figure 4.3 for one of your own relationships. As in Case 4.12, we are concerned with perceived, or psychological, equity because our actions are based on perceptions. First, pick a specific relationship you have with another person (you need not use names); it should be a relationship in which there is some level of intimacy. Figure 4.3 pictures the resources for fairness in your relationship. Think about your relationship to your other person for this moment in time. Then fill in your perceived degrees of investment for each category of resource, according to whether the input is high, medium, or low. In each blank, write the word "high," "medium," or "low" and whatever other notes you wish. After doing this repeat the process for your ideal relationship with this person, circling your answers this time.

How can you interpret the pattern in Figure 4.3? As in previous stages of this whole self-inventory, the main idea is to put your finger on the important features of intimacy relationships. No definite numerical or clinical interpretations can be made. Nevertheless, certain patterns that should sharpen our perceptions of our own intimate relationships can emerge. I now offer some suggestions that can assist in interpreting Figure 4.3.

In Figure 4.3 it is only the total of your inputs or outcomes that matters. For example, let us consider only your outcomes. In filling out Figure 4.3, you considered six kinds of rewards to make up your outcomes in the upper left corner of Figure 4.3. In equity theory, these six outcomes are all added together in your mind to form one total outcome for you. The same is true for your inputs, other person's inputs, and other person's outcomes in Figure 4.3.

**Ron's SMALL Outcomes**

AFFECTION – gets one lousy kiss per date; gets very few compliments.

STATUS – gets only six hours weekly with fiancée; is not told she is impressed by him.

INFORMATION – gets little self-disclosure from her.

MONEY – gets no money or offers of loans.

GOODS, SERVICES – gets no gifts.

SOCIAL OCCASIONS – enjoys the dates.

**Rhonda's LARGE Outcomes**

AFFECTION – gets many compliments.

STATUS – is told he is impressed by her.

INFORMATION – gets much self-disclosure from him.

MONEY – gets money; gets offers of loans.

GOODS, SERVICES – gets gifts.

SOCIAL OCCASIONS – enjoys the dates.

**does not equal**

**Ron's LARGE Inputs**

AFFECTION – gives many compliments.

STATUS – has two sleepless nights weekly; worries 20 daytime hours each week, tells her he is impressed by her endlessly.

INFORMATION – gives her much self-disclosure.

MONEY – gives her money; offers loans to her.

GOODS, SERVICES – gives gifts.

SOCIAL OCCASIONS – prepares for each date much in advance.

**Rhonda's SMALL Inputs**

AFFECTION – gives few compliments; gives only one good-night kiss per date.

STATUS – spends only 6 hours weekly with him; no sleepless nights; no daytime worrying; does not tell him she is impressed by him.

INFORMATION – gives him little self-disclosure.

MONEY – gives no money; gives no offers of loans.

GOODS, SERVICES – gives no gifts.

SOCIAL OCCASIONS – prepares one hour for each date.

**Figure 4.2.** Pattern of unfair relationship in the sad case of Ron and Rhonda (see text Case 4.12).

Another factor to consider is that a

$$\frac{\text{HIGH}}{\text{MEDIUM}} = \frac{\text{MEDIUM}}{\text{LOW}}$$

pattern can be quite fair and equitable because each party gets out *in proportion to inputs.* Suppose your "medium" input is 50 psychological units in your mind, and suppose the other person's "low" input is 25 psychological units in your mind. Then the equation

$$\frac{\text{HIGH}}{\text{MEDIUM}} = \frac{\text{MEDIUM}}{\text{LOW}}$$

becomes

$$\frac{100}{50} = \frac{50}{25}$$

in your mind.

Since 100/50 does in fact equal 50/25, the equation balances, so fairness and equity hold. Another way to describe this relationship is that you're putting a moderate amount into it and getting a high outcome, and your other person is only putting a small amount into it and getting a moderate outcome. This arrangement is fair and equitable. Note that inputs and outcomes here reside in your mind. Also, remember that Figure 4.3 reflects equity from your view. Your other person's view is

**Your Outcomes**

AFFECTION ____________
STATUS ____________
INFORMATION ____________
MONEY ____________
GOODS, SERVICES ____________
SOCIAL OCCASIONS ____________
____________

**Other Person's Outcomes**

AFFECTION ____________
STATUS ____________
INFORMATION ____________
MONEY ____________
GOODS, SERVICES ____________
SOCIAL OCCASIONS ____________
____________

**and**

**Your Inputs**

AFFECTION ____________
STATUS ____________
INFORMATION ____________
MONEY ____________
GOODS, SERVICES ____________
SOCIAL OCCASIONS ____________
____________

**Other Person's Inputs**

AFFECTION ____________
STATUS ____________
INFORMATION ____________
MONEY ____________
GOODS, SERVICES ____________
SOCIAL OCCASIONS ____________
____________

**Figure 4.3.** Fairness of relationship in Activity 4.11.

another matter. Of course, it is your view we are emphasizing.

Another part of the fairness and equity story concerns what we do when faced with an unfair relationship. Continuing with Case 4.12, consider poor Ron. According to equity theory, Ron will feel distress in no uncertain terms! What will he do? There are several ways he can reduce his distress. The first and most obvious is to get out of the relationship. As Cervantes said, "Love is a power too strong to be overcome by anything but flight."[11] However, Frederic Amiel claimed "Doubt of the reality of love ends by making us doubt everything."[12] Since doubting everything is extremely uncomfortable, we can expect poor Ron to try some courses of action before rapid depenetration.

The general goal of action is for him to try to restore equity to the relationship. Several activities follow in which Ron attempts to restore equity while still maintaining his engagement to Rhonda. Each activity begins with a strategy for our lovesick hero to patch up his hopeless engagement. Your task is to specify as precisely as you can just what he would do to pursue each strategy.

ACTIVITY 4.12.

In this first strategy, Ron attempts to restore psychological equity by grossly distorting his perceptions of his own outcomes. What would he do in this process of distortion?

____________

____________

____________

____________

____________

ACTIVITY 4.13.
Ron attempts to lessen his already large inputs. How does he do this?

______________________________
______________________________
______________________________

ACTIVITY 4.14.
Ron openly requests greater outcomes. What does he say?

______________________________
______________________________
______________________________

ACTIVITY 4.15.
Ron justifies his own exploitation. How?

______________________________
______________________________
______________________________

ACTIVITY 4.16.
Ron retaliates. How?

______________________________
______________________________
______________________________

## OPTIONS FOR ATTAINING OPTIMAL INTIMACY

Up to this point, you have taken self-inventory. We have tried to be specific enough to allow for the following:

1. Application of the six features of intimacy to real relationships in your own life.
2. Approximation of where you stand at the present time on each.
3. Comparison between where you stand now with your realistic ideal.

Hopefully, this self-inventory provides an idea of the direction in which you would like to go, if you desire changes at all.

The "direction" is general in nature. For example, "giving more self-disclosure to my best friend" is a general direction to go. The specifics of disclosure occur from moment to moment. Chapters 6 through 10 concern such moment-to-moment events, so we will not deal with them here. Rather, our concern still lies with the shape of our social life over the longer run, specifically with emotional intimacy. The goal over time is to arrange your life so as to fall within the optimal range of intimacy you set for yourself. No assumptions are made that any change is needed at present. If you *do* desire change, a greater number of options for you is assumed to be to your benefit. More options means more choices, and more choices means more potential benefits.

In addition to identifying major directions for potential change (as we have done), there is a completely different approach toward optimal intimacy. We can also ask, "Is it possible to identify situations in which intimacy is found?" Technically, the answer here is no. However, it is possible to identify situations in which the *odds* for finding human contact are greater than others. In the following section are a number of such situations, presented in arbitrary order. We begin with the delightful topic of pets.

## SITUATIONS AND OPPORTUNITIES FOR INTIMACY

### The Lost Topic of Pets

If you could have all your colleagues read one book, what book would you choose? As for me, I would oblige my fellow psychologists to discover a lost topic by reading Boris Levinson's eye-opening *Pets and Human Development.*[13] Levinson's own words set the tone:

> *Animals are a symbol of the rehumanization of society to the extent that they are allowed to function as members of the animal world, rather than as four-footed humans whose very nature is denied, and are permitted to bring their owners into that world of life, impulse, and love. The very fact that animals are regarded by so many individuals as burdens and sources of disorder indicates how far our social structure has strayed from a recognition of human needs and desires. Scientific investigation into the significance and use of pets for both children and adults has been very sparce. L. Carmichael's compendious "Manual of Child Psychology,"*[14] *for example,* nowhere even mentions the word *'pet.' . . ."*[15]

For a wealth of detail concerning the benefits and pitfalls of pet ownership, I refer you to Levinson's book. Space permits us here to consider only the broad framework of his position. Basically, Levinson's observations of clients in therapy and society in general lead him to the conclusion that pets can play meaningful roles for certain people at certain times in their lives. It is not for nothing that Americans spend five times as much each year on dog food as they do on college textbooks![16]

As a premise, Levinson agrees with the arguments presented in Chapter 2, namely, that many aspects of modern society work against human contact. In addition, our technological society begins evaluating us even as children. To make human contact in our competitive, evaluative society, a certain kind of social environment is helpful, if not necessary. What kind of social environment might that be? For Carl Rogers, such an environment "means an outgoing positive feeling without reservations, without evaluations. The term we have come to use for this is *unconditional positive regard.*"[17] But where in this day and age do we get unconditional positive regard? Our schools scrutinize us, our friends select and reject us, and our jobs judge us. Levinson says pets are one answer. I say pets come *very* close to providing unconditional positive regard, even though the variety of rewards they can supply is limited.

### Function of Pets

ACTIVITY 4.17.

Levinson argues that pets can fulfill other functions in addition to unconditional positive regard. He mentions the following functions for children: cuddliness and body contact; fantasy object, imaginary companion; the fostering of responsibility, independence, and money management skills; aid to learning and peer-group membership; and object of affection. Pick one of these functions and describe how a properly managed pet relationship might serve that function. How might the pet relationship be *mis*managed in your example?

________________________________________

________________________________________

________________________________________

________________________________________

For adults, Levinson sees several functions: preparation for parenthood, relief of prenatal stress in women, child substitute, and relief of loneliness. There are special times in many lives when pets may be particularly useful. Such times include old age and bereavement for all ages. For special populations, the companionship of a pet may be the brightest —the only—ray of sunlight in a hostile world; this is true both inside and outside of institutions. Special institutionalized populations include orphans, retardates, exceptional children, the mentally ill, and prisoners.

As with all "remedies" for increasing human contact, there are pitfalls and dangers galore. Pet contact can replace human contact to a harmful degree, as when parents come to prefer a pet over a child. Certain animals have dispositions unsuited for certain children. For example, calm pets—not restless ones—are needed to soothe. The death of a pet can be traumatic.

What can you expect from a pet? No data exist, but we can glean some speculative guidelines from informal observations. A few people might be able to satisfy all their needs for human contact through animals; but for most of us it is more realistic to expect a moderate degree of exchange of affection, social occasions of companionship, and status in relating to a pet. For certain purposes, especially the immediate alleviation of loneliness, the moderate degree of contact afforded by a pet would seem to function as psychological first aid.

### Essay on Pets

When all is said and done, Levinson provides us with one more practical psychological means for attaining a moderate degree of exchange of love, social occasions of companionship, and status in a psychology obsessed with testing overly esoteric theories. A psychology that leaves out pets leaves out an important and legitimate part of life. If one were to be stranded on a desert isle, one might rationally prefer the companionship of one pet to that of the choicest books ever written. In short, I hope that we psychologists can rediscover the lost topic of pets with theories and hard-nosed empirical data. Levinson's *Pets and Human Development* certainly seems a good starting point.

*Where animals cannot live, humans cannot survive.*

HERTER'S CATALOG.

**A Consumer Report on Growth and Encounter Groups**

Along with the recent popularity of humanistic psychology has come popularity for growth and encounter groups, which we will call *experiential groups.* On the surface, experiential groups attempt to increase personal adjustment by increasing various social skills, such as empathy, sensitivity to one's own feelings, and so on. Behind the surface, experiential groups also provide a physical setting for human contact. Such groups are now so popular that it is reasonable to treat them as a commercially available service, just like the therapy, entertainment, transportation, and hospitality industries. Given the widespread problems in attaining intimacy and the widespread availability of experiential groups in colleges and urban areas, the popularity of experiential groups is easily understood.

The function of increasing social skills in an experiential group seems legitimate and plausible. In fact, to help you increase your social skills is the main goal of this book as well. The possibilities for improving personal adjustment by participating in experiential groups have been articulated elsewhere.[18] Enough research data currently exist to show that helpful outcomes can almost surely occur.[19] However, the popularity of experiential groups has led to an explosion in demand for them, with the result that the current market is flooded with all sorts of these groups. In this section, I will present some guidelines and warnings to assist you as an intelligent consumer of services.

**The APA Guidelines**

The American Psychological Association recently adopted guidelines for psychologists conducting experiential groups. For us as consumers, these guidelines represent features that an experiential group ought to have. They are as follows:

1. *Entering into a growth group experience should be on a voluntary basis; any form of coercion to participate is to be avoided.*
2. *The following information should be made available in writing to all prospective participants:*
   (*a*) *An explicit statement of the purpose of the group;*
   (*b*) *Types of techniques that may be employed;*
   (*c*) *The education, training and experience of the leader or leaders;*
   (*d*) *The fee and any additional expense that may be incurred;*
   (*e*) *A statement as to whether or not a follow-up service is included in the fee;*
   (*f*) *Goals of the group experience and techniques to be used;*
   (*g*) *Amounts and kinds of responsibility to be assumed by the leader and by the participants. For example,* (*i*) *the degree to which a participant is free not to follow suggestions and prescriptions of the group leader and other group members;* (*ii*) *any restrictions on a participant's freedom to leave the group at any time; and,*
   (*h*) *Issues of confidentiality.*
3. *A screening interview should be conducted by the group leader prior to the acceptance of any participant. It is the responsibility of the leader to screen out those individuals for whom he or she judges the group experience to be inappropriate. Should an interview not be possible, then other measures should be used to achieve the same results.*

   *At the time of the screening interview, or at some other time prior to the beginning of the group, opportunity should be provided for leader-participant exploration of the terms of the contract as described in the information statement. This is to assure mutual understanding of the contract.*
4. *It is recognized that growth groups may be used for both educational and psychotherapeutic purposes. If the purpose is primarily educational, the leader assumes the usual professional and ethical obligations of an educator. If the purpose is therapeutic, the leader assumes the usual professional and ethical responsibilities he or she would assume in individual or group psychotherapy, including before and*

*after consultation with any other therapist who may be professionally involved with the participant. In both cases, the leader's own education, training, and experience should be commensurate with these responsibilities.*

5. *It is recognized that growth groups may be used for responsible research or exploration of human potential and may therefore involve the use of innovative and unusual techniques. While such professional exploration must be protected and encouraged, the welfare of the participant is of paramount importance. Therefore, when an experience is clearly identified as "experimental," the leader should* (a) *make full disclosure of techniques to be used,* (b) *delineate the respective responsibilities of the leader and participant during the contract discussion phase prior to the official beginning of the group experience, and* (c) *evaluate and make public his or her findings.*

(From "Guidelines for Psychologists Conducting Growth Groups," *American Psychologist,* vol. 28, 1973, p. 933. Copyright 1973, The American Psychological Association. Reprinted by permission.)

### The Altman and Taylor Warning

Social penetration theorists Altman and Taylor issue an "easy-in, easy-out" warning.[20] They fear that rapid social penetration in experiential groups cannot help but lead to the expectation for rapid depenetration as well. Even worse, as millions of people learn to penetrate and depenetrate quickly, moving from one relationship to another, Altman and Taylor predict that "ability to trust others would lessen since one could not rely on others for long periods."[21] While Altman and Taylor recognize the contemporary need to form relationships more quickly than ever before, they believe that lasting intimacy is so complicated that we can attain it only by a slow *social* penetration.

> *The ability to communicate with* one other person *requires a highly idiosyncratic, well-tuned, and synchronized communication system. It is difficult to believe that such communication can happen all at once. If this is correct, then what appears to pass for intimacy, genuineness, and respect for the integrity of others may be nothing more than a new level of superficial exchange which is only a substitute for the very things that had been rejected.*[22]

### The Flanders Warning

I become suspicious whenever a special-purpose training group or a commercially available service actually becomes "where the social action is." Perhaps it is my intuition saying that meaningful human contact ordinarily occurs in our private abodes, meetings, and social occasions. Perhaps it is the fact that the group leader's professional reputation or pocketbook is enchanced by running growth groups. Abraham Maslow agrees:

> *In the East, spiritual teachers and guides will generally also make this same point, that to improve oneself is a lifelong effort. The same lesson is now slowly dawning upon the more thoughtful and sober leaders of T-groups, basic encounter groups, personal growth groups, affective education, etc., who are now in the painful process of giving up the "Big Bang" theory of self-actualization.*[23]

Experiential groups seem to have real possibilities for *temporary* purposes, such as initiating interactions and specific skill training. Nevertheless, I am on the lookout when the occasion for specialized training becomes a major setting for experiencing human contact, as when individuals patronize encounter groups *repeatedly.*

In addition, most experiential groups usually do not possess several of the features I hold necessary for intimate human contact. First, the meeting times seldom occur on a nearly daily basis. Second, the time spent is not informal because participants all play the special, artificial, temporary role of "experiential group participant," which often implies hurried self-disclosure and other actions. Third, the accumulation of rewards over time implies exchange of a diverse range of scarce personal resources. Sooner or later, true lovers exchange all six kinds of personal resources in the Foa and Foa system. Unless the experiential group indeed becomes the center of one's social world, it stands to reason that one's scarce personal resources will be saved for relationships that endure over months and years. In fairness to some experiential group leaders, though, I readily admit that some groups do in fact endure over months and years.

### The Lieberman, Yalom, and Miles Warning

Lieberman, Yalom, and Miles did a questionnaire study of outcomes of members of 17 different experiential groups.[24] All the groups were led by experienced professionals of varied theoretical persuasions. Group members' outcomes were compared with outcomes for a control group made up of students who could not be accommodated because of scheduling problems. On extensive self-reports, group members told of significant personal changes, usually for the better. On the basis of reports by friends, however, no differences between group members and control group students could be detected. Rather frighteningly, in a follow-up done 6 to 8 months later, 10 percent of the experiential group members were described by the researchers as "casualties," that is "suffering serious psychological harm." No such casualties appeared in the control group. These authors concluded that experiential groups are potentially useful, but only if we have modest expectations concerning outcomes from participating in them.

### The Sigmund Koch Warning

Of all opponents of the encounter group movement, Sigmund Koch is probably the most caustic. He claims:

> *It* [*the encounter group movement*] *seeks to court spontaneity and authenticity by artifice; to combat instrumentalism instrumentally; to provide access to experience by reducing it to a packaged commodity; to engineer autonomy by group pressure; to liberate individuality by group shaping . . . It provides, in effect, a convenient psychic whorehouse for the purchase of well-advertised existential "goodies": authenticity, freedom, wholeness, flexibility, community, love, joy. One enters for liberating consummations but invariably settles for psychic strip-tease.*[25]

### The Abraham Maslow Warning

The warning by Maslow is quoted without comment.

> *My own belief is very strong that the salvation of mankind lies essentially in the advancement of knowledge. Also my feeling is very strong that we do not yet know enough to be good humanistic psychologists or good humanistic teachers or practitioners. I continually urge those psychologists who call themselves humanistic to regard their main task as research, that is, the advancement of knowledge of human nature. I am certainly in favor of "personal growth centers" and personal growth education and have been much involved with them from their beginning (and still am). But I should make it very clear that I did then and still do regard these primarily as experiments in the old-fashioned sense, i.e., attempts to find out more about human nature alone and in groups. I am very disturbed by those who proceed blithely to assume that we already know what we are doing and then simply apply in an unquestioning way the techniques, which have been offered as simple experimental techniques, as "trying something out to see what happens." I consider much of the Esalen-type education to be the application of a science which does not yet exist. Many of these kinds of education are used as if they were simply applying answers which had already been attained.*
>
> *I share with many other scholars and scientists a great uneasiness over some trends (or rather misuses) in Esalen-type education. For instance, in some of its less respectworthy adherents, I see trends toward anti-intellectualism, anti-science, anti-rationality, anti-discipline, anti-hard work, etc. I worry when competence and training are by some considered to be irrelevant or unnecessary. I worry when I see impulsivity confused with spontaneity. I worry when people, especially young people, overlook the fact that the proponents of spontaneity, for example people like Aldous Huxley or Alan Watts or Carl Rogers, are themselves highly disciplined, hard working people who think*

*of true spontaneity as the consequence of much hard work, as the reward for high personal development. I worry when youngsters think that this is something that you begin with, something that is easy to achieve. I do not think that spontaneity by fiat is possible. I think, for instance, that the basic encounter group, or T-group, or OD [organizational development] training is a real and important invention (of hard working scientists) and can be a blessing when well run. But it can be a disaster when incompetently run or self-run (which frequently amounts to the same thing).*[26]

### The Carl Rogers Warning

Carl Rogers, perhaps the foremost popularizer of experiential groups, remarked to Ralph Keyes, "Though I'd still do them [weekend encounter groups], that's not my choice. You can leave with a real high, but there's no follow-up. It's more costly, less dramatic and more lasting to reveal something to someone you've known for years."[27]

### The Ralph Keyes Warning

In reaction to an early draft of this chapter, Ralph Keyes wrote:

*The most sophisticated alternative [to emotional intimacy] is the transient or sexual pseudo-intimacy of encounter groups and related activities. I'm continually amazed at how the language of intimacy ("I'm experiencing a good feeling about you," etc.) can be used to hold people off as can hugs which often substitute for hits. I'm finding generally that some people functioning under the heading "Humanistic Psychology" have developed some startlingly sophisticated means to feign intimacy with no real contact at all.*[28]

### The Alternate Procedures Warning

Do experiential groups do a specific job better than alternative procedures? Julian Rappaport and his colleagues investigated this question with special reference to self-disclosure.[29] After all, there is probably no other specific result that is presumed to emerge from most experiential groups that is more important or more commonly agreed upon than increased self-disclosure after the group training is finished. Rappaport, Gross, and Lepper investigated self-disclosure after student volunteers had participated in sensitivity training groups. These groups ran for 2 hours per week over 7 weeks and were all led by experienced doctoral level trainers. Participants in these groups were compared with others who had no such training, but rather either (1) saw a 20-minute videotape of another student exhibiting self-disclosure or (2) were merely instructed to disclose themselves. The crucial question hinged on how much self-disclosure would be displayed by persons with each of the three kinds of training (sensitivity training, short videotape, or just instructions) in later group meetings. In fact, the sensitivity training did produce results. However, the researchers also "found that specific instructions alone and modeling alone were each sufficient to induce the desired performance" of self-disclosure.[30] If, in the central area of self-disclosure, 20 minutes of television or 20 seconds of instructions can produce results equivalent to 14 hours of sensitivity training, then you as a consumer of such training might do well to inquire about the specific benefits or results you may receive that have been documented to occur in addition to those you might expect from alternative procedures that take far less time.

### The Bleeding-Heart Counterwarning

Despite the value of all these warnings about experiential groups for you as consumers, it must look as though the wolves of traditional psychology are circling ever closer about the lambs of humanistic psychology. Such is indeed the case. There has been a rush to issue fearsome warnings about experiential groups while applying a double standard to the sacred cow of classroom teaching. The following discussion of classroom teaching concerns college classes in general.

There is the distinct possibility that the number of "casualties" from ordinary classroom teaching is proportionately as great or greater than the number of experiential group members who suffer psychological harm. Researchers David Johnson, Jack Kavanagh, and Bernard Lubin asked students to rate their own anxiety before and after participating in both an experiential T-group and a regular

# You can be a Saturday hero doing what you do on Saturday.

It's so easy—just include a fatherless boy in your plans each week. He'll really appreciate it, whether you're going fishing, working on the car, or watching the big game. A boy needs someone to do things with. Someone to guide him over the rough spots in life. Someone to show him he can grow up to be the man he'd like to be. Be a Saturday hero and call your local Big Brothers. Even if it's Tuesday, Wednesday or Thursday.

# Be a Big Brother.

course examination.[31] Anxiety dropped from before to after for the experiential group, but anxiety remained high for the exam group. Some college students commit suicide under circumstances closely connected to their academic fate. What can we make of all this? Should college classrooms be legally or otherwise regulated to minimize psychological harm?

The problem extends far beyond the limited settings of experiential groups and college classrooms. If government or professional agencies begin to regulate college courses in detailed ways, academic freedom goes out the window. If academic freedom is restricted, a vital national forum of expression and creativity is lost. You might as well destroy freedom of the press. So what should be done? The best solution is probably to issue public warnings (e.g., in places such as this book) about the dangers in situations where psychological harm can occur, such as experiential groups and college classrooms. A less desirable course would legally require experiential groups or college classrooms to be conducted so that no casualties ever resulted. This would be like installing a sprinkler system in your house and running it all the time to prevent a fire. Certainly no fires would break out. No casualties would result from fire. However, in the prevention process, experiential groups and college classrooms would be destroyed.

### Helping Other People as a Volunteer

It strikes me that few opportunities are better suited for opening doors to human contact than the numerous volunteer agencies, such as the Red Cross, Big Brothers (see Figure 4.4), and Big Sisters. Fortunately, there now exists a fine national organization that carefully matches up volunteers with agencies and openings in their local community: the National Center for Voluntary Action, whose advertisement appears in Figure 4.5. Upon receiving your call or letter (the address is shown in Figure 4.5), the center puts you in touch with the local Voluntary Action Center or agency nearest you. Then a match is made by the local action center or local agency. A local contact person is available in most communities in the United States. If you feel volunteer work is for you, contacting the National Center for Voluntary Action is a specific place to start.

**Figure 4.4.** Advertisement for Big Brothers, a volunteer agency for providing fatherless boys with companionship and human contact. (Reprinted by permission.)

Another way to go about entering volunteer work is to call a specific agency in your community. Some agencies, such as Big Brothers and Big Sisters, were established with the main purpose of enhancing human contact. Others, such as the Red Cross, provide a variety of services. You can contact the local units of these and other agencies by calling them directly or by contacting their national offices. To contact the National Center for Voluntary Action, see Figure 4.5. To contact the national-level Big Brothers and Big Sisters, see footnote 32.[32] For assistance in Great Britain, also see footnote 32.

### The Architectural Environment You Choose

Most of us do not think much about the influence our architectural surroundings have on us. Think about your residence. Think about your place of work. Think about the physical surroundings in your classroom. In all these settings, the architecture does not demand an immediate response from us, as people do; the influence of architecture is subtle.

In everyone's life there are a few occasions when you make a decision about your present and/or future architectural and environmental surroundings. Choosing a residence is one example. I would put such decisions along with choosing a career or mate in a category my father calls hilltop decisions. One makes *hilltop decisions* only a few times in a lifetime, and there are precious few guidelines for such decisions.[33] You might turn to books and courses on architecture, the environment, environmental psychology, and the like.[34] You might also consider an architectural solution for the city offered by architect Christopher Alexander.

In Chapter 2 we considered architect Alexander's views about how city architecture keeps people apart. The research he cited was woven into our later review of evidence on loneliness. His architectural solution to the problem of human contact in the modern city is discussed now. His goal was to design modern housing that offers the opportunity of dropping in informally on one's neighbor.

# For a few hours a week, Janet Kasem is ten feet tall.

Janet is a volunteer.

She and other members of her boating club take kids from the inner city out to have fun. And to learn about water safety.

By giving those kids someone to look up to, Janet believes she may help them grow as people. She's absolutely sure her volunteer experience is helping her.

That's the way it is when you volunteer. You start out with a feeling that you can help people. That your skill, your training, your concern can make a difference. And soon, you find the few hours a week you spend at it are precious, enriching hours for you as well.

Haven't you ever found yourself thinking how you could help people in your community? Do it. We'll help you find organizations in your town that would love to have you working with them. Join one. Or, if you see the need for a new program, start one. Call the Voluntary Action Center where you live. Or write: "Volunteer", Washington, D.C. 20013.

If you can spare even a few hours a week, why not spend them feeling ten feet tall?

**Volunteer.**
The National Center for Voluntary Action

A Public Service of
This Magazine &
The Advertising Council
Ad Council

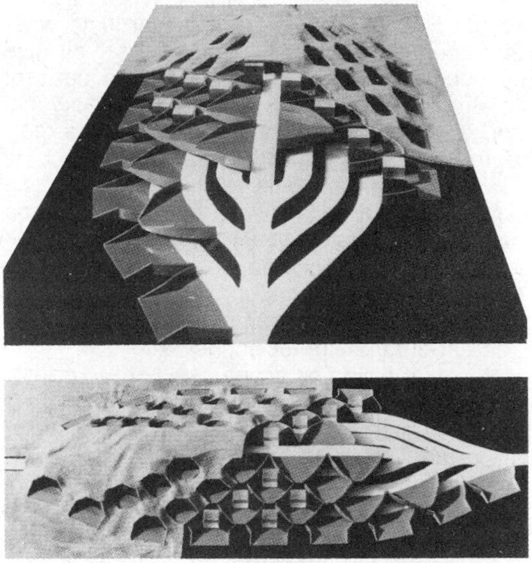

**Figure 4.6.** Christopher Alexander's architectural solution to enhance human contact in the modern city. (Reprinted from ENVIRONMENT FOR MAN: THE NEXT FIFTY YEARS, William R. Ewald, Jr., Editor. Copyright © 1967 by Indiana University Press, Bloomington. Reprinted by permission of the publisher and Alexander.)

Because Alexander believes intimacy requires frequent and informal meetings, the opportunity to have other people informally (unexpectedly) drop in is required. To allow this opportunity, Alexander presents the model shown in Figure 4.6.[35] Within each of the pod-shaped protrusions is a residence. Each residence has a transparent communal area, and occupying this area is a sign that it is OK to drop in. For privacy, "the transparent communal room is surrounded by free-standing, self-contained enclosed pavilions, each functioning as a bed-living unit, so arranged that each person in the family, or any number of people who wish to be undisturbed, can retire to one of these pavilions and be totally private."[36]

The genius of Alexander's solution is that social activities are given greater importance than, say, the mechanical efficiency of cooking a meal. Of course, Alexander's solution is radical. However, perhaps his ideas and the architectural photographs in Chapter 1 serve as useful reminders that architecture and social life are closely related. What is the practical upshot of this discussion about architecture?

You can accord choosing a residence the importance due a truly hilltop decision. Decisions about your future surroundings deserve your most careful attention. You do have choices. If seeking optimal human contact is one of your values, it is rational to award your dollars to architectural designs based on the values in harmony with your own. Whatever the case, I recommend spending some scarce personal resources to explore all the options you possibly can before deciding on, say, a residence.

## The Singles Scene

If you glance back at Figure 2.6, you will see contents of *The Single Floridian* magazine. The list of contents or "features" reflects a potpourri of concern to single people in general. We will take *the singles' scene* to mean occasions organized to promote human contact for single people. Singles lounges are organized by commercial concerns. A dance or lecture might be organized by a nonprofit organization, such as a college or sorority. A private party could be organized by you or me. What opportunities for intimacy do these various occasions hold?

One prominent part of the singles scene is Parents Without Partners (PWP). This rapidly growing organization holds discussion groups, dances, and other social activities in local chapters across the nation. After consulting and meeting with PWP representatives at length, psychiatrist Robert Weiss files a favorable report on the organization's effects on its members.[37] However, he views PWP as a temporary supporting community, not "where the social action is" over the long run.

Weiss argues that actively working hard to meet someone in the singles scene likely leads to superficial relationships and repeated loss (depenetration).[38] There is a new role and set of role expectations associated with the singles scene. This recently created role requires accelerated social penetration and acting "outside one's social context." For example, when Jack and Jane meet in a bar at 1:00 A.M. they are outside their usual social context of home, job, friends, relatives, and

**Figure 4.5.** Advertisement for the National Center for Voluntary Action, which matches volunteers to openings in most communities in the United States. (Reprinted by permission.)

so on. Because everyone is required to wear the same mask of role expectations, you give up your individuality, at least certain parts of it. Specifically, you surrender the personal and unique set of signals you are always radiating that allows another person to see you as valuable over time. The result is that you and others are robbed of whatever chance you might have outside the singles scene to develop lasting relationships. Worse yet, the easy-in, easy-out concept applies. (Here the Weiss argument is completed.) So what is good about the singles scene? A lot.

I view the singles scene as a unique opportunity for developing social skills. It offers a world of interesting people to explore plus the opportunity for self-knowledge. By definition, the *social* aspect of your personality can be illuminated only when you or someone else is there to shine the light. For the divorced, PWP offers an improvement over what was available in the good old days. For all eligibles, the singles scene can provide social stimulation. And, yet, its main limitation must be acknowledged openly: It is, ideally, temporary for most.

### Your Own Scene

After pointing out the limitations of the singles scene, Weiss goes on to suggest situations in which intimacy is likely to be found. Such situations share the common characteristics that, once inside them, you are allowed to radiate signals that accurately reflect your own self. These situations can stem from introduction by a mutual acquaintance and special-interest activities you genuinely like.

College courses and continuing education offer an excellent opportunity to meet others with whom you have at least one common interest. David Riesman wisely recommends:

> *I also urge on students of both sexes that they employ their college years to learn a lifelong sport, a lifelong musical instrument, and other lifelong interests that may stand them in good stead, whatever fate befalls them in later life. . . .* [*Anyone*] *can watch TV like anybody else, perhaps play cards like anybody else, have drinks in a bar like anybody else—but none of these activities provides more than casual access to a network of like-minded people who could become friends and, in the luck of the draw, potential mates.*[39]

In short, your interests define *your scene.* Of course, your scene and the singles scene can coincide when both encompass a given occasion.

### SUMMARY OF PART ONE AND PREVIEW

In these last three chapters, our concern focused on human contact or intimacy. In Chapter 2, a case was made for the importance of human contact for personal adjustment. In Chapter 3, I proposed six features of a general dimension running from emotional loneliness to emotional intimacy. These features included time for frequent interactions with one other person, time for informal interactions, self-disclosure, touching, accumulation of rewards over time, and fair relationship. In this chapter, you took self-inventory of where you are and where you want to be on each of these six features. We also considered other opportunities for facilitating optimal intimacy, namely the use of pets, experiential groups, helping other people as a volunteer, the architectural environment you choose, the singles scene, and your own scene.

The overall thrust of this section has been to help identify important features of human relations and where you might want to go if you want to change. Naturally, your own values play an essential role in this effort. Therefore we consider values next.

Our treatment of values will be unusual. My primary goal will not be to sell you an awe-inspiring package of values, although I will propose optimal intimacy as a value. Rather, the goal will be to aid in getting a handle on values and in making them practical. Toward this goal, the next chapter expands on the theme "your values are where you put your time." I will contend that personal values are convincingly displayed *only* when one allocates scarce personal resources. Because it is easier to get a handle on your own time or affection than it is to assess abstract concepts, the topic of values is a practical one.

# VALUES

# 5

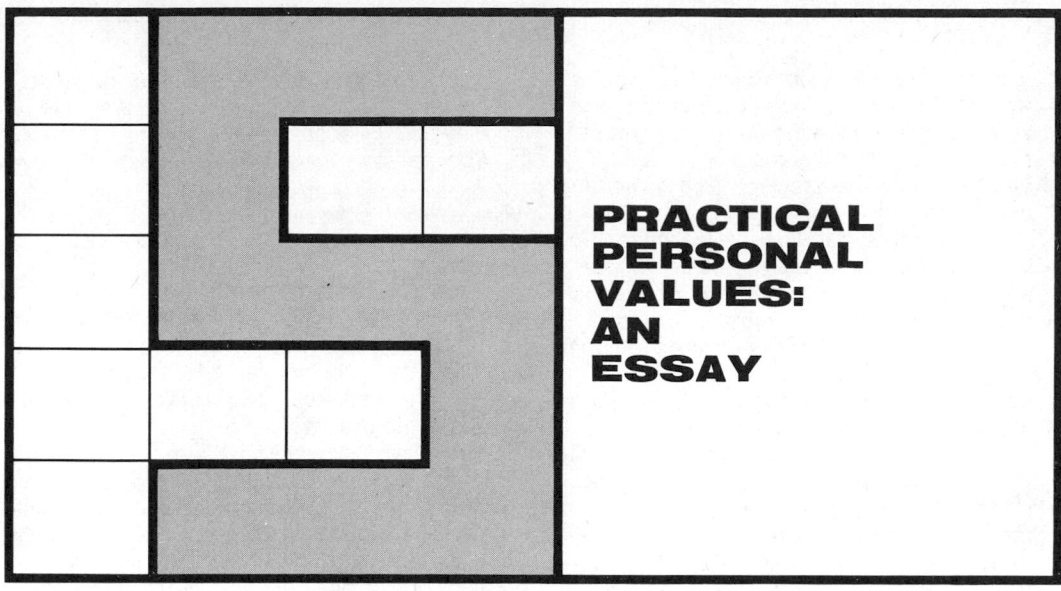

# PRACTICAL PERSONAL VALUES: AN ESSAY

CHAPTER THEME:
Your values are where you put your time.

**IMAGINARY JOURNEY INTO THE PAST AND THE POSSIBLE FUTURE**

Imagine you are taking a journey into the past, going back to the midpoint of the twentieth century in Greece. This little jaunt will be informative and refreshing because the Greeks used their time differently than Americans—then or now. A great deal in this chapter depends on how much *you like* being in Greece at about 1950. Maybe you will not want to linger. Maybe you will want to bring back a slice of that era into your own life.

Here it is, as described in Margaret Mead's book:

> *Greeks "pass" the time; they do not save or accumulate or use it. And they are intent on passing the time, not on budgeting it. Although city people say that this picture is changing, that they are now made aware of the need to use time, the attitude is still widely prevalent, even in the area of private life among the urban groups.*
>
> *The clock is not master of the Greek: it does not tell him to get up, to go to the field. In most villages, in spite of recent changes, the peasants still get up at sunrise or dawn to go to the fields, and return at sundown. The day is made for work. At night women visit and gossip; men join them or go to the coffee house; there is storytelling, and ardent political discussion; and as for any work done after dark, "the day takes a look at it and laughs." Wherever there is no law to the contrary, a man opens his store in due course, not by the clock; however, in the cities he now functions under clocked time, because he comes under government and union regulations. . . . It is distasteful to Greeks to organize their activities according to external limits; they are therefore either early or late, if a time is set at all. At church the people are not impatient while waiting for Mass to begin; and*

*the church fills only gradually. They know when to go to church; yet when a foreign visitor inquires as to the time of a certain Mass, the subject creates a discussion; and eventually the answer will be something like: "Between 2 and 3." And when Greeks who follow their traditional ways invite, they say, not "Come at 7 o'clock," but "Come and see us." To arrive to dinner on time is an insult, as if you came just for the food. You come to visit, and the dinner eventually appears. Among urbanized Greeks, this custom now seems burdensome, and there are many cartoons on the subject.*

*The dinner is not planned to appear at a predetermined time; and the housewife does not cook by the clock. She tells by the smell or the consistency, or the colour, or the resistance against the stirring spoon; or the passing of time is gauged by the intervening activities. . . .*

*Greek men and women work expeditiously, as a rule, but do this best at their own rhythm; any need to hurry is external and interfering; it introduces fuss and disturbance. Efficiency can usually be found when it is not a conscious end.*

*To introduce an awareness of time into a meal is particularly abhorrent to Greeks, though this has to be done where factories set time limits. Dinner is served when it is ready, and without regard to efficient consumption. The fish is not fileted, and nuts are not shelled, the fruit is not sliced. The eater will spend a long time removing infinitesimal bits of flesh from the head of a small fish. All this is part of the process of eating, which is more than the naked act of consumption. . . . Greeks in the city, in some circles, find the need of hurrying entering their lives. They are not at home with it. For the Greek traditionally, to work against time, to hurry, is to forfeit freedom. His term for hurry means, originally, to coerce oneself. . . .*

*In spite of the prevalence of timepieces, the church bell and the school bell, and even a cannon blast, continue to have active functions in calling adults or children to pre-arranged gatherings or communal village work. Even in the cities, people are called "Englishmen" when they turn up on the dot of meetings or appointments. People often arrive an hour late to an appointment to find that the other person is also just arriving, or, if they find him gone, they usually accept the fact with neither apology nor frustration.*

(Reprinted from Margaret Mead, ed., *Cultural Patterns and Technical Change,* pp. 90–91, by permission of Unesco. (C) Unesco 1953.)

You and I arrange our lives to pursue certain goals. Striving for optimal human contact is one such goal, upon which we focus in this chapter. We allocate valued resources such as time to attain our goals. We display our values in the process.

Humanistic psychologists in general and Abraham Maslow in particular have been concerned with helping users become fully functioning individuals. However, the emphasis has centered on the individual user to the neglect of the powerful forces, often harmful, that impinge on us from imperfections in our society. In this chapter we attempt to unite some of Maslow's ideas about human nature with the chapter theme, "your values are where you put your time." The resulting union produces a means for analyzing the forces in the larger social system that act against human contact. Practical implications for social and personal change will be discussed.

Sorting out our personal values in order to come to grips with modern life is often a rough road to travel. Modern life is often confusing. For example, with such great technology and productivity, where is the correspondingly stratospheric quality of human contact that should accompany all this technology? I shall argue that silent forces act to strongly inhibit human contact by removing or subverting the use of personal time we would normally allocate to social intercourse with other people. The source of these hidden forces lies squarely at the heart of the economic system: modern industrial technology and productivity. I most certainly will not blindly attack the high level of modern commercial technology, high productivity, or any political system. That would be simplistic. It would also ignore the many benefits of advanced technology. Technology is both modern man's greatest weakness and his greatest strength, so we will try not to throw the baby out with the wash.

By rearranging our personal lives, you and I can effect limited change in the amount and quality of personal time available for human contact. However, truly effective changes will necessarily involve the heart of the matter, advanced technology and commercial enterprises that support and depend on that technology. Words and theories by me or anyone else will not do the job. While we may use words to describe solutions, actual solutions involve changes in allocation of personal and national resources to enhance human contact.

The main goal is to make personal values practical by getting a handle on them. Our discussions will apply to any system of values, so I will not push any awe-inspiring set of values. Rather, I will argue for basic human survival and optimal intimacy, which seem required for human functioning before more esoteric values can be pursued.

### OUTLINE OF THIS CHAPTER

To help unify the train of thought in the remainder of this chapter, here is a topic outline:

I. Introduction to personal values.
   A. What you can do with personal values.
   B. Where do personal values reside?
II. Linder's theory of personal time.
   A. Linder's categories of personal time.
   B. Effects of modern technology on personal time.
   C. Where will it all end?
   D. Evaluation of Linder.
   E. Evaluation of high productivity.
   F. Out of the jungle.
III. Human needs.
   A. Maslow's system of needs.
   B. Alternate system of needs.
IV. Summary.
V. What should our personal values be?
   A. Elements of a basic system.
   B. Applying for a good life.
VI. Strategies for a good life.
   A. Personal strategies.
   B. The case of Father Polizzi.
   C. Political and economic action.
VII. The future.
VIII. Science and human values.
IX. Summary.

ADDENDUM TO CHAPTER FIVE: Possible problems in human contact

X. The possible problem of personal productivity.
   A. Statement of possible problem.
   B. Experiments in creative living.
XI. The possible community problem of motor-vehicle patterns.
   A. Statement of possible problem.
   B. Experiment in community living.
XII. The possible problem of a child's stable peer group.
   A. Statement of possible problem.
   B. Experiment in community living.
XIII. The possible problem of widespread failure experiences among young people.
   A. Statement of possible problem.
   B. Experiment in community living.

### INTRODUCTION TO PERSONAL VALUES

#### What You Can Do with Personal Values

"Personal values" can be *defined.* A personal value for you means a statement of worth or importance conferred upon something by you. However, the critical reader will immediately ask, Just how do I know when I or someone else makes a statement of worth that confers value on something? To answer this question, we must distinguish between the different things that can be done with personal values.

Personal values can be *described.* When you describe a personal value, you represent or give an account in words of that personal value. Plato described his personal values in books advocating the rule of society by an intellectual elite. You might describe your own values in a rambling discussion into the wee hours of the morning. In any case, the essence of "description" is that it is a verbal or written account.

Personal values can be *displayed.* When you display, you make public or show openly (objectively). Personal values are displayed convincingly only when one allocates scarce personal resources. Hidden from the world within each of us lie dispositions to act. Thankfully, no means yet exists for prying into our brains and assessing our personal values. Thus, until we act, our personal values remain hidden. Even when we act, there is no guarantee that much information about a given value becomes available, as Case 5.1 shows.

**Case 5.1.** Sylvia drives home from work. She sees a car by the side of the road and a woman frantically waving for help. Pulling up ahead of the stricken car, Sylvia yells back an offer to send back a service truck from the service station a mile up the road. The woman with the broken car nods. Sylvia drives on and sends back the repair truck as she had promised.

In Case 5.1 Sylvia acted to help the other lady, so we can reasonably infer that Sylvia's values include altruism, or willingness to help. However, Case 5.1 tells us almost nothing about the *relative importance* of Sylvia's willingness-to-help value. Suppose Sylvia had time to spare. Suppose she was going to spend a half hour leisurely window-shopping before going home. In that instance, we learn almost nothing about Sylvia's willingness to help. Why? Because there is no scarcity of time; even an extremely weak willingness-to-help value would have resulted in the actions we saw. On the other hand, suppose Sylvia was actually rushing home to change clothes and then dash out for an important appointment. In that instance, we could state that her willingness-to-help value is at least moderately strong because she allocated some precious (scarce) time to helping.

As Sylvia's case illustrates, we can convincingly display the importance of personal values only through the allocation of scarce personal resources. What scarce personal resources are available and open in our lives for practical consideration as users?

First and foremost among scarce personal resources is time, the great leveler. Rich or poor, powerful or weak, each of us receives just 24 hours of time per day. What we do with our time largely displays (but probably not completely) our personal values. Let us acknowledge that the equating of personal time allocation with personal values is rough because of other factors we cannot consider fully here.[1] For one thing, there are constraints on how we use our time, so an isolated look at your last week's time schedule may be misleading. Financial hardship may cause you to take on two jobs against your will for a few months. Attending night school this year might qualify you for a job next year that allows you greater time flexibility than you now have. These are obviously constraints on how time is used.

The investigation of where our personal time goes has been launched by the economist Staffan Linder. Since economics deals mainly with the allocation of scarce resources, we consider Linder's fascinating ideas in some detail later.[2]

ACTIVITY 5.1.

What else can you do with personal values? We considered only definition, description, and display of personal values. I intentionally left out a number of other things commonly done with them. Think about how the topic of values might arise in conversations you might have about love, religion, politics, race, sex, and similar topics. In such instances, what are you doing with the idea of values beyond defining, describing, or displaying values?

______________________________

______________________________

______________________________

______________________________

______________________________

______________________________

### Where Do Personal Values Reside?

Where personal values reside is a word game. In the mentalistic version, personal values reside in our heads: Your values are in your thoughts. In the biological version, values stem from vital processes of living organisms: Survival is foremost. In the behaviorist version, values reside in public behavior: Acting is valuing. In the religious versions, values come from holy teachings: The Old Testament is where values live. The mistake lies in assuming that any one version negates the others. All can exist. Our general definition of a personal value as "a statement of worth or importance conferred upon something by you" was chosen to lend itself to all systems of values. Some value systems, especially the religious ones, can exist in harmony with nearly all others. That is, in many religious systems divine revelations are assumed to underlie the specific workings of nature. Nature, with its scientific laws, runs within the larger framework of God, who runs the universe. In short, we can easily be misled into thinking personal values exist in some particular place by using a single terminology. Let us not get hung up on that word game.

**LINDER'S THEORY OF PERSONAL TIME**

In his book *The Harried Leisure Class,* Staffan Linder applies the tools of economic analysis to the allocation of personal time.[3] His analysis explains rather clearly some paradoxes of modern life: Where is the relaxed leisure time that should come with this modern age? Why do we find ourselves buying so many gadgets and material goods for leisure use? Why do we rush through meals nowadays? What can be done to alter the pressures of time that add stress to daily life?

**Linder's Categories of Personal Time**

Linder organizes his book around five ways you can spend your personal time. He assumes that your daily 24-hour ration of time is all going to be allocated somewhere. For Linder, that "somewhere" means that each minute goes into one of five categories.

1. *Working time* spent in specialized production to earn money.
2. *Personal maintenance time* spent in maintaining your possessions and/or your body.
3. *Consumption time* spent in consuming commercial resources from the business sector or social resources from other people. (The time needed for human contact falls under this category.)
4. *Culture time* spent in cultivating the mind and spirit and other noble but esoteric pursuits.
5. *Idleness time* spent doing almost nothing. Idleness time is still common in underdeveloped countries but rare in industrial countries. ("Idleness" here means passivity in the strict sense of doing almost nothing productive.)

ACTIVITY 5.2.

In the space provided after each of the five categories, list two of your activities that apply. I have filled in real examples that apply to me.

1. Working time: Writing proposal for FIU graduate program in psychology; conducting introductory social psychology class.

______________________________

______________________________

2. Personal maintenance time: Mowing the lawn; brushing my teeth.

______________________________

______________________________

3. Consumption time: Shopping for clothes; going to the beach.

______________________________

______________________________

4. Culture time: Going to hear a campus speaker; learning to play the concertina.

______________________________

______________________________

5. Idleness time: Staring into space at lunch; staring into space before going to sleep at night.

______________________________

______________________________

Linder assumes that we all allocate time to obtain the greatest "added yield" (i.e., "marginal utility") per minute. Although one might jump to the conclusion that this version of "economic man" reduces us all to satisfaction-seeking monsters, a more sophisticated analysis is easy to make. "Yield" covers the fruits from the noble actions of Albert Schweitzer and Jesus Christ, to the pleasures of Don Juan, to the bloodthirsty career of Adolf Eichmann. Taking Albert Schweitzer as an example, consider his allocation of personal time. His spectacular talents would surely have earned him fame and fortune as a medical researcher or concert organist. However, he devoted his time to practicing medicine in Africa at the expense of those other possible careers. The yield for him is whatever he got out of his career. While we cannot fathom the yield for Schweitzer beyond a superficial level, it is certainly reasonable to assume that his career of devotion to others did bring a special gratification to him.

When I apply the idea of spending time to obtain yield to myself, I can see several different yields, many of them less noble than Schweitzer's. I can easily apply the yield concept to myself by substituting "what turns me on" for "yield." Professional standing and fame in psychology turn me on; pleasant social relations turn me on; and pure physical pleasures turn me on. I feel conflict when beset by demands from work and family for time. Beneath the generally reserved exterior I generally present, a battle rages. For me, the battle seems to be conducted by conflicting brain-cell groups to capture the territory of time. The nature of the yields I obtain are very different, but the overall concept of yield applies well across the spectrum of my life.

Linder's idea about the way we function derives from classical economic theory. You allocate your time to get the greatest yield. When hungry, you eat. After a while, the added yield per minute levels off.[4] When you are full of food, you stop eating. If someone then proceeds to ram food down your gullet, the yield becomes negative. Sometimes conflict occurs. Suppose you are down to the last 5 minutes of a spy movie. You are also hungry. Your stomach growls during embarrassing moments of silence. Will you leave? It is not likely because leaving incurs the terrible cost of missing the ending of the movie. Leaving would bring a negative yield, so you stick it out and hurry to a meal afterward. The following is another, more detailed example.

**Case 5.2.** You have just received a startling phone call. A local crisis center needs people to listen to callers with personal problems. The center just landed an experimental grant that pays listeners $15 per hour just to listen sympathetically between midnight and 6:00 A.M. Despite the inconvenience, you cannot afford to pass up such a deal. However, the first night finds you barraged with a steady stream of calls. You need sleep, so you limit your services on the following night.

In Case 5.2, two shifts in your time schedule occurred as a result of *un*equal yields. In the first shift, you allocated time away from sleep (personal maintenance time) to answering calls (working time) to obtain a greater yield. Your yield could easily include benefits other than money, such as satisfaction from helping others. In the second shift, you allocated time back from answering calls to sleep to obtain yield by relieving your bleary-eyed state.

When applied to the formation of our modern society, Linder's fundamental principle provides us insight into the time pressure most of us feel. Before modern technology developed, our ancestors were accustomed to a low yield per unit of time. However, modern industrial technology has drastically altered the way we spend our time in three categories. We now examine the effect on each category individually.

## Effects of Modern Technology on Personal Time

### Effects on Working Time

Modern technology has increased productivity, which means that the added yield you get from working an hour, say, is higher now than ever before. When we apply Linder's fundamental principle to the astronomical increase in industrialization over the last century, one important prediction becomes crystal clear: As a country becomes more productive and the yield from working time displays a corresponding increase, all the other sectors of personal time come under tremendous pressure to yield much more! The chain of events goes like this: When the industrial revolution increased our productivity during working time, the yield for working time jumped up. When faced with an increased yield from our working time because we can now produce so much more, we become accustomed to a large return per unit time. We therefore try to squeeze every ounce of yield out of our remaining time as well. In some cases we try to jack up the yield in other categories of personal time, as when our consumption turns into a social and commercial whirl. In some cases previous activities cannot compete and are discontinued, as when the afternoon siesta disappears. In all cases the natural human process of seeking maximum yield heads us toward a kind of steady state. In this balanced steady state, the yields are going to be equal for every minute of the day. That is, we will tend to devote time to higher-yield activities until none are left, namely when yields from different segments of time are equal.

Yield from working time can be money, esteem, power, and so on. We modernites of the industrial revolution can and will personally do two things to maximize yield. For one thing, we may work much harder to gain the yield we get from work even more, after having our appetites whetted by increased productivity in the first place. For another, we can boost the yield in categories of use other than working time; we could consume more.[5]

Of course, you and I do not spend all our waking hours working, and we welcome the time we take to do things outside of our jobs. We do not do basic work for longer hours than persons living in less industrialized countries.[6] Therefore, compared to our ancestors in preindustrial times, we have somehow increased the yield we get out of our nonworking time. Otherwise, we would be working all the hours we comfortably could. According to Linder, some strange things indeed happen as we madly scramble to squeeze more out of our nonworking hours.

### Effects on Idleness Time

In the *poorest* countries, a person's day may contain several hours of idleness time. The year may contain dozens of religious holidays. Festivals occur and take considerable time to prepare for; there is dancing in the streets. In *developing* countries, the stretches of idle time have become short, but businessmen do not yet carry and cast worried glances at their appointment books. Greece around 1950 was a developing country. Finally, in *modern* society, the idle time all but disappears. Adults in the United States spend an average of 9 minutes resting every day; in the U.S.S.R. it is 11 minutes; in France it is 17 minutes; and in Peru it is 63 minutes.[7] In the United States, an "idle person" is to be condemned or advised about getting a job. Idle people are not mystics; they are bums. Each passing moment becomes a plum to be enjoyed with orgasmic ecstasy before it slips through our fingers.

Perhaps the conceptual opposite of the idle peasant is the chief executive officer (CEO) of a modern corporation. In a *Business Week* report on the life-styles of modern CEOs, the title—"Not Much Time for Anything but Work" —says it all.[8] Interviews with 50 CEOs from medium and large companies revealed individual differences within a common pattern: The CEO devotes most of his time and energy to working, and families and hobbies come off a poor second. Magnificent possessions are accumulated but underused by CEOs because of lack of time. Every ounce of efficiency must be squeezed out of the working hours, and the technology to help squeeze is already at hand. Already, "computers schedule salesmen's time to the last detail."[9] A Swedish inventor, Hans Hinderson, has perfected a time-sampling device to be carried in a manager's pocket for the purpose of increasing efficiency (productivity). The device beeps quietly on 30 random occasions per working day. After each beep, the manager uses its tape-recording feature to verbally answer a standard set of questions. Results can reveal that managers are spending too much time alone, too much time on trivial problems of the moment, or doing OK. Possible increases in managerial efficiency through using this device hover around 100 percent according to the device's makers.[10]

It appears that the level of idleness fluctuates opposite to the level of material well-being of nations, says Linder.[11] The poorest of nations display a time surplus. Developing (semirich) countries have time affluence. Modern industrialized (rich) countries face a time famine!

### Effects on Consumption Time

Most important of all our concerns is consumption time, which includes informal time for human contact. We can think of consumption time as consisting of two distinct components: (1) the consumption of commercial resources, that is, commercially produced goods and services, and (2) the consumption of social resources from other people. Both kinds of consumption can obviously take place at the same time, for example, as we watch television with a friend. However, we will discuss them separately in this chapter for theoretical reasons, because they suffer dramatically different fates under the pressure to increase yield. How do we increase the yield from our consumption time?

It is extremely difficult for any one person to increase very much the yield from human contact with other people. Quite simply, obtaining human contact with other people takes a lot of time, and there is not much we can do about it.

On the other hand, jacking up the yield by using up more and more consumer goods is not only possible but a process already rocketing forth at hypersonic speed. The main implication of increased productivity consists of a fantastically high consumption of goods, or *goods intensity,* crammed into our consumption time. As Linder summarizes, "By an increase in goods intensity, we push up the yield per time unit in consumption. The more goods we consume per unit time, the greater the yield. . . ."[12]

ACTIVITY 5.3.

Linder gives a number of examples of increased goods intensity. Listed are several methods for increasing goods intensity. Each method is followed by an example from my life. For each method, give an example from your life. Can you think of another method?

1. Less time devoted per consumption item. *I grab a quick lunch at McDonald's or Burger King.*

______________________________

______________________________

2. More expensive items consumed. *My next car will have an AM-FM stereo cassette player-recorder.*

______________________________

______________________________

3. Simultaneous consumption. *I drink a Dr. Pepper, watch the news on television, glance at a magazine, run the air conditioner, cook supper, and talk to my family all at once.*

______________________________

______________________________

4. Another Method.

______________________________

______________________________

Although greater productivity brings material comforts, a real tragedy results from greater goods (and services) intensity. Strange as it seems, commercial consumption competes with social consumption for time with frightening effectiveness. Examples illustrate this point.

**Case 5.3.** The time is 1900, and John's father has just passed away. John lives in a large house with a large storeroom attached. He spends half his savings and his weekends to insulate and prepare the storeroom as an apartment for his mother, whose health is beginning to fail. A year later she moves in. For a couple of hours each evening, John's family, including his mother, is together.

**Case 5.4.** The time is 1983, and John Jr.'s father has just passed away. John Jr. lives in a large house with garage attached, and he spends half his savings on a luxury car and that vacation trip around the world he and his wife have always dreamed about. Since his mother's health is beginning to fail, John Jr. takes care to see that she obtains the best health care and finds the nicest nursing home available.

**Case 5.5.** The time is 1936. The elder Mr. DiGloria sees to it that the family, relatives, and friends enjoy a traditional Sunday Italian meal that lasts for hours. (Note that although mealtimes could also be considered personal maintenance times, the analysis would be the same.)

**Case 5.6.** Generations pass. The great-grandson of the elder Mr. DiGloria is attempting to preserve the lengthy Sunday dinner, but commercial consumption is competing with him. His teenagers seem attracted to the exciting soccer games held on Sunday and to the multimedia participatory teenage theaters that have replaced the single-media movies. The youngsters do go in a social group to these exciting events, but their attention is riveted for hours to the spectacles they witness. Afterward, the topics of discussion invariably center around these shows. The specialization of commercial consumption here seems to attract a homogeneous crowd, which works against having a diversity of generations participate in a common activity.

According to Linder, two main casualties of social consumption are mealtimes and times for sex. On the run, we catch a tasteless meat pattie, which derives its savor mostly from surrounding vegetables and secret sauces.

Especially among the unmarried, sexual contacts are surrounded by rapid social penetration and depenetration. The norm of this day and age is to get to know the other person as quickly as you can. Commercial pornography, where a solitary consumer controls the time allotted, may be substituting for more time-consuming real sex. Books on the fine art of quick seduction can be found at your corner drugstore or newsstand. Although hard data on these matters still remain to be gathered, the pressure to skimp on mealtimes and love-making times can hardly be denied. Cross-cultural comparisons among different ethnic and income groups to furnish data on these matters could be done in a straightforward manner; such a project could be done by students taking this course.[13]

### Where Will It All End?

Linder believes we already live in an age where "economic growth has become an overriding end—not a mean."[14] As we approach the upper limit of commercial consumption, each new item adds less and less yield because we already have so much (satiation). Therefore we must whip ourselves into an economic frenzy to produce even more. Life will become even more hectic. The youngsters and oldsters of tomorrow will be neglected even more, and that means you and me. We will come to love our material possessions and acts of commercial consumption even more. We will rip off Mother Nature even more. Is there any hope?

In ending his book, Linder opens the curtain to reveal a ray of hope. He hopes that a change in values will somehow spring up inside the individual user. He points out that "there is already a number of dissenters rejecting the values of the consumption society."[15]

### Evaluation of Linder

How does Linder's theory stack up against the evidence? The best available evidence on use of time is found in Szalai's excellent handbook *The Use of Time,* where the results of a gigantic, worldwide project involving interviews with 27,866 respondents in 12 countries are reported.[16] Analysis revealed a rich diversity of time budgets, colored heavily by culture and custom. In the more industrialized countries, idle time drops and people spend less time resting, as Linder predicted.[17] In more industrialized countries, the time spent doing work stays the same as in less industrialized countries, although taking shorter breaks during work cuts the total working time by an hour in technologically advanced nations.[18] Unfortunately, the best available evidence does not bear directly on Linder's most important ideas.

Linder's most important ideas concern the adverse effects of being harried for time upon quality of life among the extremely productive. I predict that the main result of being time-harried is a lowering of perceived quality of human contact among those who are extremely productive in their personal lives. More specifically, such individuals should find it harder to attain optimal intimacy. Their consumption time should be marked by competing activities of a more extensive, less flexible, and goods-intensive variety. It should be much harder for them to adjust the six features of intimacy we discussed in Chapter 3 to attain optimal intimacy under their personal circumstances. For instance, a time-harried businessman may have to put in 12 hours a day at work away from home. These 12 hours may exclude informal interactions where much of any self-disclosure can occur, due to (1) contact with many other people of a superficial sort, (2) the damaging use to which personal information can be put by outside competitors or rivals within the firm, (3) norms against self-disclosure at work, and so on. Even recreational time may not allow for informal interactions in similar ways, especially if recreational activities are expected by colleagues at work. Also, a man who earns a lot of money may find it difficult to strike up a fair relationship with his wife, because he can offer her more financially than any human except a slave could return socially. The predictions in this paragraph remain to be tested.

The data in Szalai's book do not deal with mental states. Even though one researcher in Szalai's handbook reports that men and women employed in the United States spend twice as much time alone (about 6 hours) during their waking hours as do men and women employed in 8 other modern countries, these fascinating data reflect category of time use and, alas, are not related to subjective or mental states.[19] In short, the best available evidence is mostly consistent with Linder's predictions but does not bear directly on most of them.

Linder's theory applies only to advanced industrial nations, where high productivity is a problem. His theory does not apply to poor nations or poor people in any nation, because their welfare would be improved by increasing productivity. His theory is also independent of political ideology. Does Linder still have much to offer us? Definitely yes.

Linder's theory is novel and helpful to us. Using his theory of personal time, we can understand the fundamental force behind the hectic pattern of modern commercial consumption in our daily lives. That primary force is none other than high commercial productivity, made possible by advanced technology. We can understand that our idle time and social consumption time have been shifted into goods-intensive commercial consumption time. This shift also stems from commercial technology. It is not yet clear whether this shift is manifested in less hours spent socializing or in superficial socializing (low category-depth). Despite the merits of his pioneering theory, he leaves us no practical way out of the jungle.

### Evaluation of High Productivity

The single fact that high commercial productivity inhibits human contact through goods-intensive consumption should be regarded as an unhealthy side effect. But high productivity is also the backbone of industrial nations and as such, it is going to be with us. Without it, misery is certain; therefore, we must learn how to manage it. Instead of viewing productivity as a villain, we might better ask, Where is modern technology taking us? Where does modern technology come from? In what directions should future technology take us?

### Out of the Jungle

Before hastily proposing solutions to the problems of how we use our personal time, we need to take a broad look at human nature. We humans exhibit certain life patterns that must certainly be a part of any solution. Therefore we now turn to a broad consideration of human needs.

## HUMAN NEEDS

*Human needs* in this discussion means the dispositions across humanity to seek out or respond with consistency to various objects or total situations in the environment.[20] This definition says nothing about whether a need is instinctive or learned, internal or external. Human needs are near-universal dispositions, such as the need for eating. My general disposition to seek out and enjoy country music is not a human need because it is not universal, especially in academia. By the definition we are using, human needs reflect the state of nature.

### Maslow's System of Needs

Abraham Maslow's hierarchy of needs was originally intended to reflect the state of nature.[21] Because of this nature, man is said to progress from satisfying a lower need to filling a higher need when the lower need becomes mostly satisfied. Figure 5.1 shows this progression.

*Physiological needs* are physical needs, such as the needs for food, liquid, and elimination. Maslow claims that you must satisfy most of your needs at a given level before you will show concern for needs at a higher level. For instance, if you were starving, you would seek food (physiological need level)

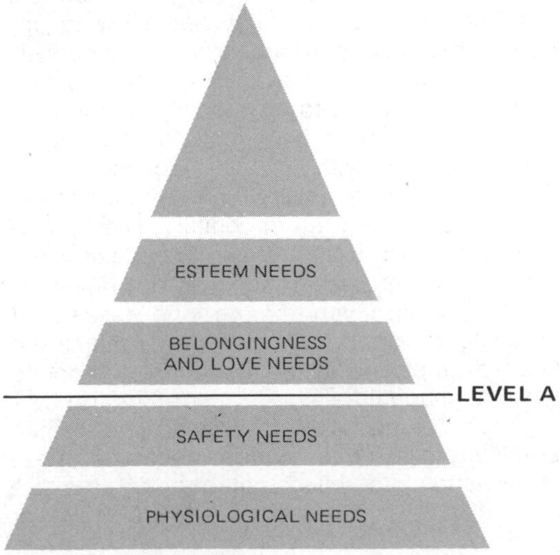


**Figure 5.1.** Maslow's original hierarchy of needs.

before worrying about how much your uncle loves you (belongingness and love need level). There are as many physiological needs as physical functions essential for life.

*Safety needs* concern protection from outside forces of nature or people who threaten us. We build warm houses and take out insurance policies to secure safety from icy winters and financial ruin from injury. In modern society, most of us have our physiological and safety needs satisfied; that is, we are functioning at least at Level A in Figure 5.1. Therefore you and I should be vitally concerned about satisfying our belongingness and love needs.

*Belongingness and love needs* refer to human contact and intimacy. In Maslow's words, the person at Level A "will feel keenly, as never before, the absence of friends, or a sweetheart, or a wife, or children. He will hunger for affectionate relationships with people in general, namely for a place in his group or family, and he will strive with great intensity to achieve this goal. . . . Now he will feel sharply the pangs of loneliness, of ostracism, of rejection, of friendlessness, of rootlessness."[22]

If belongingness and love needs are mostly satisfied, we become concerned about our *esteem needs.* Maslow states, "All people in our society (with a few pathological exceptions) have a need or desire for a stable, firmly based, usually high evaluation of themselves, for self-respect, or self-esteem, and for the esteem of others."[23]

Sitting atop Maslow's need hierarchy shines the crowning jewel of self-actualization. The core words of Maslow's own definition link *self-actualization*

> *to man's desire for self-fulfillment, namely, the tendency for him to become actualized in what he is potentially. This tendency might be phrased as the desire to become more and more what one* idiosyncratically *is, to become everything that one is capable of becoming. The specific forms that these needs will take will, of course, vary greatly from person to person. In one individual, it may take the form of the desire to be an ideal mother, in another, be expressed athletically, and in still another, it may be expressed in painting pictures or in inventions.*[24]

One crucial aspect of Maslow's concept of self-actualization is found in the word I italicized: "idiosyncratically," or uniquely. Self-actualization is your own unique thing. It is not social; it is yours. Not only that, self-actualization is a value for Maslow. Maslow says, "What a man *can* be, he *must* be."[25] Self-actualizing people, says Maslow, are generally older individuals rather than young adults; so self-actualization apparently takes decades.

From a study of case histories on people he defined as self-actualizing, Maslow gives some descriptions about what these most noble of humans are like. Using the clinical case history method, he studied self-actualizing individuals, both his own acquaintances and historical figures, as whole people. He found self-actualizers to:

- evaluate people and things accurately;
- accept imperfections in people, including themselves;
- express themselves in an easy, spontaneous way;
- center their energies around a mission in life outside themselves;
- seek solitude with some regularity;
- energize and motivate themselves from within, not from without;
- appreciate the essential experiences of life repeatedly with freshness, such as newborn babies or beautiful sunsets;
- experience mystic, "peak experiences";
- display genuine love for humanity, or "Gemeinschaftsgefühl" in desires to help the human race;
- enter into deeper intimacy with a few other people, much as children do (Self-actualizers love children. Even so, if another person really deserves it, they will terminate the relationship decisively.);
- interact comfortably with all kinds of people;
- possess definite moral standards, often unconventional;
- have an unhostile sense of humor;
- show creativity as unspoiled children show it;
- not quite belong to the culture (Symbolically, they float above the existing culture with some detachment.);
- have faults, especially occasional ruthlessness, disregard for conventional (conforming) opinions of others, temporary absent-mindedness or preoccupation, misguided

kindness, and inner conflict; and
love their work, which embodies their values.[26]

ACTIVITY 5.4.

Pick someone you know very well. Describe the degree and *specific* means by which satisfaction is achieved at each and every level of need satisfaction, as applied to him or her. Refer to Figure 5.1. At what level does he/she now stand, according to you? Feel free to conceal that person's identity.

______________________________________

______________________________________

______________________________________

______________________________________

______________________________________

______________________________________

______________________________________

### Evaluation of Maslow's Hierarchy

Maslow's hierarchy of needs has been reprinted in countless psychology and management books but rarely evaluated in textbooks at the undergraduate level. I offer two criticisms and a reformulation.

From a theoretical viewpoint, the trip to self-actualizing as Maslow describes it describes a road not worth taking in its literal form. Maslow really means actualizing oneself with only secondary regard for others. Bugental says if you really understand the humanistic psychology ethic, self-actualization as an ideal does not diminish the regard one should show for others.[27] I disagree. Self-actualization accords secondary regard for others. Even though Maslow's self-actualizing people are magnificent achievers and nice guys to boot, his pure *concept* of self-actualization is fundamentally nonsocial. And the concept lives on as mortal men cannot. As Erich Fromm claimed in *The Art of Loving,* modern interpersonal relationships bear a frightening resemblance to some aspects of the prevailing economic system.[28] The aspect of Maslow's self-actualization concept unacceptable to me is the conceptual emphasis on self. In short, Maslow's self-actualization concept is the psychological analogue to "rational" economic man. Rational economic man seeks economic self-fulfillment, while self-actualizing man seeks psychological self-fulfillment.

Another, and possibly more damaging, criticism concerns Maslow's claim that his hierarchy reflects the natural tendencies in mankind. Unfortunately, this claim stands on thin ice. To support the all-important claim that we climb up the hierarchy *in sequence,* Maslow offers not hard evidence but rather philosophical reasoning and case histories of noble people. Since he did not provide the means to gather hard data, my reply also includes reasoning similar to his.

At least two common observations cast doubt on Maslow's claim that you and your friends climb up the hierarchy in sequence, level by level. First, reversals in the level of apparent need satisfaction are so common as to render Maslow's claim of sequential progression unreasonable. Striving artisans seemingly neglect their lower esteem and love needs. Millions seek esteem and glory while settling for utter superficiality in the area of belongingness and love needs.

Second, it is easily argued that many people today are not disposed to—genuinely do not *want* to—progress beyond Level A in Figure 5.1. For every self-actualizing person, there are probably thousands of individuals located lower on his hierarchy who do not want to climb higher on the hierarchy, if the hierarchy exists at all. In other words, the claim that many lonely people today engage themselves in pursuits other than making human contact, despite the obvious satisfaction of basic physiological and safety needs, is eminently reasonable. It is also reasonable that many individuals who have their belongingness and love needs satisfied feel they "have it made" and do not aspire to lofty achievements. Rather, they enjoy life as they have it. If these claims are reasonable, then Maslow's hierarchy does not reflect the state of nature.

In fairness to Maslow, we note the existence of several studies designed to test his claim of progression up the hierarchy in sequence. Whereas a few studies[29] find limited support for this claim, most do not.[30] Lawler and Suttle, for example, looked at the importance and satisfaction of need levels at one point in time and over time.[31] Their predictions can be illustrated by a case.

**Case 5.7.** Dick is a lower-level manager in Framus Corporation, and he is on his way up in the organization. Last month he received another promotion. He is moving from satisfying belongingness and love needs to satisfying his esteem needs. He knows his family loves him, and now he is getting much more concerned about esteem from colleagues in the business community. If we look at Dick for just this moment in time, he should display the following pattern:

high satisfaction of love and belongingness needs
low importance of love and belongingness needs (because he has already satisfied these)
low satisfaction of esteem needs
high importance of unsatisfied esteem needs

If we look at Dick a year later, he should display this pattern:

Slightly higher satisfaction of love and belongingness needs
even lower importance of love and belongingness needs
higher satisfaction of esteem needs (causing) lower importance of esteem needs than prior

The relationships between the importance and satisfactions in need level shown in Case 5.7 are in fact the predictions made by Lawler and Suttle. These researchers tried but failed to detect the patterns predicted in Case 5.7 and similar patterns predicted for 187 lower-level managers in business and government over a year's time. In the face of similar results in other studies, Maslow contended that the time span of research for detecting how we move up the hierarchy must cover decades, which leaves out all existing research.[32]

In reply, it can be claimed that no research could ever definitely test Maslow's claims that (1) his hierarchy exists and (2) we climb level by level because he never offered definitive procedures for measuring need satisfaction at a given level.

In short, the research bearing on Maslow's hierarchy is not very helpful. The only really convincing data show that starving or very thirsty people become concerned about food[33] or liquid[34] and let their social relationships deteriorate. The general fact that importance of physiological needs goes down as physical well-being goes up is also well supported for both human and animals.[35] With these thoughts in mind, we turn to polishing the uncut diamond Maslow has provided us.

### Reformulation

The compassionate Maslow probably intended his hierarchy as a means to inject some nobility into the muddy mainstream of modern living. In addition, he was dissatisfied with the two prevailing themes of contemporary psychology. The Freudian theme pessimistically pictures you and me as driven relentlessly by shadowy inner forces that largely assumed their form during childhood. The behavior mod theme views human action as dominated by external forces, thought Maslow. (Our own discussion of behavior mod is in the next chapter.) Maslow's rejection of both these themes—the Freudian and the behaviorist (behavior mod)—inspired his own theory. Maslow hoped that his views would emerge as a "third force" in psychology.

For the reasons given in the preceding section, I believe Maslow's hierarchy is not well suited to describe the state of nature or the way humanity *is.* Nevertheless, it might be an exciting journey to transform his hierarchy into both a revised need theory and another theory of the way humanity *ought to be.* In the following section, Maslow's hierarchy is transformed into a different hierarchy of needs. Maslow should not be associated with the reformulation to follow because he almost surely would not agree with it.

## Alternate System of Needs

### The Flanders Wishbone

The "Flanders wishbone" reformulation (see Figure 5.2) retains three needs that closely parallel Maslow's three lowest levels of needs. The *basic needs* include physical and safety needs. Because the means for satisfaction are more or less genetically determined, the basic needs are not very modifiable.

*Physical needs* are physiological needs necessary for the internal functioning of the human body. When physical needs are not minimally satisfied, we say the person dies. If the physical needs are minimally satisfied, the person is able to move on to satisfaction of safety needs. In Maslow's original hierarchy, a need level had to be mostly satisfied before you move up to the next level. Here only minimal satisfaction is needed—an important difference.

*Safety needs* concern protection of the human body from external threat. There are as many safety needs as there are externally caused threats. The most obvious of safety needs are the needs for protection from other humans and the inanimate forces of nature. When safety needs are not minimally satisfied, we say the person is killed. Thus minimal satisfaction of both physical and safety needs is necessary for a person to stay alive.[36]

*Human contact or intimacy needs* have already been discussed. The need for human contact is social because a fair social exchange over time is required. The many different ways to express love and belongingness from culture to culture lead to my claim that cultural forces have a major role in the satisfaction of human contact needs. For example, Robert Weiss notes that in America, "individuals seem to be insecure with attachments that are not certified by sexual contact and also to feel that sexual contact is of dubious legitimacy unless justified by [emotional] attachment."[37]

Curious things begin to happen in the satisfaction of human contact needs in modern society. The primary means for satisfaction consists of a voluntary social act from another person in an interpersonal situation. ("Voluntary" here means actions that could be withheld by the other person at little or no immediate cost to himself or herself. This definition intentionally sidesteps the issue of free will.) However, note that the wishbone in Figure 5.2 branches into two directions at the level of human contact needs. These directions correspond to the means by which we attempt to satisfy our higher needs.

Going up the left branch in Figure 5.2, we see that the means for need satisfaction involves a commercial exchange whereby a unit having a standard value is used. (Money or credit need not be exchanged in commercial exchanges, as when two persons swap goods for mutual benefit.) Going up the right branch, the means for need satisfaction is a social exchange. The difference between these two branches refers to conceptually different means for satisfying the same need. We are all presumed to be carrying around a need for human contact. However, modern man has a bewildering variety of ways to satisfy this need, and not all of them are healthy.

**Case 5.8.** Dan has a need for human contact, just like the rest of us. Last week, he decided to do several things he had been thinking about for several months. He bought a sports car with a stereo tape deck, got his hair styled, had his bachelor pad remodeled, and bought a chic new wardrobe. Then Dan headed out to a singles lounge on Saturday night to stir up some action.

Human contact needs impel both commercial and noncommercial action in today's society. In Dan's case, he spent a lot of money to obtain goods to enhance his human contact. In fact, I claim that the majority of goods and services marketed in highly industrialized countries are aimed at the indirect satisfaction of human contact needs. Dan bought a car that provided far more than just basic transportation!

In other words, I am saying that the end point which causes consumption of most goods and services today consists of voluntary social responses from other persons. Such voluntary social responses cannot be sold *directly.* For example, I cannot buy a compliment from you. If I paid you for a compliment, it would not be voluntary. Thus not only are commercial exchanges nonvoluntary, but most commercial exchanges are *indirect* attempts to satisfy the need for human contact. Most are not required to keep one from dying or being killed. Dan's fancy car (a good) and his new haircut (a service) only helped set the stage. Most commercial goods and services merely help set the stage leading up to a social end point.

Today's commercial world depends mainly on a public whose needs for human contact remain only partially satisfied. The social end point cannot be reached, however, if commercial consumption is to grow. Assuming this to be the case, a radical conclusion follows: Most commercial exchange today depends on the relative scarcity of means to satisfy needs for human contact more directly—the scarcity of user information. Put another way, why would anybody buy a stereophonic, chrome-plated, fuzzy-wuzzy widget if there were *more direct* (less costly) means available

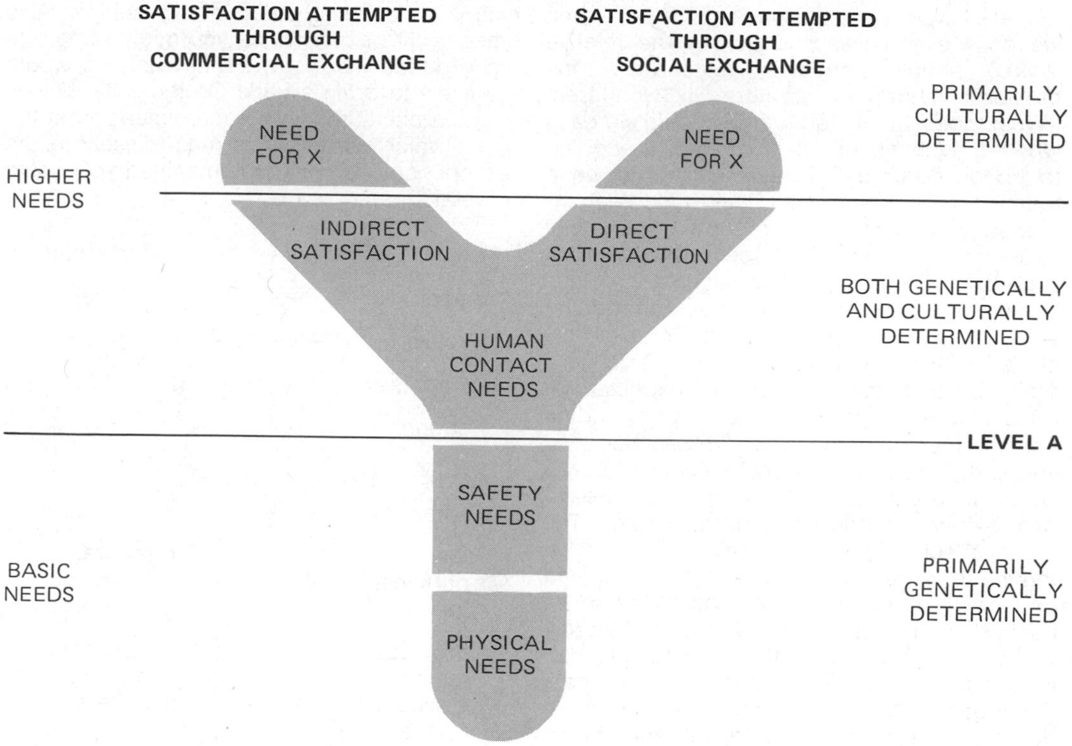


**Figure 5.2.** The Flanders wishbone of needs.

to solve that marital quarrel or meet that new person?

Of course, my argument depends on demonstrating that most modern goods and services provide more than minimal satisfaction of basic needs and somehow set the stage for satisfying needs for human contact. Such a demonstration is both feasible and reasonable. For example, more than half the current U.S. economy consists of services rather than goods in dollar value. The following list gives examples of the kinds of goods and services that help set the stage for human contact:

Expensive automobiles (say over $4000) and accessories that provide more than basic transportation.
Fancy foods that satisfy more than basic nutritional requirements.
Kitchen appliances and accessories to fix those fancy foods.
Houses and other dwellings that satisfy more than essential living requirements.
Large yards for those houses that have more space than required by children to play.
Expensive furniture.
Other expensive household items.
Most jewelry.
Most clothing, especially outer garments that reflect this month's fashion.
Fancy watches.
Most (but not all) tourist travel.
Many (but not all) magazines and books.
All other conspicuous consumption of goods and services.
All other activities that would *not* be consumed by you or me if we had to do it alone and never tell anyone about it later.

As another example of how goods and services provide more than minimal satisfaction of needs, I give you some pilot data of the most intriguing sort. My wife and I go to parks with the children fairly often. When we do, we are always struck by the relative lack of people, especially compared to the crowded shopping centers. I wondered, "What goes on inside other people's heads when they think about what they are going to do on Saturday? Does marching down a mammoth shopping mall make you feel included in some sort of group? What *social* expectations do we have about going to, say, a park, YMCA, bar, or shopping mall?"

To address these concerns, undergraduate Dave Younts did a project for one of my classes. The object was to peek inside people's minds to see what *social expectations* arise when a person thinks about spending time in four settings: park, YMCA, bar, and shopping mall. After some preliminaries, 25 young men and 25 young women rated each of the four settings on a questionnaire. The rating sheet for the park setting is shown on this page. A person's response was indicated by placing a check mark on one of the seven dashes that runs between each pair of words.

To experience what the respondents did, now read the first two paragraphs of the park description. Then place a check on one of the dashes that runs between "good" and "bad." Do the same for each of the remaining pairs.

Our goal was to get ratings comparing four settings that ran from noncommercial to commercial. Descriptions of the other settings are given on this page and the next.

PARK DESCRIPTION:

Here is a description of a setting in the Miami area. Picture a park in a location conveniently accessible for you. The park area is not confining and has open spaces available as well as sections with clusters of shrubs and trees. This park also has various recreational facilities available. There are swings and playground equipment for use of young children. Provision has been made for tennis, with two lighted courts. Also available are basketball courts with lights. Handball and paddleball courts are located there. Baseball and softball fields are also part of the recreational facilities of the park. A pool is available as a swimming facility until 9 o'clock at night. Benches and sitting areas are provided for those less active or tired.

Now imagine that next Saturday sometime you will spend an hour in this setting. Also imagine the experiences you might expect to have during that hour, doing what *you* would be likely to do in a park. On the scale below, place a check mark on each dimension at the point which corresponds most closely to the experience you have just imagined you would have at a park.

| | | | | |
|---|---|---|---|---|
| (7) | good | - - - - - - - | bad | (1) |
| (1) | small | - - - - - - - | large | (7) |
| (7) | active | - - - - - - - | passive | (1) |
| (1) | worthless | - - - - - - - | valuable | (7) |
| (7) | strong | - - - - - - - | weak | (1) |
| (1) | slow | - - - - - - - | fast | (7) |
| (1) | lonely | - - - - - - - | intimate | (7) |
| (7) | fosters personal friendship | - - - - - - - | discourages personal friendship | (1) |
| (1) | provides feeling of exclusion from a group | - - - - - - - | provides feeling of membership in a group | (7) |
| (7) | exciting | - - - - - - - | dull | (1) |
| (1) | not fun | - - - - - - - | fun | (7) |
| (7) | useful for me | - - - - - - - | not useful for me | (1) |

YMCA DESCRIPTION:

Here is a description of a setting in the Miami area. Picture a YMCA in a location conveniently accessible for you. The YMCA has three sections to the facility. In the first section there is a lobby, front desk, TV lounge, and four administration offices. In the second section—the basement—there is a complete physical education plant with a 60′ X 20′ heated pool, two locker rooms, a weight room, showers, dry steam room, in addition to attendant's basket room. Also in the basement is the Health Club area, including massage, lockers, individual workout space, steam room, infrared and ultraviolet light and nap room. The third section is a gymnasium with basketball, volleyball, and paddleball courts, and the only indoor running track in Miami. The four-wall handball courts and an informal workout room complete the physical department facilities.

BAR DESCRIPTION:

Here is a description of a setting in the Miami area. Picture an establishment in a location conveniently accessible for you, which is in business for providing a place to have a drink. On the inside there are two or three different bars able to serve you. There are also several tables where you can be seated and served. The inside is dimly lit and neatly decorated. There is a space provided for dancing. A live band is on hand to provide musical entertainment of your liking. The tables and bars are situated in such a way that you may have a choice of being in a quiet corner or sitting in a place closer to where the music or action is. This establishment is concerned with serving you in whatever way it can by providing these services.

SHOPPING-MALL DESCRIPTION:

Here is a description of a setting in the Miami area. Picture a shopping mall in a location conveniently accessible for you. Two things are very noticeable. First, the large amount of acreage the mall covers. Second is the wide variety of stores and shops. Through all of this is the prevailing atmosphere of affluence. The stores are richly decorated with a variety of interiors and expensive furnishings. Whether one wishes to buy a fishing rod or a suit of clothes, he or she has a choice of several stores to choose from. Inside the mall dozens of stores are lined up right next to each other to make it very easy for their customers to buy their products. Items are attractively displayed everywhere. It is impossible to walk up and down the mall without being exposed to hundreds of products. The mall and the stores that make it up offer a change from the world outside. The mall becomes one huge store, a world in itself.

For each of the four settings, participants filled out the same rating scales shown after the Park Description above. Average ratings are shown in Table 5.1. For each of the nine rating scales, the scores could range from 1 to 7. For example, consider "group inclusion," which hopefully relates to social intimacy and social loneliness. In the rating scale on page 108, look at the scale that runs from

provides feeling of exclusion from a group to provides feeling of membership in a group.

The numbers in parentheses there tell you which end of every scale was scored as 1 and which end was scored as 7. (These num-

**TABLE 5.1** COMBINED MALE AND FEMALE AVERAGE RATINGS OF FOUR SETTINGS ON NINE DIMENSIONS

| | Setting | | | |
|---|---|---|---|---|
| | Less Commercial | | More Commercial | |
| Dimension | Park | YMCA | Bar | Shopping Mall |
| Evaluative (bad-good plus worthless-valuable) | 4.2 | 4.9 | 4.5 | 5.7 |
| Potency (weak-strong) | 3.9 | 4.0 | 3.6 | 5.1 |
| Activity (slow-fast plus passive-active) | 3.8 | 4.3 | 5.1 | 5.9 |
| Intimacy | 3.2 | 3.4 | 5.1 | 4.5 |
| Personal Friendship | 3.5 | 4.3 | 5.3 | 4.0 |
| Group Inclusion | 2.5 | 4.2 | 5.1 | 5.3 |
| Exciting | 3.0 | 4.0 | 5.5 | 5.6 |
| Fun | 3.1 | 4.0 | 5.4 | 5.2 |
| Useful | 3.5 | 4.3 | 4.3 | 5.7 |

NOTE: The first three pairs were combined to yield evaluative, potency, and activity dimensions respectively.

SOURCE: Questionnaires and instructions are available from the author. The results from Dave Younts's term paper for PSY 370, Introductory Social Psychology, Fall Quarter 1974, are reprinted by permission.

bers were not on the original questionnaires of course.) Looking at Table 5.1, you see that the park setting experience was rated a 2.5 on the group inclusion scale, much less than the shopping mall's rating of 5.3. Thus the mall may provide feelings of inclusion that might relieve social loneliness.

Results for males and females were similar, with females showing more pronounced trends than males. For instance, the women rated the park as 3.0 useful and the mall as 5.9. The men rated the park as 4.0 useful and the mall 5.5. The sample was restricted, consisting of people Dave could buttonhole for a few minutes. The whole study should be viewed as highly tentative because (1) the sample was limited and (2) the results need to be repeated. You should browse over Table 5.1 and draw your own conclusions.

This little study indicates that commercial consumption may very well be satisfying social needs indirectly, as proposed earlier. This study provides indirect evidence; it is a tiny, preliminary piece of a giant puzzle. We now return to the wishbone (Figure 5.2) to consider the topmost human need on it.

Topping the wishbone are two need categories called "Need for X." A "Need for X" is learned, and the "X" can stand for almost anything. Given the right means, "Need for X" can often be created artificially and learned on a society-wide basis. Maslow's hierarchy expressed optimism about human nature. Mine withholds judgment, expressing neither optimism nor pessimism. To me, the world is filled with too many people doing too many downright strange things—things which dominate their lives—to say that progression toward any end is natural or somehow determined. Consider the bingo addicts or drug addicts; consider the businessmen whose lives really center around advancing corporate goals; consider sexual fetishists. Consider people whose existence centers around shiny rubber sex garments or watermelon breasts. What needs are these people satisfying? Maslow's hierarchy has no clear place for them aside from the nonexplanation that they are satisfying multiple needs. If it is possible to produce a society where large segments of the population seek satisfaction of desires not sought in other cultures, then it is possible to create truly powerful needs at will.

### The Wishbone and Human Nature

At first blush, it might appear that crowning a hierarchy of human needs with an almost infinitely plastic "Need for X" degrades man into a helpless puppet. Nothing could be more removed from the truth. In actuality, the wishbone emphatically affirms our ability to shape our destiny.

Far from degrading human nature, my hierarchy says we humans are going where we choose to go. Right at the top of my hierarchy sits a category of needs created by human beings. The "Need for X" can be viewed as a sort of void to be filled and given direction. The awesome aspect of the wishbone is the frightening responsibility we bear for guiding ourselves. The direction can lead to destruction or survival. On the one hand, it is certainly possible to create a need for large engine-displacement automobiles that will rip off Mother Nature's irreplaceable petroleum deposits in a matter of decades. On the other hand, the need to see that the needs of others nearby are taken care of can also assume a dominant role. The choice *is* yours. What is happening in modern society? What direction is the "Need for X" taking?

At present, I see the direction being utterly dominated by the modern economic system, with thinkers in psychology, sociology, religion, and other academic disciplines standing by impotently. Scholars control the descriptions of values, but businessmen and lawmakers control what values ultimately get displayed. The economy seems centered around the production of goods and services such as those we listed earlier—with a few important exceptions, such as national defense and health care. The fact that our efforts to satisfy social needs are indeed being channeled up the left branch of the wishbone through commercial exchange is confirmed beyond reasonable doubt by the nationwide neglect of populations that lack countercontrol. Specifically, the aged, retardates, the mentally ill, prisoners, and children are subject to undeniable abuse in modern nations. Examples of abuse are shown in the story and picture on page 111. The photograph is of a storehouse used for punishment of children. Both are from *Time* magazine. To illustrate widespread neglect of the aged, page 112 contains another story from *Time*.

The Rev. George von Hilsheimer, 39, a self-styled minister in the Free Religious Association, is fascinated by psychiatry. Though he has no degrees in the subject, he likes to talk about such "therapies" as electrosleep, vivid confrontation, megavitamins and hypodesensitization. What is noteworthy about Von Hilsheimer, however, is that he has been able to try out these techniques, and others as well, during his nine years as superintendent of the Green Valley School for emotionally disturbed and delinquent children in Orange City, Fla.

If a child misbehaved, for example, Von Hilsheimer would sometimes gather the students together to declare him "morally dead"; then, concocting his own version of reality therapy (which denies the importance of past traumas and encourages a patient to cope outright with his current dilemma), Von Hilsheimer and the students would force the youth to dig himself a grave and lie in it overnight. "I think it is a beautiful symbolic thing for the kids to go through," he explained. "It's a way of forcing them to look at themselves." At other times he would shackle the child, jolt him with an electroshock machine dubbed a "lalapalooza," or shut him up in a storehouse.

All this came to light last week at hearings conducted by the Senate's Permanent Subcommittee on Investigations. The Senators are probing a federal medical-insurance program called CHAMPUS (Civilian Health and Medical Program of the Uniformed Services), the benefits of which include payment for the care of emotionally disturbed children of military personnel in 486 schools and psychiatric centers round the country. Senate investigators claim that CHAMPUS administrators do not properly check out facilities before handing over money. Green Valley, they point out, has re-

ceived $1.2 million from the Government over a three-year period to perpetrate outrages that Committee Chairman Henry Jackson called worthy of "Hitler, Ilse Koch and Buchenwald."

In 1973, Florida investigators testified, the school was raided by state officials; among other brutalizing instruments, they found shackles and a brown leather whip. One nurse said she had treated numerous bruises from chains. Von Hilsheimer told TIME Correspondent Joe Kane that his young charges were "miserable, hateful, violent bastards." The school's former headmaster, Ronald E. Nowicki, could also be violent. In a fit of anger he punched a female student so hard that he ruptured her eardrums.

**Allergy Treatment.** At the hearings, former staff members testified about Green Valley's various treatments. They said that Dr. William Philpott, a consulting psychiatrist who practices in South Attleboro, Mass., believed that mental disorders stem from allergies. He tried to treat the allergies by having students inhale carbon dioxide gas. (Two of his former patients in Maryland died following carbon dioxide inhalation therapy, and Philpott was acquitted of manslaughter in 1966.) According to the former head nurse, Esther Johnson Snow, another consultant, Dr. Sol Klotz of Orlando, Fla., told her to inject a student with his own urine as a test for allergy. Klotz also made a serum of dirt, dust, and other substances and told the nurses to inject it into students as an allergy treatment.

Von Hilsheimer insists that he is being persecuted. In response to his critics, he claims that 86% of his students go on to live normal lives in the outside world, though he has done no follow-up studies. He is also proud of the fact that there was "only one" suicide at his school. In 1968 a disturbed boy named Michael Waker, 18, killed himself with a pistol Von Hilsheimer had allowed him to purchase; later the boy's mother was billed for the gun. Another boy, depressed to the point of suicide because his mother had just written telling him how peaceful it was at home without him, was also handed a gun by Von Hilsheimer, but he decided not to use it.

Green Valley is not the only school to be scrutinized by the committee. During the hearings, Senate investigators charged that at the University Center, a residential psychiatric-treatment center in Ann Arbor, Mich. (it has no connection with the University of Michigan), students who continually misbehave are locked for days or even months in a "seclusion room." The school, which has received more than $1 million in CHAMPUS funds since 1969, is also accused of being lax about widespread drug use; students who enter the institution with problems other than drug addiction quickly become hooked.

Such revelations may improve the situation at Green Valley and the University Center. But the real problem spreads much further. Senate investigators feel that there are countless private psychiatric facilities round the country that exploit their charges and even use government funds to do so. State and local agencies, which generally have the responsibility of supervising and licensing these facilities, frequently lack the funds and manpower to do an adequate job. Until something is done to change this, the nation will continue to have what Senate investigators call "commercially operated jails."

Some nations, like the Scandinavian countries, take good care of their aged. But not the U.S., where about a million American elderly spend their last years in nursing homes. In these homes, says Mary Adelaide Mendelson, a Cleveland community-planning consultant who has spent the past ten years investigating the nursing-home industry, they are often ignored, sometimes mistreated and generally exploited. Despite the $3.5 billion in federal, state and private funds that are poured into U.S. nursing homes each year, she writes in her recently published book *Tender Loving Greed* (245 pages; Knopf; $6.95), conditions in many homes are so bad that they constitute "a national scandal."

Author Mendelson, who holds a master's degree in political science, is not the first to write critically about the nursing-home industry. But Mendelson, who was hired in 1964 by the Federation for Community Planning of Cleveland as a part-time consultant to study nursing homes in Ohio, has dug deeper and come up with more dirt than other investigators. In the past decade she has expanded her investigation to cover the entire country, visiting hundreds of the nation's 23,000 nursing homes and speaking to patients, operators and employees. The book that resulted is a strong indictment of private cupidity, professional complicity and official indifference behind wholesale cheating of both the patient and the public. Author Mendelson points a finger at:

**OPERATORS.** Some homes, run by churches and other charitable groups, get good grades. But these accommodate only a small percentage of patients. Privately run homes, which care for the majority, are a different story. A few honest owners may feel forced by the difficult economics of operating a nursing home to provide substandard care; others see their operations simply as opportunities for financial exploitation of people who have nowhere else to turn. Because the pay is so low, many homes are inadequately staffed, largely with unqualified personnel. The privately run homes also generally try to maximize profits by minimizing expenditures for food, offering meals that range from insipid to inedible; one operator attempted to feed his patients on 78¢ worth of food each per day.

These are not the only abuses. One owner, without bothering to obtain power of attorney, took over his patients' bank accounts, charged them a high private rate until their resources were exhausted, then kept them on at the lower rates paid by Medicare and Medicaid. Other operators increase their profit margins by tacking extra charges onto already high bills. Mendelson reports that one Virginia nursing home listed charges of $3 per day for care of bedsores, which probably resulted from staff neglect in the first place.

**DOCTORS.** Some physicians work closely with operators, who occasionally reward them—and give them an incentive for keeping the home's beds filled—by providing them with stock in the institutions. Some doctors make "gang visits," dropping in on a home, making a quick tour of the patients' rooms and charging all of them for individual calls. Physicians have also been known to cooperate with operators in a more nefarious practice, keeping patients sedated so that they will require less attention.

**OFFICIALS.** Those charged with overseeing the nation's nursing homes have done little to improve the situation. Government agencies generally overlook such obvious violations of state and federal law as inadequate staffing, lack of safety and sanitary facilities and irregularities in accounting procedures. Ohio officials, Mendelson reports, have failed to obtain the extradition of a confidence man who fled to New Orleans after bilking several patients as well as the Government of thousands of dollars.

The nursing-home industry has reacted strongly to Mendelson's attack. Derril Meyer, a spokesman for the American College of Nursing Home Administrators, deplored the conditions described in the book and insisted that his organization was seeking to improve care of the elderly. Wiley Crittenden Jr., president of the American Nursing Home Association, attacked the book as "biased" and branded its charges "unsubstantiated." There has been no adequate response so far from government officials. State and federal authorities have been aware for years that many nursing homes have been making enormous profits while providing substandard care. They need neither investigations nor tougher laws in order to bring these homes up to par. The regulations governing nursing homes are already sufficient to eliminate most existing abuses, and the laws against fraud are adequate to jail many operators. Unfortunately, as Author Mendelson makes clear, neither have been enforced.

At this point, let us pause, take a seventh-inning stretch, and summarize.

## SUMMARY

After a brief visit to leisurely paced life in Greece around 1950, we addressed the topic of personal values. Attention centered around display of personal values, which are displayed convincingly only with the allocation of scarce personal resources. An especially important resource, personal time, was analyzed according to the theory of economist Linder. According to him, increased technology has led to increased productivity in the industrialized world. We as individuals spend our personal time to get the most yield we can. When faced with an increased yield from our working time because we can now produce so much more, we become accustomed to a large return per unit time. We therefore try to squeeze every ounce of yield out of our social and commercial consumption time as well. Since intimacy and other social pursuits take time, we tend to cram a lot of goods consumption into our consumption time. The price we pay is human contact. The foregoing argument is important because it bears directly on how each of us allocates some of our scarce personal resources.

Before rushing off and constructing an awe-inspiring system of values, we discussed human needs. Human needs reflect the state of nature, which must be reconciled with any set of values that applies to humans. Maslow's need hierarchy was reformulated into an alternate hierarchy. The alternate hierarchy should be useful for constructing a set of values: According to the Flanders wishbone, man is disposed to first survive and seek minimal human contact. Then he shapes his own destiny by creating, increasing, and decreasing needs for almost anything. An important type of man-made need was claimed to be commercial consumption for nonessentials that indirectly satisfy the need for human contact. We turn now to a consideration of what our personal values ought to be.

## WHAT SHOULD OUR PERSONAL VALUES BE?

### Elements of a Basic System

In this section I argue for a basic, or minimal, system of personal values. The basic system is essential for human functioning, so all more ambitious systems (yours certainly included) ought to be stacked on top of this one. In fact, we have already covered the elements of the basic system when discussing the wishbone. Elements of the basic system are:

1. Satisfaction of physical needs
2. Satisfaction of safety needs
3. Satisfaction of human contact needs
4. Social actualization

At the first three levels, this bare-bones basic system of personal values does nothing more than reaffirm the wishbone. If there is truth in the wishbone, then going on to pursue more esoteric goals effectively requires prior satisfaction of physical, safety, and human contact needs. Such is the state of nature. Therefore satisfaction of these three needs also comprises a hierarchy of values. In other words, we have got to cooperate with nature through the third level before pursuing needs we create ourselves.

*Social actualization,* a new concept, means that individuals see to it that the physical, safety, and human contact needs of family, friends, and neighbors are *well* satisfied. As the distance away from you in time or distance becomes greater, your responsibility for the satisfaction of other's needs becomes smaller. As I climb the hierarchy of my own need satisfaction, I incur a responsibility to see to it that others around me are almost as well off as I. Perhaps it is best to think of your social-actualizing as a shadow hierarchy of needs a notch lower than your own need hierarchy. Wherever you are, the shadow hierarchy indicates where others around you ought to be.

Social actualization is also mandated by the state of nature. The person who doesn't display social actualization will be the recipient of neglect or hate because no one in his surroundings will care enough to satisfy his needs for human contact. Obviously, if everyone wanted to and had the ability to display social actualization, the world's suffering would vanish in a few centuries.

In short, I contend that the hierarchy of four values is a realistic basic core that must be present before other values should be considered. An exception is religious values. Religious values can be put side by side or can underlie (be considered more basic than) my basic four. God can be viewed as encompassing the universe, wherein the state of nature and all life runs according to laws set up by God. Held by many religions, this view is, of course, highly compatible with my basic four. God encompasses the universe, the state of nature, and therefore everything said in this book.

**Applying for a Good Life**

Attaining social actualization on a widespread basis is sufficient for a nation's people to have *a good life.* Because life-styles differ so much, there is no such thing as "the" good life—there is only a good life.

People in industrialized nations already possess far more material resources than needed to attain a good life. One thing lacking is a rearrangement of personal time. Satisfying human-contact needs optimally takes personal time in a noncommercial relationship of social exchange; therefore an army of social workers, psychologists, and psychiatrists can never provide a good life for an individual. Only the individual himself can do it.

The satisfaction of most people's physical, safety, and human contact needs is sufficient. But if a fortunate few go on to create and satisfy esoteric needs while many suffer at the lower levels, destructive but justified conflict will occur.

**Case 5.9.** Father is saving for his quadraphonic stereo. Son is saving for a super motorcycle. Daughter is striving to become a great artist. Mother is saving for a face-lifting. Rats are chewing the toes of a ghetto-family baby 10 minutes away. Given a free press, this situation is unstable over time.

The implications of Case 5.9 and the "good-life" argument above are sweeping. The good-life argument means working toward seeing that we have our human contact needs satisfied (our own and those of our neighbors) before hitching our wagon to the star of an esoteric need, perhaps an artificially created need. But is attaining a state of social actualization really where we want to go? Is it not necessary to have people reaching for stars and attempting impossible dreams? In the final analysis, does capitalism not depend on rugged individualists who doggedly pursue their own destinies for the good of all? Case 5.10 illustrates some pros and cons of pursuing esoteric needs.

**Case 5.10.** On a distant planet sits a circle of happy hedonites. These roundish translucent creatures are devoted solely to providing pleasureful social contact to their fellows. Their society consists of just a dozen individuals. They sit in a circle, throbbing with the pleasure derived from their orange sunlight. Each one gently strokes the surface of the happy hedonite to its right in a continuous ecstasy of mutual love and orgasm that has lasted for centuries.

What shall we make of these happy hedonites? Their society marks the embodiment of human (or hedonite) contact attained. Their society also conspicuously lacks any desire to rise above satisfying needs for love and belongingness. Shall we condemn them for embracing mediocrity and scorning the glory of achievement that historians would someday praise? I think not. I think rather they should give occasional thought about alternative ways to live. Certainly they should not turn loose their one genius hedonite to create a technology for creating new needs based on marketplace demand. Suppose he creates a technology of war that is more potent than the love they share now? Suppose there is one hedonite in the group with enough latent hostility to acquire and employ that technology of war?

In contrast to the happy hedonites, modern society is burning up the earth's resources in its grasping for artificial stars. To put our house in order, personal, national, and international efforts are needed to *first* attain a good life, which means the alleviation of most human suffering. *Then,* we should decide where to go from there, on the basis of planned, not marketplace-determined, technology.

ACTIVITY 5.5.

On a separate paper, create your own system of personal values. This one is your own thing. In this exercise, feel completely free to embrace or depart from all I have said.

At this point, we have finished our discussion of value systems. Value systems are of the utmost importance because your personal values can also be your goals. If you don't formulate your own goals to allocate your time and other resources, someone else will do it for you. You could wind up addicted to 10 hours of television daily. You could wind up rich but completely devoted to a superficial social whirl and conspicuous commercial consumption. Your 24 hours daily, money, love, and other resources *are* going to be allocated somewhere.

I now make two assumptions before proceeding. Number one, you have a personal value system of your own that you will *actively* employ to guide your own life. Number two, you have included social actualization somewhere in your own system of values. Making these two assumptions allows us to embark on some strategic considerations for attaining a good life in practical terms.

## STRATEGIES FOR A GOOD LIFE

### Personal Strategies

Personal strategies for attaining a good life are carried out from plans hatched mainly inside your head. The first strategic task is to clarify your value system, which is what this chapter is all about. For values clarification, it will help to reread Chapters 1 through 5 and the epilogue (p. 257). It will help to touch bases with the great thinkers by taking courses in ethics. It will help to lock horns with friends, students, instructors, and intimates about values.

The second strategic task is to hone up your abilities to pursue whatever goals you choose. Chapters 6 through 12 will help. They are dramatically different from Chapters 1 through 5 because they concern practical moment-to-moment procedures for effecting interpersonal change in a specific other person. Other user information will surely emerge elsewhere; but it will come slowly because the factual base is still modest and research takes time. Beware especially of user information that lacks a lot of specific reference to recent research.

The third strategic task in a personal strategy to attain a good life is to use your vote. Even though this book emphasizes your personal social world, larger forces such as land use, industrial productivity, and architecture affect our most intimate dealings with undeniable power. Your vote ties you in directly with larger forces that shape your own social world, as the illuminating case of Father Polizzi shows.

### The Case of Father Polizzi

The illuminating case of Father Polizzi is given on page 116 which shows the story as it appeared in *Time* magazine.[38] For us as users, the story of Father Polizzi has three implications for improving the environment in which our interpersonal life takes place. They are:

1. Improving social surroundings takes political action.
2. Improving social surroundings takes legal action.
3. Improving social surroundings takes economic action.

Such actions were necessary in Father Polizzi's case, and I surmise the same holds in other cases. We now consider political and economic action relevant to the user concerned with attaining a good life.

### Political and Economic Action

The goal remains a good life, which I assume is common to most personal value systems. We will discuss the use of physical environmental surroundings and social surroundings, as your vote can affect them toward attaining a good life for individual users.

#### Capitalism, Economic Action, Political Action

By this point, it must seem that my arguments are leading up to an all-out attack on big business or capitalism, as is fashionable nowadays. Those hoping for such an attack will be disappointed. Rather, the two functions of national goal-setting and pursuing well-chosen national goals are distinguished.

The first function of national *goal-setting* is extremely important for us as users but often neglected in psychology. Consider the current use of land and physical environment as an important issue. I claim that land use today is largely determined on the basis of market demand. It is also safe to claim that the determination of land use by market demand is intolerable because we are devastating our physical environment.[39] A controlling technology arising from marketplace demand now exists and is largely undirected over the long haul. Worse yet, it is apparent that marketplace demand can be artificially created. The

*Many of the small and tightly knit ethnic communities that once dotted virtually every U.S. city have crumbled under the planner's rezoning and renewal schemes and the bulldozer's giant blade. One community that has successfully resisted the encroachment of urbanization is "the Hill," a 56-block, largely Italian area on the south side of St. Louis, where Yogi Berra and Joe Garagiola grew up. After a series of fierce, emotion-charged struggles with local, state and federal officials, Hill residents now boast a model community that has the lowest crime rate and the highest property values in the city.* TIME *Correspondent Marguerite Michaels recently visited the Hill. Her report:*

**POLIZZI OUTSIDE CHURCH**
*Saving a blighted cemetery.*

***BOCCIE* PLAYERS ON "THE HILL"**
*The past that works.*

In the afternoons around 3:30, Joe ("Green") Verdi, Angelo ("Foots") Colombo, John ("Detroit") Agresti and other properly and not-so-properly nicknamed neighborhood men gather at Rose's Tavern for a glass of beer from the 7-ft. wooden cooler. Then they drift out back toward the grape arbor for a game of *boccie*. On Wednesdays, Amelia Garavaglia, 76, flours her plump, competent hands in the back room of Gioia's Corner Market and begins rolling out 5,000 ravioli for sale in the front room. Each evening, Ida Galli switches on the spotlight in her front yard—not to scare away burglars, but to illuminate a 3-ft.-high statue of the Blessed Virgin. It is all part of the pleasant, unhurried flavor of life today on the Hill.

**Italian Sausage.** There is a strong sense of ritual, both religious and community, on the Hill, where 90% of the population of 6,500 is Italian and 95% Catholic. There is also a bursting pride in the rows of narrow, well-scrubbed houses and in the family-run corner stores, where links of fat Italian sausage dangle in long rows. Many residents are direct descendants of the immigrants who left Lombardy at the turn of the century to work the clay mines of St. Louis under the hill that gives the section its name. Life on the Hill is as finely woven as Ann Reistino's brightly colored, crocheted afghans.

It was not always so. In the '60s, the neighborhood's youth began to drift away. Federal and state highway officials designated the path of Interstate Highway 44 through an area of the Hill. Assuming that land values would plunge with the construction of the road, many homeowners stopped maintaining their property. A local lead company began pumping slurry into the abandoned clay mines, threatening to undermine foundations. Explains Father Salvatore Polizzi, 43, associate pastor of St. Ambrose Roman Catholic Church: "The Hill was becoming a blighted cemetery."

Polizzi determined to change things. He began delivering sermons urging the residents to regain their lost sense of spirit and pride. He also made a point of cultivating leaders of the area's strong Democratic organization.

His efforts paid off in his first encounter: discouraging the sale of land to builders of a planned drive-in theater. Polizzi sent the Democratic ward committeeman into the streets with a sound truck announcing an emergency meeting in the Big Club Hall. After a session exploring the blight that the drive-in would inflict on the area, a small army of Italian dowagers volunteered to lie down in front of the bulldozers. The sellers backed down, and the Hill's alderman quickly slipped a regulation through the zoning board forbidding a building permit for any drive-in within 500 ft. of a residential area.

Buoyed by that success, Polizzi once again rallied community support and forced the lead company to stop pumping waste into the abandoned mines. But the biggest fight was yet to come. By 1971 construction was well under way on Interstate 44. It cut off a segment of the community, isolating 150 families. Yet the state planned only one vehicle overpass. In protest, some 300 citizens piled into buses and traveled to the state capital, Jefferson City; there they argued before the highway commission for an additional overpass.

The commission said no, and the residents cannily decided to turn the problem into an "Italian issue." When Secretary of Transportation John Volpe visited St. Louis on another matter, Polizzi requested a meeting and pressed for the overpass in the same, formal Italian that Volpe had learned back home in Massachusetts. Joe Garagiola began dropping hints that he might not be available any more on the Republican banquet circuit unless the Hill got its overpass. Finally Polizzi led a Hill delegation to Washington with a check for $50,000, raised by the residents themselves, to pay for the overpass. The Hill got its bridge, and the bells of St. Ambrose rang out the good news.

Polizzi has joined 1,100 of the area's 1,500 families in a nonprofit development corporation to guide the future of the area. In its four years' existence, the corporation has found 60 jobs for new—and old—residents in the neighborhood's salami and macaroni factories, tool company and glass factory. It has set up a summer youth program and hired students at $1 an hour to spruce up the area. The students redecorated the Hill's hydrants and trash cans in red, white and green (the colors of the Italian flag). More than 1,000 trees have been planted. A system of block workers set up by the corporation makes certain that leftover ravioli lands in, not outside the garbage cans. The corportion maintains a list of Italians eager to move onto the Hill. When houses become vacant, it often refurbishes and resells them at low cost to young couples.

The money for many of these projects comes from the approximately $50,000 earned at an annual summer festival, which draws 100,000 visitors. The aroma of lasagna and meat balls fills the air, and amateur Carusos croon over the loudspeakers. There are grape-stomping contests and a step-by-step demonstration of how to make sfinge, an Italian confection. At the evening's end a spray of fireworks flares over the neighborhood as proud residents and guests clap and cheer, aware that they have seen the past and that on the Hill at least, it still works.

(From *Time* magazine, April 29, 1974, p. 27. Photographs by James A. Rackwitz. Reprinted by permission from TIME, The Weekly Newsmagazine; Copyright Time Inc.)

only sane alternative is planned land use, enforced vigorously. Otherwise a deteriorating environment will lose its value over the longer run. In other words, the capitalistic economic system is singularly unsuited for the setting of goals. Nevertheless, rays of hope abound.

The bright side here is that a vigorous capitalistic economy is ideally suited for *pursuing well-chosen national goals,* the second function. A vigorous capitalistic economy can be viewed as a locomotive that powers the train. Technology can be viewed as the tracks that determine where the powerful locomotive called our capitalistic economy is going. Naturally, the shiny exciting engine gets the glory while the controlling tracks are all but ignored. Let us look at the tracks called technology. Unhappily, today's most influential technologies derive mainly from market demand. Most (but not all) commercially funded technology is created toward the rational corporate goals of commercial consumption in the short and medium runs. Otherwise businesses would go bankrupt. Most (but not all) government-funded technology is created toward (1) reacting to visible catastrophies or (2) assisting scientists to pursue their own projects. The current flurry of research from all quarters is a recent reaction to prevent environmental catastrophy. The train tracks headed straight toward catastrophy were laid by market demand, which means continued land use without interference by enforced land planning.

### The Natural Environment and Land Use

Preserving and enhancing the natural (non-man-made) environment is potentially the most unifying force in politics today. Your personal social world depends on the surrounding environment. Attaining a good life complete with social actualization directly implies allocating your vote to candidates dedicated to preserving and enhancing the land's natural resources.

Environmentalism unifies people. Political reformers thirsting for change and staid proponents of the status quo both love the wilderness and seek natural beauty around the places where we live. Forward-looking businessmen and *Business Week* have proclaimed that environmentalism is as American as apple pie.

The state of Oregon provides a good example of environmentalism in action: As *Time* magazine reports, "In [Tom] McCall's eight years in office, Oregon adopted one of the nation's first comprehensive land-use plans, banned non-returnable beverage containers, placed its entire 300 mile shore in state ownership to protect it from developers and publicly discouraged new residents and even tourists. It also summarily closed a polluting paper-pulp plant and forced other firms to comply with tough environmental standards."[40] Former Governor McCall then infuriated party regulars by supporting the other party's candidate for the governorship of Oregon because the man agreed with McCall's *values.* McCall can teach us something in this matter.

Environmentalism requires a focus on goals. Preserving the world's natural resources would appear to be a superior goal in the platform of a given party at a given moment in time. In short, voting for candidates whose tenure in office will bring us closer to a good life means reading the fine print in the newspaper.

### The Social Environment and User Information

Just as the natural environment needs protection and enhancement, so does the social environment. Within each of us lies the social potential to take great strides toward social actualization and other social values. However, improved social consumption takes skill and hard work.

Social consumption has lagged far behind commercial consumption simply because commercial consumption now has the technology. Over the longer run, the most effective economic and political strategies toward a good life are environmentalism and the creation of user information. Throughout the history of science and technology, the pattern of discovery has been the same. The pattern holds for physics, advertising, medicine, petrochemical technology, aerospace, agriculture, communications, and many others:

1. Researcher wants to discover the state of nature.
2. Researcher attacks tough problem.
3. Critics say it is too complex. They say leave well enough alone. Critics laugh.
4. Researcher sweats.
5. Researcher fails.
6. Researcher sweats.

7. Researcher fails.

.

.

.

N. Researcher succeeds.

Often step N is not reached, but our modern age is testimonial to the thousands upon thousands of occasions it has.

The case of creating user information is no different. Certainly people are complex, but that is a difficulty, not a brick wall. I contend that the information in this book is also testimony for the creation of a viable body of user information, as discussed in Chapter 1. What might such a creation look like?

Creating a viable body of user information requires funding from government and private sectors to train and support researchers. A strong flow of user, professionally mediated, and basic research information is an absolute must. Areas of concern include:

Meeting new people or initiating interactions.
Empathy in conversation (accurate perception of other person's desires).
Changing the topic of conversation.
Giving criticism with minimum hurt.
Expressing emotions.
Eliciting emotional expression and self-disclosure from others.
Controlling one's temper for minimum hurt.
Negotiating differences in the family.
Skills in listening.
Ending a conversation.
Reducing personal fears and anxieties.
Paying compliments sincerely.

From this preliminary list, the personal benefit of user information should become apparent. Effective technologies to manipulate you and me as voters and consumers already exist in a sophisticated form; but those technologies serve organizational goals. The same ingenuity can be harnessed to serve personal, individual goals.

Once generated, user information can be disseminated in a number of ways. However, demonstrable increases in social skill will be enhanced vastly when the learning situation involves live presentations and examples of content, the opportunity for the rehearsal of new skills, and live feedback on those rehearsals. The learning situations that come immediately to mind are the public schools in grades K-12, college, continuing education, and private institutions. Especially in grades Kindergarten–12, a practical research-based curriculum of human relations may be a reality soon. This curriculum could be both exciting and useful. Perhaps instructional procedures will involve resident teams of professional actors at each school. This country has thousands of talented but unemployed actors, many of whom might find that two years of specialized preparation and then working with young people would be a fulfilling career. These instructor-actors might also be valuable in other capacities around the school because role-playing and miniproductions can be incorporated into most existing courses of study to add interest and didactic value. Some specific procedures that involve the imitation of desired performances are detailed in Chapters 7 and 10, under the label of "modeling."

In the private sector, small business ventures that aim at enhancing human contact are expanding. Singles bars flourish; people seek private therapy; and private parent-training programs enroll thousands. Such business ventures hold the promise of generating invaluable scientific research data as they develop. The possibility of large, research-based, specific skill-training services that make money in the private sector is portended by existing trends. Why would anyone buy a car with $1000 worth of useless accessories to catch someone's eye if it can be done more directly using noncommercial means that cost nothing to employ?

At this point you may perceive a clear conflict about the shape of future strategies to attain a good life. On the one hand, moving toward the apparent ideal of intermediate consumption level sounds desirable from an interpersonal viewpoint. However, any sudden moves to cut commercial productivity and (therefore) commercial consumption would create economic havoc and do untold interpersonal damage because the modern world depends on high industrial productivity. On the other hand, creating a body of user information might well lead to intense social consumption with the same stressful effects that now accompany intense commercial consumption. What is the resolution of this conflict? Is there a resolution?

The conflict will probably be resolved with

both forces just mentioned coming into play and taking their natural course: That is, as user information is generated, there will be a *gradual* lowering of consumption level, accompanied by new industries and jobs built around user information. Thus the modern economy will not be subjected to any sudden shocks. Moreover, as user information becomes available we will want to adopt a lifestyle of intermediate consumption level because the overall quality of life will be highest.

A beneficial side effect of the future scenario just sketched concerns the rise of entirely new industries that create, organize, and disseminate user information. Businessmen themselves are now caught up in the sticky web of a technology derived largely from short-run market demand to provide goods and services that indirectly satisfy social needs. That technology is by definition less effective than a body of user information that would satisfy needs for human contact more directly. User information would bring with it a whole new array of markets that do not yet exist.

Finally, I am extremely optimistic about where mankind will be headed with the coming of a viable body of user information. The bad vision of commercially supplied, artificial means to turn each other on to peak social experiences every hour on the hour seems quite unrealistic. Rather, I see myself and other humans as genetically wired up to ultimately seek out an intermediate level of consumption, both commercially and socially. With low consumption levels come the terrible hardships of starvation, lack of medical services, 30-year life expectancy, loneliness, and so on. With high consumption levels come the stressful states of information overload, environmental chaos, and pressures to achieve instant intimacy. Over the long haul of decades and centuries, the superior quality of life at an intermediate consumption level will first attract and later dominate the direction mankind takes. That direction is available, if we can survive and avoid worldwide wars.

Finally, note that social-intensive consumption is extremely compatible with environmentalism. In the process of consuming purely social resources from another person, you and I do not use up irreplacable natural resources.

## THE FUTURE

In *The Coming of Post-Industrial Society,* the noted futurologist Daniel Bell expresses concern about a replacement for the Protestant ethic.[41] According to the Protestant ethic, we work and thriftily save our pennies. Bell's vision of the year 2000 sees a continuation of the ongoing shift from producing goods toward producing services. The transition will also see a shift away from free-market capitalism toward planned technological development, with university research centers commanding a monopoly on the scientific information base that will direct society. The process of which Bell speaks can be seen now, at least in industrial nations. When material scarcities disappear, the virtues of working hard, saving, and delaying gratification embodied in the Protestant ethic are no longer needed. However, the planning of technology is not an ethic; it is a means, not an end or a goal. It merely means moving with greater efficiency toward somewhere. The values expressed in this chapter constitute a possible "somewhere" or ethic for a service economy in which scarcities are minor: the attainment of a good life for a nation's people. Pursuit of a good life may be a worthy successor to the Protestant ethic.

## SCIENCE AND HUMAN VALUES

Maslow tells us, "Science is based on human values and is itself a value system."[42] Arguments to the contrary are utterly wrong because scientific efforts require the allocation of scarce resources, just like other activities. Specifically, researchers allocate their own scarce resources of

time for graduate training
time to teach certain, highly particular classes
time to research certain, highly specific topics
money for research on certain, highly specific topics
coverage of highly specific topics *within* the highly scarce space of a given research article

Hopefully, this chapter has exposed my values and sharpened yours, whatever they may be.

We now summarize this section. The addendum to this chapter contains some possible problems that might work against human contact in your community. Solutions are proposed, but only as experiments in creative living, not dogma.

### SUMMARY AND PROJECTIONS INTO THE FUTURE

Attaining the core values embodied in a good life requires political, legal, and economic action. A vigorous capitalistic economy is needed for strength. However, a capitalistic economy derived from market demand is intolerable because then technology determines where man is going. At present, a dominant technology based on market demand is seductively leading modern men and women to allocate scarce personal resources into commercial consumption that is interpersonally deficient and environmentally devastating. *No one is in charge of where that technology is taking us.* Modern technology is controlling man; we are not controlling it. To remedy the situation, two courses of political, legal, and economic action are recommended: Both (1) environmentalism and (2) the creation of a viable body of user information comprise courses of action that lead toward a good life.

# addendum to chapter five: Possible Problems in Human Contact

A number of barriers to human contact may well exist unnoticed at the community level. In the following pages, we will state some *possible* problems. After each problem statement, an experiment(s) in creative living is proposed to test out the state of nature. In no case could a solution be proposed before the results of the experiment are determined. The experiment might turn out either way.

## THE POSSIBLE PROBLEM OF PERSONAL PRODUCTIVITY

### Statement of Possible Problem

If Linder is right, the more you get out of your working time, the more you will *want* to squeeze out of your consumption time. If you feel under pressure and generally harried, you may indeed be a member of *The Harried Leisure Class.* (Other problems might exist, but here we are concerned only with overly high personal productivity.) Linder's analysis would also predict that you can personally ease the pressure by choosing to lower your own work productivity somewhat. In fact, he ends his book by virtually suggesting this action. The results should include lowered stress and consumption. MIGHT OVERALL QUALITY OF LIFE BE HIGHEST AT AN *INTERMEDIATE* LEVEL OF PRODUCTIVITY?

### Experiments in Creative Living

To lower personal work productivity means incorporating a slice of Greece à la 1950 into one's life. Such experimentation would occur at the household level. The general plan is to try out an altered life-style in which personal work productivity is lowered for awhile on an experimental basis. The public media carry stories about harried executives and stockbrokers who drop out and become beachcombers. Magazines describing rural and other less harried life styles are springing up.[43] However, "lowering personal work productivity somewhat" does not imply dropping out of society. That is shutting down, not slowing down.

Lowering personal productivity can be accomplished in two general ways: working fewer hours or working on a job that produces less. Both mean less money, but not necessarily less yield. For example, in a high-pressure job, you may rake in 5 units of total yield—only to also bring in 2 units of negative yield through stress. Your score here is +3. In a lower-pressure job, you might earn only 4 units of total yield while incurring only one-fourth unit of negative yield through stress. Your score here is +3¾, which is better than before.

Options for lowering personal work productivity somewhat include taking a job that demands fewer hours, taking a job that entails interacting with people, moving to a small town where productivity is lower, setting up a business in which you control your working hours, and taking up volunteer work, which is often a social-intensive use of personal consumption time.

If you hold a position of authority, you can hire and reward people whose views about the use of time agree with yours. If you hold real authority, you can introduce the concept of undermanned behavior settings into your organization. Derived from Barker's theory of ecological psychology, the concept of *undermanned behavior settings* refers to a shortage of workers relative to the job requirements.[44] Barker's concept of undermanning is so important and so applicable that it is worth a paragraph.

If only two people are available to run a small grocery store or gas station, the behavior setting will probably be undermanned. When the drama teacher in a small high school decides to stage *War and Peace,* the dramatic production will surely be undermanned. Studies comparing big schools and small schools show that students in small schools enter more behavior settings, feel more needed, feel more challenged, report more self-confidence, feel they have participated in more important jobs, and even render more complex descriptions of the school settings![45] Comparisons of small versus large churches show greater participation rates in the small churches.[46] From such research, it seems that creating a small, cohesive group to battle against common obstacles can have some valuable benefits. As the most recent work on undermanning indicates, altering the number of workers per task is related to other factors in complex ways (i.e., the physical setting, task complexity).[47] Even so, work settings where small, slightly undermanned teams attack problems warrent judicious experimentation by the manager who desires to promote human contact on the job, probably at the expense of some productivity (efficiency).

Experiments today to lower personal productivity would take place in a hostile economic environment. The modern economic environment is set up to reward high productivity. Therefore be extremely careful not to bring down economic ruin on yourself—especially with experiments to set up undermanned job settings. They probably *require* being conducted in a supporting community where, say, legal protection against competition is temporarily afforded to the "mom and pop" small, but somewhat less efficient, store. I hasten to add that such legal protection seems eminently justified when (1) the purpose involves a community experiment for better living and (2) a specific date of expiration is tied directly to the result of the experiment.

**Case 5.11.** Harried Harry drops out and moves his family to Farmsville, U.S.A. He lands a job in the hardware store on Main Street. The town is deteriorating, and all the young people are moving away. Harry gets all fired up and persuades the town board to try a two-year community experiment. A modest land-use plan is agreed on. Permits for new businesses will be limited to the seven kinds of stores now needed. A siesta break of 3 hours for most businesses (but not farming) is declared for early afternoon. Schools will be closed then. Informal consent from most of the town's 327 households is obtained to patronize local merchants. Newcomers are allowed, but the land-use plan and business permits require most of them to take up farming. Harry stays, unharried.[48]

Such experiments seem to occur by accident, usually in reaction to predicted catastrophy. For example, as Father Polizzi's case shows, success is possible in an identifiable supporting community, even one inside a big city. I am arguing for small personal and modest community experiments along such lines. All are experiments because they would end at a specific time, to be evaluated by standards agreed on in advance.

### THE POSSIBLE COMMUNITY PROBLEM OF MOTOR-VEHICLE PATTERNS

#### Statement of Possible Problem

It is often said that we have not yet learned how to live with the automobile or that the automobile rules our cities and towns. Automobiles bring us together, but deadly lanes of traffic slice up neighborhoods. Little-used streets occupy a lot of real estate in prime areas.

#### Experiment in Community Living

A useful experiment for communities having mostly square blocks bounded by streets would be to block off some streets to create lots of dead-end streets. Figure 5.3(a) shows the blocks before being blocked off, and Figure 5.3(b) shows the blocked-off streets. To be sure, a few disadvantages would result, such as increased traffic flow along the unblocked traffic artery. Home deliveries would be more difficult for commercial vehicles, and a few minutes' time would be added in getting to work. However, the benefits such as fewer children being hit by speeding cars, might be tremendously high. Neighborhoods unsplit by traffic would be created, leading to viable communities. Also, acres upon acres of priceless real estate would come into neighborhood use. Even more space might become available if parking were restricted mainly to areas marked "P" in Figure 5.3(b). The creation of hundreds of miniparks could substantially improve the human contact for residents along the street because the newly created space would allow activities not possible before. Bulletin boards, play equipment for children, adult social areas, game courts, and similar *physical facilities* could be installed. *Social functions* such as garage sales, cooperative flea markets, street dances, impromptu music performances, and so on could be held. Properly engineered, a conversion of already paved real estate in the heart of cities to neighborhood use could raise the cost of living a small bit by lowering commercial productivity (efficiency); but it could also raise the quality of life immeasurably.

### THE POSSIBLE PROBLEM OF A CHILD'S STABLE PEER GROUP

#### Statement of Possible Problem

It may be the case that schools are organized in a way that enhances course learning but hurts social learning. In the process of squeezing every last ounce of efficiency out of the teaching process, children are sometimes sorted into ability groups within the school year, and occasionally reformed into new classroom groups from year to year. As a result, the grade-school child becomes accustomed to a changing group of acquaintances; this process is similar to that of the ever mobile adult, who will display high mobility and commercial consumption in later life. Human contact may suffer in the process. In fact, a major result of ability- and other efficiency-grouping techniques might well be an

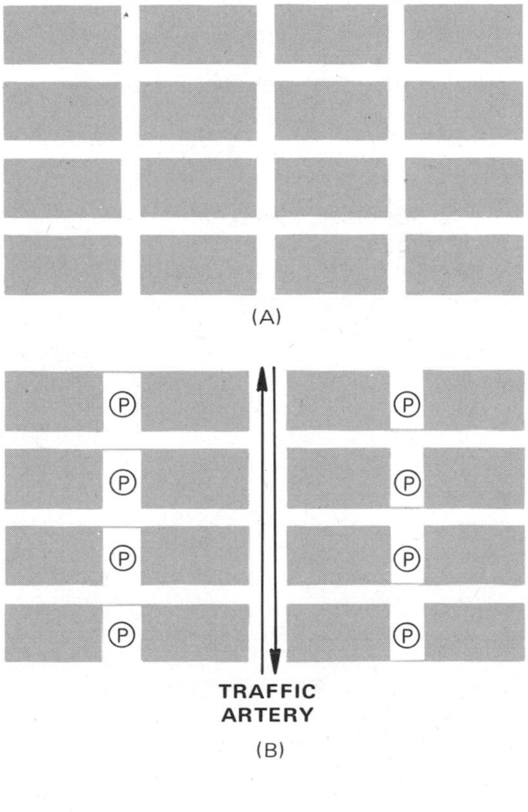


**Figure 5.3.** Block patterns (a) before and (b) after installation of barriers.

unwholesome bit of social learning. Children may actually learn that "efficiency is king. You are to excel. You are not to help those who move slower. Hired professionals will do that. Let everyone fend for himself." The adoption of these ideas may lubricate the commercial enterprise, but what is going to happen to you and me in our old age when our interpersonal world centers around a younger generation literally schooled in efficiency? (Remember it's only a possible problem, not a confirmed one.)

### Experiment in Community Living

This experiment involves the procedure of retaining stable class groupings throughout the day all the way from grades 1 to 6. If introduced on an experimental basis for half the children entering a given school or matched schools in a whole school system, the children surrounded by the same classmates should attain more optimal human contact and show greater social adjustment than the children who are bounced from group to group for efficiency's sake. The end result should be somewhat lowered scores on standard achievement tests because of lowered learning efficiency. But I predict better social adjustment for the children who experience several years' exposure to a stable peer group.

## THE POSSIBLE PROBLEM OF WIDESPREAD FAILURE EXPERIENCES AMONG YOUNG PEOPLE

### Statement of Possible Problem

Many, if not most, young people may be bombarded with needless failure experiences. Making mistakes is a part of learning, and young children should be encouraged to explore even if mistakes result. School records are kept to help teachers, but they also record for posterity the scars of mistakes or specific childhood failures. As the current system operates, grade-school success sorts children for secondary school; secondary school success sorts applicants for career or college; and college success sorts youths for postgraduate careers. The maintainence of school records assures that an account of early childhood mistakes is preserved.

### Experiment in Community Living

Two courses of experimental action exist. A community could adopt experimentally the *Guidelines for the Collection, Maintenance, and Dissemination of Pupil Records,* prepared by the Russell Sage Foundation.[49] These guidelines propose that school records be kept, but that access to them be regulated. The complicated guidelines are based on the assumption that the potential advantages of school records for whomever gets the student next (school, teacher, counselor, college, business) outweighs the costs of not seeing the records.

A more venturesome experiment could be based on the opposite assumption that the scars of failure outweigh the (1) prizes of success plus (2) benefits for whomever gets the students next. Accordingly, this experiment would require that failures or successes never be permanently recorded until an individual reaches the age of legal adulthood. (In a competitive system, one student's success implies another's failure because top grades are scarce.) At the end of each fiscal year, all school records of legal minors would be destroyed. If our adult capitalistic economic system is cold and cruel, young people would be spared the competitive and evaluative essence of the system before adulthood. (The issue of survivability and adaptability of competitive and aversive social systems is treated in the epilogue to this book on page 257.)

*ON BEING GIVEN TIME*

*Sometimes it seems to be the inmost land*
*All children still inhabit when alone.*
*They play the game of morning without end,*
*And only lunch can bring them, startled, home*
*Bearing in triumph a small speckled stone.*

*Yet even for them, too much dispersal scatters;*
*What complex form the simplest game may hold!*
*And all we know of time that really matters*
*We've learned from moving clouds and waters*
*Where we see form and motion lightly meld.*

*Not the fixed rigid object, clock or mind,*
*But the long ripple that opens out beyond*
*The duck as he swims down the tranquil pond,*

*Or when a wandering, falling leaf may find*
*And follow the formal downpath of the wind.*

*It is, perhaps, our most complex creation,*
*A lovely skill we spend a lifetime learning,*
*Something between the world of pure sensation*
*And the world of pure thought, a new relation,*
*As if we held in balance the globe turning.*

*Even a year's not long, yet moments are.*
*This moment, yours and mine, and always given,*
*When the leaf falls, the ripple opens far,*
*And we go where all animals and children are,*
*The world is open. Love can breathe again.*

# ON INTERPERSONAL CHANGE

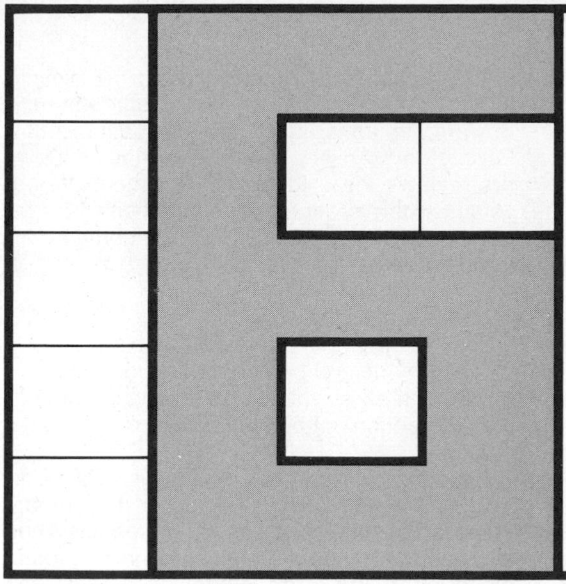

# INTERPERSONAL CHANGE

*Such is the state of life that none are happy but by the anticipation of change. The change itself is nothing; when we have made it, the next wish is to change again.*

SAMUEL JOHNSON

*A man's growth is seen in the successive choirs of his friends.*

RALPH WALDO EMERSON

*However rare true love is, true friendship is rarer.*

LA ROCHEFOUCAULD

## SELF AND OTHERS

In the previous chapters, we have been concerned with reasonably general features of human contact or intimacy. In the following chapters, our attention shifts to specific aspects of everyday interaction with others. Beginning in this chapter, we consider change in the social world of one individual: you.

The emphasis in these chapters on interpersonal change remains on serving your personal goals. Nevertheless, the social nature of the goals we are discussing and the bicycle model (Figure 1.3) both imply that if your momentary goal is to elicit a particular change in your best friend, you will probably end up changed as well. In addition, if your stated goal is self-change, you are well advised to enlist the aid of your companions. In the next two chapters, it will appear as though our approach to interpersonal change centers solely on getting your "other person" to do something or other. However, the principles for change are equally applicable to yourself. For the sake of clarity, we are nevertheless going to initially speak in terms of you eliciting action from your other person.

## WILLPOWER

The main idea in this section is that each of us can largely direct our own personal destiny, but only if we play it right. Otherwise we get knocked around by external forces.

### The Fruitless Distinction

The time-honored way to approach the idea of willpower is to distinguish between thought and action. Consider the following case.

**Case 6.1.** I have been too shy lately, I haven't even gone up and met the boss's new assistant Mary, and it's been three weeks. But then, I am a shy person and now might be an inconvenient time. To heck with such thoughts! From now on, I'm going to be an extrovert one week and my old self the next. Then I'll decide which me I like best after giving that plan a go.

This case illustrates the main problem in directing one's own life: Will intentions be translated into action by me? The relationship between the philosophy of thought and the philosophy of action as they apply to directing one's own destiny is phrased nicely by Merhabian: "It is easier to act yourself into a new way of thinking than to think yourself into a new way of acting."[1]

One philosophy emphasizing thought is distinguished from another emphasizing action. This historical distinction easily gets bogged down in similar mind-body distinctions, leading to fruitless and aimless discussions. I will suggest a different distinction—one that will, hopefully, clarify the idea of willpower.

### The Fruitful Distinction

A fruitful way to view the idea of willpower is to use the distinction pictured in the bicycle model of social life (Figure 1.3). In this model, the distinction is made between internal and external sources of influence: You or your surroundings are the focus of influence.

To apply the bicycle model of social life, our strategy as the person in Case 6.1 should be to first line up all the sources of influence. The aims in this case are to meet the new lady assistant in particular and to become more assertive in general. This case boils down to the question, "What do I do tonight to get myself on the road to reaching those aims?" We now pause to consider some specific implications of the bicycle model.

The latest research concerning the bicycle model of social life comes from Kenneth Bowers. In an article titled "Situationism in Psychology: An Analysis and Critique," Bowers reviews the evidence concerning internal versus external control of our actions.[2] In the experiments he reviews, influence comes from three sources:

1. The person (me)
2. The surroundings (physical, social)
3. The unique and personal combination of me with my surroundings (also called the "interaction" of person and surroundings)

The upshot of Bowers's review is that good evidence now exists to document the importance of all three sources of influence.[3] Thus emphasis on either "my personal actions" alone or on "the surroundings" alone ignores about two-thirds of the sources of influence that act upon me. In other words, *to effectively direct my own destiny, I AM REQUIRED to use a two-pronged attack on my life problems that involves both myself and my surroundings.*

Continuing with Case 6.1, consider two different plans of attack. Both plans will be inadequate because each will be a one-pronged attack. In the first plan of attack I emphasize mainly myself, not my surroundings. Tonight I groom myself and set out good clothes so I will look nice tomorrow. Then I think about the best way to introduce myself and choose that set of words as my line. Upon arriving at work tomorrow, I will present myself to Mary at the first convenient time and introduce myself. If this plan of attack seems ridiculous, that is because it is ridiculous. The introduction is indeed a "line," and the whole business seems artificial.

In a second plan of attack I emphasize mainly surroundings. Tomorrow I'll find out from the receptionist when Mary is free. Maybe I can get Nick to introduce us because he and Mary are neighbors. Also, I'll get Dick to fill me in on Mary's interests so I can maybe get her talking about herself. Everyone says she's such a fascinating person. Is this second plan of attack not just as ridiculously incomplete as the first?

Is a plan of attack needed at all for such a mundane event as meeting one new person? Often it is not. When should we stop to think about user information and apply principles? Apply them only when common sense fails or when a certain occasion is very important. For Case 6.1, I would argue that the occasion of meeting Mary, your new superior, is indeed important and worth a bit of thought.

The beauty of the recommended two-pronged attack is this: *Even though I am not the sole source of two-thirds of the influences on my destiny, I can largely direct my own destiny by enlisting the influence of my surroundings to aid my own personal aims.* That is willpower. Willpower means enlisting the calming influence of a quiet room, the fuzzy cuddliness of a puppy, the frustration of a traffic jam, or the compassion of a grandmother to make a melody out of life. Interestingly, this conception of willpower inseparably binds us with nature. Case 6.2 illustrates how enlisting the influence of surroundings could take place.

**Case 6.2.** Fernando is having trouble making himself study. Even though the library is fairly far away, he decides to study there for a few hours every other day. (What kinds of surroundings is he using here?) Then he is ready to gradually build up studying at home. He gets Gayle to keep track of his studying at home. He buys an old table and chair, which will be used just for studying. Then, in a series of gradual shifts, he transplants his action of studying from the library to the table at home and saves a lot of gas as well. What physical surroundings did Fernando enlist? What social surroundings did he enlist?

Incidentally, the discussion of willpower also bears on the gigantic issue of whether we are motivated from within or motivated from without. The answer is that we are motivated from both within and without, and we ought to reject any simplistic notions that we function *solely* using either internal or external motivation. While such simple answers are attractive and comforting to all of us, the day is past when we can adopt them and still keep an open mind to the output of science.

ACTIVITY 6.1.

Write down something you really need to do this next weekend. Create three plans of attack and evaluate each.

Plan 1, emphasizing mainly myself:

________________________________

________________________________

________________________________

Plan 2, emphasizing mainly surroundings:

________________________________

________________________________

________________________________

Plan 3, emphasizing myself, surroundings, and interaction of both:

________________________________

________________________________

________________________________

The considerations in this section provide a concept of willpower. The practical import of willpower will be expressed later (in Chapter 9) in the "thyself principle," which states that we can use all the practical information in this book on ourself. And we should.

## PRINCIPLES

The practical information in the next four chapters is organized around *principles,* which are general statements that predict openly (objectively, so researchers can test them). These principles will be of the form, "If you arrange for . . . , then your other person will be more likely (or less likely) to exhibit certain action." In this section, we consider some preliminary ins and outs of principles per se, because you have probably not encountered principles such as these before.

### Change and Control

Whenever any kind of practical tool exists, there is also a need to consider questions on the ethics of control of how other people act. User information is practical. But what if all the information in this book, for example, actually works for you? What if you actually have powerful information in your hands? You need not concern yourself much with the ethics of what you are doing when you simply master lofty theories from the stratosphere of science. You need to give only slight concern to your moral responsibility when you begin to intellectually comprehend the staggering problems of today's society. After all, yours is only one voice in the crowd. In stark contrast, you are heavily responsible for the welfare of others when into your hands falls information that aids your face-to-face human relations. Here you are not a bystander, but a responsible

agent of action. You are a prime mover. How can you be a morally good mover?

One approach to the issue of control involves describing the body of information, say the list of principles in the next four chapters. On the one hand, we can view the principles as basically evil tools for manipulation. This view is not only naively misguided; it is wrong. The principles themselves are ethically neutral because any practical tool can be used for good or ill. Along this line we can view the principles themselves as descriptions of the state of nature. I endorse this latter view.

Principles describe naturally occuring processes of interpersonal influence. For example, if you pay your best friend a compliment right after she does you a favor, she will generally be more likely to do favors more readily in the future. The effect of your action here, namely her doing more favors in the future, would occur regardless of whether someone formalized it into a principle or not. In other words, you exert influence upon meaningful others in your social world 24 hours a day, and there is no way in the world you can turn it off. You cannot react to any comment in a perfectly neutral way. Even your silence has an effect. Your only rational choice is to wisely manage the influence you do exert. Toward this end, we will discuss three general guidelines for ordering the response options in any given social situation.

## The HEN Guidelines for Applying Principles

When applying principles, we can assume that your previous casual actions have not met with success. Thus you are trying out new response options that have some regularity, namely, some new plans. The plans can be just ideas in your head, but they have some regularity to them. The thing to do is to order these plans according to some ethical guidelines. Otherwise a haphazard ordering of the plans might be grossly immoral.

Suppose you as a mother or father want to keep your child from running into the street (see Figure 6.1). Your requests alone have not succeeded in keeping him or her from toddling beyond the sidewalk. Spankings are obviously not as bad as the child's mutilation or death by accident; but equally obvious is the use of other actions before spankings. I know that the urge to be spontaneous and to avoid planning tiny details of our lives is strong. You and I feel it daily, and it should be strong. But in some important areas, it is just downright immoral to avoid ordering plans of action. The choice between spontaneity and a possibly crippled child illustrates this point in chilling fashion. A milder example follows.

**Figure 6.1.** Right now this youngster is deciding whether to dash across the street. To effectively minimize the odds that injury will occur in the street, there are plenty of response options open to the parents before the arrival of this critical moment. Most of the options do not involve punishment. (Photograph by Charles Blakey.)

ACTIVITY 6.2.

Suppose you want to date a certain person very much. Also suppose your casual attempts thus far have not resulted in even so much as a lunch date. What should you do to get a lunch date for next Thursday? Create three different things you could do, three plans of attack. Order these options, according to which one you would use first.

1. ______________________________

2. ______________________________

3. ______________________________

By what standards or guidelines did you order the three plans in Activity 6.2? In the following paragraph I offer you three guidelines by which you might order plans. Think of them as the HEN standards.

First, the initial plan should be *Humane.* Quite simply, this guideline has to do with pleasure and pain. Your initial plans should involve as little pain and carry as much pleasure as possible. Suppose an employee creates a disruptive ruckus in the office. Also suppose the ruckus is completely unjustified. Why embarrass or punish her if moving her desk elsewhere in the office will do the trick? An old Chinese proverb goes, "Do not remove a fly from your friend's forehead with a hatchet." Second, the initial plan should be as *Effortless* as possible. Why waste your energy? Third, the initial plans should be *Natural,* that is, as unartificial as possible. These three guidelines are discussed in more detail when we consider punishment and reward. For now, think Humane-Effortless-Natural, HEN.

### The Nature of Principles

We begin this section with an analogy. In this analogy, you are the conductor of the orchestra, which is your life. Think of principles as represented by single musical instruments. Your audience hears mainly the symphony, which results from the combining of many single instruments. But occasionally a single-instrument solo or just a few instruments can be heard, and at such times the audience can identify those single instruments. So it is with principles: They act in concert, so it takes a trained ear or a rare solo to be able to detect one principle in action alone. In the next four chapters, we will play principles in solo; that is, we shall consider principles alone, bearing in mind that applications are in concert with other principles and even other orchestras.

Principles were defined as general statements that predict openly. Open or objective prediction is needed to tell if the statement is practical or not. To illustrate, the glib advice that in your human relations you should "Smile!" is not an open prediction. The advice to smile is not even a prediction at all, because it says absolutely nothing specific about what will happen if you smile more. In contrast, principles say that if you do some specific action, some specific result will occur that you can see.

Where do principles come from? Did I create all of them? I have created a few here and there; many principles have been put forth by others; and most have some research to back them up. Indeed, after stating each principle, I summarize some of the research bearing on it. This is done because I am vitally concerned about how future evidence from research bears on my principles. Believe it or not, the essential feature of good statements in science is their capability to be disconfirmed. This is because the essential feature of science is to bring empirical research to bear on statements, which requires falsifiability. Therefore I will propose principles as openly or objectively as possible. Then both you and the professional researchers can test them.

Finally, be warned that no one will ever issue gilt-edged certificates to confirm that such-and-such is a "permanent official principle." The nature of scientific evidence about a theory or a prediction is much like the advancing edge of the Sahara Desert. The shifting sands roll on, with the grains of evidence continuously forming new landscapes of science.

### When Should I Apply Principles?

The question "When should I apply principles?" is a specific instance of the more general question "When should I apply user information?" Apply principles with a plan when plain common sense fails or when a given occasion is important to you. Using principles and user information amounts to using somewhat of a plan in human relationships, unlike what we usually do. When unplanned, casual actions on your part do not or might not bring forth desired actions from the other person, break out your list of principles. Use the list of principles (given in Appendix B) as a checklist. The policy just stated illustrates nicely the effortless component of the HEN guidelines.

### Principles Assume That Dependabilities Exist in Daily Living

In trying to squeeze some sense out of the shifting seas of human relations, I am going to state principles. Accordingly, we will assume at least some dependability in your human relations with family and friends. Dependability here means that regularities occur in our everyday actions that are governed by rules.

At this point, a strong reaction usually comes from a few students: "What? You mean you're assuming perfect regularity in my relations with *people?* I'm no machine! Hang loose and live life as it comes. There's not much regular about social life anyway." While such claims are overstated, they reflect a reaction that I feel too whenever someone applies the concepts of regularity or predictability to my life. My answer emphasizes that lack of regularity in the form of dependability would shatter the best of human relationships.

Have you ever noticed how a devoted couple or two close friends relate to each other? Along with spontaneity and creativity, there is great regularity in the form of dependability in the most positive and intimate of relationships. Intimates greet each other warmly, smile a lot, maintain a great deal of eye contact, spend a lot of time together, and so on, all with great dependability. This dependability means you can count on its regular occurrence. Of course regularity in the form of unchanging, monotonous actions can characterize an unhealthy relationship. But dependable exchange of love, for example, is essential for maintaining excellent relationships. Otherwise the relation would not continue to be positive and intimate. Do people devoted and loving toward each other alternate between 50 percent love and 50 percent hatred? Of course not. If you did not greet and make eye contact dependably with friends and acquaintances, how long would they remain friends and acquaintances? Being dependable about showing common decency is obviously required for friendship. Dependable positive interactions with your other persons are essential to the kinds of human relations that make life worthwhile.

If we accept the arguments above, what about spontaneity? Is there not some virtue in it? Yes, there is, because without some spontaneity and unpredictability, everyday interactions would become boring and grow stale. Spontaneous actions mean surprise gifts, impulsive excursions just for fun, and these are compatible with the idea of dependability as described above.

**BEHAVIOR MOD**

It is necessary that we briefly describe behavior mod as a body of knowledge because most of the principles given in Chapters 7–10 are extracted from behavior mod. Behavior modification, behavior mod for short, is widely misunderstood. Most of these misunderstandings stem from the reputation behavior mod has with the popular media. Behavior mod clearly has a bad press—and for several reasons.

Besides possessing powerful tools for changing how people act, behavior mod psychologists are usually in the business of working these tools on parties of lesser power than they or their organization, as with behavior mod programs for schoolchildren or prisoners. Thus behavior mod becomes known as the tool of the oppressors. Headlines such as "Behavior Modification under Fire" are not uncommon.[4] Also, behavior modifiers often recommend artificially created systems of control in unpopular areas. For example, even though children are supposed to like school, behavior modifiers recommend paying children for doing schoolwork when other measures fail. It is taboo to openly admit that lots of children just plain do not like school. Husbands and wives undergoing behavior mod therapy may be urged to write a formal written contract to regulate, say, their use of free time on weekends. Concerning husband-wife relations, it is taboo to write formal contracts to regulate specific behaviors in marriage. On top of all that, behavior mod psychologists often endorse Skinner's philosophical position that free will does not exist.[5] It is not at all hard to see why behavior mod has a bad press![6]

For our purposes, we will extract certain useful content from behavior mod and leave the philosophy aside for now. One dominant feature of behavior mod that we adopt is a rather descriptive approach to social events; for example, when speaking about what happens on a lunch date, our considerations will generally focus on outward actions. In behavior mod, the focus on outward actions often means that the author sees no place for internal feelings. I do see an important place for internal mental processes in psychology, but in Chapters 6–10 outward actions are emphasized for some important, specific reasons.

We focus on outward actions for two reasons. The first is pragmatic: To encourage the use of this book by a diversity of instructors and students, there is wisdom in adopting a fairly common descriptive base acceptable to individuals of varying orientations. The second reason is scientific: I judge that the scientific study of mental processes has not yet advanced to the stage to warrant a commitment by me to any one view. I look forward to the time when a given school of cognitive (thought-oriented) or physiological psychologists will come up with a Darwinian explanation of mental events that underlie our social dealings. However, until that glorious day arrives, I am playing it conservative, which translates here into a usually descriptive approach.

Our descriptive approach uses the definition of social skill given in Chapter 1: *Social skill* means success in eliciting certain actions from other people. Thus problems in human relations will have you desiring to elicit a certain action from your meaningful other person. The "action" can be any definable thing your other person does, just as long as you can clearly tell whether the action occurs or not. The action can be specific: For example, John may want Mary to tell him her unlisted phone number. The action can be general: For instance, George may want Nelson to adopt his political philosophy.

ACTIVITY 6.3.

Write down three specific instances of an "action" as discussed. After you have done this, write down another description for each of the three instances; but make the second description vague so as *not* to qualify as clearly definable action.

1a. Specific action.

______________________________

______________________________

1b. Vague description of 1a.

______________________________

______________________________

2a. Specific action.

______________________________

______________________________

2b. Vague description of 2a.

______________________________

______________________________

3a. Specific action.

______________________________

______________________________

3b. Vague description of 3a.

______________________________

______________________________

In all cases of action, we can speak of the *strength* of that action. The following are some more examples of action.

Martha going to the beauty shop.
Your eating eggs for breakfast.
Your best friend talking about himself.
Bill coming in late for work.
Maria and Fred having sexual intercourse.

In all these cases, we can think about the strength of the action. Indeed, it is possible to assign numbers to index the strength of each action, and you may wish to stop here and try that. The numbers indicating strength of "your eating eggs for breakfast" could reflect frequency of occurrence (number eggs eaten) or time spent (in minutes). For our purposes, actually assigning numbers to actions is a secondary strategy to use only when needed. Of course, for purposes of science or some special projects in this course, the assignment of numbers is usually needed.

In undertaking special projects involving numbers assigned to actions, be sure to check with your instructor. The assignment of numbers to important aspects of action, or "quantification," is a serious and often difficult matter. For example, suppose you wanted to assign numbers to reflect the degree to which "my best friend talks about herself." You would have to write a lot of definitions to define just when a statement by your friend makes reference to himself or herself. You would have to test the definition out in special ways and have at least one other person test them out as well before you could even begin to have confidence in your measure of best friend's self-disclosure.

**PROBLEM-SOLVING STRATEGY**

Here we pursue the problem-solving approach of Thomas D'Zurilla and Marvin Goldfried, who view problem solving as the means to social skill.[7] These authors employ Skinner's useful definition of what a problem is: "In the true problem situation, the organism has no behavior immediately available which will reduce the deprivation or provide escape from aversive (negative) stimulation."[8] The problem situation is one in which you have at least one existing response that would be effective, but you cannot perform it now.

D'Zurilla and Goldfried's problem-solving

steps are listed now and then illustrated in an example.

1. orientation
2. definition
3. generating options
4. decision making
5. verification

**Case 6.3.** Bill has recently broken up with the girl he has been dating for over a year. It has been two weeks since they stopped seeing each other, and the pain should have gone away. However, Bill feels restless and cannot sit down to study for long. He does not cry much, but rather spends a lot of time walking up and down the campus sidewalks and driving his car around. *Orientation:* Bill realizes he has a problem. If the present state of affairs lasts for long, he will flunk out of school for sure. He determines to do something eventually, but not jump off the deep end and do something rash right at this moment. *Definition:* Bill defines his problem as one of emotional loneliness. Since he is a member of several campus groups, he is not likely to be suffering from social loneliness. Also, his misery started when he and Linda broke up. To alleviate the situation, he thinks back to a course he took using a book by Flanders. He realizes that the specific kind of social relationship he needs involves those six features given in Chapter 3, so he must once again get himself into a steady dating situation. Thus, in defining the problem, Bill has first stated the problem and a target, or goal, as the eventual solution. *Generating options:* Bill thinks about what he might do. The first thing is obviously to meet someone to date, and here he excludes all the young ladies he knows now. They are either friends or past flames. To meet new people, there are a lot of things he could do. If he were concerned about outward appearance, he could hang around the student union; he could watch the procession of women as they stream out of classes or dormitories; he could frequent the shopping mall. Emphasizing minimum effort, he could call a friend and ask her to fix him up with a friend of hers. Emphasizing interest, he could attend meetings of special-interest groups. Emphasizing social accessibility, he could go to singles lounges and dances. Emphasizing similarity, he could put his name into the campus computer matching system. He could skim back through Chapter 11 on meeting new people in the Flanders book. *Decision making:* To make a decision after the first three steps listed means simply to order the decisions as to which will be tried first. He thinks back to the HEN guidelines and decides that none of the options are really inhumane. Maybe trailing a certain young woman home or looking for identifying parking stickers on her car is a bit sneaky, but all his friends do it. Besides, women have social needs too, and they are more hampered by society than men. Introducing himself to a good-looking prospect cold, without any introductions or known common interests, awakens a small flame of fear in him; so he opts for effortlessness as the main key to his strategy. Unlike many of his friends, he is not enamored of any special outward appearance. Besides, waiting for the ideal female appearance or even personality could take years, and Bill is hurting now. The solution must be immediate. So he decides to call Mariana for a fix-up. Mariana and he went through high school together and still remain the best of friends. They have a sort of mutual admiration society centered around enriching each other's social lives the best they can. *Verification:* A few hours later, Bill has a date for next Saturday night. He can now concentrate on his studies. The nameless restlessness seems to have evaporated. The provision for, not the actual participation in, next Saturday night's date solved his problem. However, verification means checking up on the effectiveness of the solution later. Nearly three weeks later, Bill thinks back to his decision making and the problem-solving strategy he used. Actually, the young woman who was his blind date on Saturday turned out to have a beautiful personality, but she was hung up on a religion he could not tolerate. However, he expressed these feelings to her the next week and attempted to form another relationship similar to his relation with Mariana. The girl agreed and they have both fixed each other up with friends for this Saturday night, and all is right in Bill's social world once again. This process of reflecting back onto the problem-solving strategy used is verification.

As in the case of using principles, using the problem-solving strategy is needed only when casual efforts fail or the situation is very important. Both of these conditions existed when Bill originally faced his problem. As we proceed to consider principles in the coming chapters, cases will be used to illustrate the problem-solving strategy.

### THINKING AND ACTING: PHILOSOPHICAL PERSPECTIVE

In this book I hope you will find an approach to thinking and acting consistent with my theoretically neutral intentions. Some orientations emphasize inner processes, thoughts, and feelings; some orientations emphasize outward actions. You will certainly form your own opinion as to which is best for you. Before you do, however, there is a third option: to withhold commitment and use whatever approach seems best suited to the most important task at hand, according to your values.

**SUMMARY**

Willpower was conceived of as enlisting the aid of your surroundings to aid in achieving your own personal aims. Since the next four chapters are organized around principles, several preliminaries concerning principles were considered. Principles were defined as general statements that predict specific outcomes in your life openly or objectively. Principles per se are neither good nor bad, although they may be used for good or ill. As a general procedure, initial plans to solve interpersonal problems should be as *H*umane, *E*ffortless, and *N*atural (HEN) as possible. Principles, as other user information, are employed when common sense fails or a given occasion is especially important. Although it provides valuable principles, behavior mod has a bad reputation with the public media. The usually descriptive approach to be used here allows your instructor and you to insert whatever mental events you wish into your minds. This approach is most definitely not one of scientific superiority. Rather, because of the limited means available for exploring the mind (beyond those already in use by the great novelists and philosophers), my usually descriptive approach is one of reluctant humility. Social skill will be viewed as problem solving. In solving an interpersonal problem, there are several stages in the process: orientation, definition, generating options, decision making, and verification.

*Those who are at war with others are not at peace with themselves.*

WILLIAM HAZLITT

*Life is the art of drawing sufficient conclusions from insufficient premises.*

SAMUEL BUTLER

*Your daily life is your temple and your religion.*

KAHLIL GIBRAN

*Life consists not in holding good cards but in playing those you do hold well.*

JOSH BILLINGS

# ELICITING ACTION

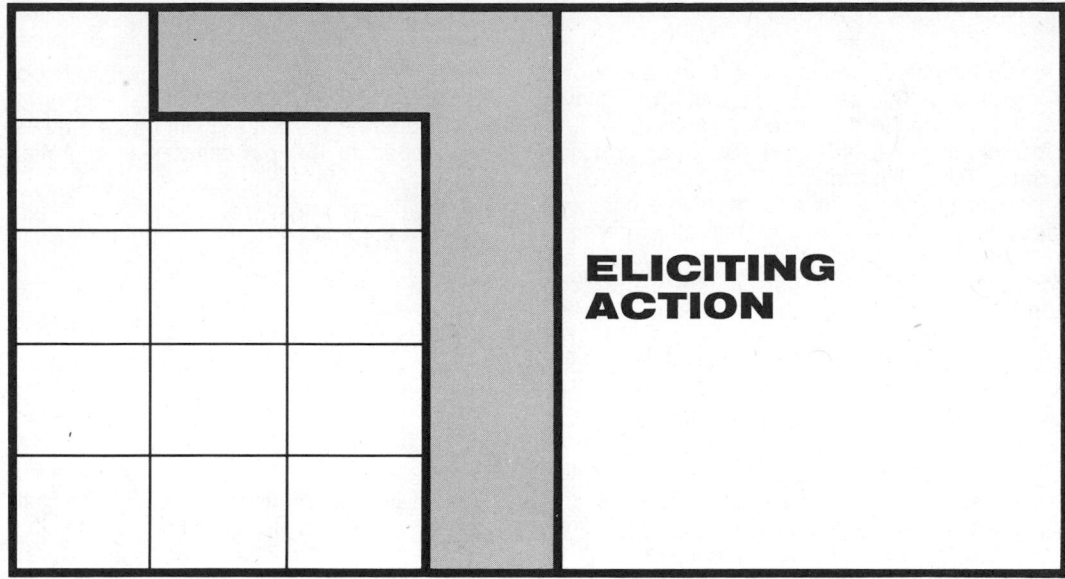

*Tsze-Kung asked what constituted a superior man. The Master said, "He acts before he speaks, and afterwards speaks according to his actions."*

CONFUCIUS

*The doer alone learneth.*

FRIEDRICH NIETZSCHE

*Men weary as much of not doing the things they want to do as of doing the things they do not want to do.*

ERIC HOFFER

## ON ELICITING ACTION FOR THE FIRST TIME

How many times each day do we wait for a certain person to take a certain action—for the first time? We can wait, but waiting does not always work. We can ask, but asking does not always work either. There is now about one chapter's worth of information in psychology for eliciting action that does not occur the first time, as illustrated in the examples below.

Picture George, the crusty manager who has for years sworn he'd not switch to computer processing. Then one day somebody says, "Well, I'll be. I never thought I'd see *George* come around." For the first time, George is taking action toward eliminating all those miscalculations in his department.

Picture a 4-year-old cherub, whose teeth are beginning to look like Swiss cheese. And the little rascal refuses to eat green vegetables. He is in your care, so how do you get him started in eating healthy green vegetables?

Patti can get across town 10 minutes faster than anyone else at the office. There have been subtle maneuverings of late to induce her to tell her secret, but none have worked. Then Fred remarks, "Hmmm. Well, *I* tried to get her to tell, and you mean *she* got it out of Patti? Hrumph!"

In each of the examples, there is a concern for eliciting action from a certain other person. In each case, I created an example where all concerned would be better off if the other person began taking the action indicated, namely, George switching to computer processing, the little rascal eating green vegetables, and Patti divulging her secret routes of travel. This chapter concerns eliciting similar everyday actions.

With this chapter we begin a four-chapter consideration of ordinary actions that are important to ordinary people. To use a problem-solving approach in these matters, we must be able to define or formulate our desires in reasonably clear terms. Recall that our conception of interpersonal skill involves success in eliciting desired actions from another person. This conception provides a way to state our desires because our desires can be stated as goals in the form of specific actions hopefully forthcoming from special other persons. In this way, vague desires translate into specific action, as the following examples illustrate.

*Vague desire:* I wish George would do his job better, especially the efficiency aspect of it.

*Specific action desire:* I wish George would adopt a computer system to handle our daily work, including input claims, processing, and output statements.

*Vague desire:* I wish my little 4-year-old would eat better and get healthier.

*Specific action desire:* As the beginning step in improving my 4-year-old's eating habits, I wish he would eat a small portion of green vegetables at each evening meal.

Translating vague desires into specific actions is only part of the problem definition process. The specific action has a *strength* of occurrence we wish to change, either by increasing it or decreasing the strength. For the moment, we will not worry about measuring, say, the strength of Alan's self-disclosure during coffee breaks. Such measurement concerns us only when we formally assign numbers to actions.[1] Rather, we will focus on what is to happen to the particular action. Action can be

elicited for the first time

built up in strength

maintained at a given strength

decreased

changed in form.

Taking first things first, we now proceed to consider principles for eliciting action that does not occur now. The order of these principles corresponds roughly to an ordering from gentle to coercive. Thus, according to the humane and effortless guidelines, the following order of principles approximates an ordering of which principles to try first. Of course, factors in your own situation will actually determine what to try first.

Coverage of each principle includes three main parts: statement of the principle, illustrations and applications of use, and support. Research results are discussed to support the principles whenever possible.

We begin with a set of principles to be employed before so-called "modeling" procedures are used. Modeling means imitation, where you arrange for your other person to see and imitate the action you want. Although each of us uses modeling procedures, such procedures are often time-consuming to arrange. Therefore, this first set of principles is concerned with procedures that take little time to employ.

## PRINCIPLES FOR ELICITING ACTION BEFORE MODELING

### Suggestion Principle

Statement of Suggestion Principle: If you arrange to suggest certain action to your other person, the other person will more likely display that action than in the absence of the suggestion.

**Case 7.1.** Mildred will surely say yes to Dwight's next request for a date, which he will make tonight. This will be their fourth date. On the previous three, Dwight has chosen what they did, but he is unsure if Mildred really wants to see motorcycle scramble races four Saturday nights in a row. His goal is to get her to express her own preference among some more peaceful alternatives for what they will do next Saturday night. First he generates several options about what he might do. He could just ask her what she would like to do. He might make the decision himself, being careful to choose a quiet activity very different from motorcycle scramble races. He might ask her best friend what she really likes. Dwight might dream up several alternatives and offer them to her. Then he decides what to do. Asking her friend is effortful and might not be accurate, so that is out of the question. His making the decision, even if he does it carefully, also misses the boat because it leaves no room for her preference. Asking her what she would like to do is OK but not very desirable because she might incorrectly assume that he wants to continue watching exciting sporting events. He decides to dream up several peaceful choices himself beforehand. Then he will offer her these choices, including the choice "or anything else you can think of." This strategy seems best to Dwight because it ensures that Mildred knows he wants a change of pace and allows her to express her preference as well. Upon hearing the several choices, if she says she has no preference, he will then ask her to express a preference (but that is the next principle, so we stop here).

When you *suggest* something, you offer an idea for your other person's consideration. When you suggest "Now would be a good time to take a break" to John, you offer the option of taking a break with John. If you suggest "Lunch at the deli might be a good idea" to a friend, you offer the option of lunch at the deli with good but vague consequences. A suggestion is an offering.

Psychologists study suggestion mostly in relation to hypnotism. In his book *Hypnotism: An Objective Study in Suggestibility,* Weitzenhoffer distinguishes between normal waking suggestions and hypnotic suggestions.[2] It seems appropriate to equate the concept of suggestion in the previous paragraph with *normal suggestion.* Likewise, we can define *hypnotic suggestion* as a special directive leading a person into a trance state or offered after a person is in a trance state. The following are examples of normal and hypnotic suggestions:

Normal suggestion: *"It's getting time to go to bed."*
Hypnotic suggestion: *"As you sit in your chair, you feel comfortable, very relaxed and comfortable. Your eyelids are getting heavy and it is becoming difficult to keep your eyes open. As you feel your eyes close, you also feel your thoughts beginning to drift away into another world, your ideas floating away into the darkness of space. . . . You are now back in your third-grade classroom. It is nearing Christmas and Mrs. Fezzywig is giving the class a party."*

Considerable research supports the effectiveness of hypnotic suggestions in eliciting action. Several kinds of hypnotic suggestions have been found to induce a hypnotic trance.[3] Once in a trance or state of heightened suggestibility, people will hold their arms out for long periods of time, will make their bodies rigid between two chairs for several minutes, will hallucinate a snowstorm and shiver, will regress in age to a third-grade classroom, and so on.[4] Hypnotically induced alterations from normal actions are so dramatic that presenting them on the stage is a part of the entertainment industry.

The documented effectiveness of hypnotic suggestions is sufficient for proposing a principle about normal suggestion because the two are related. "That hypnotism results from suggestion is not in question anymore," summarizes Weitzenhoffer.[5] There is reasonably good evidence to back up this claim.

Tests of hypnotic susceptibility have been found to predict hypnotizability and suggestibility under hypnosis quite well, even when the susceptibility tests are conducted in the waking state.[6] The fact that responsiveness to normal suggestion correlates high with responsiveness to hypnotic suggestion means that either they are much the same in nature or that some third factor causes them both, such as the expectation of reward. In either case, we have evidence to support the likely power of normal suggestions in everyday life.

Another line of research support for the suggestion principle comes from Theodore Xenophon Barber.[7] From an extensive line of research, Barber claims that normal suggestion and hypnotic suggestion are exactly the same. In other words, he says that hypnotism does not really exist apart from normal waking suggestion.[8] Throughout his research, he would first match two groups on his suggestibility scale, which measures normal suggestibility. Then he would hypnotize the persons in one group. To persons in the other group, he would merely give the same suggestions in a firm manner, but with no mention at all of hypnosis. He found, for example, that nearly 80 percent of both men and women would perform the "human plank" feat between two chairs when both groups were "told firmly and directly to make their bodies rigid and not to bend under any circumstances."[9] After finding that he could reproduce virtually all the so-called hypnotic feats in normal, waking people, Barber drew his controversial conclusion that hypnotism per se does not exist. While the researchers are still battling about Barber's conclusion,[10] the similar responsiveness of people to both hypnotic and normal suggestion supports the suggestion principle.[11]

As with all effective procedures in life, the suggestion principle can be used and abused. I see two primary means of use, one of which can be abused. First, you can use the suggestion principle to allow your other person to express a preference. That is what Dwight did in Case 7.1. Another use is to restrict the options of your other person. Although Dwight did this very gently, it seems a common procedure among salesmen, parents, and other persuaders.

**Case 7.2.** Frieda is exasperated about which dress to buy and she exclaims, "I just don't know what to do!" The saleslady has the goal of Frieda buying a dress from her, so the saleslady quickly generates a few options in her own mind before she speaks. The saleslady could (honestly) say, "I don't know which one you would like best, either." The saleslady could attempt to broaden Frieda's options: "Your interests will be served best by looking at dresses in at least two other stores. Only then will you have a decently wide selection." The saleslady could attempt to restrict Frieda's options: "Well, if you select the red one, it will fit right in with the holiday season. And if you choose the brown one, it will be nice and warm. Which one do you prefer?" After thinking these thoughts, the saleslady decides against the first two options and uses the third one because her only goal here is to make the sale.

Note that restricting the other person's options is not always bad. In Case 7.2 the successful restriction of Frieda's options by the saleslady is bad if we are worried about Frieda's having a wide range of options. However, if Frieda is very rich and if the saleslady is a poor widow with children who needs this sale to avoid having the electricity cut off in her miserable apartment, then the restriction of Frieda's options to make the sale is good.

As another example, restricting options is also used with children. I might say, "Carl, would you like to go to bed now or help me clean up the family room and go to bed in a few minutes?" These considerations on restricting your other person's options using the suggestion principle illustrate nicely the point that practical information can be used for good or ill.

### Request Principle

Statement of Request Principle: If you arrange to ask your other person to exhibit certain action, the other person will more likely exhibit that action than in the absence of the request.

Case 7.3 illustrates an appropriate use of the request principle.

**Case 7.3.** You are talking at lunch with a new acquaintance, and you both seem to like each other. However, you feel there is a small problem. This other person has the remarkable ability to shift the topic of conversation to you, and the result is your complete ignorance about her. Your goal is to get her to talk about herself. You think of several options. You could suggest, "It would be nice to learn something about you." You could command, "Talk about yourself!" You could honestly disclose your feelings: "I am getting a little uncomfortable talking about myself so much. I would feel relieved if we talk about you." You could simply ask, "Let's talk about *you* for a while, okay?" All these options are equally effortful. However, only the last option seems socially appropriate at the moment, so you ask.[12]

Research on the request principle ought to take place in natural settings, not psychology laboratories. It should involve requests by one acquaintance (not a stranger) to another of a fairly mundane sort, not of the emergency sort. Surprisingly, there has been almost no psychological research on the topic of normal everyday requests. An exception is the study of Landauer, Carlsmith, and Lepper, who studied requests made by mothers of nursery school children.[13] The study took place at the school, where each mother made three requests of three children, one of whom was her own child. The requests concerned mundane tasks, such as picking up blocks on the floor, and were phrased in the mother's own words. The researchers were interested in testing a disturbing phenomenon familiar to all parents: that their child seems to obey everyone else better than them. As it turned out, the children displayed little consistency across sexes or requests, but the experimenters' main hypothesis was supported: Of the 52 children, 44 were less obedient to their own mother than to other mothers. This study supports the effectiveness of normal everyday requests.

While the parents among us are taking consolation in the finding that ours are not the only children who listen better to others, we go on to note that the rest of psychological research bears only tangentially on the request principle. In most psychology experiments, the request comes from the experimenter as a part of the instructions, and it is assumed that all participants in the experiment will comply if they can.[14] In such cases, a special norm applies to requests by the researcher in psychology lab experiments: "This is an experiment, so do whatever ridiculous things the instructions say." This norm limits the generality of requests made in the psychology laboratory because the norm does not hold outside in the real world.

In a study by Langer and Abelson, reported under the title of "How to Succeed in Getting Help without Really Dying: The Semantics of Asking a Favor," the setting was outside the laboratory.[15] This study concerned a request for help in an emergency, wherein an actress feigned a knee injury and asked for help. Requests that emphasized the pain of the victim and requested a legitimate form of assistance were found especially effective in eliciting help. Still another special norm about requests pertains to helping in emergencies, namely, "Comply if at all possible." Such research on requests made in laboratories or real-life emergencies yields reliable evidence, but it is not relevant to our concerns here. Our concern lies with ordinary mundane requests, whereby the other person is not bound by a special norm to comply. With ordinary mundane requests the other person can and often does decline to comply.

Of much greater relevance here are some speculative but helpful proposals about making requests given by Ellen Langer and Carol Dweck in their book *Personal Politics*.[16] These suggestions typify the kinds of information that can be viewed as springboards for both action in your daily life and research by professionals.

1. The more the request is phrased to stress the helpfulness of the other person, the more likely the request will succeed.
   a. Darling, mail this for me please.
   b. Darling, would you help me and mail this for me please?
2. The fewer people there are present when the request is made, the more likely the request will succeed. This suggestion means that your chances for a successful request are best if you can catch your other person alone.
3. The more specific the action requested is, the more likely the request will succeed.
   a. Will you help me with my car tonight?
   b. Will you help me adjust the timing on my car tonight?
4. The more you look the other person straight in the eye, the more likely the request will succeed.
5. The more the request is phrased to limit your other person's choice, the more likely the request will succeed. The limitation often involves time.
   a. Margie, when could you help me set my hair?
   b. Margie, what day next week could you help me set my hair?

**Opening Principle**

Statement of Opening Principle: In the opening minute or two of an interaction, if you arrange to convey that certain actions are appropriate and encouraged, your other person will more likely exhibit that action than if you do not convey this information in the first minute or two.

**Case 7.4.** You are meeting your good friend Wendy for lunch, and you want the occasion to be

**Figure 7.1.** Pretend this picture represents you (you are seated) meeting your good friend Wendy for lunch as described in Case 7.4. Her face shows neither happiness nor any other emotion. You want her to show clear expressions of happiness. What do you do? (Photograph by Charles Blakey.)

as happy as possible. You want Wendy to show clear expressions of happiness. When she arrives, her face shows neither happiness nor any other emotion. (See Figure 7.1.) You start right out being as happy as you can—laughing, smiling, joking, and so on. She does likewise.

An ingenious experiment by Leventhal and Fischer provides us a rare look at the first minute or two when an interaction between two people starts.[17] At the beginning of psychology experiments, there is usually a get-acquainted time between experimenter and participants. Leventhal and Fischer arranged for young children to meet college-student experimenters. On the face of it, the experiment was to be a routine marble-dropping experiment, whereby the kiddies drop marbles in holes for assorted rewards. In this study, however, the researchers undertook to study the preexperimental getting-acquainted interaction of child and experimenter by using a hidden camera. Despite elaborate training to treat children as much alike as possible, each of the college-student experimenters displayed a distinctive style in interacting with his or her children. These styles had important effects on the children's actions later on, even affecting their perseverance at marble dropping. Perhaps at the outset, each experimenter acquired some kind of "social currency" or attractiveness that affected the children's later responses. Whatever happened at the outset, we have a clear demonstration to support the idea that the first minute or two is important.

Research on person perception, or impression formation, and on attitude change also supports the notion that first impressions can be dominant. In these studies, people are usually given a well-controlled series of information about a complete stranger. For example, the stranger might be described as "intelligent, industrious, impulsive, critical, stubborn, and envious" or "envious, stubborn, critical, impulsive, industrious, and intelligent."[18] The first list goes from positive to vague to negative traits, and the second series is a negative to positive sequence. The usual result of such experiments is a strong *primacy effect,* which means that first impressions dominate. Thus, participants who get the first list rate the imaginary stranger more positively than do participants exposed to the second list.[19] However, different instructions, contexts, and other procedures can wipe out primacy effects. Why do primacy effects occur? One theory says first impressions affect how we interpret later information.[20] The other theory says we simply tend to ignore later information.[21] Whatever the underlying, mental mechanism turns out to be, there is ample experimental evidence to support the opening principle.[22]

From the research described in the two previous paragraphs, we can draw a conclusion: Unless some influence is there to contradict first impressions or to emphasize later impressions, first impressions will dominate.

Turning now to brass-tacks applications, consider what happens at cocktail parties. A fascinating rationale for the importance of the opening is provided by Leonard and Natalie Zunin in their book *Contact: The First Four Minutes.*[23] On the basis of astute but undocumented clinical intuition, the Zunins claim that 4 minutes is the average interaction time between two people before either decides to continue the interaction or split (e.g., at a cocktail party conversation).

Eugene Weinstein, an ingenious sociologist, has some equally intriguing propositions. Imagine a bustling office party before the year-end holidays. You have just walked over to your favorite person at the office. According to Weinstein, the very beginning of this and other interactions is characterized by a jostling about to achieve a *definition of the situation.*[24] Defining the situation means you are not only acting to create a set of expectations in your own mind about status, roles, topics of conversation, how long you two should be speaking, and so on in your own mind; you are also thinking about the *projected* definition of the situation, namely, the other person's definition of the situation. As the bicycle model of social life would imply, you and your favorite office mate engage in communication about the conversation to come, often using some common tactics.

Weinstein calls one such tactic "preinterpretations," or *printerps* for short.[25] For example: "Don't take this wrong, but I've really got the inside scoop on. . . ." or "Not that I agree with it, but. . . ." or "Objectively speaking. . . ." Another common device Weinstein names is the "preapology," or *prepalog.* For instance: "I haven't really got all the facts yet, but it seems obvious that. . . ." or "I'm really lousy at these things, but I'll give it a try." To my knowledge, no systematic research has been done on the effects of printerps or prepalogs inside or outside the laboratory. Did you catch the prepalog in my last sentence?

My own theoretical rationale for the opening principle begins like this: Imagine you are going into a small shop to buy a pair of slacks. You are just about to speak to the salesman. In this opening situation and all others, there lies a set of rules.[26] Such rules are more flexible early in the interaction. Therefore the best time for you or the salesman in this case to change or establish rules defining the situation comes in the first minute or two. However, harsh reality imposes some constraints on you or me as we are opening a conversation. First, a *time constraint* is automatically imposed because an opening minute or two does not allow much time for expression. Second, a *social appropriateness constraint* reflects the reality that some definitions of the situation just do not lend themselves to becoming a part of the conversation gracefully. Looking back to Case 7.4 and Figure 7.1, can you see yourself saying, "Hi, Wendy. Please be kind enough to act happy for the duration of our meeting. Also smile at me because it makes me feel good"?

As we all know, nevertheless, these two constraints are solvable, because it *is* possible to start new conversations smoothly. How do we do it? We use the method suggested by Les Giblin, who recommends that you "assume the attitude you wish the other to take."[27] In Case 7.4, if you want happiness from Wendy, you act happy yourself right away. Giblin's suggestion overcomes the time restraint because you can display either a businesslike or a very merry set of actions at the very outset. His suggestion overcomes the social appropriateness problem because you do not have to ask the other person for anything. You can convey your desires clearly and without a request.

ACTIVITY 7.1.

In Figure 7.2 you see a typical weekly staff meeting. Assume that you see the situation exactly as pictured in the figure. You are about to enter this situation as part of this staff. Suppose this is your working group of people, and you know each one well. In the spaces provided, write down five unwritten rules pertaining to this staff meeting. Try to draw each rule from your own experience, transposed from your own life and applied to this staff meeting.

Rule one: ____________________

Rule two: ____________________

Rule three: ____________________

Rule four: ____________________

Rule five: ____________________

Sometimes unwritten rules can be conveyed by the demeanor of one person at the outset. For example, suppose a good friend appears extremely anxious when he sits down to join you for dinner. His demeanor might suggest the following rules: Begin speaking in a soft voice. Speak slowly. Avoid unhappy or negative topics at first. Do not become anxious yourself. Don't laugh a lot at first. Address your friend with some expression of friendship to reassure him. Before long ask him if there is something worrying him. Devote your attention mainly to him and don't get distracted.

**Surroundings Principle**

Statement of Surroundings Principle: If you arrange for your other person to enter surroundings where certain action is clearly appropriate and encouraged, the other person will more likely exhibit the action there than elsewhere.

**Case 7.5.** You wish to invite a very special other person to a major occasion for a week from Saturday. Your goal is a yes response. If accepted, it would be the first date of any consequence for you two. Acceptance of the date is the action you want, and the other person wants to accept the date. Where should you make the request? You could ask at work. You could make a phone call and catch your other person at home. However, work is stressful for your other person. Also, you will have no idea of your other person's mood at home if you call on the spur of the moment. You decide that the best surroundings are when you are in each other's company coming back from a lunch date.

**Case 7.6.** You wish your two little toddlers to play together peaceably. All they want to do is demolish what is left of Grandmother Ramrod's antique table. Your goal is to elicit nondestructive play. *She* wouldn't have stood for such nonsense. The action you seek is appropriate play not centered around the table. You could yell requests. You could plead with requests. You could declare the living room off limits for children. You decide that your children's precious social development will proceed more smoothly without that nuisance of a table around. You put the table into storage and childproof the rest of your house while you're at it. You engineer surroundings.

**Case 7.7.** You have been office supervisor for more than a year now. That Hazel has a sharp tongue and has just made one cutting comment too many. Your office operation would work much more smoothly if Hazel would begin to make positive comments about her co-workers. As it is, she's solidly negative in her comments. Your goal is to elicit positive comments from her and hopefully stop the negative ones. You decide to use the request principle because more subtle suggestions have failed. The question is where to make the request. You could make it in the weekly staff meeting. You could approach her at her desk. You could get together with her and her best friend, Joanne, to make the request. However, all these possibilities entail surroundings where Hazel might be unduly embarrassed, even humiliated. You decide to take advantage of the physical and social surroundings inside your office. Giblin and other popular writers recommend that you criticize in private and praise in public.[28] You use the privacy of your office as surroundings optimal for requesting a change in Hazel.

Remember the bicycle model of everyday social influence? Do you recall the exact words having to do with "surroundings?" If not, glance back at Figure 1.3 and you will see the words "social and physical surroundings." For us, surroundings equals situation

**Figure 7.2.** A weekly staff meeting, typical of those attended by millions each week. (Photograph by Charles Blakey.)

equals setting. Surroundings contain both tangible physical elements and intangible social elements such as rules. For example, in *any* physical setting, Grandmother Ramrod would have certainly expected you to avoid swearing. Her expectations are as much a part of the surroundings as the arrangement of furniture.

In one of the classic experiments of all time, Schachter and Singer changed not only body state but surroundings as well.[29] Some of the people in this study were injected with adrenaline, which creates body arousal, and some were not. Some entered anger-arousing surroundings by filling out an insulting questionnaire and being exposed to another supposed participant (really an actor) who got mad. Other participants, or subjects, entered euphoria-eliciting surroundings. Results of subjects' actions and reported feelings showed two main results: (1) The surroundings produced either euphoria (silliness) or anger. (2) Subjects injected with adrenaline displayed more actions and *more inner feelings of whichever emotion was present in the surroundings.* In another study, by Schachter and Wheeler, similar injections increased humor in subjects while watching a slapstick comedy film.[30] To the despair of those who would narrowly view all action as flowing from internal emotions and thoughts, these results show again the joint interplay of surroundings and inner states. For our purposes, the main implication comes from the demonstrated effect of surroundings.

Convincing empirical support for the surroundings principle comes from the research of Roger Barker and his colleagues. Barker and company moved into a small Kansas town and became a part of the community. Then they began to identify situations that involved fairly stable patterns of action, such as auctions and high school basketball games.[31] The findings generally show that "the characteristic behavior patterns in [behavior] settings are generated and maintained *in spite of* the great variety of interior conditions inhabitants bring to settings."[32] While the precise *degree* of influence exerted by internal personality characteristics versus influence of external surroundings currently ranks as one of the hottest controversies in psychology, the heavy influence of surroundings can safely be assumed.[33]

To illustrate further, consider a real group of people consisting of yourself and your favorite companions. Imagine yourselves being whisked from situation to situation, as the ghosts of Christmas did with Scrooge. See yourselves in the following settings: halftime at the Superbowl, attending a funeral, and at a wild party. Your actions would, of course, be dramatically different from situation to situation. When you think about it, this example becomes more and more remarkable. There you are—completely different individuals with widely varying backgrounds. You were all behaving differently in different surroundings, but reasonably like each other within each situation. Think about it. I could predict your actions better from knowing just the surroundings alone than by knowing just you and not the surroundings!

A final rule of thumb may help in applying the surroundings principle: Enlist the aid of a force known to be influential upon the other person. Such forces might be third parties, tangible objects, opportunities, mood-creating environments, and so on (as every businessman knows).

### Timing Principle

Statement of Timing Principle: If you arrange to time your efforts to elicit action to coincide with certain internal states of body and emotional disposition within your other person, the other person will more likely exhibit that action than if you randomly time your actions. Case 7.8 illustrates *not* applying the timing principle.

**Case 7.8.** Joe, a salesman, has his top client out for dinner. His goal is to make a sale. She is famished. Although she has stuffed down 23 saltines, she still feels a bit uneasy in the stomach. She has just finished a bitter 10-minute speech on what is wrong with the world in general and her company in particular. Joe salesman eagerly starts his pitch. To his dismay, she does not buy.

How might Joe improve his timing? The next case illustrates better timing.

**Case 7.9.** Ruth is reading the newspaper one weekday morning, and one of the ads catches her attention. Her favorite department store is having its annual clearance sale and there it is, the washing machine of her dreams at half price. Having failed in previous attempts to get her husband to agree on a replacement for the old clunker they now have, Ruth decides to use the best timing she possibly can. Her goal is to get Dave to go downtown and look at the washers on sale. She could bring up the topic during the morning routine, but Dave has not had his coffee yet. She could bring up the topic after supper, but Dave feels harried after a workday, even after a good meal. She decides to bring up the topic on Saturday morning. Therefore, on Saturday morning, Ruth wakes up early, goes to the kitchen and prepares a "miner's special" breakfast for Dave: orange juice, four pancakes, two eggs, bacon, honey, and coffee. When she comes back from the kitchen, Dave is awakening. She kisses him and puts the big tray on the night table. When he finishes his feast, she says, "Honey, that sale ends today and they have washing machines for half price. Ours is really in bad shape. Darling, it would be the greatest help if we could get a good deal on a new one. Let's go see the new models later today, OK?"[34]

In both Case 7.8 and Case 7.9, the other persons are more likely to say yes after being well fed than otherwise. Just as surroundings are important, there are more favorable times to try to elicit action. When calling to make a lunch date, for example, when is it best to call? If the recipient of the call about to be placed in Figure 7.3 lives alone, she might be more receptive late at night, when she might feel like talking to someone. Then again, a late call might disturb her and make her angry.

To support the timing principle, we need evidence about the specific effects of changing bodily states in an otherwise constant situation. Not surprisingly, Berkowitz and Geen and Hanratty, O'Neal, and Sulzer have found that angered study participants imitated an aggressive person more than nonangered participants.[35] And Kimbrell and Blake showed that thirstier subjects more readily violated a rule not to drink.[36]

## MODELING PRINCIPLES FOR ELICITING ACTION

### The Idea of Modeling

Recently the ordinary handshake has given way to a variety of handclasps and greeting slaps. Think back to the first time you saw someone greet or congratulate someone else by saying, "Gimme 5!" and slapping palms together. In this case, you were an observer watching a modeling performance.

*Modeling* is imitation. In my review of the literature, "A Review of Research on Imitative Behavior," I attempted to provide a useful framework for looking at imitation.[37] Initially, an observer views a model exhibit some action. Initially, you viewed two people exchange a novel hand greeting. You were the observer and they were the models who acted for you.

Later, you had the opportunity to imitate by using the new hand greeting on a friend. The modeling framework is exceedingly useful because we can conceive of virtually every action as a modeling performance for potential imitation. In the sections that follow, our attention will focus on the other person as observer and you or someone else as model.

Modeling provides a unique means for eliciting action because your other person merely observes passively. There is no need for action from the other person during exposure, nor is there need for a direct request by you.

### Reward-to-Model Principle

Statement of Reward-to-Model Principle: If you arrange for your other person to observe a model who is rewarded for exhibiting certain action, the other person will more likely exhibit that action than if exposed to a model receiving less reward or to no model.

**Case 7.10.** A cousin of mine is having trouble with his job. He is receiving no promotions, while employees having college degrees are being hired and promoted over him. My goal is to get him to truthfully say he is considering enrolling in college. I could ask him what is wrong at work, but he is extremely sensitive on this matter, so mentioning failure or even approaching the topic directly is out of the question. The next time the topic of work comes up, I could mention that for better or worse, going to college seemed to bring rewards on the job for my friends Paul and Mike. Here my cousin (other person) is called the *observer* who observed Paul and Mike get rewarded with promotions for the action of going to college.[38] Paul and Mike are the models.

The reward-to-model principle allows for the model's action during training to be in person, viewed over television, heard by word of mouth, read in a letter, and so on. "Observing the model" thus connotes all manner of occasions where the observer is exposed to some action of the model. In other words, the *medium* by which the model's action and reward come to the other person is left open. In Case 7.10, did my cousin observe the action directly? No. The modeled action was

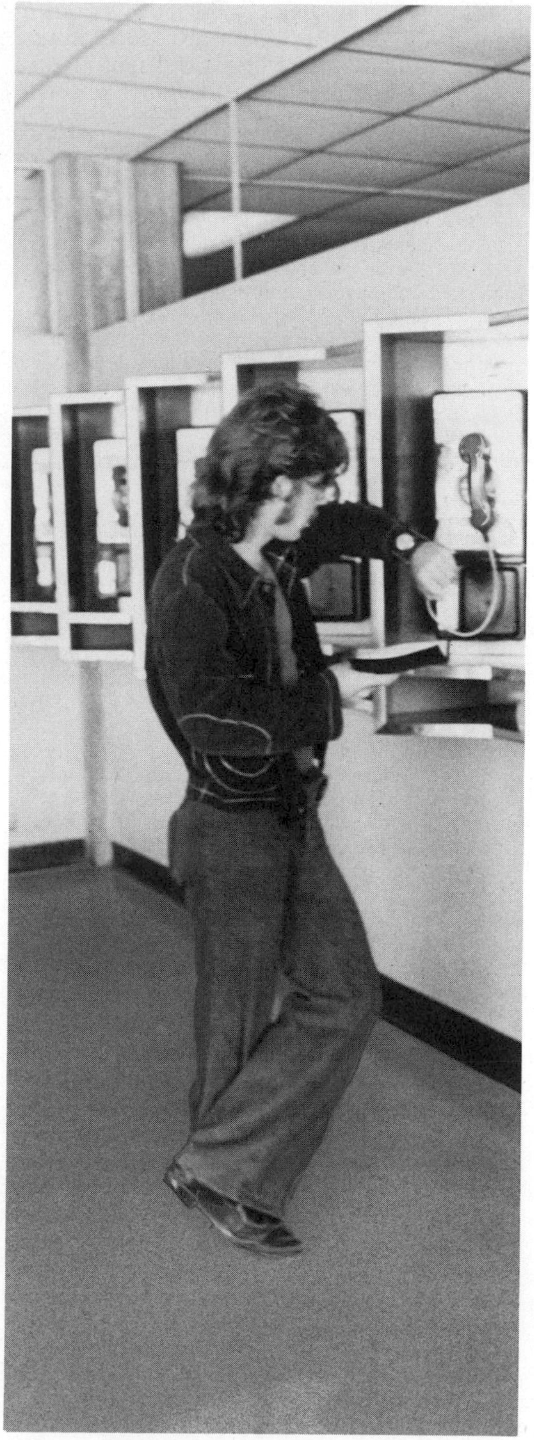

**Figure 7.3.** To call now or not to call, that is the problem. This young man is wondering if this is a good time to call for a lunch date. When is it best to call? (Photograph by Charles Blakey.)

going to college, which I related by word of mouth. Thus my cousin's exposure to the model's actions was indirect in Case 7.10. To illustrate live or direct exposure of observer to model, Case 7.11 and Case 7.12 are given.

**Case 7.11.** Ted has been late for work 3 days in a row. You are on probation as the supervisor in this purchasing division, and you fear others may start using Fred as the model. Your goal is to get Ted to arrive at precisely 8:15 A.M. Although you could use several options for approaching Ted directly, you decide to try out the reward-to-model principle as an experiment for self-improvement of your interpersonal skills. Therefore you decide to praise Martha for always being on time for work in Ted's presence. Here Ted is the observer who views the model, Martha, get rewarded with praise for the action of being on time for work.

**Case 7.12.** Mrs. Watson wants her husband to take his own dishes into the kitchen after dinner, as her brother does in his home. Actually, her husband has a dozen or so little things she would like to change, and not taking the dishes out into the kitchen is just one. However, she has a happy marriage and does not want to barrage George with a string of requests because that would be seen as nagging. No, she decides against the option of requesting. Because even subtle suggestions might rub him the wrong way, she decides to use the reward-to-model principle on the next appropriate occasion. The next time her brother and his wife are over for dinner, her brother takes his dishes into the kitchen as usual. Mrs. Watson casually tells her brother how much she appreciates his help. George then takes his dishes into the kitchen. Here George is the observer who observes the model, Mrs. Watson's brother, get rewarded with praise for the action of taking his dishes into the kitchen after a meal.[39] (Although this written description may seem a trifle involved for such a simple matter, the whole business took at most 15 seconds, including Mrs. Watson's thoughts beforehand.)

**Case 7.13.** Hilda and Bertha bicker constantly, and bank tellers had not ought to do that in front of customers. They may lose their jobs, and you would not like to see that happen. Your goal is to elicit friendly conversation between them. You are a bank teller too and thus do *not* have authority over them. It would be fruitless to try to overpower them with a demand for change. You make a point of describing to each of them an incident in which a soap-opera star won her lover by ceasing to bicker constantly and starting to converse in a civil manner on the job. Only you phrase the tale a bit more gently than my description. Who were the observers here? Who was the model? What was the medium by which the model's actions and resulting reward were transmitted?

A good rule of thumb for applying the reward-to-model principle is to catch a model at being good; that is, you catch the model acting the way you want your other person to act.

There is overwhelming hard data to support the effectiveness of reward to the model. Increased imitation in the laboratory has been shown following exposure to models who receive rewards such as knowledge of success on a task,[40] a researcher saying the word "good,"[41] praise by the experimenter,[42] maternal affection,[43] and other rewards.[44]

Alan Kazdin studied two pairs of schoolchildren who were sitting side by side in class.[45] Within each pair, one child was praised for paying attention to schoolwork with remarks from the teacher such as "Good, Ken, you're really doing nicely!" or "Jane, that's really good." Kazdin was interested in looking at the effects of praise on Ralph and Laura, who sat next to Ken and Jane respectively. Ralph and Laura were observers who received no praise for attentive study themselves, but merely observed. Ken and Jane were models who got praise heaped on them for listening. Kazdin's findings showed an increase in attending to studies for Ralph and Laura (unrewarded observers) that paralleled that for Ken and Jane (rewarded models). Thus reward to the model had an effect in the classroom.

Reward to the model, or *vicarious reward*, as it is also called, seems to affect both good and bad actions. Observing someone else can increase charitable donations,[46] but it can also increase rule breaking.[47]

Notice also how the reward-to-model principle leaves the kind of reward open. Suppose you with to interest Judy in going back to school. You arrange for her to have coffee with Joan, who raves about the benefits of going to school. Going back to school is the action here. Joan is the model. The "benefits" could be social or financial, tangible or intangible.[48]

In the preceding paragraph, you might have noticed yet another aspect of this principle. Did you notice that, in this case, *you* need not have had coffee with Judy and Joan?

Just as the principle stated, you "arranged" for the exposure of Judy to Joan. Look back through all the previous principles to see if the word "arrange" is in the statement of those principles. If so, what are the implications?

### Emotions-of-Model Principle

Statement of Emotions-of-Model Principle: If you arrange for your other person's exposure to a model who displays clear and positive emotional expressions as a clear consequence of exhibiting certain actions, the other person will be more likely to exhibit that action than if exposed to a model who displays no such emotions or to no model.

**Case 7.14.** You have a certain other person, Irwin, in mind for a glorious weekend at the beach. Your goal is for Irwin to accompany you to the beach this next weekend or the weekend after that. You could just ask. You could subtly suggest. However, despite the reasonable likelihood that these approaches would work, you want to try out some of the modeling principles. By adding some variety to the ways you are able to successfully elicit action, you feel you can increase your social skills and make life more interesting. You arrange to go shopping with Irwin and another couple, Margie and John. John brings up the experience of still another couple: "You know Bill and Susie? They went to the beach a couple weekends ago and loved it! They still talk about it, and now I'm getting excited too. Say, what about it? How about us four going this weekend or next?" Irwin says yes. It paid you to have Margie and John as friends. In this example, who is the model? There are two models, namely the third couple. Why are *they* models? Because the models displayed the action, namely, going to the beach for a weekend. The models were also reported to exhibit emotions because of going to the beach. The medium of observing the models is word of mouth. If John or Margie had not brought up the topic of Bill and Susie's excursion to the beach, you would have brought it up and thus arranged for modeling to occur. Is this case an exception to the hint about making requests of the other person when he or she is alone? Why or why not?

**Case 7.15.** Kim is a nurse trying to provide the best possible care for a new patient on her floor. The problem is that the new patient is a stoic, elderly farmer who has never been to see a doctor before and now, inside the hospital, is not about to disclose much about himself. She does not desire to pry deeply into his private life, and indeed she hasn't the time to do that. Kim's final goal here is to elicit enough self-disclosure from him so that he will at least tell her when he hurts and provide other information so that he can be given the best of care. As of now, he says almost nothing about himself, let alone about his feelings of pain. Kim decides to first pursue a limited goal of eliciting statements of a superficial sort from him about his daily life. When she has 5 minutes to spend with him, she joyfully recollects her own idyllic summers as a girl on the farm, sort of like Knulp's nostalgia about his boyhood. Then she asks him about his farm, and he answers. She easily achieves her final goal, but does not pursue topics other than his farm life and his medically relevant feelings.

ACTIVITY 7.2.

You want your youngster to brush his teeth every evening. In the space provided, complete this case using the emotions-of-model principle. Remember to supply several "you could"-type options before describing the option chosen.

________________________________________

________________________________________

________________________________________

________________________________________

________________________________________

________________________________________

Credible empirical support for the emotions-of-model principle would come from experiments that meet several tough standards: (1) The emotion to be displayed must be stated in advance. (2) The emotion itself and the connection between the model's action and the emotion must be clear enough for independent judges to check them out reliably. (3) The critical comparison between modeling display without emotion versus identical modeling display with emotion ought to show increased imitation as a result of adding the emotion. These standards are hard-nosed, but remember that they apply to supposedly rigorous scientific research and not informal applications.

In one experiment that met standards 1 and 3, Berger and Johansson asked college students to play an extrasensory-perception guessing game.[49] During the training period, some students saw a "model [who] expressed delight at being correct or annoyance at guessing incorrectly."[50] Other students witnessed identical modeling displays, but without such emotional expressions. Still others witnessed no modeling displays at all. If the model's emotions really increase imitation, the last two conditions should have elicited less imitation than the first one. True to predictions, results showed that "observers watching the emotional model participated longer [imitated more] than subjects in either of the other two treatment conditions."[51] Thus, when emotional expressions were "stacked on top of" modeling displays, imitation increased. This finding illustrates the emotions-of-model principle's effect—an effect in addition to the separate effect of reward to the model.

Emotions of the model can also act to *reduce* the separate effect of reward to model. in another experiment to study emotions of the model, 8-year-old boys and girls watched models who were rewarded for giving in to temptation and playing with forbidden toys. Half the models displayed positive emotions (smiles), while the other half displayed negative emotions (crying). In this study, Slaby and Parke found that the negative emotion of crying reduced the effect of a rewarding outcome, so rewarded models who cried were imitated less.[52] Thus a display of negative emotions can have a separate effect that subtracts from the effect of the reward-to-model principle. In short, the most imitation will occur when the model gets rewarded and is clearly joyous about it.

Theories of social learning give two clear roles to the model's emotions. First, they grab the other person's attention and focus it on the model's action. According to social learning theorist Walter Mischel, our lifelong learning history results in our assigning a *subjective value* to cues such as emotions of a model, reward to a model, and other cues that turn us on.[53] In short, we all learn to attend to what turns us on.

A second role is that of enhancing memory. In an extensive review, *Emotions and Memory,* David Rapaport cites abundant research to show that positive emotions enhance our memory.[54] (With negative emotions, the situation seems more complicated. While negative emotions can both increase and decrease memory, there is as yet no hard evidence to support the idea of repression as Freud originally formulated it.[55] That is, even though negative emotions can make memory selective, no evidence exists to support Freud's claim that once in memory, ego-threatening facts tend to get bounced from consciousness into the unconscious or to stay locked in unconscious memory.)

ACTIVITY 7.3.

This activity can be done with a friend if you like. Write yourself a definition of "a clear and positive emotion." Then watch television for an hour. Count positive emotional expressions during commercials and regular programming. Time the commercials and programmings. Calculate positive emotional expressions *per minute* during commercials versus during programming. When you finish, you should have two numbers. One number should indicate the number of positive emotional expressions per minute for commercials, and the other for number of such expressions per minute for regular programming. Put these numbers in the appropriate boxes that follow. Does Madison Avenue use the emotions-of-model principle to sell, sell, sell? Share your findings in class.

Definition of "a clear and positive emotion":

________________________________________

________________________________________

Number of positive expressions in commercials: = A

________________________________________

Minutes of commercials: = B

________________________________________

Number of positive expressions in regular programming: = C

________________________________________

Minutes of regular programming: = D

________________________________________

| | | |
|---|---|---|
| Number of positive emotional expressions per minute for commercials | $= \frac{A}{B} =$ | $\square$ |
| Number of positive emotional expressions per minute for regular programming | $= \frac{C}{D} =$ | $\square$ |

### Control of Resources by Model Principle

Statement of Control of Resources by Model Principle: If you arrange for your other person to observe a model who controls resources that can possibly be shared with the other person, the influence of the model will be greater than for a model having fewer resources.

**Case 7.16.** Pat, a friend of yours, wishes to invite company over on one weeknight per week. Her goal is for her husband to willingly participate in these weekly occasions. She arranges for her husband, Dave, to observe the actions of Dan, a neighbor. Not only do Dan and his wife invite company over at least one weeknight each week, but Dan has a large collection of books about World War II history. Books about World War II fascinate Dave, and Dan lends his books willingly. Here Dan is the model, and the action is inviting company over on at least one weeknight per week. Dan's collection of World War II books makes up the resources to be borrowed and used by Dave. Dan's book collection induced Dave's visit and subsequently Dave's exposure to Dan's social habits. Other resources might be friends, children, personality characteristics, objects such as boats, influence, and so on. In this case, the resources were distinctively nonsocial, despite their employment in furthering Pat's distinctively social goals.

A review of empirical research turns up good support for this principle. For example, in one study of control of resources by the model at the present time (versus the future), more imitation of such models was found. In a study by Bandura, Ross, and Ross, children imitated an adult model more if the model controlled a magnificent collection of toys.[56]

In another study, the resources were social rather than tangible and concrete. Joan Grusec found children to imitate a model more who was warm and friendly and asked questions about the child versus an aloof model.[57] Other research indicates that control of resources in the future also enhances a model's effectiveness. In a study by Grusec and Mischel, children showed increased imitation of a model who was to be their future nursery school teacher versus a substitute teacher.[58]

**Case 7.17.** As office manager, you notice that Fran seems to be down in the dumps. You know enough to believe that Fran's mood is socially caused. Her work is not suffering, but the last thing you want is an unhappy person in your office —or anywhere else for that matter. Your goal is to make Fran happier. You turn to the effervescent Marilyn Kay, who is always full of happiness. Her outstanding characteristic is possession of seemingly endless social resources. You arrange for both of them to cooperate on some task for a while. Would you have to be the manager or supervisor in this case? I think not.

We can use Case 7.17 to illustrate some ins and outs about application. In this case, your goals were entirely humane because Fran's work is not suffering even though Fran is suffering. Of course, it would be possible for Fran's depressed mood to drag down her work and the work of others. In such a case, your efforts would serve both personal and organizational goals. This case illustrates the possibility that individual and organizational goals can coincide, despite the current zeitgeist (spirit of the times) where large organizations often get a bad press.

Another problem in Case 7.17 concerns timing. A crude application of the control-of-resources principle would have you rushing headlong to bring Fran and Marilyn Kay together as soon as you noticed Fran's depression. A more sophisticated version would allow you to scout the territory before taking reckless action. If Fran were mourning the loss of a loved one, timing is of the essence. Clearly some time should be allowed to pass before Fran's exposure to the delightful Marilyn Kay. The thrust of these ins and outs of applications is that possible clumsy application or misuse does not invalidate principles. To the degree that such principles accurately reflect the state of nature, they remain our best guess to attain the most compassionate of goals.

### Status-of-Model Principle

Statement of Status-of-Model Principle: If you arrange for your other person to observe a model who has high status, the influence of the model will be greater than a model with less status.

**Case 7.18.** You want your teenage son to attend *any* church regularly. You arrange to take him to a church that one of his favorite star athletes regularly attends.[59]

With the status-of-model principle, as with the control-of-resources principle, the main point of application concerns selection of who the model is to be. There is a catch, however. We can realistically expect this principle to hold, but only up to a point. Beyond a certain level, higher status of the model will not produce more imitation but less. The reason is that the gap between the status of the model and the status of the other person can become too wide. For example, very poor people may resent very rich people. Indeed, Mary Rosenkrans found that preadolescent boys imitated a peer model less on a war strategy game when the model was presented as having a different background and different interests.[60]

Considerable research supports this principle. The critical aspect of such research is that increased status alone leads to an increase in imitation. In a study by Harvey and Rutherford, school children imitated peers whom they had rated of higher status on a questionnaire more than peers who received low status ratings on an art judgment task.[61] Lefkowitz, Blake, and Mouton did a famous study wherein young adults walked across an intersection against the red light.[62] With high status defined as being richly dressed and low status defined as wearing shabby clothes, pedestrians more often imitated the models dressed for high status by violating the stoplight themselves. Violating the stoplight is shown in Figure 7.4, where photographer Blakey caught medium status models being imitated on a corner in downtown Miami. In an unusual laboratory experiment, Klinger found increased imitation of a trained actor when he displayed achievement-oriented gestures and other high-status nonverbal actions.[63]

Warning: In the status-of-model principle, we have an example of a procedure that, in the short run, can be used to further humane aims. However, using status of model may be undesirable in the long run if the larger society awards status on questionable grounds. Specifically, in the United States high status is accorded largely on the basis of power, money, and technical skill. More pointedly, high status is *not* accorded on the basis of behaving in ethically desirable ways toward others. Thus the use of high status as currently determined may aid us as individual users right here and right now, but it may also strengthen a questionable status system over the long run.

With this warning we have completed our coverage of principles involving modeling. If modeling principles do not work to elicit the action you desire, there are more possibilities. These possibilities I have called principles for eliciting action after modeling. If modeling fails and you still desire certain action, you may wish to use the principles in the remainder of this chapter. I advise using them after you try modeling, because these principles to use after modeling are more effortful and less humane than preceding principles.

## PRINCIPLES FOR ELICITING ACTION AFTER MODELING

### Priming Principle

Statement of Priming Principle: If you arrange to (1) ask your other person to exhibit certain action, (2) closely and visibly monitor the occurrence of that action, and (3) make sure a potent reward follows that action, the other person will more likely exhibit the action than in the absence of these combined procedures.

**Case 7.19.** Juanita, a beginning bank teller, wishes her friend Leah to take an interest in folk music so they both can attend folk music concerts regularly. Juanita offers to treat Leah to the pizza of her choice if Leah will accompany her to the concert next Friday.

The priming principle is based on the idea of priming a pump. It's the "Try it, you'll like it" idea. In simple terms, this means you put your other person through the action by offering a strong reward. The priming principle does not mean punishment and coercion because, if the other person refuses, the matter ends.

As is the case with most behavior mod procedures, the priming principle has been most effectively demonstrated in institutional set-

**Figure 7.4.** Pedestrians are shown violating the stop light and imitating the models who first walked against the light. (Photograph by Charles Blakey.)

tings, such as mental hospitals. In a field experiment supporting this principle, Ayllon and Azrin rewarded mental patients heavily for "going for a walk, watching a movie, and attending a music session."[64] These activities were later used as rewards themselves, and trying them did in fact lead to greater partaking in them later. Here we see also an example of the field researcher's dilemma: Either use captive subjects, retreat back into the laboratory, or do no research. Skinner pricked the national conscience when he noted that all manner of oppression and misery (not just participation in research) is generally foisted upon five classical types of hapless populations: children, the aged, the mentally ill, the retarded, and prisoners.[65] Caplan and Nelson twist the knife in the belly of psychological researchers by pointedly noting that "there is a lack of data on landlords, bankers and city officials" and similar populations.[66]

Warning: When handled crudely, the priming principle can lead to anger. If forced on the other person by using strongarm tactics, anger can easily result. The priming principle should be used only when you wish to convey that "I'm going to take note of whether you exhibit certain actions, and a substantial reward will make it worth your while."

Is using the priming principle bribery? Before you answer, consider that bribery connotes not only giving someone a reward, but also perversion of judgment or corruption of conduct in the process. Thus it is moral wrongdoing that sets "bribery" apart from "influence." Clearly, bribes can be bad. However, suppose you were to treat a group of people to a superb meal after they toured a hospital. Then after the meal, you requested their help as volunteers to work with crippled orphans. Clearly, the use of the priming principle and "influence" can be good. And that is where the matter stands. As usual, no simplistic moral universals apply.

### Coercion Principle

Statement of Coercion Principle: If you arrange to (1) ask your other person to exhibit certain action, (2) closely and visibly monitor the occurrence of that action, and (3) make sure a punishment would follow if that action were not performed, the other person will more likely exhibit that action than in the absence of these combined procedures.

Last and least desirable of the principles for eliciting action is the coercion principle. Here it is the "Try it or else" idea. In simple terms, this means putting the other person through the action by threat.

Warning: Usually there is not enough justification to warrant the use of coercion. If there is not *any* reward that would elicit the action you want, there is a good chance that the action is not worth eliciting.

Warning: There is a natural human tendency to use coercion prematurely, that is, before trying more humane plans.

**WHAT IF I BOMB OUT?**

As with everything else in life, applying these principles sometimes results in failure. Failure here means that the actions you desire still do not occur. The first question you should ask after failure is, "Is it worth it to continue?" If no, stop. If so, ask the second question: "Is my other person *able* to come up with the action I want?" We normally restrict failures to act to children, as in the case of physical motor skills like walking or certain intellectual skills. On the other hand, we adults certainly had to be given special training to be *able* to perform certain motor skills, such as riding a bicycle, playing a guitar, typing, pipe fitting, repairing a car, and sewing.

Returning to the idea of social skill, we adults are likely *not* able to perform certain social tasks without special training. How do you tell when a good friend wants to deepen the intimacy between you? How do you detect when a child would enjoy affection? How do you detect subtle social obligations? How do you decide when to stop talking? How do you tell when it is time to terminate an interaction and leave? How can you make guesses about the attitudes and values of others so as not to hurt them? Might not a whole training program be developed for each of these skills? Who among us has not learned much of what he or she knows through painful trial and error? These examples should bring home the idea that even full-grown adults may be lacking in certain social skills. Thus our other person may not be *able* to exhibit the action we want.

What do you do when your other person is not able to exhibit the actions you want? You can only arrange somehow for the other person to learn the actions. Beyond this general strategy, the problem now consists of a *learning* problem, and you are on your own.

**THE ETHICAL PROBLEM OF USING SUBTLE MEANS**

The principles suggested in this chapter and other procedures can be used with extreme subtlety; that is, your other person may never know of your intentions unless you state them. The modeling principles are perhaps the most subtle of all because they divert attention away from you. Back in Case 7.14, who would be given credit for inducing Irwin to go to the beach? You? No, your friend John made the request and still other persons acted as models. Thus they and not you get the credit (or blame). Cannot such subtle means of influence be abused? More personally, "When I use subtle procedures, am I doing something bad?"

As with all ethical questions, there is no absolute answer. On the one hand, subtle procedures are all around us. We cannot help but influence others in subtle ways. When we complete later discussions about nonverbal communication, it will be staggering to realize how much more we can communicate than we intend. Our unwitting use of such influence is unavoidable and thus not always bad. Likewise, it is not always good.

When *is* the use of subtle procedures bad? Unfortunately, no general standards apply. I can offer you only one warning: The goals of a person who could not ask the other person for certain action are likely suspect.

**PRINCIPLES AND PLOYS**

What is the difference between principles and ploys? Principles can be viewed as testable claims about the state of nature. That is the scholarly view of principles. A practical view of principles sees them as describing interpersonal tactics. A *tactic* can be described as a device for accomplishing an end, often on a small scale. Similarly, an *interpersonal tactic* is an interpersonal device for accomplishing an end, often on a small scale. A *ploy* can be described as a kind of interpersonal tactic intended to embarrass or frustrate an opponent. As crony is to friend, ploy is to interpersonal tactic. A crony is a kind of friend labeled as bad. A ploy is a kind of interpersonal tactic labeled as bad. You might say there are as many ploys as there are people who pin bad labels onto interpersonal tactics. (After someone cries "ploy," look at both the label*er* as well as the label*ee*.)

For a chapter summary, see Appendix B, in which a list of principles is given in place of summaries for Chapters 7 through 10.

# 8

# BUILDING UP ACTION

*A wise lover values not so much the gift of the lover as the love of the giver.*

THOMAS A. KEMPIS

*He who has more learning than good deeds is like a tree with many branches but weak roots; the first great storm will throw it to the ground. He whose good works are greater than his knowledge is like a tree with fewer branches but with strong and spreading roots, a tree which all the winds of heaven cannot uproot.*

TALMUD

## BASIC REWARD PRINCIPLE

Statement of Basic Reward Principle: If you arrange for your other person to receive a reward after exhibiting certain action, your other person will increase that action over the shorter run and/or maintain it over the longer run.

### Illustrative Cases

Case 8.1. You are rooming with your best friend. Recently Jack has taken to reading quality nonfiction rather than escapist paperbacks. Your goal is to engage him in an all-night bull session over weighty topics. To achieve this goal, you could allude to how much fun all-night bull sessions are; you could point to friends who have had all-night discussions and enjoyed them. But these options seem not to address what is happening. "What is happening" is that Jack is already increasing his reading of quality nonfiction and the desired action of talking with you about it, an action you want to build up. You decide to continue doing exactly what you are doing and what comes naturally: Namely, you react with a pleasantly enthusiastic response after his every comment. In this case, the action consists of Jack's comments, which you want to extend far into the night. Your positive comments and occasional complimentary remarks in response to his statements are the rewards.

**Case 8.2.** You consider yourself an excellent wife, and you try very hard to look especially attractive whenever your husband is home. In spite of this, he only rarely seems to notice your efforts. Your goal is to build up his giving you compliments. You could ask for them, but a request seems inappropriate. You could use some of the modeling principles, but the action you want already occurs now, so your problem is one of building up rather than eliciting. You begin to pay very strict attention to everything your husband says. You then make it a point to reward even the slightest hint of a compliment with an affectionate smile, hug, or kiss. Your husband gradually begins to notice and compliment you on your appearance more often. In this case, you rewarded your husband's actions of giving compliments with smiles, hugs, and kisses.[1]

**Case 8.3.** Mick does not want to join the family on vacation this year. In some previous years, he went along; but this year he wants to stay home and hang around with the gang. His mother, Pat, wants him to go this year and in future years as well. She arranges to meet former neighbors from New York, who also have teenagers, at a resort in North Carolina. The resort offers activities for all age groups, including a canteen for teenagers only. Mick changes his mind and decides to go, and a good time is had by all. Here the action is Mick's accompanying the family on vacation, which is rewarded by the opportunity to socialize with peers. Note that Pat arranged the reward but did not herself give the reward to Mick.[2]

**Case 8.4.** You have been going to lunch with a new member of the supervisory team, Juanita, for about a week now. The whole team lunches together. She is so shy, but she is beginning to open up and enter the conversation. Your goal is for Juanita to join in the stream of conversation as a full-fledged participant. You decide to reward her every statement. When should you reward? Right after she has finished speaking. What kind of reward should you employ? Here there is no end of the variety possible for the socially creative. Any positive reply from you might suffice. Charlie Chaplin or Groucho Marx might respond with a raise of those famous eyebrows, followed by a broad grin. Another possibility is self-disclosure of some fact about yourself, if it is called for. Still another reward is for you to later make clear reference to something Juanita said earlier. You could make this reference at the end of the luncheon gathering. Since *something* follows Juanita's every remark, it would seem that rewards are rather like the nitrogen in the air—all around us, although usually we don't notice these rewards very much.

## The Concept of Reward

The idea of reward is probably the most practical concept in current psychology. It is also, therefore, quite important and extremely controversial. Accordingly, we will go into some detail about it.

### Origin

The basic reward principle found its popular origin as Edward L. Thorndike's famous law of effect: "Of several responses made to the same situation, those which are accompanied or closely followed by satisfaction to the animal [or human] will, other things being equal, be more firmly connected with the situation, so that when it occurs, they will be more likely to recur."[3] In the years since Thorndike made his statement (1911), a more general definition has emerged.

### Definition

A *reward* is any event that strengthens the action which immediately precedes its occurrence.[4] Rewards are also called "positive reinforcers," wherein *reinforcement* means any events that strengthen or weaken the action they follow. We are interested in defining "reward" as a verb, that is, as the *operation* whereby reward comes after the action. We are not concerned here with defining reward as an effect, namely, the resultant strengthening of the action in question.[5] In other words, we are interested in the concept of rewarding an action, that is, the operation of following some action with a consequence which ought to strengthen that action.[6]

At this point, please skim over Cases 8.1 through 8.4 to review what the action was and what the reward was in each. What rewards do you think will follow and strengthen your action of reading this book, *Practical Psychology?*

## Kinds of Reward

### The Wide Variety of Rewards

In line with our emphasis on the practical, it would be most helpful to supply a useful system for describing rewards. We could then use the system as a mind jogger to help us generate rewards as options for ourselves. Reinforcement in general and reward in particular stand as the keystones of behavior mod. However, behavior mod practitioners have preferred to focus on how rewards affect the strength of the action. Accordingly, they mainly supply lists of positive events for use in specific situations, as in the elementary school classroom.[7] These lists are great for those specific situations, but several larger questions remain unanswered—even unaddressed.

We will conceive of rewards as they are related to the situations where they are used. In the course of any given day, say today, in your life, you will likely enter a variety of situations, each calling for use of different rewards. When you grab a quick lunch with a certain friend, there is a set of unwritten rules that limits what rewards you can use. The rules vary. Sometimes they are strict. After receiving a compliment, you don't reward with a $10 bill. Rather, you reply in like kind with a social reward back to your friend. This situation limits your response rather strictly. Sometimes the rules are broad. With my father and mother, I have laughed, intellectualized, danced, prayed, chopped wood, hiked, wept, and done hundreds of other things over the years. Since these actions followed a parent's action of "being with Jim," we can conceive of my varied actions as rewards of a sort. Thus a great diversity of rewards were acceptable in the situations where a parent was near me. In my life and in others, it is reasonable to suppose that my utterly different actions often carried the common meaning of love.

Here is a tough question: How can it be that the same reward can affect the action of your other person so differently? For instance, when Jack gives Jill $10, he might get back the words "And have a nice day, sir," or he might get a hearty slap in the face. This common observation that the exact same rewarding event can functionally affect in different ways the action it follows means that active and complex information processing is going on inside the head of your other person before the other person emits action. Therefore it behooves even the staunchest advocates of behavior mod to seek the structure of that processor of information—the mind.

### Structures in the Mind about Reward

Discovering the mental structures we use in thinking about reward is a practical matter. The complexity of life forces your other person to classify situations and rewards into reasonably finite categories, just as you and I do. If we could discover a system of relatively few categories we use to think about rewarding events, we would have a handy way to describe rewards in social situations. Such a system would also serve as a mind-jogger to help us be creative in thinking up rewards as well.

In their comprehensive book *Societal Structures of the Mind,* Uriel and Edna Foa supply us with such a system.[8] We can best view their system as a mental map. As the child grows up, his or her mental map *differentiates* from simple to complex. Doing justice to their entire theory would take a book, so we will glean only those aspects directly relevant for reward or resource exchange.

Foa and Foa speak of face-to-face social situations as characterized by exchanging interpersonal resources. They define an *interpersonal resource* as "any commodity—material or symbolic—which is transmitted through interpersonal behavior."[9] We now consider the Foa and Foa system for classifying kinds of rewards. This theory probably comes closest of any to being a system of *situations,* about which psychologists have always dreamed but have found so difficult to create.

As we grow into adulthood, we differentiate our mental map along the dimension of interpersonal resources. Foa and Foa muster limited evidence to support the developmental sequence leading up to the mature adult's mental map of interpersonal resources, which is pictured in Figure 8.1.[10] Let us consider each kind of resource in detail.

*Love* means affection, so love resources convey affection. For example, "I love you" and "I enjoy being with you" convey affection. Here, "we should remember that the resource classes are categories of *meaning* and not a classification of action. Consequently, each class covers a wide range of actions, all conveying the same resource. For example, one can convey his liking [or love] for the other by verbal means, by a smile, a kiss, etc."[11] Love here means something a bit narrower than intimacy or human contact as conceived earlier; a broadly based intimate relationship with a lot of category breadth and exchange of rewards over time would certainly involve exchange of status and services as well as affection per se.

*Status* means respect, so status resources convey respect. For example, "I hold your opinion on this matter in high regard," "You did a really good job," and "I admire your tennis backhand" all convey status. Can spending your time at a particular place convey status on your other person?

*Information* means factual content that does not convey love or status. For instance, "You get to the corner of State and Main by going to the first stop sign and turning left three blocks" and "My advice is not to buy at this time" convey information.

*Money* is any token that has a standard unit of exchange. The credit card, however, comes as close to information as it does money, say Foa and Foa, because it conveys information about the solvency of its owner.

*Goods* are tangible objects.

*Services* "involve those activities on the body or belongings of a person which constitute labor for another."[12] For example, "I repaired it for you," "I ran that errand for you," and "I will do that for you" convey service meaning.

ACTIVITY 8.1.

For each of the kinds of interpersonal resources we have just defined, identify one example of an exchange in your own life today where you gave (or will give later in the day) each kind of resource. In each exchange, be sure to identify the other person and the resource given by each of you.

1. Love: ____________________

____________________

2. Status: ____________________

____________________

3. Information: ____________________

____________________

4. Money: ____________________

____________________

5. Goods: ____________________

____________________

6. Services ____________________

____________________

**Relationships Between Kinds of Rewards**

Gaze back over your responses in Activity 8.1 and try to answer this question: Did the other person in each exchange give you back the same kind of resource or one from a neighboring kind, as shown in Figure 8.1? They should, according to Foa and Foa, because the situation usually dictates the exchange of similar resources. We now consider a few of the properties of the Foa and Foa theory that make it a unified system rather than simply a list.

Our mental map of resources ranges along two dimensions, as shown on Figure 8.1, according to Foa and Foa. The *particularism dimension* reflects how personalized or person-specific the resource is. Naturally, love is the most particular because love is most closely tied to one particular other person. Why is money the least particular? Are services done for you more particular than goods you purchase? Is your haircut (service) more particular to you as a person than the hairbrush (goods) you buy?

The other main dimension of interpersonal resources is *concreteness,* which ranges from tangible to symbolic, or abstract. Here commercial goods and services are the most concrete. Can you think of examples? Foa and Foa state that "love and money are exchanged in both concrete and symbolic forms and thus occupy an intermediate position" on the concreteness dimension.[13] Can you think of some juicy examples? With these dimensions in mind, we now consider some specific properties of these kinds of resources as they apply to everyday social situations.

According to Foa and Foa, our social institutions are set up to formalize the exchange of resources. Schools and banks are set up for the exchange of information and money. We should be able to locate each social institution and every interpersonal situation in our everyday life somewhere as a point on

Figure 8.1. However, a lot more goes on in a school or a bank than mere exchanges of facts or money. Obviously, romances spring up, insults are hurled, and lunches are eaten —none of which constitute sheer information or money. Therefore Foa and Foa propose that a range of acceptable resource exchange surrounds the point of location (on Figure 8.1) for every social situation. For example, suppose you are buying tomatoes in the express lane of your neighborhood supermarket. You do not know the checkout cashier. This situation is located squarely between money and goods because you are giving money and the cashier is giving goods. The situation allows you to exchange information and status. You can ask for directions or pay certain kinds of compliments. Can you exchange love now? Not much. Can you exchange any but the most superficial services? No. In short, the situation allows you to operate within a prescribed range of resource exchange. Inside that range, you are safe. Outside it, you are in trouble for violating unwritten rules associated with the supermarket situation.

To support the particular ordering of resources shown in Figure 8.1, Foa and Foa present some strong evidence. In their questionnaire research, they have asked hundreds of participants to identify the more appropriate resources for exchange in specific situations, such as "mother's behavior to child (love)" or "barber to customer (services)."[14] The results provide strong support for the ideas that (1) social situations can be located on Figure 8.1 and (2) the resources people *think* are more appropriate to exchange are closer to that location, and vice versa. In addition, the Foas have staged controlled situations in their laboratories wherein an actor takes away a resource. For example, the actor takes status away from the participant by saying, "If you had been less clumsy, we could have finished long ago."[15] The findings indicate that we tend to retaliate to being deprived of a resource by withholding from the other person a resource inside the acceptable range. Finally, the Foas have even confirmed the invariance of their system of interpersonal resources across cultures by testing people in the United States, Israel, Greece, India, and Senegal. Although the customs and institutions were found to differ, the relationships shown in Figure 8.1 were supported.[16]

Can we say anything about the range of acceptability across situations in our daily lives? Yes we can, according to the Foas. As the location of the situation becomes more particularistic, the range shrinks. This means that we are more likely to exchange love for love, while we are not likely to give money to get similar money. When you are lonely, you seek another lonely person to share the same kind of love. If you are a pauper, you do not want to meet another person who lacks money.[17] When you spend money, you ultimately want to get something else besides money, and the range is wider than for love.

ACTIVITY 8.2.

Foa and Foa also claim that we exchange more particularistic resources in smaller groups.[18] Look back to your answers to Activity 8.1. For each of the six situations you wrote down, now estimate the number of people who would *eventually* know about the exchange. You will probably have to guess here. The numbers below correspond to those in Activity 8.1.

1. ____ 2. ____ 3. ____ 4. ____ 5. ____ 6. ____

### Ways to Use the Foa and Foa System of Interpersonal Resources

***As a Way to Describe Situations.*** If, as Foa and Foa claim, society has drummed the

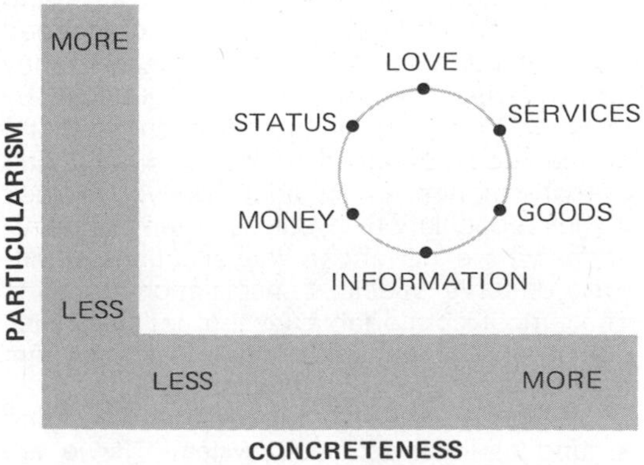


**Figure 8.1.** Kinds of interpersonal rewards or resources. (From J. L. Turner, E. B. Foa, and U. G. Foa, "Interpersonal Reinforcers: Classification, Interrelationship, and Some Differential Properties," *Journal of Personality and Social Psychology,* 1971, *19,* p. 170. Copyright 1971 by the American Psychological Association. Reprinted by permission.

mental map of Figure 8.1 into our heads without our thinking about it very much, their system provides us a means to describe the social reality of situations. I have no difficulty in locating my own commercial transactions and my relationships with colleagues at work on Figure 8.1. My relationship with my wife covers the entire range at some time or other. Does this last fact invalidate the usefulness of their system? No, it does not, because when I think of *specific* situations involving my wife and me, I can usually locate them at some point in the Foa and Foa system.

***As a Way to Help Create Reward Options.*** An entirely different interpretation of the Foa and Foa system casts it as a motivational theory of needs and rewards to satisfy those needs. By this interpretation, we all came to acquire six need systems. Through socialization, we all emerge with internal needs for external rewards of love, status, information, money, goods, and services. However, each of us develops a unique and personal *optimal range* of need satisfaction for each category of need. For example, consider John, a "poor little rich boy."

**Case 8.5.** John was well supplied with everything but affection. As soon as they could, his parents packed him off to boarding and military schools, a clear refusal to spend their time with him. In military school, he again received no affection and cried for long hours at night, sometimes in the company of other boys who felt the same way. He turned to stealing, to drugs, and finally to a drug program that enabled him to enter college. (This is a true case.)

In John's case, Foa and Foa *claim* that the optimal range for his need for love would be affected strongly by having experienced semistarvation for affection as a child. They further *speculate* that he would adjust by lowering his upper limit for affection, so that a normal dose of affection would swamp and overwhelm him as an adult. Do you agree? If their speculation is correct, then acquaintances who experienced little affection as children deserve special consideration from us. Their most comfortable level of intimacy may not be very deep, and getting to know them may best proceed at a cautious rate.

We can view our other person as carrying around at least six need systems. If we are genuinely concerned about our other person's welfare, we will try to see that his or her needs are satisfied within the optimal range for each need. By using the Foa and Foa system, we can—hopefully—create and use rewards that enhance our other person's welfare in the process of building up the action we desire (satisfying our needs).

One way to use the Foa and Foa system involves adding category breadth to a relationship. If the office crew is planning a birthday party for the boss, it might help to go around the circle of Figure 8.1. so as to include exchanging resources of all kinds except money. A silly song could convey some love. The gift of a new tie (goods) could be accompanied by someone tying it (service), and so on.

ACTIVITY 8.3.

Does social exchange parallel monetary exchange? For example, when you give out some money for a ride on the bus, you have less money right afterward. Does the same thing hold for love?[19] That is, after you give out and get some love, is your supply of love possessed depleted somewhat after the exchange in a manner similar to the exchange of money? Or are you somehow richer?

________________________________________

________________________________________

________________________________________

For two more exercises, see Figures 8.2 and 8.3.

## Controversies Surrounding Reward

### The "Reward Is Evil" Controversy

We can hardly complete our consideration of reward without touching on the controversies that surround this topic in the annals of science. In our discussion of each controversy, we shall either dismiss it outright or give it back to the professionals as a technical matter of little concern to us as users. Each heated issue is first stated and then treated.

The "reward is evil" controversy views reward as a fiendishly powerful tool of evil, used mainly by "the system" of large organizations to oppress the common man. To be sure, a glance through the books and journals of behavior mod would not refute the idea of reward as evil. The person doling out reward is usually superior to the other person in power and status, as seen in the reward technology used by schoolteachers, supervisors, and administrators in mental institutions, and so on.[20] Even the settings for research on interpersonal social behavior involve captive populations, such as college students coerced into participation.[21] What can we say?

First, psychologists have been forced into such research, perhaps because of the rewards that follow the very activity of doing research on reward. (What might such rewards be?) Second, the power of reward is virtually unquestioned. Third, there is a crying need for research (1) in everyday settings where (2) the applier is equal or *in*ferior in status and power to the other person. Such research is probably essential for carrying out former American Psychological Association President George Miller's idea that we give psychology away, that is, make it available on a free and widespread basis.[22] Thus we throw this hot potato back to the professionals to extend their limited but impressive data base.

Another aspect of the reward is evil controversy sees reward as bribery, pure and simple. What could be more nauseating than the view of rich and intimate interactions between human beings as nothing more than exchanging superficial bribes called rewards? This question about bribery overemphasizes tangible rewards. A bewildering maze of social rewards forms an indispensable part of everyday life. Attaining optimal intimacy for ourselves and our other persons would be inconceivable without a number of social rewards flowing both ways, to and from the other persons. I dismiss the bribery claim as simplistic.

A final implication of the reward is evil controversy views reward as evil because it is powerful. As a powerful procedure, reward is of course both good *and* evil. Hence we can likewise dismiss this claim as simplistic.

### The "Universality of Reward" Controversy

The "universality of reward" controversy attacks the question of whether reward is always necessary for learning or personal change. Since reward is merely one concept of many, I see no reason to claim that rewards must accompany all learning or personal change. For example, a recent theory about learning began with the words, "The theoretical formulation wholly discards the response-reinforcement principle."[23] Such theoretical positions use the unsavory tactic of trying to build up the importance of inner mental process by cutting down the importance of observable public action. Both mental processes and public actions are worthy of study. This controversy belongs back in the halls of science.

ACTIVITY 8.4.

Some behavior mod psychologists have elevated the basic reward principle from a clear-cut tendency to a universal mandate. They claim *all* human actions are determined solely by actual or expected consequences, such as reward and punishment. From your own experience, list three human actions that are *not* determined largely by actual or expected rewards. Before plunging ahead, think about it for a few minutes because rewards take a wide variety of forms. Do we not buy gas-guzzling monster cars for expected (rewards of) comfort, highway safety, and reactions by friends? Are not religious actions influenced by expectations of divine rewards? Are not antisocial actions in teenage gangs determined by social rewards (or punishments) from peers?

Action 1. ______________________

Action 2. ______________________

Action 3. ______________________

### The "Consummatory Reward" Controversy

The "consummatory reward" controversy points to the fact that certain rewards accompany rather than follow actions, such as a little girl eagerly enjoying a new doll. Surely the delights of fine food and sex cannot be separated from the very actions of consumption. Again, however, the precise definition of reward is a professional if not a literary matter, so we give this one to the professionals.

### The "External Control" Controversy

The "external control" controversy attacks all deliberate reward procedures as fostering excessive dependence on external as opposed to internal motives. Suppose you promise your daughter dessert if she eats the asparagus soufflé. According to one view, you are turning your little one away from internal control and toward external control by sweets or by Big Brother as an adult. This possibility clearly exists. However, the needed long-term research to resolve this controversy has not been done; so we toss this one too back to the professionals. There *is* enough research now to say with some certainty that any view which emphasizes either solely internal motivation or solely external motivation is too simple. In fact, the data show support for the influence of both.[24]

With major controversies now disposed of, though hardly resolved, we can again turn our attention to application. The rest of this chapter concerns the ins and outs of rewarding.

## GENERAL PRINCIPLE

Statement of General Principle: All principles for eliciting action the first time are also effective in building up action over the shorter run. (We covered principles for eliciting in the last chapter.)

**Case 8.6.** In the case of Fran's low mood at the office (see Case 7.17), you have discovered that existing work assignments make it impossible to pair her up immediately with Marilyn Kay. Upon surveying the situation, you decide to do the next best thing, which is to shift the seating arrangements slightly so Fran sits next to Marilyn Kay and Jamie. In this way, all the social goodies Marilyn lavishes on Jamie become much more available to Fran than otherwise. Here the surroundings principle is being used to build up, in addition to elicit, happy actions from Fran.

**Case 8.7.** Priscilla and her husband want to induce their son Alan to read the daily newspaper more and discuss his reading with them. They decided to bring up and discuss stories that would interest him at the dinner table. They began to discuss between themselves those articles that they thought would interest Alan. Finally, one evening he interjected with information he had got from the paper. Alan began to read the paper

**Figure 8.2.** What rewards or resources are being exchanged here? (Photograph by Charles Blakey.)

**Figure 8.3.** Here the bargains of the days are being discussed. What rewards are being exchanged? What reward is it permissible to exchange in your town at a location similar to that pictured here? (Photograph by Charles Blakey.)

more, and the discussions became more enjoyable for all. Here Priscilla and her husband used the reward-to-model principle to build up the action of reading and discussing the paper by Alan.[25] They both modeled the action and received rewards from each other as models. Did they use the basic reward principle as well?

Support for the general principle comes from two sources. First, the empirical studies cited in the previous chapter rarely made a distinction between eliciting and building up and thus apply to both. Second is an extension of the theoretical argument made by Jacob Gewirtz, who claims that reward to model and reward directly to the other person convey precisely the same information. Gewirtz says there is no distinction between what is going on when you reward a model and when you reward the other person. Your other person gets the same message in either case, namely, that "this action brings on consequences that I *like.*" If Gewirtz is right, this message should act to both initiate and build up whatever the action should happen to be.[26]

## REWARD-SELECTION PRINCIPLES

In many cases, we rack our brains to discover what a certain other person likes. The assumption underlying the three principles on selecting rewards is that the preferred activities of your other person carry certain characteristics that label them as preferred.

### Other-Person-Preference Principle

Statement of Other-Person-Preference Principle: In the process of identifying events that are rewarding to your other person, if rewards are selected that consist of events for which your other person has clearly expressed a desire, then such events will be more effective than events selected by you without the benefit of such information.

**Case 8.8.** Mabel continues to dress sloppily for the office, despite a slight improvement in appearance after your using the reward-to-model principle. You have racked your brains without the slightest progress to fathom what's going on inside her brain. Soon you decide that an honest, direct approach is best. You invite her into your office and say, "Mabel, I'm going to lay a small problem right out on the table, and I would like your help. The last two office evaluations by those guys upstairs have given our operation good marks for production but also mentioned a couple of minor things to be corrected. One is the way you dress, which they say is careless. You know and I know that you are downright good-looking but you wear old, old clothes that don't do you justice. What are your thoughts? Is there anything you want that I can do?" Mabel sits for a few moments staring blankly out the window and then informs you that she wants a desk near the window. She has a touch of claustrophobia and the sunlight helps her complexion. You agree to make the change after she starts to dress appropriately.

**Case 8.9.** This case is true. One night my son Carl was making a ruckus before going to sleep. My wife asked him what she could do so that he would lie quietly. He asked for a piece of cheese and after getting it, went right to sleep. Getting the cheese was harmless enough, but suppose he had asked for something bad? What should we have done then? Depending on the request, we might have agreed, refused, or negotiated some compromise acceptable to all.

**Case 8.10.** You have taken Kathy on 17 dates so far, having gone someplace different each time. But there are only so many places to go in this midwestern town, so for your next date you just ask her preference. She replies with a desire to visit a night court in a nearby city, an activity that would never have occurred to you.

The empirical support for the other-person-preference principle is covered under the token-reward principle (p. 169), whereby the preferences of the other person are paramount.

### High-Frequency Principle

Statement of High-Frequency Principle: In the process of identifying activities that are rewarding to your other person, if rewards are selected that consist of events of which your other person partakes *often,* then those events will be more effective than less frequent events.

**Case 8.11.** You know Stu is the jock of the department. Everyday he jogs for an hour. You bring up athletics as a topic of conversation whenever possible during the first few coffee breaks you share together. The topic of athletics was identified as rewarding to Stu because he participates in them with such high frequency.

**Case 8.12.** Lorelei is a relative newcomer to town, and she wants to make friends. Recently she met Ruth, who has the qualities she likes in a friend. Lorelei soon discovers that Ruth is an expert in needlepoint and spends most of her spare time doing needlepoint. Now, when the two arrange to meet, Lorelei always asks about Ruth's latest work. Since Lorelei has an interest in handiwork, they build an interesting friendship based on an activity Ruth finds rewarding.[27]

The high-frequency principle simply says that we all engage in preferred activities when given a choice. Solid support for this principle, also known as the "Premack principle," comes from animal studies. David Premack has shown that one can build up nonpreferred (low-frequency) activities in laboratory animals by using preferred (high-frequency) activities as reward.[28]

The high-frequency principle also receives support in the field setting. In a classic field experiment, Homme, C'deBaca, Devine, Steinhorst, and Rickert increased sitting quietly and looking at the blackboard by grade-school children by using the opportunity to run and scream as the reward.[29] These scientists had noted earlier the high frequency of "running and screaming," which identified this activity as a good bet for reward.

ACTIVITY 8.5.

Try applying the high-frequency principle to your beloved instructor. From your observations thus far in this course, inside and outside of class, what high-frequency activities have you noticed that would mark them as good bets for reward?

________________________________________

________________________________________

________________________________________

### Equal-Interval-Between-Participation Principle

Statement of Equal-Interval-Between-Participation Principle: In the process of identifying activities that are rewarding to your other person, if rewards are selected that consist of events in which your other person participates with more equal intervals of time in between, then those events will be more effective rewards than others.

**Case 8.13.** To support and illustrate this principle, I know of only one case history in the clinical literature, but it is interesting indeed. Israel Goldiamond was doing therapy with a husband and wife, both intelligent professionals who were socially at ease in their community. Their problem was sexual relations, which they had about twice each year. The wife was afraid she would be driven into an affair, but both parties were Roman Catholics determined to save the marriage if possible. In fact, they thought that once they got the ball rolling, their problem would solve itself. Unfortunately, "various procedures were assayed by the subjects, but proved ineffective. Fondling was repulsed. *Playboy* was recommended to initiate amorous activity, but the husband fell asleep reading it."[30] Finally, Goldiamond hit on an ingenious idea. He noticed that both husband and wife went to the barber shop and beauty shop respectively on an equal-interval basis. He got them to agree to use these appointments as a reward for an honest attempt at sex during the week. Here sex was the action, so to speak, and beautifying activities served as the reward. These and other procedures proved successful.

(Reprinted with permission of author and publisher: Goldiamond, I. Self-control procedures in personal behavior problems. *Psychological Reports,* 1965, *17,* 851–868. [Monograph Supplement *3*–V17.])

In this case, the curious reversal of action and reward adds some humor, but it also illustrates an important and serious point. Just what activities are really rewarding depends on the other person and not on you. A whole lifetime of learning has preceded any given moment for each of us, and what we like is determined by our actual life, not what someone else *thinks* we like. This idea finds expression in such expressions as "Take people as they come" and "You've got to get where *he's* at to reach him."

## REWARD-ADMINISTRATION PRINCIPLES

### Immediate-Reward Principle

Statement of Immediate-Reward Principle: If you arrange for your other person to be rewarded immediately after displaying certain action, the reward will be more effective than if given after greater delay.

**Case 8.14.** You have 2 days off per week, and one of them you spend doing volunteer work with crippled orphans. Little Stevie has been blind since birth. He seems to respond mainly to being held and spoken to. You drive up to the shabby old building. As he hears your voice echo down the dimly lit hallway, he lunges forth from one of the wooden chairs that border the hall. You scoop him up, toss him gently into the air, and tell little Stevie that you love coming to see him more and more each time—*immediately* after he flies into your arms. After some actions it would be a shame to delay responding.

In this case, you and Stevie are clearly exchanging rewards of love. His action of running to meet you should be strengthened; and the more immediate your response of taking him in your arms, the more his action is strengthened. Your action of going to see him should be also strengthened, and the more immediate his response of lunging forth to greet you, the more your action of coming to see him is strengthened.

Support for the immediate principle comes mainly from a few studies that compare immediate with delayed reward. In some tightly controlled animal studies, more immediate rewarding of rats with food clearly led to increased learning.[31]

This principle reflects the fact that a reward relationship is one of time. The power of rewards derives from an "if . . . then" time relation: If action, then reward follows (closely in time).

Actually, most psychologists take the immediate-reward principle for granted as a truism based on everyday experience. To illustrate this point, imagine yourself going around giving verbal replies and smiles *randomly* rather than after or during appropriate speech by your friends. They would think you were crazy. Even crazier, think what it would be like if you waited 5 minutes before laughing at (and thus rewarding) a good joke. People have been institutionalized for less!

### Continuous-Reward Principle

Statement of Continuous-Reward Principle: If you arrange to reward the other person after each and every time certain action appears, that action will increase more rapidly than if reward comes on an intermittent basis.

**Case 8.14 (continued).** While holding little Stevie in your arms, as you do for minutes at a time, you reminisce back to the days when you two first met. At first he was hardly responsive to your speech. In fact, he would not even pay attention unless you held him. How satisfying it was when he first began to open up, even if just a single word every few minutes. If you had not expressed lots of affection *continuously* at first, he might never have ventured out of his shell.

The continuous-reward principle works only for building up action. In fact, continuous reward seems to lose its power after a while, when satiation sets in. Too much good food leads to satiation. Too much socializing with other people can lead to satiation, accompanied by the desire to be alone. When satiation sets in, action is best maintained by occasional or intermittent reward; but that is the topic of the next chapter.

Managers in industry know well the power of continuous reward. Here the reward is pay, and the action is work. Contracts, strikes, tempers, and union wage-agreements often revolve around just how continuous the pay is going to be. For example, consider the proverbial widget factory where thousands of wonderful widgets are manufactured daily. There are two basic ways to set up the pay schedule.

1. Suppose you are a worker and you get paid $1 for each widget you make. The pay schedule is a continuous ratio schedule of reward, because the ratio of reward is one-to-one with every unit of action, namely every widget you crank out. In such a *ratio schedule,* reward or reinforcement becomes available after so many units of action, in this case after every single widget. In industry, such a ratio schedule is called a *piece-rate* schedule of pay.

2. Suppose you are a worker and you get paid $225 per week. This pay schedule is an *interval schedule* of reward because your pay becomes available after a given interval of time, namely 1 week. In such an interval schedule, reward becomes available after so much time has passed since the last reward (payday). In business, interval schedules of pay are called *wage-rate* schedules.

Managers have already experimented with real workers in real industries by replacing wage rates with piece rates. When the switch is made, production generally rises from 10 to 20 percent, clearly supporting the continuous-reward principle.[32] However, squeezing more work out of employees is not often greeted with open arms by those being squeezed.

In fact, workers strongly resist piece-rate systems with mixed success. They recognize only too well the likely effect of working under a piece-rate system of reward. When questioned about it, workers fear that a continuous one-to-one piece-rate schedule will be "stretched" into an intermittent one, whereby more work is required for the same reward.[33] As an example, how would you react to the memo, "Notice to all wonderful widget workers: Starting next Monday, the schedule of pay will change from $1 per one wonderful widget to $1 per two wonderful widgets produced"? Here the one-to-one fixed ratio schedule, or FRI, was stretched or thinned out to a FR2 schedule, and you would likely get hopping mad.

**Open Reward Principle**

Statement of Open Reward Principle: The more clearly you arrange to inform your other person about the relationship between his or her action and reward, the more effective that reward will be.

I hasten to describe two kinds of application of this principle. The first is crude, as with the awkward request, "C'mon and talk for a few more minutes. Then I'll feed your ego and turn you on with a neat response." Crude applications such as this indicate that this principle holds only up to a certain level of openness or obviousness. Past that point, the exchange becomes so obvious that the interaction takes on a mercenary quality, as in the example just given.

More sophisticated applications take the form of expressed feelings and hope by you. "Tell me some more about working for such a big company. It's something I've thought about a lot." "Boy, is that impressive!" In applications such as these, the reward of your continued interest is implied but not stated. Here your interest is sincere. In addition, you are expressing something about yourself, the road to similar but gradual self-disclosure by the other person. In fact, Les Giblin has speculated that the most potent social reward you possess is to let the other person know you are impressed by her or him.[34]

Support for the open reward principle comes from a study about how to reduce disruption at lunchtime in a grade school. MacPherson, Candee, and Hohman trained six aides—housewives from the neighborhood—to heavily reward appropriate lunchroom actions.[35] However, upon talking while an aide was speaking, getting out of one's seat, or quarreling, a disruptive child would lose privileges (e.g., movies or playing outdoors). These procedures were standard across time and constituted a baseline. The researchers were really interested in looking at the effects of two other procedures stacked on top of the standard baseline conditions. So, periodically, some added rules went into effect. Rule One stated that misbehavior would result in the offender having to copy over a "mediation essay," an essay that stated in no uncertain terms the lunchroom rewards and punishments of which the offender had run afoul. Thus, Rule One forcefully applied the open reward principle. Rule Two required the offender to copy pages from books in the library, a frequently used punishment in schools. In brief, the lunchroom was governed by one of the following three conditions, alternated over time:

1. Baseline rewards and punishments plus Rule One (open reward)
2. Baseline rewards and punishments plus Rule Two (copying as punishment)
3. Baseline rewards and punishments alone

Results showed the clear superiority of the first condition, strongly supporting the open reward principle. The results lent themselves nicely to the interpretation that the baseline rewards and punishments wiped out disruptions from all except a few die-hards. For these hard-core offenders, adding punishment was *not* effective, while using the open reward principle to make clear (or drum in) the unwritten rules of lunchroom life was.

### Reward-Contract Principle

Statement of Reward-Contract Principle: In the process of rewarding certain action by your other person (and after informal reward procedures have failed to build up the desired action), if you arrange to secure a clear and mutual agreement with your other person regarding the relation between that action and the reward to follow, the action will increase more than without such formal agreement.

**Case 8.15.** Fred keeps hitting his younger brother Michael, and your task as a mother is to (1) stop this aggression and (2) ultimately, build up friendly interaction between the two, which occurs now only occasionally. You inform Fred that television time is available to him only if he does not beat up little Michael.

A lot of empirical evidence stands behind the reward-contract principle. In *Behavior Modification in the Natural Environment,* Roland Tharp and Ralph Wetzel detail dozens of applications using successful contracting. For example, in one case, a teacher enlisted the aid of an older brother to curb the disruption and raise the underachievement of a young boy in school.[36] The older brother agreed to give praise (genuine in this case) and money upon completion of classroom assignments by the young boy. Also, the teacher gave out stars that earned the boy television viewing time at night for acceptable social behavior in class. In this case, the relation between action (completing assignments, acceptable social behavior) and the respective rewards (praise and money, television time) was made clear by using a contract with the boy. As a result, his failure rate at spelling dropped from 84 to 6 percent. He also earned a star for good behavior in class on 60 percent of the class days after the contract went into effect. Incredibly, despite these improvements, the boy's grade in spelling remained the same, and his citizenship grade actually dropped, a fact his teacher was unable to explain when confronted with the facts.

A final hint for the application of reward contracts is that they must be adhered to with consistency over time. Otherwise they fail.

### Token-Reward Principle

Statement of Token-Reward Principle: In the process of rewarding certain action from your other person (and after informal procedures have failed to build up the desired actions), if you arrange to use token rewards that can be exchanged for a variety of known rewards, the use of such tokens will build up the action more effectively than the use of any single reward by itself.

**Case 8.16.** Laurie is a teenager on probation and does not go to work every day, as she should. Ilene is the probation officer for juvenile offenders; her goal is to build up the action of Laurie going to work. Ilene knows that Laurie loves horseback riding, but Laurie also has no transportation to the stables. Ilene negotiates an agreement whereby Laurie receives points for showing up for work. These points can be accumulated and exchanged for transportation to the stables or for other rewards desired by Laurie. The points are the tokens.[37]

The use of this principle amounts to setting up what is known as a "token economy,"

**Figure 8.4.** What resources are being exchanged here? What is the all-time greatest token in the history of the world? Money is. (Photograph by Charles Blakey.)

whereby tokens are accumulated to earn more potent "backup" rewards. What is the all-time greatest token? See the caption of Figure 8.4 for the answer. Tokens can be money, points, paper scrip, or any other convenient symbol that stands for something else. And credit cards are tokens for tokens.

What are the advantages of tokens? Tokens can indeed be given immediately after a child, for example, responds as desired, whereas the backup reward of a movie on Saturday night is delayed. Also, tokens can be given piecemeal, whereas the backup often must be consumed in one time block. Points might be accumulated toward a special meal, which must be consumed in one time block.

There is overwhelmingly solid evidence that tokens can shape a variety of actions by other persons. In mental institutions[38] and public schools,[39] token economies have been set up to regulate both task-oriented and social actions.[40] Tokens used have included points, Mexican currency, U.S. currency, gold stars, teacher's initials in a notebook, slips of paper, and so on. The power of such miniature economic systems is evident, even to the point of showing economic ills such as bribery, extortion, stealing, and inflation.

When the impressive power of a token point system can be implemented with relative ease in all sorts of institutions, the scientists who invented the system in the first place are obligated to study its side effects. The *main effect* of token economics has been well established, to the point where you can now go out and buy wall charts and the other means to set up a token economy for your children, or whomever is under your care (and under your power). The *side effect* of generalization has not been investigated much, and behavior modifiers are now being urged to do research on the carry-over, or generalization, of token systems into related actions.[41] For example, would giving Laurie points and pay to keep her attending work (Case 8.16) carry over or generalize into her social life, so she does not get convicted again? In addition to the generalization side effect of token economies, there is another side effect, perhaps more subtle and elusive that warrants our attention.

Does using tokens undermine intrinsic interest in the desired action? Will paying your son to make his bed each day and mow the yard undermine his later interest in taking responsibility for family tasks? If so, a dangerous longer-range side effect of using tokens as rewards may exist. This danger is especially worrisome because the short-range rewards may seduce the parent, teacher, or administrator into using tokens to produce mere obedience at the risk of thoroughly messing up the other person's values over the long haul. What does the evidence say?

Envision yourself coming into a psychology experiment and working on a series of challenging puzzles. The experimenter pays you some money for each puzzle you solve and leaves you in the room alone with the puzzles and also some recent issues of *New Yorker, Time,* and *Playboy* magazines. The question here is how much longer you keep working on puzzles. And, there's a second experimenter hidden around somewhere to see what you do. This procedure has been used by E. L. Deci in a number of studies, with variations in the kind and amount of reward.[42] If getting paid for puzzles undermines your interest in them, you should come to like them less and spend less time on them when left alone. Their results consistently show this outcome, with one interesting exception. When given a bit of praise rather than money, college men came to prefer the puzzles. In the whole series of experiments, the only procedure that increased liking for the challenging task was praise (for men). With achievement-oriented men especially, the *perception* of freedom of choice may be all important. When paid with money, perceived freedom goes down; when praised, it does not.

Other studies support this interpretation. In one study, Collins and Hoyt had students write essays contrary to their own opinions.[43] The *most* opinion change occurred under conditions of *low* pay and *high* personal responsibility, wherein participants signed statements acknowledging full responsibility for their essay. To add some confidence to these findings, we note that other Deci studies took place in a field setting, where students created headlines for a college newspaper for pay and for free, with payment leading to less intrinsic motivation later on.

In a classroom study, Lepper, Greene, and Nisbett found that rewarding children for performing an already interesting drawing activity undermined interest in it.[44] When given free access to the drawing activity at a later time, schoolchildren who had been earlier rewarded with a certificate spent less time on it than did others who had received no reward. This and other studies resulting in similar conclusions are summarized by Fredric Levine and Geraldine Fasnacht in "Token Rewards May Lead to Token Learning."[45]

What do all these results about the side effects of using the token-reward principle mean? This research means that long-term effects, such as undermining interest in now-attractive activities, very likely result from using tokens in association with those activities. No long-term research exists on the topic. Therefore it would seem reasonable for those of us concerned about individuals being subjected to formal token economies to request, if not require, long-term research on the side effects.

If you are going to use a token economy, there are some agreed-on hints for enhancing its power: Make all aspects of the procedures clear, always pair a social reward with giving a token, and eliminate tokens as soon as possible. These procedures should minimize long-run side effects of token economies and make the need to use tokens as short as possible.

In short, it may be wisest to use tokens only to build up actions that your other person is going to get legitimately paid for later on in life. Otherwise, token systems may seriously alter in unknown ways the values of those whose actions are controlled, especially in bureaucratically administered systems (e.g., mental hospitals, prisons, schools, nursing homes), where obedience is paramount and disruption is deadly to those in charge. Ironically, these ideas imply paying school children for certain actions.

Finally, it can be argued with some legitimacy that the preceding critical thoughts about token systems represent a bleeding-heart attitude for overcontrolling a useful tool. After all, token economies run by psychologists are but miniature versions of the real-world economy run by national government. A national economy is also a token economy. If institutionalized people can be bruised in a miniature token economy, all manner of psychological slaughter can surely result from exposure to the real thing. Therefore we can use the effects of the national economy as a kind of standard against which to judge the ill or good effects of token economies. If a psychologist's token economy produces less harmful effects than the real national economy produces, then we can hardly condemn or restrict the psychologist's version.

### Sacrifice Principle

Statement of Sacrifice Principle: In the process of rewarding certain action from your other person (and after informal procedures have failed to build up the desired action), if you arrange for voluntary sacrifice by your other person of a known reward until desired action reaches a certain level, that action will increase more rapidly than if the reward is made freely available to your other person.

**Case 8.17.** Marvin wants badly to cut down on smoking. He asks your help as a trusted friend to give him all the support you can in the difficult transition period just ahead. Reliance on self-determination has already failed. He agrees to count honestly the number of cigarettes per day he smokes. He further agrees to give up $14 at the beginning of each week. If he succeeds in smoking one less cigarette each day, then you give him $2 back each day. Otherwise, you donate it to the charity of his choice. He also sports a pipe now to satisfy his oral needs.

**Case 8.18.** Helga, your sister, is about 20 pounds overweight by her own admission and wants help in reducing. First she sees a doctor to settle on a medically acceptable diet. Willpower has not worked. Neither of you want to adopt such powerful procedures for self-improvement that a health risk exists, so seeing a doctor is a must. But the doctor's concluding remarks leave her still without the self-will to change. Helga and you settle on a plan. She will count calories meticulously. She will initially sacrifice the pleasure and convenience of eating a dessert on her Saturday night date if she fails to follow the doctor's advice for reducing calories daily. Otherwise, she may eat the dessert. She is, in fact, *earning back* the opportunity to eat dessert.

The voluntary sacrifice idea was proposed and supported by Thomas Tighe and Rogers Elliott.[46] This principle seems especially suited as a temporary measure to break troublesome bad habits. The general idea is always the same. The other person always sacrifices some desired reward or puts some money into holding in an escrow account. Then the sacrificed reward is earned back, bit by bit, with a periodic (e.g., daily) display of the desired action (e.g., consuming only 500 calories).

A number of projects from students in my classes have used the sacrifice principle as exemplified in the rather typical cases above.

## SINCERITY

When relationships deepen between two people, there is always the danger that one or both parties is "insincere." Insincere here means putting on a false *positive* front. Such an insincere false front is called *ingratiation,* whereby one party distorts and exaggerates his or her own attributes to make the other person more favorable toward him. Some excellent research by Edward E. Jones clearly points to the use of tactics such as agreeing with the other person and false flattery as ingratiation tactics.[47] The use of such tactics becomes a problem if you are willing to grant that each of us might use these tactics unwittingly as well as knowingly; that is, there might be a natural tendency, about which we know nothing, to ingratiate ourselves to others.

To be sure, reward procedures are perhaps necessary in building a lengthy relationship, but here they are being prostituted into self-serving methods to control the other person.

In *Pairing,* Bach and Deutsch discuss the problem of mutual self-delusion at length, whereby societal expectations are unwittingly translated into false fronts displayed by *both* parties.[48]

**Case 8.19.** Victor and Lucille are getting to know each other. He thinks she wants an achievement-oriented, successful husband. Because he likes her, he begins to display achievement motivation. She thinks he wants a career wife who can contribute to family finances. However, he actually desires only a modest income, and she wants to rear children for the next few years and then decide what to do with her life. They both put on the false front they think the other wants. They marry, and he climbs the ladder of occupational success, while she does likewise. They never discover their mutual delusion.

Case 8.19 shows that insincerity can be unintentional as well as intentional. The critical question is how can we tell when a relationship is insincere.

ACTIVITY 8.6.

The following is a list of characteristics claimed by Bach and Deutsch to indicate insincere, exploitive relationships.[49] Your task is to add to the list. Examples from the dim dark past should not be hard to find.

1. Absence of reference to the future, especially to the future of the relationship at hand.
2. Absence of negative or critical comments about the other person, you or him (her).
3. Absence of feedback and responding to important requests.
4. Encouraging of dependence of one party on the other. (What *is* dependence, anyway?)
5. Absence of self-disclosure of feelings, emotions, hopes, and fears.
6. Superficial verbal exchange accompanied by physical advances. (I added this one to their list.)

7. ______________________________

8. ______________________________

9. ______________________________

10. ______________________________

## CONCLUDING COMMENTS ABOUT REWARD

This whole chapter expounds the ins and outs of the basic reward principle. While it may be stretching the point a bit, the array of rewards you can arrange for your other persons probably comes close to comprising your social assets. Hopefully, this chapter will provide a guide for creating and using rewards in your own personal life.

For creating rewards in especially tough situations, here are two aids: (1) Look at Figure 8.1, where the Foa and Foa mental map of rewards is shown. (2) Glance over the list of principles in Appendix B to jog your mind. Used as a checklist, these devices should help you generate options.

*Giving and receiving love cannot be done in a hurry; it requires time and even some leisure. Money, on the contrary, can change hands very rapidly. In an environment providing an overload of stimuli, those resources that require a longer processing time are more likely to receive low priority.*

URIEL AND EDNA FOA[50]

# 9

# MAINTAINING AND REDUCING ACTION

*Nothing so needs reforming as other people's habits.*

MARK TWAIN

*A man who reforms himself has contributed his full share towards the reformation of his neighbor.*

NORMAN DOUGLAS

## THYSELF PRINCIPLE

The principles considered up to this point always had you effecting some change in your other person. However, suppose the person you desire to change is none other than yourself? Can you apply principles to yourself? The answer is yes, and the "thyself principle" formally states this fact. Should you apply principles to yourself? To the degree principles reflect the state of nature, we apply principles on ourselves 24 hours per day. Thus you already are applying principles on yourself. In addition, if you are willing to use the latest and most powerful procedures to influence others, including your loved ones, then you ought to be willing to use those same powerful procedures on yourself as well.

Statement of Thyself Principle: The procedures in all other principles are also effective when you and your other person are one and the same, that is, when you want to change your own actions.

**Case 9.1.** Joe Bruiser loves to loll around and relax on the weekends. Weekends should mean hammocks, fishing, watching the game, playing with the kids, and yard work. Joe loathes yard work, but a yard with a decent appearance is necessary. He decides to enlist the aid of his wife, who says she'll grant him one wish of his choice the first several times he does Saturday yard work. In this example, Joe Bruiser is both the central person and the other person. He applied the basic reward principle and the other-person-preference principle on himself with his wife's help.

**Case 9.2.** At the University of Wisconsin, an announcement went out in psychology classes and men's residences advertising for men who had a common social problem: fear of meeting girls. Those men who answered were screened. Those chosen had reasonable social skills but evaluated themselves negatively or avoided meeting girls out of fear, according to researchers Lynn Rehm and Albert Marston.[1] These 24 young men were normal clinically except for a mild fear. (This fact is important!) Some participants were put through a self-reward procedure that had been found effective in previous studies. Rather than climbing the fearsome Mount Everest of going out and meeting new girls right and left, these men were carefully guided up some gentle hills. Each one made up a series of four situations that, for them personally, gradually approached a feared situation. For example, one participant made up these levels: "sitting down next to a girl in class," "meeting a new girl while with a group of your friends," "phoning a girl to ask her for a date," and "dancing with a girl while on a date." Between the first and second training sessions, the men were to try entering the first (least fearful) level of situation on their own list (e.g., sitting next to a girl in class). After success at that level, they were to reward themselves with points and think positive thoughts. In the next session, the trainer asked for reports and lavished rewards of praise for improvement. Compared to other participants, those in the self-reward treatment showed greater improvement. In short, rewarding themselves for gradually approaching feared situations relieved those fears better than other procedures or no training at all.

From the Rehm and Marston study and many others like it, we can safely conclude that self-reward is effective. At the time of this writing, the research in *Behavior Change Through Self-Control*[2] and *Behavioral Self-Control*[3] clearly shows that ordinary users can be trained to (1) define personal problems clearly, (2) observe and count their own actions, (3) administer self-reward, (4) administer self-punishment, and (5) control thoughts. Unfortunately, as in Case 9.2, procedures such as self-reward are mixed up with other procedures, such as praise from the trainer. Hence the crucial elements are obscured. In addition, skills (1) through (5) seem to be learned only with practice and to be useful mainly when used in combination with other procedures. Thus a user hoping to use the thyself and the sacrifice principles to cut down on food intake would probably have to throw out snack foods in the house as well. Nevertheless, the thyself principle shows so much promise that two books devoted solely to applying behavior mod principles on yourself have been published: Mahoney and Thoresen's *Self-Control: Power to the Person* and Watson and Tharp's *Self-directed Behavior*.[4] Surely others will follow.

Present and future parents take note: Behavior mod enthusiasts are using the thyself principle to speed learning in the schools. Students are generally programmed to gradually take over the tasks of determining the reinforcement, determining the task, evaluating performance, administering the reinforcement, and writing a contract that spells out all these procedures. Contracting is generally used, with Lloyd Homme's *How to Use Contingency Contracting in the Classroom* as the standard reference.[5] There seems to be nothing harmful in these procedures per se. In fact, Stephen Johnson has used contracting and self-reward in classrooms to build up the rewarding power of positive self-evaluations, such as "I was right."[6] Despite these noble efforts, your children should not be misled into thinking that they are running the whole show if they are merely choosing the road to a goal selected by an outside authority.

## PRINCIPLES FOR MAINTAINING

### When Do We Maintain Action?

Think about these things:

Good will from the boss.
Good kissing between husband and wife.
Employees who come to work on time.
A friend and fellow employee not getting fired for an outburst of temper.
A little girl whose eyes light up and who flies into your arms after you have been away a few hours.
Thinking about meeting new people as a worthwhile adventure.
Good variety in sex.

These items are slices of life belonging to a special category: worthwhile actions we have already built up and would like to maintain over the longer run. In the last chapter, we dealt with building up action or getting a good thing going. In the rest of this section, we focus on *keeping* a good thing going once started.

### Intermittent-Reward Principle

Statement of Intermittent-Reward Principle: If you arrange for your other person to receive a reward on an intermittent basis, your other person will maintain those rewarded actions longer than if rewarded on a continuous basis.

"Intermittent" reward means not rewarding every occurrence of the action you want, but on occasion. A true personal example illustrates this idea.

**Case 9.3.** In my childhood, my friend Tim had a paper route. Every Saturday morning, he would turn in his money to the downtown office and get paid. He told me about the lady down at the office with whom he dealt, and I remember his description to this day. After every utterance he made, she would have the same smile plastered across her face, a broad grin. She always displayed this expression, and it positively infuriated Tim! He thought she was a phony put-on. And this took place when Tim and I were only in grade school.

Case 9.3 illustrates the continuous use of perhaps the most common social reward—smiling. We smile normally, but only at certain times. Usually we time our smiles to either set the mood or act as rewards. This lady's continuous smiling was so awkward it made interacting with her strange and evoked hostility in a grade-school boy.

**Case 9.4.** Julie is a nurse. She has an hour for lunch every day and does not like to spend all of that hour at a restaurant. Therefore prompt service is essential. She invariably sits at a table served by Mary, the waitress. When Julie first started to go to this restaurant, she used to tip 25 cents. Then she raised it to 35 cents. However, after a few months, Mary began to slow down on the service. Here the action Julie wants to maintain is prompt service from Mary. Julie feels that a higher tip is not warranted. She could ask for better service, but Mary looks harried enough already. She could go elsewhere, but this restaurant has the only excellent French onion soup in town. Julie decides to occasionally (intermittently) leave a 50-cent tip. After she begins doing this, prompt service is restored.[7]

**Case 9.5.** Carolyn is your secretary. She's a bright enough girl, but lately she has been lackadaisical and forgetful. Your goal is to somehow maintain her alertness on the job. Coupled with a request, you invite her out to lunch once in a while. You make sure she gets extra interesting work periodically, and she begins to do a good job.[8]

Empirical support for the intermittent-reward principle is abundant. The usual result seen is that intermittent reward leads to increased "resistance to extinction," which refers to how long it takes for action to fade away after reward is stopped. The classic studies of Ferster and Skinner demonstrated that intermittent reward produces *greater* resistance to extinction of bar-pressing by pigeons in laboratory cages.[9] Lewis and Duncan showed a similar effect with humans on an imitation task.[10] On a slot machine game, subjects kept pulling the lever longer after winning on 25 percent of their previous tries than did other subjects who won 100 percent of the time. Thus an intermittent schedule of reward produced increased resistance to extinction here.

ACTIVITY 9.1.

Behavior mod researchers have devoted a lot of attention to describing the main varieties of intermittent reward. We have already introduced the most fundamental concepts bearing on intermittent reward in the last chapter's discussion of pay schedules. Recall that in a *ratio* schedule, reward becomes available after so many instances of the desired action; in an *interval* schedule, reward becomes available after an interval of time has passed. In this activity, you see these two main kinds of intermittent reward, each subdivided in two. In each box you see the name and an example of that kind of reward in real life. Your task is to complete the examples on the next page.

As the examples in Activity 9.1 show, both ratio and interval schedules can be either fixed or variable. In *fixed* schedules, reward becomes available after a fixed (constant) number of actions or fixed time interval. In *variable* schedules, reward becomes available again only after a variable (changing) number of actions or variable time interval. For example, Donald Whaley and his associates wanted to build up and maintain the action of pausing for 3 seconds in a young boy who literally talked all the time.[11] First, Whaley built up pauses by rewarding each and every pause (continuous reward). For reward, he used tokens that were exchanged later for a cap

| | Ratio Schedule | Interval Schedule |
|---|---|---|
| fixed schedule | *fixed-ratio schedule*<br>1. $500 commission per car sold.<br>2. 2 points per exam question.<br>3. .<br>4. . | *fixed-interval schedule*<br>1. $300 pay every Friday.<br>2. Greeting by pastor every Sunday as you leave church service.<br>3. Weekly quiz for extra credit.<br>4. .<br>5. . |
| variable schedule | *variable-ratio schedule*<br>1. Slot machine payoff.<br>2. Smiles from a friend.<br>3. .<br>4. . | *variable-interval schedule*<br>1. Visits from Aunt Martha, who visits on impulse when she gets lonely.<br>2. Randomly determined bonus at work, given unexpectedly about every six months.<br>3. .<br>4. . |

Filling in the variable-ratio and variable-interval schedule examples may seem a little tricky, but remember the rules. In variable-ratio schedules, reward becomes available after a varying *number* of actions by you. With the slot machine, you must pull so many times; with your friend, he smiles after so many smiles from you. In each case internal programming of the slot machine and inside your friend determine when you can get a payoff. With the variable-interval schedules, you can get a reward only after a variable *time* has elapsed. Aunt Martha starts getting lonely about two months after her last visit. Bonuses at work are given sometime after four months have elapsed since the last bonus.

pistol, caps, and the opportunity to massacre everything in sight using said pistol. Then the action of pausing was maintained by rewarding every fifth pause. Here a fixed-ratio schedule was used because reward came after every fifth pause, which means after a constant number of actions.

The power of intermittent reinforcement is obvious. Using the intermittent-reward principle, you can maintain action more effectively than by using continuous reward—and you use less reward to boot. In general, people create the fixed schedules, while the variable schedules are more naturally occurring events. As a salaried professor, I will get paid on a fixed-interval schedule, a man-made schedule. A salesman who sells on a straight commission basis is solidly on a fixed-ratio schedule, another man-made schedule. The nomadic tribe wandering from oasis to oasis finds water on an irregular basis, a naturally occurring variable schedule. The playboy or playgirl who succeeds in seduction on an irregular basis is on a naturally occurring variable-ratio schedule of rewards, whereby each seduction is a reward.

**Unpredictable-Reward Principle**

Statement of Unpredictable-Reward Principle: If you arrange for your other person to receive reward on a more *unpredictable* intermittent basis, your other person will maintain those rewarded actions longer than if rewarded on a more predictable basis.

**Case 9.6.** Every Friday night for the past 10 years, Steve's wife has gone shopping with her friend. This left Steve with the house to himself so he could invite his friends over for a good game of cards. Occasionally and without warning, Steve would buy his wife a present as a reward for her kindness. In this case, Steve used the unpredictable reward principle to maintain the action of his wife's Friday shopping.[12]

**Case 9.7.** Bill is a successful insurance salesman. He is married but headed for divorce unless he can somehow maintain the waning affection between his wife and him. Therefore he decides to romance her once again. He calls her at 3:00 P.M. to tell her he will be home at 6:00 P.M. He begins to praise and give gifts unpredictably, but not to excess. She responds with affection and their marital happiness returns.

Unfortunately, I can't offer you a book-length treatise on regaining a lost love. Nevertheless, it seems to me that marriages and friendships slip into the rut of stale predictability with surprising ease. Unpredictability of reward is one of the spices that adds to the variety of living.

The unpredictable-reward principle is consistent with two lines of reasoning. First, what is likely to be going on inside the head of the person facing an intermittent reward schedule? What is the car salesman thinking? He knows that about every fiftieth customer, say, will buy. He is uncertain but has hope, so he must keep responding to prevent loss of rewards, car sales in this case.[13]

Second, consider the would-be Romeo and the woman who is stringing him along. He think she is interested, but she says no unpredictably when he asks her for a date. She lets him proceed on his romantic advances but stops him unpredictably. His association with her has become an adventure with excitement at every turn. Unpredictability virtually defines adventure of every kind, and romantic adventure is no exception.[14] He is hooked but enjoying every minute of it.

According to many behavior mod authorities, superstitions and other folk customs probably have their origins with unpredictable, accidental rewards that happened in ancient times. Bachrach tells of the magic lore and magical rituals that have grown up surrounding fishing in the open sea surrounding the Trobriand Islands.[15] Such fishing is unpredictable and adventurous; fish are caught on an unpredictable schedule. In contrast, lagoon fishing provides a stable schedule of reward, since fish can always be caught there. No magic lore or magical rituals have grown up concerning fishing in the lagoon.

In short, unpredictable reward often leads to feelings of adventure and mystique surrounding the associated activity, be it romance, fishing, or climbing a mountain. These feelings are far more than the perceptions of isolated individuals at the time of action. Rather, powerful norms and customs arise, such as the norm for conquest and achievement that dominates industrial nations today. Both (1) the likely thoughts of the person facing an unpredictable reinforcement schedule and (2) the excitement and adventure associated with possible conquest of an uncertain task provide ample basis for proposing the unpredictable reward principle.

When we try to apply these ideas of unpredictability and intermittent reward to everyday life, we come up with spontaneity. Sidney Jourard recommends being spontaneous all the time, as do many other humanistic psychologists.[16] I suspect that spontaneity fosters the feelings of freedom, free will, free choice, and fun despite some constraints necessarily present in any situation.

Do not be deceived. The examples in this section have been ordinary, but the principles for maintaining are so powerful that they can be dangerous addicting. I refer specifically to the addicting properties of unpredictable intermittent reward. Consider the case of addiction to gambling. The addicted gambler's life can be as horribly devastating as the hard-drug user's. There are tremendous individual differences in susceptibility to gambling. With some, a malignant obsession with the unpredictable rewards of gambling grows to the point of addiction. The results are huge debts, sobbing wives, and shattered children, resentful and in conflict.[17] There are Gamblers Anonymous groups in many cities to assist addicted gamblers. The magnetism of gambling is so powerful that it requires regulation by law. In fact, many states and countries put gambling and alcohol in the same category for all practical purposes. Both are regulated and dispensed through state dispensaries or are state-licensed, with the state reaping some of the profit!

Going one step further it is only a matter of time before business organizations heed the words of Nord and start instituting lotteries and surprise bonuses on a massive scale.[18] Imagine the effects of $1000 lotteries held on unpredictable dates annually at your workplace, with only five people in the running for each $1000. Such a lottery would probably pay for itself with decreased turnover and absenteeism. If instituted, in addition

**Figure 9.1.** Emotions at the racetrack, illustrating the excitement that accompanies unpredictable schedules of reward. (Photograph by Charles Blakey.)

to existing pay policies, such applications of the unpredictable reward principle might well result in addictive loyalty to the company. So be on the watch for organizational abuse of the unpredictable-reward principle.

Adventure and "where the action is" seem to be composed, in large measure, of unpredictability. In his typically fascinating essay, "Where the Action Is," sociologist Erving Goffman pictures a variety of situations that fit this description.[19] They include Karl Wallenda walking the high wire, gambling, crime for fun, financial speculation, soldiering, political life, racing, bullfighting, hustling, conning, and so on. From Goffman's essay, it is reasonable to speculate that doing or even watching such actions is maintained in substantial measure from big consequences, slim odds, and utter unpredictability (see Figure 9.1).

Case 9.8. John is a compulsive gambler. He has tried many times to break his habit. His wife finally hit on a plan. Each week he was to give her a certain amount of money to hold, and he would bet using it during the week. The kind of betting and pay off odds would be created by them jointly to resemble those of the bookmaker. That way, he would satisfy his urge to gamble and still not lose his money.[20]

ACTIVITY 9.2.

Be especially observant for a day or two about when one or two particular other persons smile at you. Can you easily fit their pattern of smiling into the chart in Activity 9.1, or does an adequate description require more explanation? In the space provided (1) describe their pattern of smiling and (2) answer the question just posed.

## Surprise Principle

Statement of Surprise Principle: If you arrange to directly give your other person a series of clearly positive events (unpredictable surprises) not as a reward for any certain action whatsoever, the effectiveness of all other principles involving you will be greater than in the absence of such surprises.

**Case 9.9.** You have been married to your faithful wife for seven years, the supposed telling point in marriage. Lately you think maybe you have been taking her for granted. You want to maintain a high level of affection and fidelity between you, so you arrange to leave the children with your in-laws for a weekend. You then come home Friday afternoon and ask your wife to pack for the weekend, and off you go for a surprise-filled, romantic weekend.[21]

**Case 9.10.** Nelson and Mary have been dating off and on for some time now. With no advance warning, Mary calls Nelson at 7:00 P.M. on Tuesday with a surprise invitation to go out for a fabulous meal Wednesday evening. (Liberated women arise!) In fact, the reservations are already made. Nelson has to work late Wednesday but wisely requests a rain check for Thursday night. She changes the reservation and gladly gives him a verbal rain check for Thursday.

**Case 9.11.** Your little daughter is quietly playing by herself. It is an ordinary afternoon. All of a sudden you say, "C'mon, darling. You are such a wonderful person and I love you so much that we are going out to get us an ice cream cone." And you mean it.

The surprise principle simply states that we all love and respond to a surprise. A surprise here means a positive event so unpredictable it cannot be readily classified into a schedule of rewards. The specific implication is that "respond to a surprise" means becoming more responsive to the person who gives us a surprise. Be sure to notice that a surprise is not a reward. Rather, a surprise is given for no specific reason other than loving or positive regard toward your other person.

Empirical support for the surprise principle would come from comparing surprisers with those who do not give surprises, which would mean looking at the different reactions evoked from relevant other persons. For example, one could compare outward affection and inward feelings of love from spouses who are being surprised versus comparable spouses who are not being surprising. I claim that not only are surprises a great way to break monotony in life, but surprises offer a simple and powerful way to deepen intimacy between two people (see Figure 9.2).

As with many things we do, giving a surprise carries along with it implications beyond the simple act of giving. I claim that giving out surprises has several implications, which you can test informally and professionals can test formally. Specifically, the other person will come to hold these perceptions about you more with surprises than without them:

You give out spontaneous actions.
You enjoy spontaneous actions yourself.
You give out rewards and goodies in general.
You enjoy getting rewards and goodies in general.

**Case 9.12.** All year long little Leah has looked forward to Christmas. And it indeed comes to pass that on Christmas day Leah receives the toy of her dreams, a chrome-plated, fuzzy-wuzzy, quadraphonic framus. The day after Christmas, what is Leah playing with? You guessed it. The box in which the framus was packed. She lost interest in the toy itself on Christmas day.

The events in Case 9.12 illustrate *satiation,* or loss of effectiveness with repeated use. Satiation is all around us. It has even been rumored that the thrill of sex in marriage is subject to satiation after a few years. Indeed, falling into routines probably leads to boredom and occasional dramatic reactions to boredom (e.g., changing jobs, changing mates, mental illness). The issue concerning us is practical. Beyond changing *schedules* of rewards, what can I do personally to ward off the cancer of satiation of rewards for meaningful activities I truly want to continue?

### Arabian Nights Principle

Statement of Arabian Nights Principle: If you arrange for the nature and kind of reward to your other person to change, your other person will maintain those rewarded actions longer than with less varied rewards.

**Case 9.13.** Leona is head nurse on the floor. Being a generally positive and pleasant person, she is constantly letting each employee know he or she did a good job. But the effect of words and smiles seems to be wearing off. With her own money, Leona buys flowers for the ladies and silly coffee mugs for the men. She gives these gifts for good work on impulse.

**Case 9.14.** Jeff wishes to maintain a high level of friendship with his friends. Lately, however, he has become a bit self-conscious about speaking up, fearing that he has nothing original or appropriate enough to say. To apply the Arabian

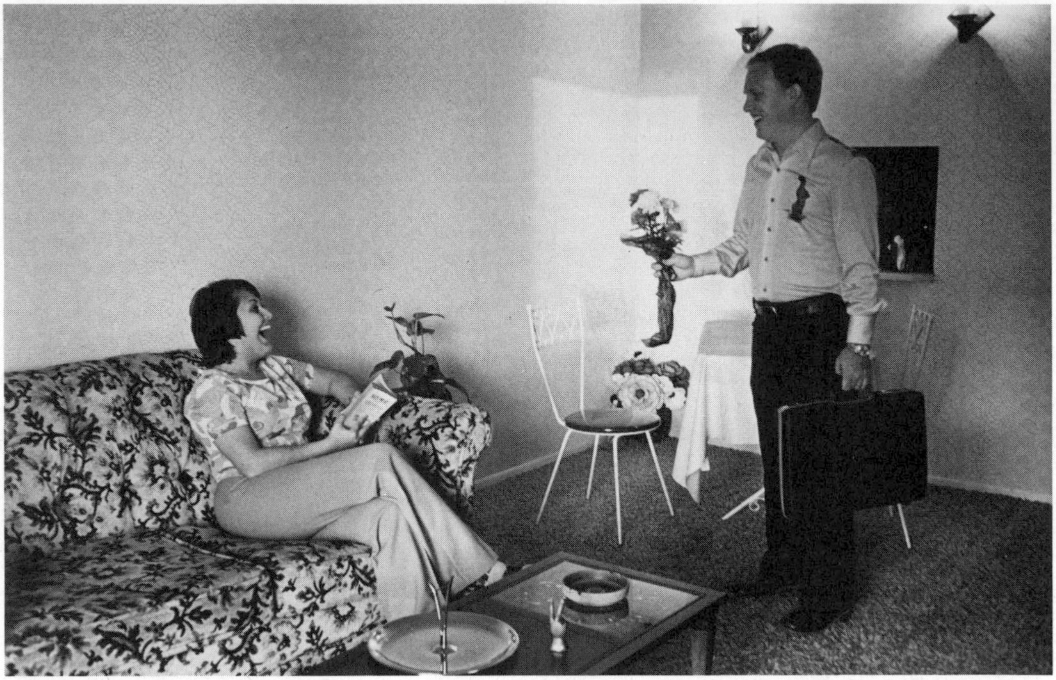

**Figure 9.2.** Application of the surprise principle. (Photograph by Charles Blakey.)

Nights principle, he begins to express his feelings spontaneously. Whatever the mechanism, it works. His spontaneous thoughts are accepted as adding variety to the conversation, and his friendships continue.[22] Would this procedure always work?

**Case 9.15.** Frank works for the county as a recreation leader. He enjoys the work immensely because he loves sports generally and tennis especially. He was recently offered a supervisory-type position, and he came to see Diane, his boss, to discuss it. She emphasized that in the present job he is doing what he loves to do and has a lot of freedom. In the other position, he would have to wear a suit and work inside, doing mostly paperwork. He turns down the new position, even though it would have paid more.[23] In this case, the employee's present work action was maintained because of the variety of activities it offers.

We would all like to be socially creative. The socially creative person has taken the tip from the Arabian Nights idea and is armed with 1001 creative ways to respond socially, especially 1001 ways to reward. The most popular people I know not only reward massively, but they use a seemingly endless variety of rewards.

ACTIVITY 9.3.

Imagine you are waiting with one other person for the bus. You have nothing with you to read and are getting bored. Suddenly the other person turns to you and asks, "Say, have you got the time?" List five different things you can say to maintain the conversation in the process of giving her the time.

1. ________________________

2. ________________________

3. ________________________

4. ________________________

5. ________________________

**Least-Powerful-Reward Principle**

Statement of Least-Powerful-Reward Principle: In the process of maintaining certain action from your other person, your use of the least powerful reward will be more effective than if you use a more powerful reward.

**Case 9.16.** Doris, a teacher, wishes to maintain the action of doing math problems in all of her students. She decides to time her interactions with students as she moves around the room during math time. Her results show she was spending an average of 38 seconds with each pupil. She decides to first raise the amount of time per pupil to 50 seconds, but this dramatically increases the goofing off. She then decides to use the least-powerful-reward principle and cuts down on the contact to 20 seconds per student. To her amazement, the goofing off drops.

Case 9.16 describes results of a real experiment by John Scott and Don Bushell, Jr.[24] Note that social interaction was defined as goofing off, or "off-task," behavior. Note also that the students' actual progress in the math program remained the same throughout. Case 9.16 shows that more "on-task," good social behavior resulted when the teacher supplied *less* reward in the form of less teacher attention.

In a related study, K. Daniel O'Leary and his colleagues found that soft reprimands quelled disorder in the classroom more effectively than did loud reprimands.[25] Once again using less of a reinforcement, punishment in this case, maintained action more effectively than using more of the same reinforcement.

The least-powerful-reward principle was named by Kopel and Arkowitz, but it has been around in social psychology for some time.[26] Indeed, Collins and Hoyt emphasized its practical implications after finding that participants who were paid less changed their attitudes more. "It is those very stimulus conditions which would minimize response occurrence in training environments (low financial inducement, high choice, high consequences) which maximize internalization, attitude change, stimulus generalization, and response generalization."[27] These authors are stating a fairly complicated and important point, so we will take a paragraph to elaborate.

Collins and Hoyt are underscoring the point that maintaining is a whole different ball game than building up. In building up an action, you want to pile the rewards on heavy, limit the other person's choice, and emphasize how important the action is (e.g., disclosing personal information to you) to you and others. On the other hand, to maintain action, you go as easily as possible, keeping outside external inducements to a minimum. The whole business fits nicely with Kopel and Arkowitz's interpretation that to maintain action over time, your other person must be convinced that he or she is really choosing to do it of free will. In their review, Kopel and Arkowitz cite abundant research to support the idea that maintaining action of all kinds is enhanced if an individual is convinced that he has chosen a particular course of action himself.

In short, the least-powerful-reward principle entails the perception that "I have chosen to do this action myself." This perception seems to be a crucial mediator (mental event) for maintaining action over the longer run.[28] Indeed, who among us would not embrace this perception as a description of how we usually act in our own life?

## REDUCING UNWANTED ACTION

### What Are My Chances for Change?

How do you get rid of actions you don't want, especially bad habits? There are two primary views on this matter. The first was expressed by a young man about to participate in an experiment I was doing at Walter Reed Army Institute of Research. We were just passing the time waiting for the others to show up, and our conversation turned to changing the actions of adults. He had strong feelings on this topic and made several points, finishing with the emotional conclusion, "You can't change someone's personality!"

Another view is expressed by the following exchange between Goldiamond and one of his clients in therapy:

> *During the course of one of the sessions,* S *started to talk about his childhood and was summarily cut off. "Shouldn't I talk about this with a psychologist?" he asked. "Isn't this one of the things that interests you? Doesn't it affect me now?" "Look," I said, "a bridge with a load limit of three tons opens in 1903. The next day, a farmer drives eighteen tons over it; it cracks. The bridge collapses in 1963. What caused the collapse?" "The farmer in 1903," he said.*

*"Wrong," I said. "The bridge collapses in 1963 because of the cracks that day. Had they been filled in the preceding day, it would not have collapsed. Let's discuss the cracks in your marriage."*[29]

(Reprinted with permission of author and publisher: Goldiamond, I. Self-control procedures in personal behavior problems. *Psychological Reports,* 1965, *17,* 851–868. [Monograph Supplement 3-V17.])

Obviously, these two views about change are the end points on a scale of optimism about changing ourselves. Where along the scale will you put your opinion? As for me, I'll put my money nearer to Goldiamond's optimism. For one thing, the pessimistic view that adults cannot change is uncomfortably fatalistic. For another, there is ample evidence in the clinical psychology literature (see any clinical journal) that adults can change. Maas has documented the claim that having had a chum in preadolescence is not necessary for the "development of a capacity for intimacy in adulthood."[30] Thus you need not feel doomed by past experience. Also, it is abundantly clear from research that parents can learn new ways to deal with their children.[31] Of course, I cannot give you odds on personal change because the failures almost never get printed. However, the possibility of change is real. In fact, this chapter and this book reflect high (but not blind) faith in the possibility of personal change for the better.

## Reviews

### Orchestra Review

Once again it is imperative to bear in mind that when we consider principles individually, we are listening to the second cello playing a solo and not the whole orchestra. Specifically, in this chapter we will neglect the all-important emotional aspects of change. This neglect is remedied in the next chapter, which is devoted mainly to emotional change. It will be best to master at least this chapter and the next chapter and then check with your instructor before embarking on a personal-change project.

### Strategy Review

Nowhere is the guideline of using a *humane* initial plan more relevant than when applied to plans for reducing unwanted actions. There are a lot of means to reduce, say, a bad habit other than the "cold turkey" way. The HEN guidelines apply to this section on reducing unwanted actions more than to any other in the book. Initial plans should be as humane, effortless, and natural as possible. Accordingly, the principles in the following section constitute a rough ordering of strategies for changing undesired actions, with earlier principles best used earlier. However, the ordering is rough, so even the optimal plan of attack on a particular problem will not be perfect.

## Constructive-Alternatives Principle

Statement of Constructive-Alternatives Principle: For reducing unwanted action in your other person, if you arrange for explicit exposure to a reasonable alternative activity, all other procedures for reducing action will be more effective than in the absence of such constructive alternatives.

**Case 9.17.** Gil wants to reduce smoking, and he has noticed that he smokes most when he's with other people. He is afraid to quit cold turkey because he might start doing nervous things with his hands or mouth. Before he even begins to plan how to reduce smoking, he needs to provide constructive alternative actions for his mouth and hands in the company of friends. What might he consider here?

**Case 9.18.** Pete is home with his little toddler. While he's having coffee with his buddy Tom, the little girl toddles her way into the kitchen. Before long she is burrowing her way into the cabinets, cans start rolling onto the floor, and pans come clattering out. Pete simply requests her to stop it. Unless Pete gives her something better to do, who would expect her to stop? She is doing something fascinating, and she is close to her father as well.

**Case 9.19.** Ted is a nurse, but he keeps showing up late for his shift, an action you as head nurse must decrease. You could punish him, perhaps dock his pay. You could request change, but that has failed before. You decide to give him something better to do. One morning a week you throw a 5-minute party for the whole crew beginning promptly 5 minutes before the shift starts. The party features small portions of the best pastry in town for everybody.

**Case 9.20.** Carl broke up with a girl to whom he was engaged. This made him very uptight and nervous, a physical and mental condition he needed desperately to reduce. He could not eat and did not want to do anything except think about his misery. He decided that he needed some constructive alternatives to occupy his thoughts, so he made up a list of things to do each day. His constructive alternatives included cleaning the apartment, washing the car, and generally going out with friends and trying to have a good time.[32]

**Case 9.21.** GI Bill runs the office with an iron hand. This veteran soldier is actually a pretty fair guy, but he conveys all his desires in the form of commands—and he knows it. One time at lunch, he mentions this problem to you in passing. Before the opportunity slips away, you remark that the problem seems more one of words and phrases than any deep personality thing. Rather than issue commands, he could get better results by asking questions that start with "Do you think you could . . . ?" and "Will you . . . ?" And, besides, everyone in the office thinks Bill is an all-right guy with the exception of this carryover from the military. If he wants, you'll keep him posted on the commands and questions he gives tomorrow morning.

The appropriate test for the constructive-alternatives principle involves comparing identical procedures for change with and without clear provision for alternative actions to replace the ones to be reduced. Curiously, there seems to be little or no good evidence of this sort. It may be that the constructive-alternatives principle is so obvious that researchers have assumed it to be *logically necessary* and not in need of proof, just like the request principle. That is, to change there must be alternative actions to replace the undesired ones. In his introduction to transactional analysis in *Games People Play,* Eric Berne pointedly reminds us that our other person's time is going to get structured or filled up with *some* action, regardless of what we do.[33] Thus forcibly stopping some undesired action will not lead to a vacuous state of suspended animation but rather an alternate set of actions.

In decreasing the action of overeating in obese clients, Ferster, Nurnberger, and Levitt found that many overweight people eat when they are depressed.[34] For mildly depressed people, the researchers recommended the age-old remedies of taking a walk, going to a movie, going on a bus ride, and so on. These producers were only a part of treatment, which was comprehensive and personalized in each case. In another example, a friend of mine who has quit smoking cigarettes now sports a pipe. He never smokes the pipe, but it seems to help him.

In a "self-directed program for weight control," Mary Harris instructed her subjects to practice taking breaks during meals, starting with short breaks near the end of each meal.[35] Besides being incompatible with eating, taking such breaks provides a bit of self-mastery as reward.

Many programs of weight control begin with the temporal control of eating before even beginning to alter the amount of food eaten. Snacking several times a day could ruin any effect of reduced eating at meals. So first, snacking is limited gradually to, say, one large snack to dull the appetite at mealtime.[36]

### Request Principle Revisited

To be sure, the nastiest of habits (e.g., smoking, snacking) will not go away just because you request it. However, the possibility exists that your other person does not know what you want. The mere request that you want a change may indeed be sufficient for the change to occur, as in the case where you shift your taste preferences so that you want your hamburgers medium well rather than well done. In two studies, Steinman found that children in his experiments would stop imitating specially programmed mannerisms of an actor (model) immediately upon being requested to do so.[37] "But," you ask, "were the mannerisms in this case rather trivial, and is it not likely that such requests work best to reduce rather minor actions?" The answer is affirmative, and this is just the point. Even if the odds that a simple request will work are 1 in 1000, a request is worth a try.

### Distraction Principle

Statement of Distraction Principle: In reducing unwanted action of your other person, if you arrange for your other person to be distracted, the unwanted action will decrease more over the shorter run than in the absence of distraction. Distraction here means your other person's immediate and usually temporary exposure to an attractive event of which she (he) can partake where such exposure is incompatible with the unwanted action.

**Case 9.22.** Connie hates going to the supermarket because Kathy always throws a fit. Somehow the little girl becomes transformed upon being placed in the shopping cart and begins acting like a little hellion, screaming and all. But today is going to be different, Connie decides. Before entering the store, Connie proposes that Kathy is now big enough to have something to say about which foods are to be bought and would she like to help choose? Upon entering the store, Connie begins a tour-guide spiel about various aspects of the store to entertain and distract Kathy. (Why shouldn't we be entertaining to friends and family?) Going down the aisles, Connie allows Kathy to choose which vegetable to buy, which of two similar brands to buy, and so on.

**Case 9.23.** It's coffee-break time at the hospital office and your gang is busy talking. However, the conversation turns to rumor and backbiting that focuses on John, who just happens to be off today. You think very hard to come up with a more interesting topic of conversation, one which is not so nasty. You bring up the latest political scandal, and the conversation shifts away from John.

There is a fairly large body of recent evidence concerning distraction, but it has mainly to do with using distraction as a means to change attitudes. As such, the distraction technique seems to work effectively and enhance attitude change, but the nature of the distraction clearly has to be tailored to a highly particular situation.[38] Distraction is also used on television commercials. Ownership status distracts you from gas mileage in luxury cars. Economy distracts us from low crashworthiness in lightweight cars. Animated cartoon characters distract children from the nutritional value of cold cereals. Brand names distract us from product quality, as quality would be rated in *Consumer Reports* magazine.

### Extinction Principle

Statement of Extinction Principle: If you arrange for unwanted actions from your other person to be ignored without insult or putdown to your other person, the undesired actions will decrease more than if present consequences continue.

**Case 9.23 (continued).** The backbiting and nasty comments about John resume, and you are racking your brain to find a more engaging topic of conversation—without success. Finally, you decide to just ignore the comments and see if they stop.

**Case 9.24.** A certain married couple are among my friends. The husband has an annoying habit of making nasty little remarks about the wife every so often. These nasty remarks comprise the unwanted action to be reduced. I began to notice that the wife's reaction was really no reaction at all (extinction procedure). But as far as I could tell, her ignoring of his cutting comments had no effect at all.

The fact that extinction procedures (i.e., something you do) *alone* will often not do the job does not mean they are ineffective. But extinction procedures are best used in combination with other procedures. Note that "extinction procedures" means something you do, not the effect of what you do.

**Case 9.25.** If you were trying to quit smoking at home and your spouse reacts to you in the same manner whether you are smoking or not, you are being rewarded similarly for both smoking and not smoking. To apply the extinction principle (and some other principles as well), you ask your spouse to ignore you while you are smoking.

In this last case we might wonder if the extinction procedure is not actually punishment, namely, being ignored by your spouse for a few minutes. Indeed the *experience* of receiving extinction procedures and receiving mild punishment may be the same in some cases. However, there is a legitimate distinction to be made between the external operations of extinction and punishment. *Extinction* procedure means following action with no consequences, that is, consequences that are neither positive nor negative. *Punishment* means following action with negative or aversive consequences.

Extensive support for the extinction principle exists in laboratories and in the field, in studies with animals and humans. For example, one field study concerned a 4-year-old boy who would cry excessively at the drop of a hat.[39] The researchers successfully reduced crying by instructing the parents to ignore it. Of course, the researchers also instructed the parents to attend to legitimate hurts the boy suffered.

### Unchaining Principle

Statement of Unchaining Principle: If you arrange to disrupt the chain of actions leading to the unwanted action, your other person will reduce the unwanted action more than with less disruption.

The unchaining principle assumes that *many unwanted actions occur only after a reasonably fixed chain of events has occurred.* Here are some examples of chains. GI Bill issues commands only after he has physically entered the office premises. Gil smokes only after buying cigarettes, obtaining matches, and entering a social situation. Your child becomes disruptive, say, only after playing with toys for 20 minutes and then becoming bored. Fights between marriage partners occur, say, only after one or both parties have entered an unpleasant emotional state, have not left that state, and have physically situated themselves in private surroundings.

**Case 9.26.** Dedra has a problem when she enters a modern shopping center. It seems there are magnets tugging at her money, and she can dream up the most ingenious excuses to buy the most useless items. Upon pondering the unchaining principle, she decides to eliminate an early link in the chain by leaving credit cards and most of her money at home. She carries only one check already made out to the supermarket, but not signed, so she can get groceries on the way home. Thus Dedra disrupted an early link in the chain leading up to the unwanted action of squandering dollars in the mall: the placement of money or the means to obtain credit in her wallet.

**Case 9.27.** You want to stop eating those fattening but delicious Italian pastries that you buy at a special bakery and consume while watching the late show each night. You decide to take a new route home from work every night to avoid passing that bakery because you feel you are in its irresistible clutches whenever you get near it. Here the usual decision about which route to take home is disrupted well before the final fattening action can take place.[40]

ACTIVITY 9.4.

List at least 10 links in the original chain described in Case 9.27. The original chain ended with your consumption of Italian pastry during the nightly late show.

1. ______________ 6. ______________

2. ______________ 7. ______________

3. ______________ 8. ______________

4. ______________ 9. ______________

5. ______________ 10. ______________

ACTIVITY 9.5.

From your own experience, pick an unwanted action exhibited by yourself or someone you know well. Identities can be changed to protect the guilty. In the spaces provided, write the final unwanted action in space number 10. Then work backward and list some links in the chain as far as you can go. Is it easier to construct the chain when you work backwards?

1. ______________ 6. ______________

2. ______________ 7. ______________

3. ______________ 8. ______________

4. ______________ 9. ______________

5. ______________ 10. ______________

ACTIVITY 9.6.

From the links you have listed in the chain you created in Activity 9.5, now pick the link you would disrupt if you wanted to reduce the undesired action. In the space provided, briefly describe how you would go about breaking this chain. Would you succeed if you really wanted to?

______________________________________

______________________________________

______________________________________

______________________________________

Actually, the unchaining principle is somewhat of a parody of the usual approach involving chaining. In usual applications to child rearing or classroom situations, for example, chaining is cast as a procedure for bringing several actions of the other person under the control of one final, powerful reward. For example, if Connie wants little Kathy to help dry the dishes during the week, she might make drying the Friday evening dishes necessary for watching Saturday morning television. The chain is drying Friday dishes ——► Saturday television. This chain could obviously be built backward through the week to, say, Monday. How?

Rather than casting chaining procedures as control devices, I would rather view *unchaining* as a means to disrupt harmful chains that have already formed as a function of one's life history. As always with user information, the agent served is—hopefully—an individual person and not necessarily an organization.

### Time-Out Principle

Statement of Time-Out Principle: If you arrange for your other person's unwanted action to be followed by his (her) temporary physical transfer from the surroundings in which the unwanted action occurs into other surroundings where bland or boring actions are appropriate, the unwanted action will decrease more than in the absence of this transfer.

**Case 9.28.** In this true case, my young son Carl and I went to see the movie *Cinderella.* Suddenly he started screaming for candy and could not be induced to stop by any words I had to give. I picked him up and carried him, screaming, to the lobby. We waited there for about 5 minutes and he was ready to return.

"Time out" is a mild punishment. Obviously, it will find more use when the other person is a child rather than one's boss or mother-in-law.

In an experiment conducted by Zeilberger, Sampen, and Sloane, a mother and father brought their son to the experimenters for help. Their 4-year-old boy displayed "screaming, fighting, disobeying, and bossing" at home.[41] The researchers instructed the mother to remove toys and other interesting objects from a bedroom and put the son in it for 2 minutes after each instance of undesired action. Coupled with a program to build up constructive play, this program reduced the problem.

### Overcorrection Principle

Statement of Overcorrection Principle: If you arrange to overcorrect an unwanted action, the unwanted action will decrease more than in the absence of such procedures. Overcorrection here means instituting overly repetitive or overly correct performances.

**Case 9.29.** Ralph's young son Rusty constantly bothers him to watch television at all hours. Ralph decides to use overcorrection, starting this weekend. Before the weekend, Ralph and his son agree to watch television "all the time this weekend." Starting after supper on Friday, they begin watching. When Rusty begins to doze off at 10:00 P.M., Ralph gently keeps him awake for a few more hours. Then, bright and early Saturday morning, the regimen begins all over again, lasting far into the night. By the end of the grueling weekend, Rusty has even begun to dislike watching television.

Nathan Azrin and his colleagues have been experimenting with overcorrection with retarded mental patients.[42] Putting objects into the mouth was overcorrected with using an overly detailed oral-hygiene procedure of toothbrushing and face wiping after every bad object was put into the mouth. Hand clapping was overcorrected by first making the child wait for a length of time without clapping hands and then clapping the hands in overly correct, robotlike fashion. Thus far, the results seem promising; Azrin's overcorrection yielded more permanent effects than either reward or punishment used alone.

### Punishment Principle

If you want a precise statement, you will have to write it yourself. There will be no documentation of the effectiveness of punishment here. The annals of history survey rule by punishment, whereby subtle social pressures and the horrors of war and torture have served to maintain social classes and the identities of nations; such techniques are, of course, still used. Rather, our treatment of punishment will focus on why it should be used last and similar matters.

Go to any public place and you will see

unskillful, uncreative parents punishing their children instead of first trying to entertain and distract them. The HEN strategy means using punishment last and stopping it as soon as possible. (See Figure 9.3.)

Numerous scientists, such as Fred Keller and B. F. Skinner, have pointed to other disadvantages of punishment in addition to its painful character.[43] First, the effects of punishment are often temporary, as when spanking a child. Second, there are often emotional side effects that would not occur if the HEN strategy were used. Children subjected to more corporal punishment tend to become more aggressive outside the home.[44] Thus the long-range effect of punishing children seems to be an *imitation* effect, not a *suppression* effect. *Punished children are more likely to become punishers.* Third, punishment may lead to the other person's avoiding or escaping from you when given to chance. Children run away from home, children drop out of school, and adults may cross international borders to avoid punishment.

An even more subtle effect of punishment may come to pass with the widespread availability of user information. With such availability comes provision for a specific ordering of procedures to try *before resorting to punishment.* For example, as office manager, you will no longer have an excuse for heatedly chewing out a subordinate's sloppy work because constructive ways to improve the work are public information. Accordingly, using punishment too soon or using overly strong punishment will *implicitly* convey one or both of the following messages to your other person:

1. I do not care enough for you to use means better than punishment.
2. I truly want to hurt you.

These messages will be read between the lines when you or your other person are familiar with user information.

If you *must* use punishment, be sophisticated; the clumsy use of punishment abounds, even among professionals. In a well-known behavior mod book I shall not cite here, the author describes projects undertaken by his students involving applications of punishment techniques with schoolchildren. Study 12 tells the case of Glib, an 8-year-old boy who disrupted his class by talking out of turn. The college student doing a project with Glib decided to stamp out this unwanted disruption by making Glib work three extra math problems as punishment. I always ask my students, "What was Glib really going to learn?" The same reply always comes back: "To hate math." The college student was not only modeling punishment actions, but he was implicitly telling the child that math problems are so bad they can be used as punishing events. And this study was published as exemplary. I hope no one ever applies user information in that way!

Punishment is generally treated as a consequence that weakens the strength of the action it follows. Viewed in this way, a typical diagram about how punishment works as a consequence might go like this:

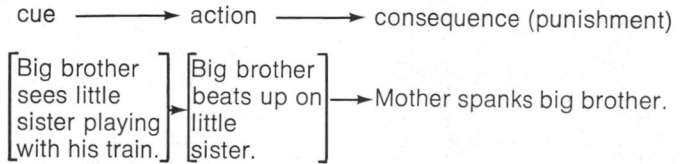

cue ⟶ action ⟶ consequence (punishment)

[Big brother sees little sister playing with his train.] ⟶ [Big brother beats up on little sister.] ⟶ Mother spanks big brother.

The punishment process consists of following certain action with events that are usually aversive or painful. However, the punishment process can occasionally function in a different way, with completely opposite results. Specifically, Sandler and Davidson review research to show that punishment can function as a cue which actually strengthens the action on occasion.[45] We will look at this process in animals and humans to show how people come to do some apparently strange things, such as punish themselves.

In a laboratory study, Holtz and Azrin first demonstrated the usual response-suppression effect of punishment.[46] Upon being shocked as a punishment consequence, pigeons reduced their ratio of pecking at a circle in their cage. (Nothing unusual so far.) However, in

the second part of their study, electric shock was associated with the availability of reward; so the birds came to rely on shock as a cue for reward. Now the functional sequence is:

[shock (cue that reward is available)] → [pigeon pecks at circle] → [food]

Then extinction of pecking at the circle began. When shock was turned on again during the final extinction procedures, the birds began to peck *literally* like "crazy." There were those crazy pigeons pecking to get shocked. Of course you and I, knowing their history, know that shock meant the availability of rewards for those birds. However, if you or I were to look at the birds in this final stage without knowing what came before, we would swear those birds were crazy masochists bent on destroying themselves.

One real-life counterpart of this view of punishment as cue concerns so-called bondage and discipline as variations of sex. As Fenicel states, "Certain experiences may so firmly have established the conviction that sexual pleasure must be associated with pain that suffering has become the prerequisite for sexual pleasure."[47] Here the sequences are:

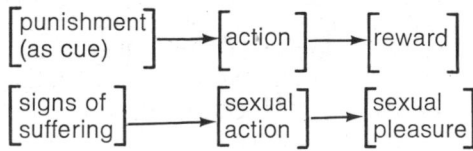

[punishment (as cue)] → [action] → [reward]

[signs of suffering] → [sexual action] → [sexual pleasure]

The signs of suffering here assume all manner of holding another person helpless and inflicting pain. Pornography stores sell the details.

Does the functioning of punishment as a cue explain other human actions as well? Are bondage and discipline advocates crazy? Might the strange actions of psychotics become logical once we understand their view of the world and their lifelong learning history?

### Group Surrender Principle

Statement of Group Surrender Principle: After all else fails to break a personally dev-

**Figure 9.3.** "I've had enough and I'm leaving!" yells the husband in this episode involving punishment. (Photograph by Charles Blakey.)

astating, habitual action of yours, if you use the thyself principle to submit to the demands of an organization that requires you to surrender to group methods to control the habit, you will more likely break that habit than otherwise.

If you have a drinking problem, for example, you might join Alcoholics Anonymous. Using the group surrender principle is the last resort, but it may be needed. It demands that you sacrifice your own will, your own rationality. To solve devastating personal problems, organizations like Alcoholics Anonymous have flourished and have performed a valuable service. How do such organizations wield their influence once you join? John Wallace paints a useful picture of the steps used in Alcoholics Anonymous to help curb problem drinking:[48]

1. Admitting personal incompetence (I am helpless to aid myself).
2. Request for help from the group (I want help).
3. Expectations that submission to group methods help you.
4. Viewing group members as similar to yourself (similar in past, common fate in future).
5. Submitting to heavy rewards for complying with group methods; rituals.
6. Discouragement of critical, analytical thought on your part in favor of blind compliance with group methods.

Such *formal* procedures are common to drug rehabilitation programs, Take Off Pounds Sensibly, Weight Watchers, certain religious conversions, military indoctrinations, and political groups around the world (see Figure 9.4). The procedures render the individual susceptible to group pressure and "soften him up." Used sensibly and *specifically*, as in Alcoholics Anonymous, these procedures can save lives. Misused and applied on a *nonspecific* basis, the procedures themselves can foster blind obedience to political leaders.

This discussion wraps up our consideration of individual principles to reduce unwanted

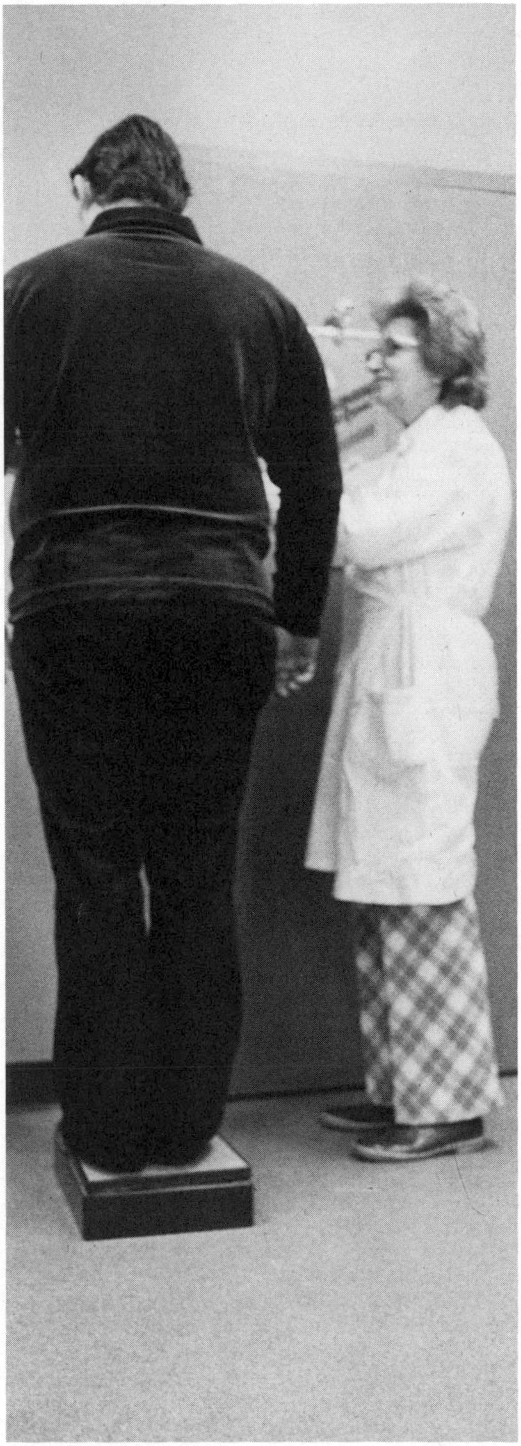

**Figure 9.4.** Picture of weighing in a group to which participants surrender selective aspects of their will in the hope of reducing the unwanted action of overeating. (Photograph by Charles Blakey.)

action. We return to the general principle for some practice at putting the principles together into some semblance of an orchestra.

### The General Principle Revisited

Case 9.30. Goldiamond tells of a case of disharmony in marriage. Two years ago the husband suggested that his best friend keep his wife company while he went to study in the library. The best friend and the wife committed adultery that night. "Since that time, whenever he saw his wife, *S* screamed at her for hours on end or else was ashamed of himself for having done so and spent hours sulking and brooding."[49] Goldiamond proceeded to try to significantly change the everyday situations in which the two interacted. He viewed their interaction as the problem rather than as a symptom of something deeper. They moved all their furniture around. The wife bought new clothing. The bedroom lighting was changed so that the only light ever turned on was a yellow night-light. According to reports from the couple, these procedures produced a marked change in their home surroundings. To resume conversing in a civil manner in private, the couple dined at new restaurants and began talking about topics that would not lead to arguments but rather mutual rewarding. One more problem remained. If conversation started and yelling stopped, that would be all well and good. However, "since in the absence of yelling at his wife, *S* sulked . . . , *S*'s sulking was in danger of increasing. *S* was instructed to sulk to his heart's content but to do so in a specified place. Whenever he felt like sulking, he was to go into the garage, sit on a special sulking stool, and sulk and mutter over the indignities of life for as long as he wished."[50] On the day before all these procedures were put into effect, the man had sulked for 7 hours! But the story has a happy ending. Goldiamond concludes, "At the end of the [10-week] period, there was no sulking in the garage and the partners were able to commune."[51]

(Reprinted with permission of author and publisher: Goldiamond, I. Self-control procedures in personal behavior problems. *Psychological Reports,* 1965, *17,* 851–868. [Monograph Supplement 3-V17.])

ACTIVITY 9.7.

On a separate sheet of paper, write down all the principles used by Goldiamond in Case 9.30. For each principle, supply a brief phrase indicating the specific means of application (who did what to whom). As an alternative to writing down the principles Goldiamond used, you might make another list, one for the supposed friend of *S;* that is, supply the details for the seduction scene and list the principles applied by whoever seduced whomever.

#### Final Reminder

Always accompany any program for reducing unwanted action with a tandem program for building up desired action. *Your other person must have available something better to do.*

### THE ETHICS OF PUNISHMENT

A question foremost on the minds of many parents is, "If I use punishment on my youngster, how ethical is it?" Similar questions can be raised about control in classrooms and control by governments. As with all such sweeping ethical issues, no pat answer is available. On certain occasions, punishment is justifiably used on a temporary basis to suppress especially disruptive actions. Fortunately, there are two guideline questions that can give us a lot of help: "What other procedures have I tried before resorting to punishment?" "While using punishment, am I trying out alternatives to punishment occasionally to see if punishment can be withdrawn?"

If I have honestly tried other procedures before resorting to punishment, I at least have the consolation that my attempts to reduce unwanted action are somewhat humane. If not, my action of using punishment prematurely is itself an unwanted action to be reduced by using a humane plan of attack.

The only way to tell if I am *continuing* to use punishment when the job could be done with more humane procedures is to try replacing punishment with more desirable procedures on a regular basis. The absence of attempts to replace punishment is itself an undesirable action needing reduction.

### LOOKING AHEAD

We have now covered a basic set of behavior mod procedures. You should realize that your everyday life usually involves complex applications of these principles, whereby many principles are applied at the same time. Looking ahead to the next chapter, we will begin to apply several principles at the same time.

Looking ahead in our lives, we can indeed

get a lot of mileage out of the principles. The principles do indeed apply to a wide variety of important events in our lives in addition to our interpersonal relations. A number of such applications are illustrated using the following rhetorical questions: Do newspaper reporters get rewarded for reporting specific facts that can be checked with reality or for making vague statements? For what kind of statements and promises do political candidates receive campaign contributions? What actions by prisoners are rewarded in prisons? Are prison wardens and guards rewarded for eliciting rehabilitation or obedient action from prisoners? What means does a 4-year-old have to reward and punish his parents? What new set of consequences was introduced by no-fault divorce legislation, already a reality in Florida and other states? By no-fault auto insurance? If you were twice as religious as you are now, what new rewards and punishments would apply to you? Are aggression and hostility ever rewarded? When? By whom? Can pain cues from a victim become rewards in and of themselves for the aggressor?[52] To what degree has the total array of rewards available to you at this moment been influenced by your mother and father?

Let us now turn to emotions, the topic discussed in Chapter 10.

*Instead of loving your enemies, treat your friends a little better.*

E. W. HOWE

# 10

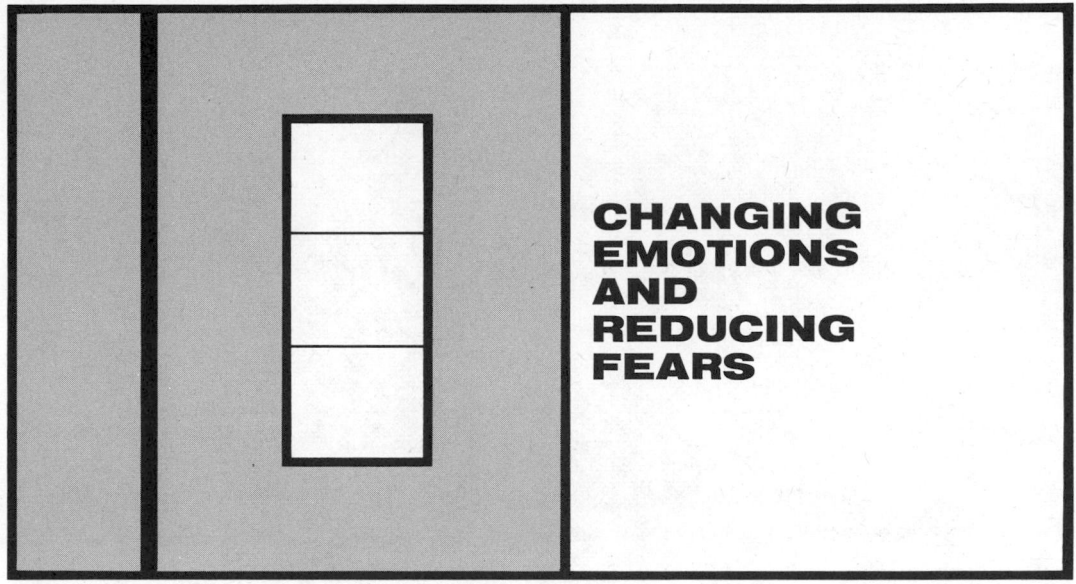

# CHANGING EMOTIONS AND REDUCING FEARS

*Half the things that people do not succeed in, are through fear of making the attempt.*

JAMES NORTHCOTE

### CAUTION

Do not use any of the procedures discussed in this chapter until you know the whole chapter (and its warnings) cold and have reality tested your plans with another person you trust.

### EMOTIONS AND ACTION

In the last four chapters we emphasized outward actions. The price we paid was the neglect of inward emotions. Dealing with actions we can see is a logical enough way to approach everyday life, but emotions are too important to be ignored any longer.

*Emotions* are affective feelings. Emotions are perhaps our most personal and private possessions. Emotions such as joy and physical pleasure and pride accompany the events that make life worthwhile. The private agonies of despair and pain and embarrassment signify if not define the darkest reaches of human existence. It follows naturally from our earlier ideas about willpower and self-direction that we should be optimistic about our own emotions.

John Bowlby reminds us that "no form of behaviour is accompanied by stronger feeling than is attachment behaviour. The figures towards whom it is directed are loved and their advent is greeted with joy."[1] In accord with our overall emphasis on human intimacy and practicality, our emphasis here will come to rest on procedures by which a nonprofessional user can change his or her emotions for the better. Specifically, we

**Figure 10.1.** One person is being introduced to another by a third party. This situation might never have happened had it not been for the third party because a perfectly normal, mild fear might have kept the two from introducing themselves. (Photograph by Charles Blakey.)

will focus on altering emotions that keep people apart, as defined by the user himself.

Our emphasis on changing emotions reflects the desire in each of us to experience more positive and less negative emotions. From your personal experience and from the tragic annals of clinical psychology, there is surely strong reason to believe that emotions can get in our way and be harmful as well as delight us. Has not the emotion of mild fear kept each one of us from speaking to several hundred potential acquaintances and friends? "No," we say privately, "I might be ignored or even ridiculed. I am better off to stay inside my invisible shield. I'll play it safe. I'll say nothing and stare at the floor." Sometimes we overcome such fears and sometimes someone else helps us, as shown in Figure 10.1. Sometimes we are not so fortunate.

Our perspective will be one of realistic optimism. The bicycle model compels me to consider the whole range of my life experience as it bears on my emotions. A limited perspective, such as just sitting there in my favorite easy chair and drooling over my favorite fantasy, is not going to bring that fantasy and its wonderful emotions into reality because I am not using willpower to enlist the support of my surroundings. Along similar lines, we are not going to expect instant changes in emotions as a rule. Rather, our approach will include careful considerations of (1) our private thoughts in a relaxed state in that easy chair, (2) our actions out there in the real world of dizzying emotions, and (3) practice over time, which means real effort. We first consider how our emotions come to be.

**PREVIEW**

At this point, we will conceive of emotions as learned associations. Because of the enormous complexity of human thought processes, it is possible to learn a practically infinite variety of emotions. This is so even if we use only classical conditioning, verbal association, and higher-order conditioning as devices to explain the learning process. Unfortunately, harmful emotional reactions are learned as well as beneficial ones. In this chapter, we emphasize reducing harmful fears using self-desensitization.

The research to date gives us three kinds of desensitization for reducing unwanted fears. All three use the desensitization principle. This means taking a cautious and extremely gradual approach to the object of fear while you experience an emotion that is incompatible with fear. In armchair desensitization, the feared thing is approached via a series of mental images while you sit still relaxed in an armchair. The incompatible emotion is deep muscle relaxation. In role-playing desensitization, you approach the object of fear in a series of practice scenes in which everyone involved knows the purpose is 100 percent rehearsal. In in vivo desensitization, you enter a series of situations in the real world that gradually approximate the object of fear. In all cases, the graded series of scenes approaching the feared thing is called the fear hierarchy. In all applications the approach to the object of fear is cautious and slow. It cannot be hurried or crammed into a single session or two.

## THE ORIGIN OF OUR EMOTIONS AND FEARS

### Instinctive Emotions

To convince us that at least some emotions have purely instinctive origins, John Bowlby marshals some convincing evidence. However, the hard evidence directly concerns only attachment in animals. "For mammals other than man, rigorous evidence that attachment behaviour can develop and be directed toward an object *that provides none of the traditional rewards of food, warmth or sex* is available only for guinea-pig, dog, sheep and rhesus monkey."[2] For instance, in John Paul Scott's research, puppies were reared with mother and siblings but in total isolation from humans.[3] Just after the puppies could crawl, they would immediately approach a man who was sitting down and spend 10 minutes with him. In Scott's and other animal research, animals approach and follow objects of attachment who are unfamiliar and who do not provide rewards beyond companionship.[4]

Does this research mean that our emotions are likewise instinctive? The answer is no because similar experiments have not been done with human infants for obvious ethical reasons. However, Bowlby does present an impressive case to document the strength of the attachment process in nearly all children. The key concept here is emotional *selectivity.* Given a chance, the human child forms a strong attachment to one (occasionally two) specific adults. The youngster is especially sensitive to clues that separation might occur. Upon separation, the child puts up a protest. Upon long separation or loss, the child lapses into plastic emotional indifference (sometimes anger) toward everyone.[5]

Since Bowlby popularized the attachment process, there has been renewed interest in Freud's emphasis on the emotional experiences of childhood. However, the interest now carries an optimism not present in Freud's stage theory of human development. In Freud's theory, adult emotional patterns are all but fixed by childhood experiences over which the adult has litte control at present. In contrast, learning theorists are optimistic that harmful emotions can be unlearned. They reason that, if harmful emotions can be learned in the first place, then helpful new emotions and actions can be learned by adults. These helpful learning processes are the focus of this chapter.

### Learned Emotions

#### Learning Emotions by Association

The process of association underlies the learning of emotions. The nature of the association may be simple or complex. Accordingly, the classical conditioning principle and all the other topics discussed in this section have to do with association. What is associated? *Association* here means the connection between a neutral cue and an existing emotion.

#### Classical Conditioning Principle

Statement of Classical Conditioning Principle: If you associate neutral cues with a given emotion in your other person, these cues themselves can come to elicit the emotion.

***Examples of Classical Conditioning Principle.*** The following true case was written by one of my students, Maria Ana Alvarez.

**Case 10.1.** At age 9, I was involved in a very serious traffic accident in which a cousin of mine, 20 years old at the time, lost his life. Our car was hit with the tremendous impact of an ambulance running at full speed to pick up some injured person somewhere else. I heard the siren real close. The next thing I realized was all that chaos around me, the blood and the sharp pain of my arm—fractured in three different places, as I learned later—along with the terrible news of the death of that cousin, of whom I was very fond.

Ever since that day, probably the worst in my whole life, I can't help evoking a chill of terror, maybe for a couple of seconds, when I hear a siren. I always experience the same thing. Yesterday a police car passed by us on West 49th Street in Hialeah when my husband and I were returning home from the movies. Listening to the siren, I had that uneasy feeling so familiar to me now! I get over it almost immediately, but I can't help experiencing it over and over again. It is definitely a case of direct association.

This case is presented with the permission of Maria Ana Alvarez.

Examples in real life are easily found. The mere sight of a dog can come to elicit intense fear. The smell of food makes our own saliva flow. A stern glance from your boss can produce discomfort. The mere sight of a sexually attractive other person can produce arousal of all sorts. The sound of distant firecrackers can evoke a chill of terror in a soldier veteran of night patrols. The comforting smile of a loved one can create a pleasant feeling of well-being in you. In all these cases, the cue was neutral once upon a time; but through continued association with an existing emotion, it has acquired its current properties. Such associations can be made and unmade. Unmaking such associations is our major concern in this chapter.

Note also that in the *original* marriage of neutral cue and given emotion, the emotion was there because of some other cues that were definitely not neutral. The original dog bit you, let us say. The original pairing was definitely not neutral. The original sight of food accompanied eating a delicious meal. Stern glances came from your boss that first time, way back when he originally raked you over the coals for that mistake. Sex cues surrounded some original sex experience. The veteran had witnessed his best friend blown to pieces by a land mine on the original night patrol, when faint bursts of gunfire punctuated the night stillness. The comforting smile of your mother, say, was often associated with relief from the frights of childhood.

***Evidence for the Classical Conditioning Principle.*** On the positive conditioning side, there is good evidence to show that associating a positive event with a neutral cue leads people to like that cue. Jum Nunnally and Terry Faw gave 14 girls and 10 boys in the third grade the association between a "make-believe word" and 2 cents.[6] In a game setting, the child would choose among lids labeled GEX, MYV, and CIJ. On the back of each lid was a sign that said "Earn 2¢," "Pay 2¢," or nothing at all. The game was played until each child chose the label that earned 2 cents for six choices in a row. Thus, when the choices were over, one neutral label should have taken on a positive value and one should have taken on a negative value relative to the label that still remained neutral. After the choices and conditioning were over, the children were allowed to express preferences for stick figures having the three labels. They were also given a chance to push buttons that lighted up the same three labels in a picture box. Results clearly showed that the children preferred the stick figures and lighted up the labels that had earned them 2 cents earlier. In this study and a series of others, Nunnally has shown that associating a positive event with a neutral cue leads both children and college students to prefer that cue over others.[7]

On the negative conditioning side, there is also good evidence that associating a neutral cue with an aversive emotion results in the cue later eliciting that emotion. In a classic experiment, Solomon, Kamin, and Wynne gave dogs a terribly strong shock.[8] Afterward, the dogs were observed on hundreds of occasions to avoid the whole area (cue) where shock was delivered, long after the shock was turned off. Maria Alvarez's story in Case 10.1 relates a similar example of so-called one-trial traumatic learning. In short, there is abundant evidence that neutral cues come to elicit emotions with which they have been associated.[9]

***Associations from Associations.*** At this point, someone usually objects, "The simple process of association cannot possibly be responsible for the complex emotions I and other adults feel." This objection seriously underestimates the impressive ability of humans to build on and elaborate from classically conditioned associations. The growing child will feel emotions from not just one, but from a whole range of many cues that have some association with particular emotions. As verbal abilities develop, a capability to form verbal associations develops too. The name of a Ku Klux Klansman can come to elicit fear in an area where the Klan is strong —all through verbal association. On top of all these ways for associations to form, there is higher-order conditioning as well.

In *higher-order conditioning,* a neutral cue comes to elicit a given emotion by association with another cue that was once neutral but now has emotional value. Remember the Nunnally and Faw experiment with the nonsense words and pennies? Neutral nonsense words were paired with 2 cents, but what is the 2 cents? Do 2 pennies per se carry positive values? No, the pennies were once neutral but have acquired the properties of reward themselves. Thus the Nunnally and Faw study demonstrated higher-order conditioning.

In summary, the evidence and arguments in this section support the idea that even if classical conditioning were the only means to acquire emotions, we adults would walk through a dazzling world of emotions. The countless associations accumulate over the years so that when pressed, almost everyone has a preference or opinion about everything around him. Coupled with our enormous abilities to form associations mentally on the basis of words, picture images, and other symbols, we are easily capable of deriving a practically infinite range of personal emotions from the classical conditioning principle alone.

ACTIVITY 10.1.

Describe an example of the classical conditioning principle you have experienced or witnessed in someone else in the past month.

________________________________________

________________________________________

________________________________________

________________________________________

________________________________________

***Implications of the Classical Conditioning Principle.*** The classical conditioning principle specifies a basic process that is probably responsible for many of the emotions we feel as adults. If we have indeed learned our current emotions through conditioning, then we can also learn to change harmful emotions through relearning. This implication is extremely important, because *it is necessary for optimism about personal change*. Note that the "relearning" process is not tied to any one theory. Thus relearning can be viewed in the perspective of any theory that has something to say about emotional associations.

Also, the process of change will usually be slow because the process of original learning is usually gradual. Beyond traumatic learning and religious conversions, instant change in human adults is the exception rather than the rule. The implication is that emotional self-change is usually a matter of hard work.

## REDUCING FEARS USING SELF-DESENSITIZATION

### Background for Desensitization Principle

The desensitization principle is a specific *procedure* that employs the process of classical conditioning. The desensitization principle assumes that it is difficult, if not impossible, to actually experience a positive and a negative emotion at the same time. To be sure, we can intellectually think about two opposite emotions, but "to actually experience" them means a physical state of being. When in a conflict between two opposite emotions, one usually wins out or we alternate between one and the other. Suppose the bride's mother is torn between losing a daughter and gaining a son-in-law. On the one hand, she may be happy throughout the wedding, but not ecstatic. On the other hand, she may also alternate between bursting into tears and radiating joy.

The general procedure by which one emotion comes to replace another is called "counterconditioning." In his book *A Glossary of Behavioral Terminology,* Owen White defines *counterconditioning* as "any of several specific behavior therapies in which new conditioning procedures are instituted for the express purpose of counteracting previous conditioning."[10] In fact, systematic desensitization is a specific subvariety of counterconditioning. Desensitization is a tool that, until now, has been used in therapy. For this reason, we address the issues in regard to making it public.

A number of my colleagues have advised me not to write this book in general and this chapter in particular. The practical procedures for reducing fears make up some of the most effective tools in the repertoire of the modern-day therapist. Writing this chapter might be the equivalent of dispensing prescription drugs without a prescription, they say. I reply with two arguments. First, the content here is more like first aid, which everyone can use to keep relatively small problems from growing into larger ones. Second, the alternative is to concentrate the ability to alter emotions over time in the hands of psychologists, whose professional help is available mostly to those who can afford to pay for it. Since concentration of power is needed to abuse it, the antidote to concentration is widespread dispersion by giving psychology away, as George Miller recommends.[11] The whole idea of giving psychology away strikes me as similar to the idea of democracy, whereby power is distributed widely—at least in theory.

I further contend that forces outside our control have powerfully influenced all of us during our upbringings. Some of us were fortunate, but some of us were not so fortunate. Some of us may have suffered humiliating, crushing defeats in early attempts to get close to another person. Some of us learn to react to frustration with instant rage, a poor response at best. The least that social and clinical psychologists can do is to provide us with some practical means to affect and direct our own destinies, especially in how we identify and strive toward personal levels of optimal intimacy.

We will assume that negative emotions can easily stand in the way of positive emotions. In other words, before enjoying our positive emotions, we have to wipe out our negative emotions for at least awhile. The main emphasis will be on reducing the negative emotion of harmful fear. We will use the term *fear* rather than anxiety because *anxiety* means discomfort about things in general and in the future as opposed to a specific fear. All of us have some fears, and certainly a lot of fears are healthy. For example, we ought to fear falling into the open ditch.

We will view fears as emotional reactions to given cues. The feared cues can range from a specific fear of purple earthworms to a more general fear of meeting new people. Some fears are mild, as when we are about to ask the waitress to take back a glass of tainted tomato juice. Other fears can be so strong as to dominate, warp, and ruin a human life.

I do have sympathy for the position that loosing powerful therapy tools upon the corner newsstand requires some moral consideration and perhaps regulation as well.[12] However, before psychologists and politicians whip themselves into an ethical fury and envelop certain user information in a cocoon of restrictive regulations, they ought to look at the environment of psychology very carefully. In the outside world, extremely powerful forces are often free and unregulated to do untold emotional damage (and good). We adults knowingly create overmanned high school football teams and assembly lines where, sooner or later, everyone learns that he is expendible as a participant. The psychological damage for the majority in such settings is certainly enormous, especially in a society that stresses achievement by males. The advertising industry has succeeded in creating a nationwide breast fetish among males. Pornographers are reasonably free to create others. Parents are free to psychologically torture young children, as long as it is done *verbally*. The point I am making is that real-life opportunities to foster good positive emotions also allow opportunities to foster unhealthy emotions. Restricting the one also means restricting the other. The upshot is that instant legal restriction of certain user information (e.g., who can use desensitization) is unwise. The best policy would be to shine the light of new evidence wherever possible so that harmful and ineffective procedures are exposed.

In fact, the premature restriction by any professional or legislative organization of who can apply user information would probably be illegal. For example, if a law were passed saying that only doctoral-level therapists could employ desensitization, attention would soon focus on regulating where those unwanted emotions come from in the first place. And regulating the origins of harmful emotions would require placing restrictions on how parents can rear children and other hallmarks of freedom. In short, restricting the application of user information is likely unworkable.

A far better policy is to disseminate user information as widely as possible.

The best means for seeing that procedures for emotional changes are not abused when published in the public domain is an intelligent body of user-consumers. Specifically, you should look for several features in such information:

1. Detailed instructions for when the use of certain procedures is appropriate.
2. Instructions about when to seek professional advice.
3. A context of human values (versus mere details about a "tool you can use on yourself or your friends").
4. Reference to recent *research* results (theories rest on the results of research; the reverse is not true; that is, when good research is in conflict with theory, you throw out or change the theory, not the data).
5. Specific information about dangerous procedures and the dangers of misusing the recommended procedures.

Even after all those cautious considerations, systematic desensitization emerges as the perfect candidate for reducing unwanted fears in user information. As therapist Gerald Rosen concludes, "It would appear that self-administered systematic desensitization is generally 'safe and effective when used as directed.' "[13]

Please accept my apologies for all these preliminaries, but they were needed. Now we consider the desensitization principle itself.

## Desensitization Principle

Statement of Desensitization Principle: If you arrange for your other person to experience an emotion incompatible with fear while at the same time exposing him (her) to a graded series of cues that more and more closely resemble a feared cue, that feared cue will gradually lose its power to produce fear.

The desensitization principle is a slightly broadened version of Joseph Wolpe's "reciprocal inhibition principle: If a response inhibiting anxiety can be made to occur in the presence of anxiety-evoking stimuli [cues], it will weaken the bond between these stimuli and the anxiety."[14] Wolpe is generally credited with the invention of desensitization.[15]

On the one hand, there is heated controversy about the relative roles of physical, mental, and social processes in desensitization.[16] On the other hand, there is general agreement that a great deal of good evidence from clinical research studies supports the effectiveness of properly conducted desensitization procedures. The numerous experiments are thoroughly reviewed elsewhere.[17]

A confusion often arises about the distinction between extinction and desensitization. In extinction, there is no series of cues that leads gradually up to the most feared cue; the feared cues are simply presented alone. In contrast, desensitization always involves (1) a series of cues, (2) an emotion incompatible with fear, and (3) pairing the cues with the emotion in the manner we shall now describe.

## Armchair Desensitization

### Illustrative Case

**Case 10.2.** Mary is afraid of tests to the point she may flunk out of college and wreck her life plans (see Figure 10.2). It began about a year ago, when she resoundingly flunked a test. Since that time, her fear of tests has snowballed and now she begins to tremble the day before a test. She cannot sleep the night before, and her mental processes are severely lowered during the test session. Mary has no other major life problems. She seeks help at the counseling center. In the interview, her counselor ascertains that this fear is a fairly isolated and specific fear. The counselor explains that many fears are emotionally conditioned through association and often seem illogical to the person herself, as in Mary's case. In view of Mary's past history of personal competence, Mary is put on a program of self-desensitization.

The first step in her program is to learn deep muscle relaxation. She is given a manual that instructs her about how to relax her muscles gradually. Such gradual, or progressive, muscle relaxation means relaxing one particular group of muscles at a time. The manual was written by Gerald Rosen, a therapist-researcher skilled in the area of teaching people to desensitize their own fears. The manual is reproduced as Appendix A in this book (you should now skim Appendix A). The manual proved especially valuable for Mary, who could barely spare time to attend her classes, let alone spend hours learning to relax. So, she took the manual home to learn relaxation before going to sleep. However, after three sessions, she found that turning the pages of the manual interfered with relaxing her arms. She

**Figure 10.2.** Here college students are taking an exam. For some the exam situation is routine; but for others, such as Mary in Case 10.2, it is traumatic. (Photograph by Charles Blakey.)

called her counselor to ask what to do. Although this difficulty was rare, the counselor had heard it before. She noted that Mary should have learned the relaxation program well enough beforehand to ensure that absolutely no physical activity would be needed in armchair desensitization programs. She advised Mary to make her own tape recording from the manual, but only if Mary had trouble remembering the relaxation program. Then she could listen to it and not move at all.[18] Mary did so and mastered deep muscle relaxation soon after. It was a gradual learning process; but after several practice sessions, she learned to become relaxed within just a few minutes.

Another step in self-desensitization was the construction of Mary's own personal fear hierarchy. When desensitization actually begins, explained the counselor, Mary would first relax deeply in an armchair. Then Mary would approach the feared situation, an exam in her case, using mental images. Mary's *fear hierarchy* is simply a personalized series of scenes that gradually approach the feared situation (test for Mary). Mary still wasn't sure how the whole process worked, but she made up a list of scenes:

1. I walk in the classroom door to the test.
2. I think about happier days.
3. The instructor hands out the test.
4. I receive my test paper.

Full of pride, Mary took this list to her counselor and asked if she could begin to use it. The counselor diplomatically told Mary that a few improvements would be needed, but that this fear hierarchy was a nice beginning. Then she gently described some desirable features of fear hierarchies as they relate to Mary's list of 4 steps. Fear hierarchies should have a fair number of steps, with 10 or 12 being about right. There is always the danger that the steps will be too great. The difference between steps 2 and 3 seems quite great, and Mary would do well to make out a 12-step hierarchy with smaller steps throughout. A second problem concerns ordering the items inside the hierarchy. In fact, thinking about happier days is far *less* frightening than entering the classroom, Mary admits after thinking about it; so step 2 should have come before step 1. A final problem is that step 2 is really too vague to be a scene. Mary learns that vivid and specific words should be used, so step 2 will be eliminated. So she tries once again and comes up with the following list:

1. The letter *E* in red.
2. The word "exam" in soft white letters.
3. Filling out a form that registers me for a course.
4. Getting out of bed for the first class session in the course.

5. Driving to school on the first day of class.
6. Entering the classroom on the first day of class.
7. Receiving the course outline that contains the exam schedule.
8. The instructor finishing class by reminding students that the first exam is one week away.
9. Getting out of bed on the morning of the first exam.
10. Entering the classroom and taking a seat on the exam day.
11. The instructor handing out the first exam paper to another student across the room.
12. The instructor handing me my exam paper.

Mary's counselor approves this hierarchy with delight and tells Mary that she is now ready to desensitize her fear. Mary is to go home and relax as usual. When she is fully relaxed and her mind is a blank, she is to imagine scene 1 for about 5 seconds. If she can easily picture the scene for 5 seconds, she is then to imagine it for longer intervals, gradually working up to 30 seconds. When she can imagine it for 30 seconds, she makes her mind blank for 30 seconds and moves up to follow the same process with scene 2. If at any time she begins to feel fear or discomfort in the least degree, she is to blank her mind for 30 seconds and drop back to the previous level. In short, she is to work her way up the hierarchy totally at her own speed. If her mind wanders or she feels the slightest fear, she is to stop, blank her mind, and resume at a safe (nonfearful) level.

Mary goes home that night for a self-desensitization session that will last the usual 30 minutes. The next day, she excitedly calls her counselor to inform her that she made it up to step 3 with no problems at all. The next week, Mary does run into a problem. She is at step 9 and cannot make it to step 10 without some real fear. Her counselor tells her to insert three steps between current steps 9 and 10 so the gap won't be so great. Mary creates the following scenes and proceeds through to step 12:

9a. Driving to school on the exam day.
9b. Walking from the parking lot toward the classroom on the exam day.
9c. Entering the classroom building on the exam day.

Mary continues self-desensitization until she can imagine step 12 without discomfort. Her counselor praises this accomplishment. Mary goes on to take her next real classroom test with only a minimum of fear.

### Ins and Outs of Armchair Desensitization

***Test Fears.*** Case 10.2 is a composite of similar cases that are true. In fact, desensitization of test fears has even been automated. In "Automated Group Desensitization for Test Anxiety," Donner and Guerney report that they brought groups of students together in a dimly lit room filled with padded leather chairs.[19] The students then learned to relax and ascend a *common* fear hierarchy, all using tape-recorded instructions. Because the same hierarchy had to be used for all students, the steps had to be small. So the hierarchy was beefed up to 29 scenes. The researchers found an improvement in grade-point average after these procedures were followed, as compared to a waiting-list control group that was treated later.

***Evidence about Self-desensitization.*** In both Case 10.2 and the Donner and Guerney research, the "self-desensitization" really amounted to carrying out instructions under the guidance of an expert (see Figure 10.3). At the time of this writing, there is abundant evidence that college students can (1) learn to relax and (2) ascend a fear inventory under the tape-recorded guidance of an expert without ever coming face-to-face with that expert during relaxation or desensitization.[20] Research using automated self-desensitization procedures has generally been done in the laboratory. These "minimal therapist contact" procedures have been successful in alleviating fears of snakes,[21] mice,[22] dissecting laboratory animals,[23] wooden kitchen matches,[24] public speaking, driving, and authority figures.[25] The reduction in fear is usually measured convincingly in a real situation where the feared thing is actually approached.[26] In the research of Peter Lang, the research has also included measures of heart rate, perspiration (measured by skin conductance of electricity), respiration rate, and self-reported feelings of fear on questionnaires. Reduction in fear was lasting, as indicated by a follow-up from 6 to 10 months later.[27]

A few controlled studies have looked at the effectiveness of completely self-administered desensitization at home using materials pro-

**Figure 10.3.** Armchair desensitization in progress. After learning the procedures for relaxation, he will no longer use the tape recorder. The young man will close his eyes when visualizing images. (Photograph by Charles Blakey.)

vided by researchers. These results are just beginning to filter out from the research labs, but the general finding is that about half of the people with specific fears are able to desensitize at home and eliminate their fears.[28] In short, there is every indication that self-desensitization can work. In cases in which it did not work, the possibility of unskilled application or otherwise ineffective procedures exists. Therefore we now consider some important details of armchair desensitization in the form of a checklist.

***Desensitization Checklist.*** Considerations and procedures in this chapter are meant to be used by users, but only on well-defined emotions and only after reality testing with someone, hopefully your instructor. By reality testing I mean telling someone you trust exactly what you plan to do. Before using desensitization to reduce fear or changing other of your emotions, go down the following checklist. Satisfy yourself that you are abiding by the recommendations in each category. In this list, I usually replace the term "fear" with "emotion," because later in the chapter we briefly consider the alteration of other emotions.

—1. Can I change an emotion or should a professional do it? To be a candidate for change by me, an undesired emotion should be simple and not devastatingly strong. "Simple" means that I can label it and also label the occasions on which it occurs. For example, if I feel depressed with life in general and cannot pinpoint when such feelings occur, the emotion is not simple. If the emotional problem is not simple, a professional is needed to identify it. Imagine the danger if the object of fear were not correctly identified! The same holds for powerful emotions. Remember that user information is somewhat like first aid.

—2. Am I avoiding all aversive procedures and punishment when changing fears? If I or a loved one presently experience fear, the last things I want in my self-change procedures are negative or aversive events. (More on this subject later.)

—3. Am I really relaxing? Wolpe reports that failure to relax is common and needs to be checked.[29] The usual procedure is to work on arms, head, neck, shoulders, back, legs, and so on before any desensitizing takes place. See Appendix A for details. The first several sessions are devoted solely to learning to relax. A helpful procedure is to ask a friend to help check your relaxation.

—4. Is my hierarchy simple? Does it rather completely cover the range of situations in which I am afraid? Wolpe reports that multiple fears exist and are interrelated. For one man he treated, two lesser fears were derived from an overriding fear of death. If the answer to either question is no, do not attempt to change it yourself. Seek professional help.

—5. Does my hierarchy consist of small steps? One never knows in advance. If fear is experienced at a particular step, add steps to make sure the steps are small enough. Then resume at a safe (nonfearful) step.

—6. Will changing an emotion of mine have effects on others I care for?

—7. Am I able to actually visualize images? Some people are not, so armchair desensitization will not work for them.

—8. Am I progressing at a rate that is comfortable for me? If no, slow down. The following are some figures provided by therapists Joseph Wolpe and Hal Arkowitz to indicate approximate time dimensions involved in desensitization:[30]

a. Length of visualized scenes: Each scene is visualized for 3–5 seconds at first, always terminated immediately when the negative emotion is felt; length is gradually worked up to 30 seconds per image before moving on to the next scene.
b. Interval between scenes: 10–30 seconds.
c. Length of each session 15–30 minutes without interruption.
d. Number of presentations of each scene before moving up to a higher level in the hierarchy: 3 or 4 is usual, with 10 or more not unusual.
e. Number of sessions ranges from 6 to over 100.

—9. Do I know this chapter and all its warnings cold? If not, review.

—10. Have I got a buddy to help me?

—11. Have I included the following elements into my procedures?

a. Clear definition of the emotion to be changed by specifying the nature of the cues that cause it to appear.
b. Construction of a fear hierarchy.
c. Specifying the emotion incompatible with fear that is to be used. (The incompatible emotion is deep muscle relaxation in the case of systematic desensitization.)
d. Review of all earlier principles as a checklist for procedures that might be helpful (as illustrated in examples later in the chapter).
e. Review of this checklist.

—12. Have I checked out the procedures I plan to use with at least one trusted other person for reality testing? If not, before plunging in, I should.

—13. Am I avoiding overly high hopes? This danger, called the "negative placebo effect," is probably the biggest danger in self-desensitization; it is discussed in the following section.

—14. Am I continuing to run down this checklist every few days, whether I am making progress or not? If not, do.

***Negative Placebo Effect.*** A wise caution comes from Steven Kopel and Hal Arkowitz concerning overly high hopes, or the *negative placebo effect:* "The negative placebo effect refers to cases where the client receives a drug with strong expectations of improvement. To the extent that the client does not actually improve, he may then infer that his problem has actually gotten worse, since even a powerful drug did not help him."[31] In conversation with me, clinician Hal Arkowitz has wisely advised to spread the word that initial failures in self-change procedures are to be expected. So be warned to expect generally slow and gradual change if the procedures work at all. In the absence of change, his clients sometimes began to feel "I must be terribly sick, perhaps going crazy" when nothing of the sort was true. In all likelihood, the procedures simply did not work, sometimes because of mistakes in applying them (e.g., steps too far apart in hierarchy).

Beyond the negative placebo effect, there seems to be an absence of harmful results that can be traced to desensitization procedures per se. Used properly, desensitization appears to be relatively harmless.

While falsely high expectations and impatience may sabotage self-desensitization, being somewhat optimistic at the outset seems to make no difference. In a carefully executed program of research, McGlynn and his colleagues have exposed fearful persons to a variety of expectations before and during automated desensitization.[32] The curious but consistent result has been that desensitization procedures reduced fears and that expectations had no effect. Although their results are strikingly consistent, they may apply mainly to volunteers for experiments who may possess some measure of hope before allowing themselves to be participants in research in the first place.

### Illustrative Nursing Case

**Case 10.3.** The following case study is presented word-for-word as it appeared in the *Journal of Consulting and Clinical Psychology;* it was written by Max W. Rardin.

*History and clinical data. The client was an 18-year-old single female in the first year of a nursing program and had been a student in an introductory psychology class taught by the author. At the encouragement of her nursing instructors, she contacted the author about the possibility of controlling her fear of blood. An interview indicated that she had a limited phobia. She reported no dissatisfaction in other areas of her life, was achieving above average grades, and had good relations with family, peers, and faculty.*

*The following history of the problem was gathered during the first scheduled session. The client indicated that she had been fearful of blood and generally squeamish for several years but her fears had not been a serious concern until she entered nursing—a career goal for her since childhood.*

*Her reaction to blood and possible physical injury varied from moderate discomfort to dizziness and nausea depending on the topic and circumstances. The immediate concern was her reaction to the films shown in nursing classes which vividly depicted various medical conditions. On a number of occasions, she had to put her head down or leave the room. She felt she would faint or vomit if she continued to observe the film. This reaction was interfering with her performance in the classes in which the films were shown, and the nursing faculty was beginning to question her suitability for the profession. Both S and her instructors felt it was imperative that she gain control over her reactions before the start of clinical classes in the hospital or she would not be able to continue in the program.*

*Treatment procedure. During the latter part of the first session, S was given a detailed description of desensitization as it would apply to her situation. The next three sessions were devoted to training in relaxation and construction of a fear hierarchy. The client was capable of deep relaxation and apparently experienced vivid imagery. The 16 items in the fear hierarchy involved increasing amounts of blood due to injury, surgery, and childbirth.*

*Except for changes in the placement of some items in the hierarchy, desensitization had proceeded routinely through seven items during the next four sessions when the school term ended. The seven items completed were: a scraped elbow; a torn hangnail; squeezing out one drop of blood; a cut in the sole of the foot; compound fracture of the leg; needle in the skin for a stitch; and a gash in arm with flowing blood.*

*The remaining nine items which had not been dealt with were: bleeding from nose and mouth due to internal injury; a sucking chest wound; seeing a blood sample drawn; blood foaming from mouth; water breaking for childbirth; head emerging and effect on mother; blood flowing after birth; delivery of placenta; and stitching after delivery. At this point, in order to continue treatment, the client was faced with the alternative of commuting 100 miles or attempting an experimental self-desensitization procedure suggested by the author.*

*The experimental procedures were explained as follows. The relaxation technique and the general style of the monologue accompanying the presentation of each item was reviewed. She was reminded that the goal was to imagine increasingly vivid and personally relevant scenes. The importance of not proceeding if anxiety interrupted her relaxation was stressed. She was given general examples of monologue to accompany the rest of the items. On request, the client was able to produce additional appropriate examples. The possibility of arranging an observation of childbirth at a hospital was discussed. After further assurance that contact with the author would be available if there was difficulty, the client decided to attempt this program.*

*It was agreed she would work on the hierarchy each night when in bed under the following conditions. She was instructed to retire in her usual fashion, induce relaxation, and to begin with the highest item already completed. Work with the items was to be limited to approximately 1 hour. She was told to omit the procedure if she were sick, unusually tired, or disturbed by other matters. She later reported engaging in self-desensitization 5 or 6 nights a week for 6 weeks.*

*At the end of the 6 weeks, she contacted the author and reported being able to imagine comfortably all of the items on the list and having visited the hospital maternity ward. She was late for the delivery but did see the cord being cut and the delivery of the placenta. At that point, she felt mildly faint and left. She requested that she be allowed to use smelling salts at her next birth observation since her dizziness was not accompanied by nausea. Because she attributed this faintness more to excitement than anxiety, she was given permission to use smelling salts with the condition that she not force herself to observe if she felt highly anxious. She observed her next delivery successfully. The last session occurred after her return to school and was primarily a review of events to complete the case history. She reported having observed a complete delivery, successfully taken blood samples, and having her own blood sample taken. One year later she was a student nurse on an obstetrics ward fully assisting in deliveries to the point of dabbing blood between vaginal stitches. Surgical repair after delivery had been the highest item on her hierarchy.*

*Discussion. The client's progress with self-desensitization was apparently routine with no report of difficulty other than the incident which resulted in the request for smelling salts. At the conclusion of the self-desensitization procedure in a tape recording describing her thoughts on the experience, she revealed a technique she had improvised for maintaining control of her fear when approaching an anxiety-arousing situation. As she neared the situation, she would subvocally repeat to herself phrases abstracted from the desensitization monologue. The phrase "it's not me" was most often used. Her use of this phrase as an aid to discrimination appears similar to that of "it's just a dream" applied in the treatment of a recurrent dream reported by Greer and Silverman.[33] Both studies suggest that perhaps the discrimination process is crucial in controlling phobic reactions.*

*The need to use such phrases might raise a question about the degree of desensitization. Since she was doing so much of the work on her own, it may well be that desensitization was continuing at the time she reported her impressions. She later reported a decline in the use of the phrases.*

*This case suggests that self-desensitization may be a useful variation from the usual technique for clinical application. In research, it offers a method by which the contribution of the therapist to desensitization might be more precisely defined.*

Max W. Rardin, "Treatment of a Phobia by Partial Self-Desensitization: A Case Study," *Journal of Counseling and Clinical Psychology,* 1969, *33,* pp. 125–126. 

### Role-Playing Desensitization

In armchair desensitization, you are physically relaxed in an armchair while you mentally move up your hierarchy. *Role-playing desensitization* involves moving up the fear hierarchy, but in a way physically different than in armchair desensitization. It means moving up the fear hierarchy in a "safe" role-playing situation, wherein all participants realize that the purpose is for practice and training. No muscle relaxation is required,

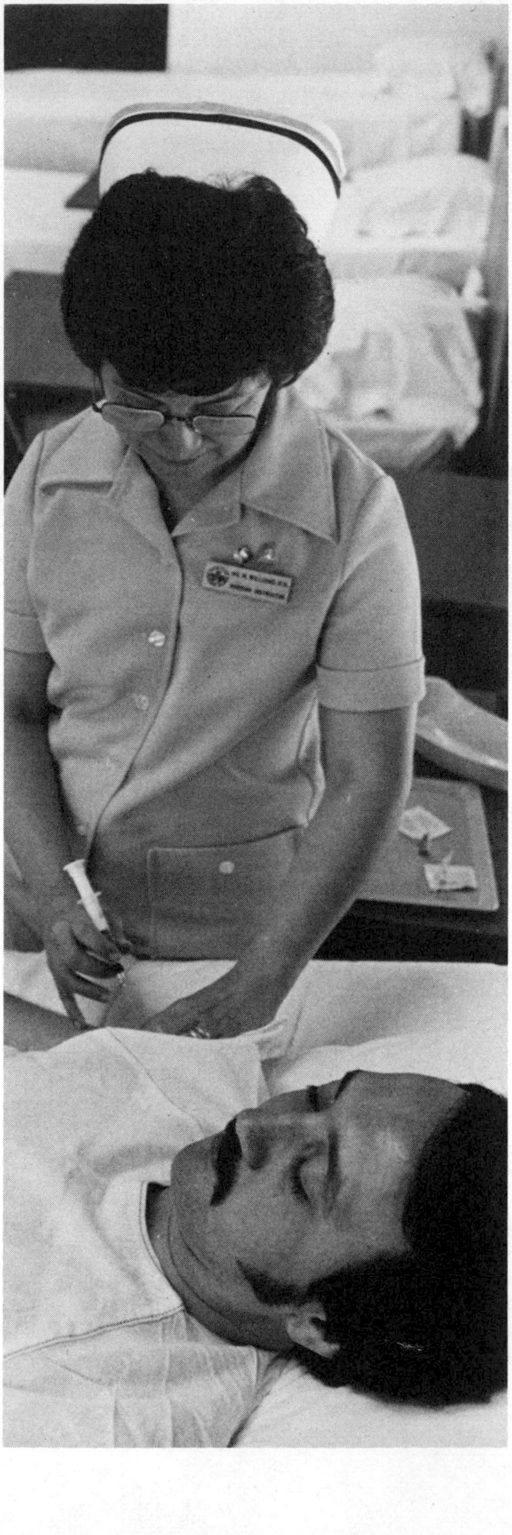

but there is a fear hierarchy. Instead of a scene to be imagined mentally, each scene is acted out for practice in role-playing desensitization. Rules for going up the hierarchy remain the same. For example, when fear is felt, the scene is stopped immediately and progress resumes at a nonfearful level. Role-playing desensitization procedures are discussed later (p. 213). We can view role-playing desensitization as being halfway between the armchair and real life.

### In Vivo Desensitization

Desensitization can also be carried out in the real world, rather than in the make-believe worlds of role playing and armchairs. In in vivo desensitization, the fear hierarchy is ascended in surroundings where at least one other person does not realize the training aspect of your actions. *In vivo* means in real life, in contrast to *in vitro,* which means in an artificial or test-tube environment. In other words, in vivo desensitization is for real; you travel around and actually enter real-life situations (see Figure 10.4). In vivo desensitization is covered later on starting on page 215. We now summarize briefly.

### Summary

Up to this point, we have considered emotions as learned associations. Because of the enormous complexity of human thought processes, it is possible to learn a practically infinite variety of emotions. This is so even if we use only classical conditioning, verbal association, and higher-order conditioning as devices to explain the learning process. Unfortunately, harmful emotional reactions are learned as well as beneficial ones. In this chapter, we emphasize reducing harmful fears using self-desensitization.

The research to date gives us three kinds of desensitization for reducing unwanted fears. All three use the desensitization principle. This means taking a cautious and extremely gradual approach to the object of fear while you experience an emotion that is incompatible with fear. In armchair desensitization, the feared thing is approached via a series of mental images while the person is relaxed in an armchair. The incompatible

**Figure 10.4.** In vivo desensitization in progress. This student nurse has nearly completed ascending her fear hierarchy in real-life situations and is now watching an injection. (Photograph by Charles Blakey.)

emotion is deep muscle relaxation. In role-playing desensitization, you approach the object of fear in a series of practice scenes in which everyone involved knows the purpose is 100 percent rehearsal. In in vivo desensitization, you enter a series of situations in the real world that gradually approximate the object of fear. In all cases, the graded series of scenes approaching the feared thing is called the fear hierarchy. In all applications the approach to the object of fear is cautious and slow. It cannot be hurried or crammed into a single session or two.

**DESENSITIZATION STRATEGY**

### What Actually Happens in Desensitization?

In our thinking up to this point, we have treated desensitization as a procedure for rewiring our emotional associations. According to this view, desensitization causes beneficial changes in the passive person. However, another view is available, and it gives more credit to you as a person. Marvin Goldfried claims that "it would seem more appropriate to construe systematic desensitization as more of an active process, directed toward learning of a general anxiety-reducing skill, rather than passive desensitization to specific aversive stimuli [events]."[34] Goldfried's view greatly expands the ways we can look at what is happening in desensitization; the skill for conquering fears can have muscular aspects, visceral aspects, mental anticipation aspects, self-confidence aspects, and so on. Any strategy you might have about desensitization would do well to consider all these aspects because all may play some role.

In particular, mental self-perception may play a large role. Think what fear is like. Think what it would be like to feel the chill of fear and your stomach sink as you extend your trembling hand to meet a beautiful member of the opposite sex. The self-perception of past failures would likely breed future failures as well. On the other hand, conquering the molehill called step 1 on your fear hierarchy would certainly lead to some mental changes as well as a rewiring of your emotional electricity. You would have at least one success. Climbing up the hierarchy means repeated successes, and your self-perception would include not only dismal past failures but also some growing successes. There is some good evidence that watching yourself master a painful challenge leads to mental changes later on.

Kopel and Arkowitz paid 45 female undergraduates at the University of Oregon $2 each to be in an experiment to study electric shock. One-third of the women role played calm reactions during shock.[35] Another third role played upset or disturbed reactions during shock. The final third did not role play at all. In a final series of judgments after the role playing was over, the women became more similar to their earlier role-playing performances, relative to women in the control group who did not role play at all. Those who had merely acted calm earlier actually displayed higher tolerances for shock later on, and vice versa. In short, they acted themselves into a new way of thinking *and* a new way of acting.

Obviously, it is not certain that changed self-perceptions are essential for desensitization to work. However, there is evidence that our self-concept is based at least in part on what we see ourselves doing, as the bicycle model implies. In fact, Lazarus reports greater success in desensitization when a definite series of hurdles is set up. Among other things, the series of hurdles probably provided his clients with some bona fide success experiences.[36]

To support his own theory of self-perception, Bem induced college students to act out a variety of actions that they would not otherwise have performed.[37] In one study, the students were induced to claim that certain cartoons were funny, when in fact those very cartoons had been rated as neutral by the same students some weeks earlier.[38] The results showed that when the students were later asked for their honest ratings, they rated the cartoons as funny. Using a variety of similar tasks, Bem has produced evidence to indicate that our attitudes about ourselves come in part from what we see ourselves doing and acting.

### Desensitization Toward Reality

We will now assume that improvements in self-perception toward a view of self as calm and competent are part and parcel of successful desensitization of all kinds. We will also assume that your perceptions of social reality are accurate. These assumptions imply a strategy of desensitization toward reality.

It is reasonable to assume that going up a desensitization hierarchy in vivo is more convincing *to the doer* than going up that same hierarchy using role playing or doing it while relaxing in an armchair. Therefore it is probably most effective to start out with in vivo desensitization and resort to role playing and armchair procedures (in that order) only when needed. HOWEVER, remember that this strategy remains a prediction because the appropriate research has not been done.

In other words, we can theorize that the progression from armchair to role playing to in vivo desensitization is in itself a larger hierarchy leading toward reality. This larger, or metahierarchy, is certainly headed in the correct direction because the goal of any and all fear desensitization is fearless performance in vivo. This general strategy implies some tactics as well.

The tactical starting point for desensitization, then, ought to be as close to reality as possible. Thus try in vivo desensitization first. If you still feel fear, recheck your procedures. Especially important is making step 1 extremely free of fear, even to the point of being absurdly funny. If the fear of heights is the problem, let step 1 be standing on a piece of paper. Humor might just be an effective incompatible emotion. If success eludes your best attempts at in vivo desensitization, don't lose heart because you have backup procedures available. In such a case, drop back one level to role-playing desensitization. If success escapes you here as well, there is one more retreat: armchair desensitization.

So much for retreats. There are also advances you can make toward reality. Once fairly well along in, say, armchair desensitization, you may be able to advance one level to role playing. In this case, it would certainly be best to start at the lowest possible step in the role-playing hierarchy, while finishing up the armchair hierarchy separately. Therapists in fact employ mixtures of armchair, role playing, and in vivo desensitization. They do role playing in their offices and give in vivo homework assignments.

Remember that the tactics discussed are but reasonable predictions submitted for your judgment. They are all subordinate to the overriding consideration in desensitization that you never experience discomfort. Therefore if discomfort appears at even the lowest steps on an in vivo hierarchy, for example, it is best to play it safe and begin with more comfortable role-playing or armchair procedures.

We will return to these matters of tactics in later examples of specific applications. At present, there are tactical considerations we must give to reward and modeling procedures.

### Reward in Desensitization

In the desensitization checklist given earlier, "review of all earlier principles" was given as an element of desensitization. Clearly, advancing even the least amount up a desensitization hierarchy deserves a handsome reward. All indications about the effectiveness of reward predict that progress in desensitization will be greater if improvements are rewarded. Therefore reward your own improvement and progress in desensitization, especially at the beginning. For example, learning to achieve deep relaxation more quickly or advancing a level on the hierarchy surely deserves a substantial reward. Of course, the reward should be administered after the desensitization session so as not to disrupt it. And there will surely be individuals for whom the knowledge of their own accomplishment will be reward enough. These people will not want to use any external reward at all; rather, they will want to keep careful records to document their progress. *Self*-reward will likely work best.

### Modeling in Desensitization

Research on desensitization has shown modeling to be an effective ingredient of desensitization. Perhaps the classic study here is that of Bandura, Blanchard, and Ritter. They took snake-phobic individuals into the laboratory and exposed them to one of three treatments. One group got standard armchair desensitization. Another got automated armchair desensitization that used a reversible movie projector, which was controlled by each individual to provide a visual image rather than a mental one. The third group received live modeling with guided participation. "At each step, the experimenter himself performed fearless behavior and gradually led subjects [participants] into touching, stroking and then holding the midsection of the snake's body with gloved and then bare hands. . . ."[39] This third treatment proved most effective; the other two provided an intermediate level of relief. What does this research show?

The research on modeling in desensitization has generally been done in a hybrid situation that is halfway between role playing and in vivo, namely, approaching the real thing in a laboratory. Both automated and live modeling seem to work. Also, the experimenter's companionship seems to help. What do these conclusions imply?

Modeling procedures probably assist in desensitization if they are correctly used. "Correctly used" means at least three things: (1) At any given level of a particular hierarchy, observation of a fearless model before you join the scene at that level will probably make it easier for you to join the scene. (2) The model must be fearless or calm while acting. (3) The model ought to be faded out of the scene before long; otherwise, the model might become essential. All these implications are in line with a broad area of social psychological research about the effect of companions in anxious situations. The broader area of research shows that companions reduce stress, but only if they are calm or otherwise interfere with the fearful person's reactions.[40]

The strategic and tactical thoughts in this section apply to self-desensitization in which you perform the tasks of private, sergeant, and general alike. We now turn to the specific fear that keeps people apart more than any other: fear of other people.

## NEW ASSERTIVE ACTIONS TO REPLACE OLD FEAR REACTIONS

### The Fear of People

ACTIVITY 10.2.

Imagine you are standing in line at a theater. Suddenly somebody pushes in front of you in line. What would you do? Would you act differently if you thought the ticket supply were about to run out? Would you act differently if accompanied by your spouse or date?

______________________________

______________________________

______________________________

______________________________

ACTIVITY 10.3.

You are at an office cocktail party and you notice the boss's wife wearing a strikingly beautiful bracelet. What would you do?

______________________________

______________________________

______________________________

______________________________

ACTIVITY 10.4.

You order a steak medium rare, but the waiter brings you one you could grind up and sell for lampblack. What would you do?

______________________________

______________________________

______________________________

______________________________

In Activities 10.2, 10.3, and 10.4, something called "assertiveness" is called for. You would be expected to assert yourself. Assertiveness in the appropriate situations is healthy, and a lack of assertiveness keeps people apart. Oftentimes a general fear of other people blocks the establishment of healthy interaction. Is such a fear real? Is it widespread? Everyday experience says so, and some preliminary research agrees that social anxiety is real and fairly common.

Researcher Thomas Borkovec and his associates report that "at the University of Iowa in 1971 and 1973, 15.5% of the introductory psychology males and 11.5% of the females report some (or greater) fear of being with a member of the opposite sex and 32% of the males and 38.5% of the females feel some or greater fear of meeting someone for the first time."[41] Not only is fear of people seemingly real and common, but it also seems to be vague and stubborn. (Of course, specific fears of people also exist, such as fear of authority figures or fear of one certain person.)

Several studies show that a generalized fear of people is more stubborn to reduce than a more focused fear, such as a fear of water. For one thing, reactions reflecting a generalized fear of people do not weaken very much with repeated exposure,[42] whereas a fear of spiders, for example, does.[43] For another, general social anxiety seems to yield less to desensitization than do specific fears.[44] Generalized social anxiety appears related to a lack of assertiveness and probably loneliness as well. Recall that the young men in Vello Sermat's research who rated social situations as more fearful also described themselves as more lonely (Chapter 2).[45] We now go on to describe the antidote to nonassertiveness and fear, namely, assertiveness.

### Healthy Assertiveness Defined

In their popular book *Your Perfect Right: A Guide to Assertive Behavior,* Alberti and Emmons distinguish between assertiveness and aggression. "Behavior which enables a person to act in his own best interests, to stand up for himself without undue anxiety, to exercise his rights without denying the rights of others is called *assertive behavior.*"[46] Wolpe emphasizes the expression of your emotional feelings in his definition of assertiveness when he states, "Assertive behavior is defined as the proper expression of any emotion other than anxiety towards another person."[47] The inability to disclose such emotions probably acts as a major block in attaining optimal emotional intimacy, wherein self-disclosure is important.

According to Alberti and Emmons, standing up for your rights is not always easy. By being assertive, you may encounter reactions of grumbling, tantrums, psychosomatic illnesses, and overapologizing from the person who is exploiting you. These you can ignore, they say.[48] But the other person may react with hostility or seek revenge, which cannot be ignored.

Let us at once affirm the right to be nonassertive if you so choose. However, the concern here is with problem nonassertiveness. *Problem nonassertiveness* causes discomfort to you and often the other person. When we exhibit problem nonassertiveness, we often reward another person for taking unfair advantage. In short, problem nonassertiveness always warrants change by the definition given in this paragraph.

### Origins of Nonassertiveness

#### The Social Skill Viewpoint

Before plunging headlong into the available procedures, we must first evaluate two very different views about the causes of problem nonassertiveness. If valid, each would imply different procedures for change.

The social skill viewpoint says that low assertiveness exists because the person never learned the appropriate actions. As D. Richard Laws and Michael Serber claim, "There are many cases where the appropriate interpersonal responses are not in the subject's repertoire. This is more than a failure to be assertive; it is a total behavior deficit."[49]

**Case 10.4.** Doug has always admired Rita. She represents the ideal date and possibly mate. Doug has never approached her, although he would like to ask for a date. Once he was asked why he did not just call her up and ask for a lunch date. He replied by blurting out several excuses, but admitting he did not really know. Tonight his roommate got him to go to a party. Later in the evening, his roommate introduced him to Rita and then left the pair alone. Doug became tongue-tied. After a painful silence of several seconds, Doug looked at the floor and asked her a question about the weather. She replied, "Oh, yes," and drifted away to refill her glass. Doug felt bad and left the party to mull over his failure to engage Rita in conversation. He mulled and sulked for weeks.

According to the social skill viewpoint, Doug probably never learned how to engross another person in conversation. This viewpoint is supported by survey data concerning the background of certain college males. In summarizing a self-report survey of "nondater" college males who seldom dated, William Martinson and James Zerface found that nondaters exhibited misinformation and/or a lack of information concerning dating behavior. "It appeared in some instances that an *S* [a nondater] had simply never 'learned' to date."[50] Actually, far from sounding pessimistic, Martinson and Zerface's position clearly implies that some dating inhibitions can be remedied by skill training in the dating area.

#### The Anxiety Viewpoint

Another viewpoint holds that low assertiveness comes from blockage by a brick wall called "anxiety." In other words, if the anxiety were removed, Doug (Case 10.4) would clearly have been able to engage Rita in conversation. He had the skill but was overcome by anxiety and fear.

Research by Arkowitz and his colleagues

supports the anxiety viewpoint.[51] In a comparison of nondaters with daters, all were volunteers and the nondaters wanted to date more. Arkowitz could find no differences between the groups on a battery of tests concerning social skill. But to his surprise, he found striking difference in how nondaters versus daters *perceived* their social skill. Nondaters underestimated their social skill, while daters overestimated their social skill. When participants were requested to estimate social skill in others, overestimations and underestimations failed to appear.[52] Socially anxious people even remember more of their faults than nonanxious people.[53] Thus nondaters downgraded themselves, but not others. Even when provided with a ringing success (highly positive interview with a female), the nondaters attributed their own success to more external causes than did the daters.

In short, the picture emerging from Arkowitz's line of research suggests not a skill deficit but rather a tendency to be overly self-critical on the part of nondaters. Possibly, the nondaters were more sensitive to negative social feedback and needed desensitization—literally. The anxiety viewpoint about low assertiveness is also optimistic, however, because its advocates assume that the anxiety can be lessened.

### Evaluation of the Two Viewpoints

Given the current data, the relative importance of social skill versus anxiety in low assertiveness remains unresolved. Both factors likely exist. Arkowitz's emphasis on perceptual factors entails some problems because the finding that daters and nondaters do not differ in social skill might be due to his use of insensitive instruments to measure social skill. In fact, Arkowitz is quick to acknowledge "that in many cases, there may indeed be an important factor of social skill deficiency."[54]

In practice, the two viewpoints imply different procedures for change. If social skills are lacking, then change means skill training. If fears are present, then desensitization is called for. In fact, most treatment programs play it safe and supply both.

Most treatment programs for low assertiveness include portions of seven components listed by Eileen Gambrill: the pinpointing of specific actions to be increased or decreased, modeling displays of appropriate assertiveness, imitation of modeling displays, feedback on that imitation, training in self-reward procedures, assignments to behave in new ways, and praising the advantages of assertiveness.[55] In addition, desensitization is often used.

## Increasing Assertiveness

### Armchair Desensitization

**Case 10.5.** Jeff has a mild fear of asking small favors from others. In his upbringing, he was taught not to impose on other people. He intellectually realizes that his other persons might welcome the opportunity to do him a favor so they might, for example, get a ride home with him when they need it. But his fear remains. When faced with his own need to ask a ride home with a fellow worker, Jeff fails to summon up the courage to make the request, which results in getting home late at night. Jeff embarks on a program of self-change to increase his own assertiveness. He carefully reads Chapter 10 of this book several times and gets a roommate to assist in reality testing his program. (His roommate is the one person of whom Jeff can ask favors without fear.) For reasons of his own, he feels safest with armchair desensitization. He constructs a hierarchy, masters deep muscle relaxation, and employs the procedures for armchair desensitization described earlier. His least feared situation is asking a friendly supermarket clerk for five dollar bills in change rather than a five-dollar bill. His most feared situation is asking his rather aloof boss for a change in the date he will take his yearly vacation. Jeff kept a log on his progress to assure himself that he was indeed responsible for his self-change, even though change came ever so slowly.

### Role-Playing Desensitization and Assertive Training

**Case 10.6.** Emilio possesses a mild fear of asking girls for dates. On his very first attempt years ago, some friends played a cruel trick. They assured him that Amelia was hoping he would ask her out, while in fact Amelia harbored no such hopes. Upon being called and asked out, Amelia ridiculed Emilio, laughing at and taunting him. Since that time, Emilio has feared asking girls for dates, even when *he* intellectually knows they will say yes. Enlisting the aid of his older sister and her husband, Emilio constructed a hierarchy. Rather than the recommended 12-step hierarchy, they decided to construct a 10-step hierarchy but to use it in different ways. The first step in the hierarchy was "talking to his sister about her job." The final and highest step was "asking a girl out for lunch." Under the encouraging eye of his brother-in-law, Emilio and his sister were to spend several evenings role playing the interactions in his hierarchy. The first evening they planned to role play, Emilio wisely called it off because he felt tense and anxious from a trying day at work. After the sessions finally began, the role playing in each situation proceeded only if Emilio felt fearless and comfortable, free from anxiety. His incompatible emotion was a feeling of masterful calmness. Since reactions from the girl were important to Emilio, they decided to first go up the hierarchy with the assurance that his sister would role play eager acceptance. Then they went up the hierarchy with his sister always giving an inconclusive reply but asking him to call back. Upon first being faced with these delaying tactics, Emilio immediately felt fearful; so they stopped playing the scene. They decided that his sister would again give an inconclusive reply but would exhibit eager acceptance when he called back. Using successively more negative reactions from his sister, Emilio ascended his fear hierarchy using role playing four times in the following ways:

1. Sister enthusiastically accepts.
2. Sister asks him to call back and accepts upon being called again.
3. Sister politely refuses.
4. Sister curtly refuses.

In between the sessions, Emilio skimmed Chapters 7 through 10 for practical information. One procedure that came to his mind was to have his sister and brother-in-law reward him after he moved one step up the hierarchy. However, he was progressing satisfactorily and felt no need to employ any external source of reward. He taped each session on casettes and played them while commuting to work. Feedback in the form of hearing his own successes replayed on these tapes seemed to make him feel better than feedback coming from others.

Before going on, try your hand at creating a fear hierarchy right now.

ACTIVITY 10.5.

Suppose a good friend of yours has a mild fear at first meeting and talking to attractive members of the opposite sex. He (she) is beginning to worry about the fear itself. Make up a 12-step desensitization hierarchy that he (she) could use in armchair desensitization, role-playing, and real-life assertive training. Also describe the tactics and procedures to be used in sufficient detail so someone else could repeat these procedures. (Hint: Use the checklist on pages 204–205.) It may help to begin at the extremes (steps 1 and 12) and work toward the middle steps to assure even intervals between steps.

1. ____________ 7. ____________

2. ____________ 8. ____________

3. ____________ 9. ____________

4. ____________ 10. ____________

5. ____________ 11. ____________

6. ____________ 12. ____________

Tactics and other procedures:

______________________________

______________________________

______________________________

______________________________

______________________________

### Combining Procedures

**Case 10.7.** Aida has a mild fear of initiating interactions at cocktail parties. She wants to increase the scope of her acquaintances, and this fear is getting in her way. Also, she can think of only two levels in her hierarchy, namely:

1. Aida introduces herself and gets a positive response.
2. Aida introduces herself and gets a negative response.

She realizes that in this hierarchy, the difference between the two steps is far too great. Even if she were to ascend this two-step hierarchy using armchair desensitization, she anticipates that actually attending the party would elicit anxiety. She calls on her friend Dick. Together they create a new hierarchy containing many more steps that are much closer together:

*Steps 1–6, armchair desensitization.*

1. Introduction to stranger is performed by Dick; stranger is highly positive toward Aida.
2. Introduction to stranger is performed by Dick; stranger is neutral toward Aida.
3. Introduction to stranger is performed by Aida herself; stranger is highly positive toward Aida.
4. Introduction to stranger is performed by Aida herself; stranger is neutral toward Aida.
5. Introduction to stranger is performed by Dick; stranger is negative toward Aida.
6. Introduction to stranger is performed by Aida herself; stranger is negative toward Aida.

*Steps 7–12, role-playing desensitization.* Steps 7–12 are the same as steps 1–6 except the scenes are played by Dick and Aida in a role-playing situation. Dick role plays the stranger's part.

*Steps 13–15, in vivo desensitization.*

13. At the next real party, Dick introduces Aida to an acquaintance of his whom she has not met.
14. At this party, Aida introduces herself to a person whom she has not met while Dick looks on from a distance.
15. At this party, Aida introduces herself to a person whom she has not met. Dick has left the room.

In Case 10.7, it is possible that the distance from 12 to 13, from role-playing to real life, might be too large. In such an event, added steps might be inserted concerning the physical approach to real-life party surroundings. As in the previous examples, Aida would do well to keep a log of her progress to assure that she has indeed made progress. (See Figure 10.5 for an illustration of combining procedures.)

Case 10.8 is an example reported by Arkowitz. When faced with this case, therapist Arkowitz decided to play a supervisory role, assigning the client major responsibility for self-change. I reproduce this true case verbatim to illustrate the combined use of armchair and role-playing desensitization procedures.

***Case 10.8.*** *Ted was an 18 year old freshman who sought treatment at the Psychological Service Center on campus. He reported feeling anxious and depressed, with occasional thoughts of suicide. He felt unable to concentrate on his school work, and unable to seek out social relationships on campus. The immediate stress seemed to involve his relationship with his girlfriend who was attending a distant college. She was the first and only girl he had dated, and he found himself preoccupied with thoughts about her, as well as having extremely explosive and jealous reactions to her casual dates with other men. He often made massive and impulsive bids for reassurance from her through highly emotional letters and telephone calls. Ted was also concerned that he was sexually impotent. He had attempted intercourse with his girlfriend several times, and each attempt had ended unsuccessfully with either premature ejaculation or loss of erection.*

*Ted was seen by the author [Arkowitz] for a total of 15 sessions over a six month period. The first 14 sessions were primarily directed toward exploration of his feeling about his relationship with his girlfriend, rational decision-making strategies, and role-playing and homework assignments directed toward increasing his social comfort and participation on campus. At session 14, Ted reported that he had broken up with his girlfriend. At this session, he appeared extremely anxious and agitated. He was concerned that his resolve might weaken, and that he would return to the relationship despite his preference to end it. Ted also discussed his anxieties about heterosexual relationships and his fears about his sexual performance. At this point, the therapist decided to*

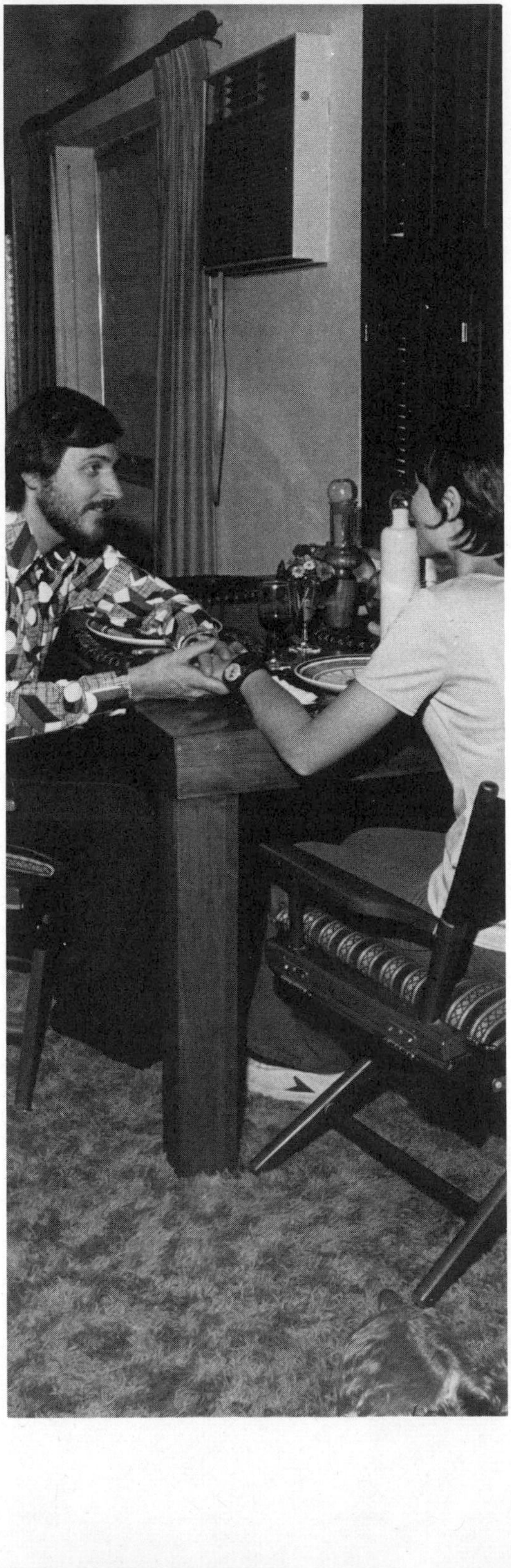

Figure 10.5. Combination of desensitization and assertive training procedures in progress In this scene, a restaurant situation is being role-played in the apartment of the man, who is well along in desensitizing his fear of dating situations. (Photograph by Charles Blakey.)

*initiate a self-desensitization program to help reduce these anxieties. A self-desensitization program was chosen, in part, to help Ted increase his perceptions of control over his feelings.*

*The self-desensitization took place over the course of the last nine weeks of treatment. During this time, Ted designed and executed the program on his own, between meetings with the therapist. The meetings with the therapist were primarily concerned with problem-solving for difficulties encountered in the self-desensitization program, and a discussion of progress. The therapist's role during this time was structured as one of "technical consultant" to Ted in his self-directed program.*

*The first step in the program was having Ted read about the rationale and procedural details of desensitization from a book. The second step was training in muscle relaxation. The first relaxation session was conducted by the therapist in his office. Subsequent relaxation sessions were conducted by Ted in his room, using a tape recording of the relaxation instructions which the therapist provided for him. After about four hours of practice with the tape, Ted was able to relax himself very effectively, and no longer needed the tape to induce relaxation. He found that he was able to relax himself at this point simply by thinking about the relaxation instructions, and without going through the tension-release exercises. The third step involved hierarchy construction. Ted generated three hierarchies on his own. The first two were concerned with situations associated with his ex-girl friend which elicited anxiety and ruminative thoughts. Some sample items from these two hierarchies included "hearing from a friend that Susan (the ex-girlfriend) was dating another guy seriously," "the telephone rings in my room and I think it might be Susan calling." The third hierarchy was concerned with social and sexual contact with other females. This included such items as "starting a conversation with a girl in one of my classes," "a girl invites me into her apartment after a date," as well as higher items reflecting increasing degrees of sexual contact through intercourse.*

*The fourth step was the actual desensitization which involved self-directed exposure of the hierarchy scenes with self-administered relaxation. The self-desensitization sessions were conducted by Ted in his room. He typically began each such session with five to ten minutes of relaxation. When he felt sufficiently relaxed, he opened his eyes and read the first hierarchy item from a stack of hierarchy cards on an adjoining table. Next, he closed his eyes and imagined the scene. He reported that this procedure did not disrupt his relaxation. Ted started each new scene with brief exposures and moved on to longer ones if he did not experience anxiety. If, during the exposure of any scene, he did begin to feel anxious, he terminated the scene and relaxed. After two successive repetitions of a scene for about thirty seconds without anxiety, he would move to the next hierarchy item.*

*For the most part, the procedure worked smoothly for Ted. One problem which he reported concerned his anticipation of later scenes in the hierarchy. During one period, he reported that he became increasingly tense between scenes, because he began to anticipate the exposure of more anxiety-arousing scenes much later in the hierarchy. The solution which he devised for this was to utilize positive thoughts and relaxing images between exposures, so that he would not begin thinking about the later items.*

*One further problem which Ted experienced was an apparent lack of generalization for some items. That is, even though he had sufficiently passed an item in the imaginal hierarchy, he still often experienced noticeable tension in the real-life situation. For this problem, Ted decided to utilize role-playing desensitization procedures. For example, this problem was especially marked for the item "the telephone rings in my room and I think it might be Susan calling." For this item, Ted enlisted the aid of his roommate who telephoned Ted from an adjoining room on a pre-arranged signal. First, Ted relaxed himself and then signaled for the telephone to ring. Ted let the telephone ring a few times, and during this time focused on relaxing himself. He also varied the volume of the telephone bell to gradually approximate the standard one. With two such role-playing sessions, Ted reported that he felt quite comfortable about the telephone ringing and that it did not lead him to thoughts about his girlfriend. This type of role-playing procedure was one which Ted successfully employed on several occasions for especially troublesome items.*

*Ted reported many changes consistent with his progress through the hierarchies. He was able to confront situations and cues relating to his ex-girlfriend without getting anxious and depressed; the frequency of his ruminative thoughts and preoccupation with that relationship markedly decreased; his schoolwork improved; his social participation on campus increased; and he began dating more frequently. In addition, he became less concerned about his sexual performance. He began to date one girl somewhat regularly and felt quite comfortable with kissing and petting, although they had not attempted intercourse. Finally, he appeared less impulsive and explosive, and was no longer considering the kinds of extreme actions which characterized his earlier behavior.*

*The therapist sent Ted open-ended letters for follow-up information at six months and one year following termination [of therapy]. . . . During the year following termination, Ted reported that the changes which were described above were maintained. He reported that he continued to be free of depression and anxieties and his preoccupation with his ex-girlfriend. He was dating fairly frequently and doing well academically. Ted reported that he had utilized the self-desensitization during this year for several minor anxiety problems which arose. These concerned test-anxiety one quarter, and tensions concerning the uncertainty of his long-range career plans. In both of these cases, he utilized a combination of imaginal and role-playing desensitization as described earlier. Ted reported that in both cases, he successfully reduced his anxieties and felt that the use of self-desensitization had helped prevent these from becoming more major problems for him.*

*In a letter from Ted 2½ years after termination, he reported that he was married. He had been married for almost a year at this point and wrote that "I feel that I can have a lasting and meaningful relationship with a woman without the kind of uncontrollable emotions I experienced before." He reported that their sexual relationship was a good one and that intercourse had not presented any problems for him.*

From Hal Arkowitz, "Desensitization as a Self-Control Procedure: A Case Report," *Psychotherapy: Theory, Research, and Practice,* 1974, *11,* 172–174. Copyright 1974. Reprinted by permission of author and publisher.

### Components of Assertiveness

Alberti and Emmons discuss general and situation-specific nonassertiveness.[56] General nonassertiveness seems more resistant to change. The examples in this chapter have concerned mainly low assertiveness in situations that are fairly easy to specify. However, it may turn out that only a professional can define and change general nonassertiveness across many situations; or it may turn out that users can do it by themselves or under supervision. The relevant research concerning the ability of users to improve general assertiveness has not been done. It might be well for users who wish to increase their assertiveness in general to have a go at it themselves. However, I would caution anyone who is hurting acutely to seek professional advice without delay, if they feel it is needed.

The list that follows this paragraph presents typical situations used for increasing assertiveness. The usual procedure is to ask the individual to respond to each situation as he (she) would normally react. Then training in how to respond assertively is given, usually with role playing, modeling, videotape, and so on. Using feedback and rewards, this general procedure has thus far increased the assertiveness of individuals as measured in the laboratory by researchers Richard Eisler, Michael Hersen, Peter Miller, and their colleagues.[57]

*SOME SITUATIONS WARRANTING ASSERTIVENESS*

1. *You have just come home from work and, as you settle down to read the newspaper, you discover that your other person has cut out an important article to get a coupon on the other side. Your other person says, "I just wanted to cut this coupon out before I forgot it." You respond.*
2. *You are in the middle of an exciting television drama. Your other person walks in and changes the channel, saying "Let's watch this quiz show; it's supposed to be real good." You respond.*
3. *You are in a crowded grocery store and are in a hurry. You have picked up one small item and get in line to pay for it when a woman with a shopping cart full of groceries cuts in line right in front of you. She says, "You won't mind if I cut in here, will you? I'm late for an appointment." You respond.*
4. *You have just bought a new shirt, but upon putting it on the first time, you notice that several buttons are missing. You return it to the sales clerk who sold it to you. The clerk says, "May I help you?" You respond.*
5. *You are in a drugstore and buy something that costs $.75. You go to the cashier to pay for it and hand her a five-dollar bill. She rings up the sale and hands you $.25, change for only $1. The cashier says, "Thank you. Here's your change. Have a nice day." You respond.*

Adapted from Richard Eisler, Peter Miller, and Michael Hersen, "Components of Assertive Behavior," *Journal of Clinical Psychology,* 1973, 29, p. 296. Reprinted with permission.

If assertiveness can be displayed across situations, there should be cross-situational characteristics that apply to occasions where assertiveness is warranted in general. To assist in identifying such components, I present two lists. The first list was given by Andrew Salter, whom Wolpe calls "the pioneer of assertive techniques."[58] This list presents six ways of acting that should be helpful in improving low assertiveness.[59]

*SALTER'S LIST OF GENERAL ASSERTIVE MODES OF ACTION*

1. *Talking about feelings, manifested by expression of emotions now being experienced.*
2. *Facial talk, manifested by display of facial emotion.*
3. *Contradict and attack, manifested by expressed disagreement, plainly stated with as much emotional responsiveness as feasible.*
4. *Use of the pronoun "I" as much as possible.*
5. *Expression of agreement when you receive praise.*
6. *Improvisation, manifested by spontaneity, whenever needed.*

A similar list comes from the Eisler, Miller, and Hersen research group.[60] However, you should be aware that this second list was derived from ratings of videotaped responses by 30 male psychiatric patients. The characteristics listed were found to statistically differentiate between the 15 higher-assertive versus the 15 lower-assertive men.

*THE EISLER, HERSEN, AND MILLER LIST OF COMPONENTS FOR ASSERTIVENESS*

1. *Latency of your response in seconds. The more quickly you respond (shorter latency), the more assertiveness.*
2. *Loudness of your speech. The louder you speak, the more assertiveness displayed.*
3. *Compliance content. The less compliant you are, the more assertive you are.*
4. *Requests for new behavior. The more new, alternative actions you request, the more assertive you are.*

These two lists are clearly meant to be taken with a large grain of salt. They are presented to assist in clarifying what assertiveness means across different situations. The lists are best viewed as reasonable but incomplete and unvalidated by research in vivo.

What is the difference between being assertive and being a bully? Are they the same thing? No they are not. Being assertive means standing up for your legitimate rights, which means assuring a fair relationship as described in Chapters 3 and 4. So receiving more than a fair return from a relationship may indicate excessive assertiveness. Also, excessive forcing of one's will on another person and use of physical force characterize the bully. Being a bully means excessive assertiveness, which is always relative to the situation.

## PRESCRIPTION PROCEDURES FOR PROFESSIONALS ONLY

### Aversive Counterconditioning

In all the preceding pages of this chapter, we have been dealing with situations for which classical conditioning is used to neutralize an unpleasant, fearful cue. However, there are occasions where exactly the opposite may help. The compulsive smoker may want to make certain cues negative, such as the now pleasing act of reaching for cigarettes. In the case where a chain of pleasing or neutral events leads up to something that is harmful but enjoyable (bad habit), aversive counterconditioning is often used to break the links in the chain. In *aversive countercon-ing,* an aversive event is paired with a neutral or positive cue to make that cue more negative. The process involves classical conditioning. Here is an example.

Consider the following chain:

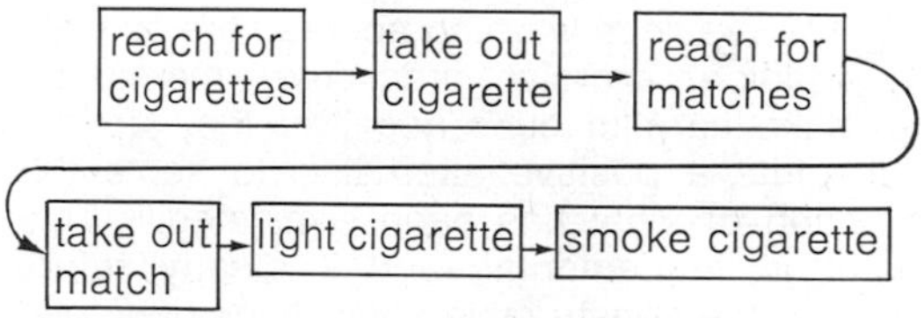


To break this chain, volunteers often undergo excruciating shocks paired with an early link in the chain. For example, a strong shock might be given when the volunteer opens the cigarette case. Here the classical conditioning principle is being used to disrupt one link in the chain, specifically, "take out cigarette." Similar chains and aversive events have been used to successfully treat sexual fetishism, transvestism, homosexuality, exhibitionism, gambling, obsession with thinking about foods, excessive smoking, and drinking.[61] (Note that "successfully treat" means some success, not 100-percent success.) Pain has been induced using shocks, foul-smelling liquids placed in the nose, nauseating chemicals to be swallowed, and so on.

WARNING: Aversive counterconditioning should be used only by professionals. Only under the eye of a professional is the danger alleviated that the aversive event will not spread beyond the specific link in the chain or otherwise get out of hand.[62]

### Covert Sensitization

An interesting subvariety of aversive counterconditioning is called "covert sensitization." Here the aversive event is not externally administered but rather is imagined. In this technique, the client is relaxed in the armchair and, say, wants relief from a craving to eat doughnuts. He is instructed to imagine some links in the chain leading up to eating a doughnut, such as just being served one by a waitress. Then he commences to vividly imagine an absolutely sickening and detailed scene in which being served the doughnut leads to nausea. When the scene ends, the restaurant is practically engulfed in a sickening tide of little green particles and puke and snot and mucus and vomit. The repeated association of *symbolic* aversive events has been reported to be effective in treating alcoholism,[63] smoking, obesity,[64] and sexual disorders.

As with all aversive procedures, covert sensitization is not a procedure for users to try. The previous warning applies here as well. In addition, aversive procedures merely try to make harmful cues negative; they do *not* substitute a positive alternative to serve the function of what has been eliminated.[65] This point is fundamental, and it clearly refers back to the constructive-alternatives principle.

### Implosive Therapy

#### Description of Implosive Procedures

Radically different from all the procedures discussed so far, *flooding and implosive techniques* actually try to overload the fearful person with fear cues. The lady afraid of a snake may be put alone in a room with several snakes. Or she may be told to imagine scenes such as being slowly swallowed by a mammoth anaconda or having a poisonous coral snake alive and writhing around in her stomach, biting her mercilessly. The rationale behind these procedures is simple and logical enough at first blush. Stampfl and Levis reason that prolonged exposure to fear cues will eventually result in satiation and weakening of the fear reaction.[66] To illustrate, imagine that you and I have been out for a nighttime walk and our eyes have adjusted well to the dark. As we return and suddenly enter a brightly lighted room, the light blinds us and is painful. However, with exposure to these initially painful cues, our eyes adjust and these very cues become neutral. In like manner, fear cues will lose their power to hurt. Even Wolpe is "now convinced of the wide efficacy of the method,"[67] although he advocates caution.

#### Evaluation of Implosive Procedures

Implosive therapy has given rise to what could best be described as a running battle in the clinical literature. Critics claim that implosive therapy (1) provides the fearful with even more to fear than before, (2) leads to a worsening of fears for some, and (3) is altogether less preferable than desensitization.[68] Advocates charge the critics with being uninformed and claim that implosive therapy works.[69] The best advice for users is to subject yourself to implosive procedures only with the guidance of a professional. The evidence is not in yet, and aversive procedures for emotional change are for professional use only.

## CHANGING EMOTIONS IN THE FUTURE

In this chapter, we have focused on the removal of fears because clinicians have done the research on changing emotions and their clients have wanted their fears removed. However, in the broader perspective of all healthy emotional change, this focus on removing fears is rather like looking for the lost keys at night only where the light from the porch lamp falls; that is, we have looked at the desensitization of fears as the main kind of emotional change because the light of current research falls largely on this topic. Three other extremely broad realms of emotion change will probably appear before long, two healthy and one not so healthy.

One healthy realm of emotion change concerns making a good emotion better. For example, if your heart skips a beat when a certain other person approaches, after mastering Chapter 10 in this book you have the means available to increase the positive emotional value of that person. The same relaxation and cue association procedures for taking the sting out of negative cues can likewise be used to enhance the positive value of an already attractive cue. We saw this process at work in the Nunnally research cited earlier (see p. 198).[70] Thus, when the attractive cue happens to be a certain other person, a happiness hierarchy can be created ranging from mildy pleasant to fantastic ecstasy. Going up the hierarchy here means increasing the positive emotional value of that person, namely liking or loving him (her) more.

Another healthy realm consists of using cue association procedures to make a neutral cue positive.

**Case 10.9.** The in-laws have come to retire in the small cottage at the back of John's property. Overall, his in-laws are neutral to him; his good and bad experiences with them have balanced out. Intellectually, John realizes that the current situation is perfectly acceptable, but he would like to like his in-laws a bit more. He could easily use relaxation and a hierarchy of positive-cue-association scenes to increase his liking for his in-laws.

Case 10.9 illustrates a less than optimal application because, obviously, the best strategy for John is to engineer real-life positive experiences with his in-laws. But the point is that he could use the association methods if he wished.

Last and least of the future realms of emotional change concerns the possibility of people running around motivating themselves for dubious purposes by willfully creating in themselves all sorts of crazy associations. For example, using appropriately personalized procedures, Bernie Backstab could establish positive associations that would pervert his motivation on the job into a blind and ruthless climb up the executive ladder. Willie Weaselton could transform himself into the willing servant of a politician by rearranging his own emotions. Blindly devoted employees and "true believers" are not unknown in politics and business. Clearly, the reality of creating undesirable associations already exists. Although Bernie and Willie may fully intend to change themselves back later, the critical question is whether they will *want* to change at a later date. If you make yourself love Big Brother now, then how likely are you to *want* to tear yourself away from Big Brother or his lieutenants later on?

So now you know why a few of my colleagues have fear (pardon the expression) about my providing information about procedures such as desensitization to users. No doubt you, if you are disposed to do so, could practice, create, and perfect the means to rearrange some of your own major emotional attachments in a few months' time. The procedures we have discussed are certainly no cure-all, and they are to be handled as you would dynamite.

## SEEKING PROFESSIONAL HELP

### Reality Testing

When in doubt, always seek reality testing from friends and professionals. Social reality resides in our minds and, as such, it has a slippery quality about it. Without reality testing by bouncing ideas off of other people, our perceptions can easily become distorted. What seems to be a problem may actually not be a problem at all.

All the procedures for self-change can be seen as specific tools in a toolbox. Sometimes the problem turns out to be nothing, so no tool is needed; sometimes several tools are needed; sometimes the wrong tool is applied; and sometimes no tool in the toolbox is capable of doing the job. And, sometimes, only a professional is capable of doing the job.

### You as a Consumer of Professional Help

It is curious indeed that when one seeks out professional help for problems in living, he expects to patronize just one therapist who will help him. When we go to a medical doctor, we do not expect that one drug or one doctor will cure us. Rather, we expect a competent diagnosis and then treatment, often administered by another doctor to whom the first referred us. As editorial consultant Phil Zeigler commented on an early draft of this chapter, there is none to whom one can go who will say, "Well, this problem is handled most effectively by psychoanalytic therapy. This other problem ought to be handled using behavior mod. And for this third one, we ought to use nondirective therapy." I can offer a few suggestions along these lines.

The most important advice for the seeker of professional help is to realize that he or she is really a consumer having a choice of what to consume. A lot has happened since Freud invented psychoanalysis. New techniques such as desensitization have come into being. Different therapists have different techniques and different personalities to go with them. After settling on any therapist and method of treatment, give it a fair chance; no treatment will work if not given a fair chance. On the other hand, the consumer ought to be king. Upon being given a fair chance, some therapy may not work whereas another will. Above all, do not lose hope simply because one treatment administered by one personality failed. In short, the sublime medium lies somewhere between the ridiculous extremes of rigid loyalty to one therapist and playing musical therapists every couple of weeks.

During the first interview with a therapist, be sure to inquire about his or her qualifications. Be assertive. The qualified therapist will take pride in his or her training. Generally, a Ph.D. in psychology and a residency in clinical psychology are required for independent practice in *clinical psychology.* In *psychiatry,* the M.D. plus residency in psychiatry are the usual requirements. In the area of *social work,* the MSW (master of social work) is usually required. In addition, experienced masters-level psychologists doing therapy and masters-level psychologists who work under the supervision of a certified or licensed therapist are becoming common. Degrees are not guarantees. Rather, the absence of degrees or other comparable qualifications is a handy indicator of possibly inadequate training. Check for qualifications in your locality. Also check with your local and state psychological and medical associations for listings of licensed and certified practitioners, because official certification and licensing is usually a matter of state law.

The question always comes up, "Is the M.D. or the Ph.D. better?" In response, there are competent therapists with both kinds of training. The M.D. is a medical degree with basic foundations in physical medicine. The Ph.D. in clinical psychology is an applied research degree with basic foundations in human behavior and clinical research. The practical experience required for both degrees should enable the holder of either to make referrals, as in the case of a clinical psychologist who suspects that a physical problem exists. The best way to judge is on the basis of the individual therapist, not the Ph.D. versus M.D. degree per se.

A few schools offer a Doctor of Psychology (D.Psy.) degree, which is equivalent to the Ph.D. degree. Here you may want to make sure the awarding institution is approved by the American Psychological Association in Washington, D.C., a nongovernmental professional association.

During the beginnings of treatment, be assertive enough to get an explanation of why the particular treatment is being used instead of others. The competent therapist can provide an excellent rationale for you. You would certainly want to get a similar explanation if you were thinking about, for example, surgery. Why should it be any different with therapy? The method of treatment ought to be tailored to specific goals, and the goals should involve in vivo, not just armchair, changes.

For the treatment of reasonably definable fears and anxiety, go to someone who can use desensitization because it has been shown to be more effective in reducing fears than any other treatment.[71] Beyond desensitization, there is no other specific clinical procedure that has produced such resoundingly favorable results while being applied in so many different ways.

The personality of the therapist is not to be ignored. In fact, in addition to the preceding suggestions and other advice you can glean, the personality of the therapist might be the most appropriate characteristic on which to decide. Deal with someone you personally feel you can trust.

Finally, expect *transference,* which means emotions directed toward the therapist. Transference in therapy is perfectly natural and to be expected. The competent therapist is supposed to use these feelings to produce real changes in your life outside the office, not to create a permanent customer with them. So expect to come to like the therapist and occasionally get angry at him or her. Cooperate with the direction the therapist gives to these emotions.

Above all, remember that the professional helper is supposed to act as your agent. Therefore try to strike the sublime medium between being rigidly loyal to one therapist and playing musical therapists.

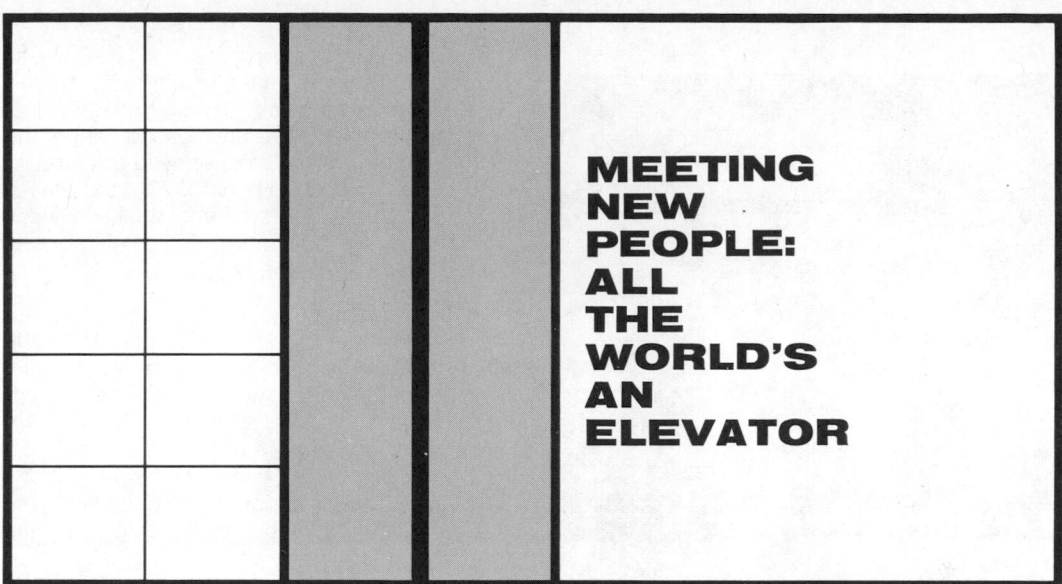

# MEETING NEW PEOPLE: ALL THE WORLD'S AN ELEVATOR

**AN ELEVATOR ESCAPADE**

Sunny Saturday for shopping. Department store full of people and sound. Talk, talk, talk. Wish they'd keep it down; sounds like high noon on a chicken farm. Better take the elevator up. It'll get me there faster than the escalator. Here it is. Guess it's not as empty as I thought it would be. WOW! Did somebody turn off the world? Somebody sure turned off the people. It's as quiet as a cave in here. A bit humid too. Breathe deeply, breathe quietly. Whew, what a relief—it's starting to move. Why do they all face the door? Why am I facing the door? A-ten, HUT! That little blonde lady over on the right, I bet she's got a sharp tongue. Tiger Tongue. What a big fellow that bear of a man up front is. Arms crossed and all closed up. You try to talk to him and he'd let you know who's boss. Bite your head off. The teenager? He's anti everyone over 20 and sure 'nuf anti me. Second floor. Why don't they leave? Quiet idiots! Why don't they talk? Even that married couple won't. Hold your breath, breathe silently. My god, you could cut this silence with a knife! Seems like I'm starting to sweat. Talk about the invisible shield between people. The elevator is an egg carton and we're all in our eggshells. Wonder if they talk at home? They must. But lots of homes have communication problems. Number one family problem they say. This is absolutely crazy. I'd get killed if I said anything. Suppose I caught the eye of that big man and said "Hi." He'd growl something, maybe even be polite, and that would be the end of it. Then silence. Then that blonde and the teenager would start to chuckle, and before long the whole rotten crew would be howling and laughing at me. Like a cartoon character, I'd shrink down to 6 inches tall. All mocking me, making fun. Shot right out of the sky. Any one of them would crush me. Agony of agonies. Aaaggghhh!!! There's no pain like loneliness, except maybe being laughed at. When those rotten———are howling at me and belly laughing at least I know who my enemies are. Enemies, all of them. They say those who aren't for you are against you.

Trapped in an elevator surrounded by zombies, the walking dead. Worse yet, enemies! I better get out safe and sound while the getting's good. Ah, that honeyed breathe of natural fresh air conditioning. Ah, that saving grace of double doors sliding briskly. Sweet, sweet relief. Seventh floor. Out that door like a SHOT! Oops, sorry lady.

In this chapter, we take a short breather from principles and the usual rigors of science to explore the frontier of meeting new people. With tongue in cheek, we will view the modern world as a giant-sized elevator in which there exist unwritten rules that discourage meeting new other persons or even being civil to them. As Murray Davis has noted, the transition from the static communities of a century ago to the highly mobile society of today has foisted the need to create one's own social world. "Whereas in the community a person found his set of close associates to be ready-made, in the [mobile] society he now finds that he must *make* his own friends, loves, and spouse."[1]

For some while, I have been fascinated with the process by which each of us comes to meet an other person the very first time. I am convinced the topic is extremely important. In the only book on the topic, *Contact: The First Four Minutes,* Leonard and Natalie Zunin nicely capture the reasons for their interest in this topic:

> *There is a sequence through which all of our activities and encounters must pass. In this sequence, phase one is Contact; phase two is a midterm of varying degree; and phase three is the ending or "good-bye." . . . It is my contention that phase one, contact, is the key to the door of social success, family harmony, business achievement and to some extent, sexual satisfaction.*[2]

## THE STATE OF THE ART

### The Great Need

For social success, you have to choose your friends and intimates with care. In regard to marriage, it seems likely that those people who have a broader range of acquaintances from which to choose their mates will

**Figure 11.1.** Standing at attention in the elevator. (Photograph by Charles Blakey.)

be able to make a better selection and be less apt to get divorced. Who would have a better chance to choose a compatible friend or mate? A young adult with 20 acquaintances or one with 200? In regard to work, who would be more successful at getting a job or getting the right person to come to work for her (him)? A person with 20 acquaintances or one with 200? The topic of meeting new people is important because *it is logically necessary to meet a new person for the first time before that person can become your acquaintance or friend or a loved one.*

But meeting new people oftentimes requires freedom from fear and some skill as well. Recall from the last chapter that a study by Borkovec et al. found that "32% of the males and 38.5% of the females feel some or greater fear of meeting someone for the first time."[3] In addition, social psychologist Philip Zimbardo and his colleagues at Stanford University demonstrated convincingly that shyness is widespread.[4] In a survey of 817 students in the Stanford area, over 40 percent described themselves as presently shy. Only 1 percent said they had never been shy, and 82 percent reported having been shy in some past situation. Outwardly, shyness is marked by silence, absence of eye contact, generally avoiding others, and speaking softly. Inwardly, the person exhibiting shyness has feelings of self-consciousness, worry about controlling one's own actions in a skillful way, worry about others' unfavorable evaluations, worry about shyness, heart pounding faster, blushing, perspiring, and butterflies in one's stomach.[5]

For most of us, the fear of rebuff varies in strength. Sometimes we overcome it, but sometimes not. For some, this fear represents an ever present barrier in the course of each day. For some, meeting a new person has been a traumatic learning occasion, with long-lasting effects. Case 11.1 illustrates such an occasion. It is a verbatim excerpt from a paper written by a former student of mine in reaction to an early draft of this chapter.

**Case 11.1.** I literally trembled, stuttered, and had moments when my mind went blank. . . . The most important obstacle, I found, was fear of rejection. . . . I was haunted by the memory of visiting a teen dance [television] show in Newark, New Jersey, in 1966 (I was 17) when the set director announced that it was 10 seconds to showtime and everyone should get ready to dance. I summoned every ounce of courage I could muster and went up to an average looking girl and asked her if I could be her partner. She broke into laughter, called to her friends who were nearby, and loudly exclaimed something to the effect of "*this guy* wants to dance with me?!" My heart sank as I hurriedly left the studio. . . . The New Jersey incident still sends chills down my spine when I think about it. . . . When two adolescents clash, and neither knows how to handle social situations, there is danger that one, or both, will be scarred for life.

Zunin and Zunin's *Contact* is a popular book emphasizing the importance of the first 4 minutes of all encounters. Laced with many insightful suggestions, *Contact* devotes 12 pages to the opening, or outset, of the interaction; those pages constitute the most systematic treatment of the subject to date.[6] Other discussions about meeting new people are woven into popular books in which the main focus is sex and seduction.[7] And in the literature of psychology, you will find absolutely nothing. In the research literature of sociology, you will find only one paper—that by Emanuel Schegloff, who studied the openings of conversations in a police department.[8]

In this chapter, I incorporate the original suggestions of others into a pretheory of my own. Hopefully, the pretheory will open up "meeting new people" as an area for research. There are volumes upon volumes about ingenious flexible plastics for better trash cans and bearings. There are volumes upon volumes in psychology about how to get more work out of people. There ought to be volumes upon volumes about how to meet people.

### The Reaction Against

Not long ago in one of my classes, I took a small survey about meeting new people. The questions asked students how they met new people. I was astonished at such reactions as these: "I don't really use strategy. I try to be natural." "I don't believe in seek and ye shall find. A watched egg doesn't hatch. One naturally finds someone." "To hell with my 'strategy.' I'll be honest and seek myself as others stand with me." When asked about how they might select a mate, a typical answer was, "I think mate-seeking, as such, is ridiculous." Clearly, the very idea of looking at meeting new people systematically is downright upsetting to a few and possibly anxiety arousing to many. Why?

Several reasons come to mind. For one thing, cultural norms against meeting new people surely exist. These norms evolved to serve a purpose. Children should not accept rides with strangers; girls would do well to refuse offers of transportation by strangers at the bus terminal. Such norms likely developed to (1) avoid exploitation and (2) maintain existing social classes. Moreover, meeting new people is a mildly fearful business for many. Many do not feel confident, but most of us would like to improve. Curiously, attempts to apply *any* sort of planning to meeting new people is seen by some as anti free will or somehow dehumanizing. Finally, the area of meeting new people is virtually unexplored and therefore presents difficulty. Difficulty means work. And the unknown has always been cloaked with all sorts of superstition.

In light of reactions such as these, *should* we proceed to try to make some sense of meeting new people? I strongly believe so, and the three paragraphs that follow tell why.

### Arguments for Meeting New People

#### General Argument

As I argued in the chapter on values, morality is highly social. The bicycle model of social life would imply as much. For now, we shall assume that nearly every worthwhile goal requires the aid of other people at some point. Even with goals that do not, a greater range of acquaintances could only help. Because (1) more acquaintances are so instrumental in reaching most goals and (2) meeting new people means more acquaintances, meeting new people means more reaching of noble goals—whatever you (the reader) define those goals to be. To the extent that we can discover some order in this area, we are further along in attaining noble goals.

#### Personal Argument

We all need friends and intimates. We all need at least one intimate to whom we can express our feelings and with whom we can do reality testing. Other persons need you in the same way. The number of hours per day and years per lifetime severely limits the time you can spend with friends and intimates. So, to best satisfy your own social needs, you need to make the best selection you can. To make the best selection you can, it is best to have as large a number of acquaintances as possible. Meeting a lot of new people with ease means more acquaintances for you. Thus, finding out more about how you meet new people means better filling your own social needs.

#### The Unique Value of Acquaintances

Acquaintances are full of potential benefits. They can become your friends or intimates. They can help you out. They can ask you to help them out. You can become their friend or intimate. Acquaintances have almost no disadvantages because they do not take up much time or effort. There are almost no drawbacks associated with carefully chosen acquaintances. Of course you may wish to take the time to develop friendships and intimacies from your pool of acquaintances. Therefore we should make as many acquaintances as we possibly can.

## STATE OF THE CULTURE

Remember the egg carton and eggshell image of the elevator at the start of this chapter? In their book *Pairing,* Bach and Deutsch pick up this idea when speaking about harmful cultural pressures that squeeze young adults into the courtship-for-marriage mold. "For the courting culture looks to a chance proximity for human contact. It is not 'proper' to break one's shell deliberately. One must wait for Fortune to drop an egg. So one waits eagerly. Who will be in the next seat on the airplane? Who goes to the same church, joins the same club, has the same mutual friends, rents the apartment next door?"[9] I would go on to argue that precisely this process of waiting for fate's perfect moment is harmful when it interferes with the development of certain intimate relationships. Specifically, the harm comes when the opportunity to meet potentially excellent friends, intimates, and mates is blocked.

So we wait. But must we wait? Is there a way to avoid waiting without running afoul of the culture? Yes, there is. The key is found in this sentence: Cultural norms discourage you from initiating an interaction *where no reason for the interaction exists.* Fortunately, in a great many situations it is possible to take advantage of a culturally appropriate reason to meet or to create one on the spot.

**BEING PROPER**

Thus you have my plan of attack: I will proceed to spell out meeting occasions that are legitimate according to the cultural norms of today. I will identify and classify situations for initiating interactions that are *culturally appropriate.* With a foundation of sufficient ingenuity and tact, these situations are many indeed.

A safeguard for all such situations should be that the other person has the right to terminate at any time. If the other person moves to another seat, walks away, turns away, requests openly, or otherwise indicates a desire to terminate, then stop immediately. With this safeguard for the other person's privacy and dignity in mind, there should be no fear about hurting anyone. Everyone has facts and feelings they want to express. Almost no one will rebuff an honest attempt to make small talk. Almost everyone likes a smiling face and wants to talk about something.

ACTIVITY 11.1.

Make a list of meeting opportunities for persons like yourself in your area. Define "persons like yourself" and "your area" with some exactness.

ACTIVITY 11.2.

Is there someplace near you where meeting new people is institutionalized? Somewhere that people go especially to meet other people? Go there with a friend and just sit back to observe. Take out your list of principles on eliciting action. Go over them one by one. Are the principles incorporated in this place? What is the role of the *physical* surroundings, such as arrangement of furniture? Share in class.

**THEORY OF INITIATING INTERACTIONS**

**Definition of Initiating an Interaction**

For our purposes, *initiating an interaction* is the same as meeting an other person the first time. You can initiate an interaction with a given other person only once. After that first meeting, you two can meet again, but never for the first time again.

What is necessary to say that you have met the other person? Is saying "Hello" in a reception line a meeting? Considering the present state of ignorance about meeting new people, it is wise to give ourselves a definition with some flexibility. Thus the definition should allow one to fill in some of the variables. And the definition is not black-and-white, but rather allows realistic shades of gray.

The degree to which you initiate an interaction with an other person varies in relation to the length of conversation or to the information elicited from the other person. In other words, initiating an interaction is a matter of degree, like everything else in life. The degree of meeting is reflected in one of two outcomes.

**Outcomes of Initiating an Interaction**

The first outcome of a newly initiated interaction is simply how long your conversation with the other person lasts. The conversation starts with the first reply by the other person. Before that time, we could not say that a conversation exists. The conversation ends with the final communication by either party to which the other attends. This outcome may seem simple, and it is. Nonetheless, time is enormously important.

The second outcome consists of the information the other person gives to you. The information can be biographical, such as first name, last name, nickname, hometown, brothers, sisters, and so on. The information can be small talk about hobbies. It can concern current employment. It can express feelings, attitudes, or emotions. It can be personal, such as marital status or information about future contacts between you two. Of course, we can and should turn the tables in our perspective here: Whatever holds for you also holds for the other person.

What about thoughts and feelings you both experience but may not express? Such thoughts and feelings very likely enter into your interaction. In addition, feelings and thoughts are so important that they have a central place in the value context that surrounds meeting new people. However, for the present chapter we will have our hands full just laying the groundwork in this uncharted area within value contexts that are sanctioned by society.

## Segments of Initiating an Interaction

We can view meeting a new person as having three segments. First comes the *approach segment,* in which you physically approach or telephone the other person and make an opening statement.[10] From the time you begin your opening statement to whenever the other person first replies makes up the approach segment. It generally takes only a few seconds and is deceptively subtle in importance because it passes so quickly. Moreover, the reply (if there is one), the remainder of the interaction, and the possibility of an acquaintanceship depend on the approach segment. Accordingly, the rest of this chapter is devoted to the approach segment.

The remaining *conversation and ending segments* of initiating an interaction are not to be deprived of importance. We will take up conversation as the major topic for the next chapter.

## Kinds of Meeting Opportunities

In this section, we will touch on four kinds of meeting opportunities that are all culturally appropriate. They are not independent. Thus you will find yourself putting them together.

### Special Momentary Need for Help

If you or the other person has a special momentary need for help, it is often appropriate to initiate an interaction. For instance, you might ask the time of day or request directions. Note that not all special needs for help carry a mandate for meeting the other person like emergencies do. Also, asking for help on a specific task does not automatically lead to a conversation of any length, as Davis notes.[11] You could find out the time of day for yourself; you could buy a map for directions.

### Common Task

If you and the other person must or can possibly work on a common task, initiating the interaction is often appropriate. The occasion may be on the job where you both work or in the class where you both study.

### Common Interest

If you and the other person have or even might have a common interest, a meeting may be appropriate (see Figure 11.2). The interest can be any topic at all. Nearly everything is fair game, from what the fat lady over there is wearing to what is happening in your immediate surroundings. Davis suggests that a bit of information picked up about the other person can comprise a common interest. Also, certain settings such as singles lounges, Parents Without Partners, club meetings, and so on can clearly imply that everyone in attendance has a common interest and is free to be approached.[12]

### Introduction by a Common Acquaintance

It is perfectly appropriate to take advantage of introduction by a common acquaintance. As you might imagine, the introduction can be spontaneous or arranged in advance. A valuable feature of introduction by a common acquaintance is that the introduction can often be made for purely social purposes. For example, you can fix up one friend to go on a date with another for purely social purposes.

**Figure 11.2.** What common-interest topics are available for openings here? (Photograph by Charles Blakey.)

## Major Aspects of Initiating Interactions

One major aspect of initiating an interaction with a new person concerns the degree to which the appropriate circumstances for the opening exist; they may already exist or they may be made to exist. To be sure, the truth about whether a meeting occasion occurred by chance or was artificially and intentionally created may be a private matter hidden deep in the heart of one human being. The degree to which the circumstances are ready-made for an opening by either party involves the degree to which one or both parties go out of their way to arrange the social and/or physical surroundings ahead of time so that initiating the interaction would be most likely to happen. In practice, "most likely" can be interpreted to mean falling into one or more of the four categories in the previous section. The lady who drops her handkerchief and the man at the party who ambles over to the far side of the room, ostensibly to open a window, are both classic examples of arranging surroundings ahead of time.

Another major aspect of meeting new people has to do with the use of physical props that engage attention. Such props are technically a specific instance of arranging physical surroundings ahead of time, but they are important enough to warrant independent consideration. There are whole shops devoted largely to selling such props: attention-grabbing bumper stickers, jewelry, pin-on buttons, custom-made T-shirts, pictures, objects to hang on the wall, black lights, decals, sew-on patches, and so on. In addition, people are painting their automobiles with wild designs and carrying around curiosity-arousing objects like controversial books more today than ever before. While no hard data on the subject exist, I strongly suspect that if other persons never reacted to novel props, the businesses that sell them would dry up overnight.

Does this discussion on props seem a bit corny? Are not gaudy sweatshirts and other props only for the socially immature? Some students and colleagues have advised me that mature adults do not use props to facilitate meeting new people. In reply, I remain unconvinced. The form of the props changes from gaudy and garish to subtle, and the older folks have their own equivalents to teenage fads. Often the prop is subtle, as in the case of expensive custom-tailored clothes, shoes, and jewelry.

**CREATIVE ACTIVITIES**

In the remainder of the chapter, your ideas and creativity take over. Your task is to take inventory of your own situation by creating all possible combinations of the aspects about initiating interactions we have discussed. For each example, create or describe a real or realistic other person. The first person is always yourself, so the range of situations to be explored constitutes a rough survey of the opportunities for initiating interactions that could realistically come your way. In short, include four elements in each brief example: yourself, your other person, physical surroundings, and social surroundings. Social surroundings here means other people or activities in the situation, such as a common friend or a meeting of a certain club. I have answered the first one as an example.

ACTIVITY 11.3.

Special momentary need for help, opportunity for initiating interaction already exists, no props. I pass a lady with a flat tire on the way to work three blocks from the college campus. I stop to help.

ACTIVITY 11.4.

Special momentary need for help, opportunity for initiating interaction already exists, props (props can be yours or other person's).

ACTIVITY 11.5.

Special momentary need for help, opportunity for initiating interaction is made to exist, no props.

ACTIVITY 11.6.

Special momentary need for help, opportunity for initiating interaction is made to exist, props.

ACTIVITY 11.7.

Common task, opportunity for initiating interaction already exists, no props.

ACTIVITY 11.8.

Common task, opportunity for initiating interaction already evists, props.

ACTIVITY 11.9.

Common task, opportunity for initiating interaction is made to exist, no props.

ACTIVITY 11.10.
Common task, opportunity for initiating interaction is made to exist, props.

ACTIVITY 11.11.
Common interest, opportunity for initiating interaction already exists, no props.

ACTIVITY 11.12.
Common interest, opportunity for initiating interaction already exists, props.

ACTIVITY 11.13.
Common interest, opportunity for initiating interaction is made to exist, no props.

ACTIVITY 11.14.
Common interest, opportunity for initiating interaction is made to exist, props.

ACTIVITY 11.15.
Introduction by a common acquaintance on the job.

ACTIVITY 11.16.
Introduction by a common acquaintance solely for social reasons (not necessarily mate-seeking).

ACTIVITY 11.17.
Just how unfriendly are other people? Just how difficult is it to create the opportunity to initiate an interaction all by yourself? Ask 20 people wearing watches for the time of day. Use identical verbal requests but smile at 10 and be straight-faced with 10. Alternate smiling and not smiling. Do not attempt to start a conversation at this time, but do not refuse. If possible, go with a friend who can observe and record reactions (especially advisable for females). What percent in each group reply? What percent smile at you? What percent try to converse beyond the reply? Share in class.

ACTIVITY 11.18.
Design and carry out a simple exercise like the one in Activity 11.17 to learn something about how people react to you.

## OVERCOMING FEAR OF MEETING NEW PEOPLE

Fear of meeting new people is common. In the terms we have been using for the last two chapters, this fear translates into problem nonassertiveness in the approach segment of initiating an interaction. If this fear troubles you, Chapter 10 offers practical procedures for replacing fear reactions with assertive action. In using Chapter 10, remember to master all of it thoroughly before starting self-change procedures. Remember the warnings.

## SUMMARY

Meeting new people the first time was viewed as an important area of concern. An acquaintance can become a friend or loved one, but we must meet another person the first time before even acquaintanceship can begin. The widespread cultural norms against meeting new people at will exist for purposes such as the protection of children; but these same norms also work against our finding the most compatible friends and loved ones. However, with enough ingenuity it is possible to greatly expand the existing situations in which cultural norms do permit meeting a new person. To do so requires identifying those situations and then recognizing and/or creating those situations in everyday life.

A theory of meeting new people was advanced. The theory views meeting a new person as consisting of three segments: the approach segment, the conversation segment and the ending segment. Social norms in industrialized nations permit meeting a new person in four kinds of situations:

1. One party's special momentary need for help (e.g., flat tire).
2. Work on a common task (e.g., joint school project).
3. Common interest (e.g., your surroundings, service club organization).
4. Introduction by a common acquaintance.

Each of these four situations can (1) be recognized as it already exists or (2) be made to exist with some ingenuity. The creative activities in this chapter afforded a chance to recognize and create meeting opportunities for you in your everyday life.

# 12

# CONVERSATION AND LISTENING

> *In an age of Television and Cinema we are in danger of losing the art of talk and with it much more. For, through conversation, we find friends and keep old friends and are not old friends often the best? In time, all artificial entertainments bore and weary but true companions, to whom you can talk without second thought, are never dull.*
>
> ELLIOT RUSSELL

**Case 12.1.** I am the world's most skillful individual. I use the principles discussed in Chapters 7 through 10 with uncanny ability. I am considered superb at conversation. My broad knowledge enables me to discuss almost any topic you choose, and be stimulating to boot. I can be serious, hilarious, informative, or light. I am responsive to you and considerate of your feelings. If you feel even the slightest offense or discomfort, I immediately switch to another topic without arousing your anger. In fact, perhaps my greatest virtue is that you are completely safe when you relate to me. I will not embarrass you. I will not punish you. I will not humiliate you. And, most important of all, I will never, never desert you. I am your tireless friend. Really, I am. I have only one possible fault: I am possibly too skilled in my relations with people. With my tireless energy, I am ready to take over your social functions by displacing the time given you by your intimates. I may have done so already. For a picture of who I am, turn the page.

## INTRODUCTION

I have some strong feelings on the topics of conversation and listening, as who doesn't? I feel bad and almost guilty every time I break apart a conversation to analyze and dissect it, and that happens a lot. For better or worse, nevertheless, the best way to learn to become sensitive to other people in conversations is to take some elements of conversation apart and then practice putting them together. In this chapter, our solution will be to put separate components of conversation back together as soon as we can for life-like realism. However, be warned that the burden of adding life-like realism to what-

**Figure 12.1.** Your constant friend. (Photograph by Charles Blakey.)

ever I can give you on the printed page rests on you because printed words come to you via a medium that is different from our actions in everyday life. The real action is going to happen or not happen when you take what you can from what I give you and go it alone.

### WHAT IS CONVERSATION?

*Conversation* is two or more people talking to each other or otherwise communicating with each other on a moment-to-moment basis. Can you communicate with another person without conversation? Certainly. You can write a letter.

Think of everything that goes on when you are talking, other than the words you speak. You are barraging the other person with information. Your voice changes tone. You gesture. You assume a body position. You make use of space. We can call your tone of voice and timing of speech *vocal communication.* What you do with your body we can call *nonverbal communication.* These nonverbal signals relay basically *emotional messages* and other information about the *relationship between persons.* On the other hand, we view the words you speak as *verbal communication* that conveys all the other information you are transmitting. In fact, your emotional messages will be transmitted nonverbally even if you utter words to the contrary, as Case 12.2 illustrates. In this example and from here on, we consider the two levels of communication described in this paragraph: the nonverbal (emotional) level and the verbal (mostly factual) level.

**Case 12.2.** The gray clouds seemed to Roger to be rolling over the earth like a steamroller. He was on his way to an intimate dinner with Susan. With his fingers, he tightly surrounded a small package nestled in the left pocket of his sports coat. Later on that evening, he and Susan were about to top off their dinner with sherbert served in glistening goblets. He could resist no longer. "Have you made a decision about the transfer to Europe for two years?" he asked, curling hidden fingers for the security of the small package. "Yes. I've given it a lot of thought and concluded that it's a once-in-a-lifetime opportunity." Her eyes dropped to the off-white disk of china supporting the goblet. "I'm going," she continued, "but don't worry. We can write and still keep in touch. That'll be OK, won't it?" Roger's eyes clouded and he felt beads of sweat starting to form on his forehead. A strange suction tugged downward on his stomach. "Oh, yes, yes," cracked his voice. "That'll be OK with me," he said, looking her straight in the chin and dreading the return to the jewelry shop.

In Case 12.2, there was a clear conflict between Roger's final statement, "That'll be OK with me," and his nonverbal actions. To any observer, his nonverbal actions contradicted and reversed this final statement like a tidal wave flips over a rowboat and crashes forward. When there is conflict between nonverbal messages and verbal messages, the nonverbal messages are generally more credible.

Another major aspect of moment-to-moment interaction concerns segments. The *approach* segment was covered in the previous chapter. In this chapter, our attention focuses on the *conversation* segment and, briefly, on the *ending* segment.

The end result of conversations includes the tenderness of emotional intimacy that (to me) makes life worthwhile. To attain optimal intimacy, we need to talk, talk, talk. Machines will simply not do the job. Watching television for a while may indeed provide some relief for us after a socially hectic day, so watching television may well allow us to *lower* our level of social stimulation to attain optimal intimacy. However, watching television is not the means by which we *raise* our intake of certain social stimulation to attain optimal intimacy, because such social stimulation requires conversation with another person. Talk is the tree on which the fruits of emotions are cultivated and grow.

## THINKING OF SOMETHING TO SAY

### Conversation as Climbing a Tree

In Figure 12.2, conversation is pictured as climbing a tree. The whole tree corresponds to having a conversation. The major limbs correspond to major topics, such as Topics A, B, and C. The smaller limbs and branches correspond to further subdivisions of a given topic. The process of entering a conversation corresponds to you climbing up the tree. Climbing up limbs corresponds to your pursuing topics as you go along.

Thinking of something to say is usually not a problem, but occasionally it is. Long silences tend to be embarrassing. However, lulls in conversation among the best of friends are perfectly normal. In fact, these pauses allow time to think of something to say, which means selecting a branch on which to climb. The "Russell thought drift" will be useful because its purpose is to help you create and pursue topics of conversation. The topics are assumed to be ordinary small talk for the most part.

### The Russell Thought Drift

#### Drifting

Most of the time, I find no trouble thinking of topics and things to say. However, every once in a while, my mind goes blank at the worst times. I stumble or sit there with my mouth hanging open (it seems like forever) through an awkward silence. For me, it is only occasional, but at such times I really wish for a topic to come to mind. It is for such tongue-tied moments that Elliot Russell's "thought drift" may help.[1]

We probably go from one topic to the next by association. The Russell thought drift con-

**Figure 12.2.** Conversation as climbing a tree.

**Figure 12.3.** Lining up at the bus stop. What aspects of this situation help produce conversation (or lack of it)? (Photograph by Charles Blakey.)

sists of using free association to *actively* think up topics related to the one you are on now. Nothing more.

**Case 12.3.** You are conversing about inflation. As you listen, your mental thought drift goes inflation→groceries→Russian wheat deal→foreign products→imported cars→saftey versus economy and dependibility→safety of loved ones→the other person's family→family vacations→trouble finding time for doing things as a family→decline of most churches' memberships→need for agencies to supply moral guidance to society→corruption in politics→local politics→defeat of bond issue for parks→recreation→games people play, and so on.

ACTIVITY 12.1.

Let your imagination go, and create your own thought drift consisting of 10 topics. Start with the topic of "love."

ACTIVITY 12.2.

Think of a recent conversation you have had. Write down a topic you discussed and go through a thought drift.

### Freeing the Mind

Russell treats thought drifting as a process of letting your mind go. He proposes that our minds are already disposed to free association if we only allow it. His strongest statement is that "*Failure* [to think up topics of conversation easily] *is chiefly due to the fact that efforts to think of something are blocking the efforts which their minds are making to suggest something. GET THAT.*"[2] So, it may help to think of your thoughts as wild mustangs thrashing around in a corral. Your thoughts need no pushing. They are ready to go if you let them. Thought drifting means opening the gate and allowing the penned-up horses to stampede out. The key point is that a conscious effort to grind out topics will hurt, not help.[3] Viewing our minds as already active and freely associating will help a lot. (See Figure 12.3.)

### Branching

Another feature of conversation that Russell clarifies for us is the degree to which we pursue any given topic. After using the thought drift to find a topic that interests our other person, we either branch out within the topic, switch topics, or end the conversation. If you detect that branching out within the topic is best, then Russell has another commonsense suggestion: "When you detect a response to the general topic you have introduced—while your friend or friends are discussing it in the usual conventional way—your mind should be dividing the topic into its categories."[4]

**Case 12.4.** While riding in an airplane one time, I began to talk with a man who sold light bulbs. Never having thought much about light bulbs before, I wanted to find out some of the ins and outs of the strange kind of yellowish lighting in downtown Miami at night. I came up with a branching diagram with the following categories:

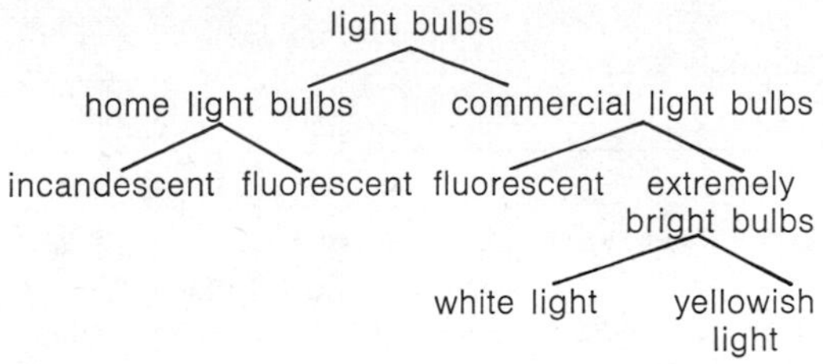


ACTIVITY 12.3.

Imagine that you have just taken a seat on an airplane or bus and notice that the person sharing your seat has a name tag saying "President, College Recruiting Corporation." You have no idea what kind of recruiting he does, but you would like to find out. In the space provided, classify the topic of "college recruiting." Begin with the general category "college recruiting" and create a branching diagram comparable to the one I created in Case 12.4 about the light bulbs.

college recruiting

ACTIVITY 12.4.

Create a branching diagram below where you break the topic "means of transportation" into sub-categories:

means of transportation

ACTIVITY 12.5.

Tape-record 10 minutes of a good talk show. In the space provided, create a branching diagram for the conversation. If the entire conversation is too complex, create your diagram to cover only a manageable portion of it.

ACTIVITY 12.6.

Tape-record an hour's worth of a good talk show. Then go down the list of principles in Appendix B and see how many were used somewhere in the show. Do this on a separate paper.

## MAJOR CATEGORIES OF NONVERBAL ACTION

### Major Categories Must Be General

Major categories of nonverbal actions in conversation must be general to be helpful to us as users. There are two good reasons for this. Both tell us why an overly microscopic analysis of nonverbal communication is not very fruitful.

First, to accurately decode whatever message the other person is sending to us requires a context of time. This fact is especially relevant for our efforts to *accurately* empathize with emotional messages. When asked to name the emotion being shown in a still picture, observers frequently disagree.[5] (See Figure 12.4) However, upon being provided a context that lasts for some length of time, accuracy seems to improve.[6] Some researchers have reported extremely high accurarcy in identifying emotions from still pictures; but subjects chose one of six emotions already written down by the researchers rather than labeling the emotion with no help beforehand.[7]

Second, context often determines meaning completely. To illustrate this fact, complete Activity 12.7.

ACTIVITY 12.7.

Ask most people what a smile signifies, and they will reply that a smile means happiness or pleasure. But is the meaning of a smile all that simple? After each of the following examples, write down what *you* think the smile means. The context changes in each case, and you can assume that the smile is exactly the same smile throughout.

Greg is 12 years old. He bites into a delicious piece of candy. He smiles.

________________________________________

________________________________________

The math teacher asks Greg to give the class his solution to problem number seven. Greg has not the foggiest idea of the solution because he could not work number seven at all. He smiles.

________________________________________

________________________________________

Greg feels destructive and mean. He has just been hurt, and he wants to hurt someone else. He hauls off and hits the boy who lives next door for no outward reason at all. He smiles.

________________________________________

________________________________________

### Listing the Categories

In order to take context into account, we will adopt the general categories of nonverbal behavior given by Paul Ekman and Wallace Friesen.[8] The following are the five categories, and they also form the next five sections.

1. *Body words* have a direct verbal translation and thus stand for a word or phrase. For example, flashing the peace sign is a body word that means "peace."
2. *Illustrators* are tied directly to speech and emphasize or otherwise illustrate what you are saying. For example, you sweep out your arm to its fully extended length to emphasize a concluding point you are making.
3. *Nonverbal emotions* convey affect or our emotions.
4. *Regulators* control who speaks and for how long. You may say "mm-hmm" and nod your head to keep the other person speaking. You might also look at the floor to get the other person to stop talking.
5. *Adaptors* maintain comfort and harmony between you and your environment. Scratching an itch, driving a car, and smoking are considered to be adaptors.

### Body Words

*Body words* have a one-to-one direct verbal meaning.[9] They can be replaced with a word or two. Most people in the given group or culture could immediately say the word or two upon seeing the body word.

According to Ekman and Friesen, body words can be shared by a whole culture, specific group, or just two people. Body words can occasionally be accidental, as when a man unknowingly clenches his fist in the presence of a person he purports to like. These authors have detected obscene body words during conversation. Upon being questioned afterward, the sender firmly denied sending any such message.

ACTIVITY 12.8.

Identify or make up body words that might be used in each of the following situations. Describe them in writing here, and be prepared to act them out in class.

Body word that means "committing suicide."

______________________________________

______________________________________

Body word transmitted by ground-crew member who is guiding an arriving airplane toward its position at the gate. The message sent to the pilot is "come closer and a little to the pilot's right."

______________________________________

______________________________________

Body word that is unique to just two people in a situation of your own choosing.

______________________________________

______________________________________

A particularly ingenious student of nonverbal behavior, Albert Scheflen gives us a provocative list of possible body words in *Body Language and Social Order*.[10] As you read the list of Scheflen's body words here in this paragraph, try to picture a situation in which the body word is being used. According to Scheflen, showing the palm of your hand

**Figure 12.4.** What message do you think this pretty smile conveys? (Photograph by Charles Blakey.)

to a member of the opposite sex is a courting body word. Similarly, preening your hair is courting. Grooming the other person, such as adjusting her jewelry pin, adjusting his tie, or flicking lint off clothing, is also courting. The eyebrow flash of recognition is claimed to be a universal, cross-cultural body word signifying recognition. In this body word, you first look at the other person, then lift your eyebrows high, and open your eyes wide for just a moment. Your hands can send body words. Your hands can indicate a specific size, say the specific length of 30 inches. Your hands can indicate "cutting" as when you draw a hand with fingers together across your other hand at a right angle. Scheflen also claims that drawing your index finger under your nose while you are talking means "I'm not telling the truth" or "I don't like it." Do you agree?

Another aspect of body words derives from the influence of body adornments, such as clothing and props (portable items about you). The activity that follows concerns the meaning of clothing and props. You will be asked to speculate about what the clothing connotes. As you do, think about aspects of clothing such as color, sloppiness versus neatness, amount of skin exposed, where the skin is exposed, stereotyped clothing of certain groups, and texture (hard, rugged Western denim versus soft, cuddly cashmere).

ACTIVITY 12.9.

Speculate about the connotations of the clothing in Figures 12.5, 12.6, and 12.7. To the extent that your speculations are shared, those shared connotations turn from speculation into social reality.

Figure 12.5. ______________________________

______________________________________

Figure 12.6. ______________________________

______________________________________

Figure 12.7. ______________________________

______________________________________

To jog your mind a bit, suppose photographer Chuck Blakey approached you at this

**Figure 12.5.** (Photograph by Charles Blakey.)

moment to ask you to pose for a new picture to accompany Activity 12.9. What would readers' reactions be to your dress? Would the reactions be changed by the props about you? What is connoted by the book you are reading? By the other physical adornments about you?

A final claim by Scheflen is worth noting before leaving the subject of body words: that a cultural function of body words is to maintain the *existing* social order.[11] He speaks of the need to limit *lateral mobility* so people do not leave an existing twosome, a family, a peer group, or an institution. For example, a twosome at a party will often stand with their body torsos parallel to indicate that "we are together and not to be separated." Scheflen also speaks of *vertical mobility* over time, noting that each social class has its distinctive collection of body words. Within the social class of vice-presidents of BC Corporation, there might be a distinctive style of dress, trim of facial hair (which might well change every so often), type of attaché case, and key words and phrases unique to that particular business. Anyone hoping to break into the ranks of vice-presidents at BC would have to master and display the appropriate collection of body words before being seriously considered.

ACTIVITY 12.10.

Refer to a specific work, social, or family group of which you have been (or are now) a member. What body words are characteristic of that group, if not distinctive of it?

As we go on to consider the other major categories of nonverbal action, it is important to bear in mind that the category of "body words" and the four categories to follow are not always independent from one another. A given action can easily fall into more than one category.

### Illustrators

*Illustrators* basically augment (emphasize, clarify, or contradict) what is being said. In

**Figure 12.6.** (Photograph by Charles Blakey.)

**Figure 12.7.** (Photograph by Charles Blakey.)

contrast to body words, illustrators cannot be used without conversation. We are less aware of when we use illustrators, and we would be less certain about their verbal translation if asked. Ekman and Friesen give us the following list of illustrators.[12] To clarify them, each is followed by a verbal statement which that illustrator might accompany.

*Batons* emphasize a certain word or phrase. "What this country needs is change *now,* not later but right *now.*" (fist pounded when speaker says "*now*")

*Ideographs* trace the direction of ideas and thoughts. "I don't enjoy living on the ground floor and would rather live on a *higher* floor."[13]

*Pointers* point. "It's right over there."

*Spatial movements* depict spatial relationships. "Well, I'd say you need to plant those hedge bushes about this far apart."

*Rhythmic movements* show rhythm and pacing of an event. "And the professor lectured on and on and on." "In my type of work, we're moving that inventory out *fast,* and I mean *fast.*"

Ekman and Friesen treat the different illustrators separately, but also say that they are not independent. Thus the rhythmic movement in the last example could also be a baton.

## Nonverbal Emotions

### On Emotions

Over the centuries, more has been written about love than any other topic. From ancient poetry on papyrus to modern pornography in pulp paperbacks, love has dominated all other topics. As we have discussed them, body words and illustrators serve only as *means* to aid communication. In contrast, such emotions as love can dominate a conversation because the like–dislike relationship is often the primary topic or *goal* of conversation.

Assume that most emotional meaning, including information about love, is conveyed nonverbally. This assumption is reasonable from a commonsense viewpoint because, if verbal and nonverbal messages concerning emotions are in conflict, the nonverbal overrides the verbal. In fact, some empirical studies have tried to pit a given verbal message against a conflicting nonverbal message. The findings support common sense. Merhabian and Ferris and Merhabian and Wiener derived the following formula:

$$\text{Total liking} = 7\%\ \text{verbal liking} + 38\%\ \text{voice liking} + 55\%\ \text{facial liking.}$$[14]

In other words, your other person may well draw conclusions about how much you like her (him) mostly from your voice and facial expressions, not the words you speak.

Assume also that we do not think a great deal about our nonverbal communication. Of course, sometimes we do. But elementary and secondary schools do not teach much of anything about nonverbal communication as a part of the formal curriculum; rather, verbal and written communication are emphasized. The enhancement of skill in accurately communicating what one wishes using nonverbal means would seem an appropriate domain of user information. If you put all the ideas in this section together, you will conclude that a lot of emotional information is likely to "leak out" without our knowledge. In fact, the idea that hidden thoughts and feelings can slip out unintentionally is a major factor motivating the study of nonverbal communication. In short, nonverbal emotions are extremely important topics in their own right.

Several scholarly books that review the various theories of communicating emotions have appeared recently: for example, Dittman's *Interpersonal Messages of Emotion* and Strongman's *The Psychology of Emotion.*[15] Dittman and Strongman agree on one main conclusion: Besides the good–bad dimension, no other dimension of emotional meaning has been convincingly demonstrated to exist. The only other contender that consistently turns up in study after study is a dimension of meaning which runs from passive to active.[16] Although the level of activity shown does not seem to be an emotion, there is good reason to suspect that level of or changes in level of activity often signal (but do not guarantee) that "I am sending out an emotional message."[17] Therefore, under the category of nonverbal emotions, we will consider messages of good-bad and active-passive.

### Liking and Disliking

As we discuss liking and disliking, our movement will take us from some rather solid conclusions to semisolid conclusions to speculative propositions. Beginning with solid conclusions, we note that some actions have been consistently associated with more liking. These findings are solid (at least for now) because they have been found repeatedly. In addition, these actions have been found to convey liking from the viewpoint of both sender and receiver. In the experiments of Merhabian and of Merhabian and Williams, young people were asked to show liking by acting out their emotions.[18] By *en*coding their own liking into action, Merhabian captured the viewpoint of the sender. (The sender's viewpoint corresponds to you when you want to show a lot of liking to, say, a new colleague at work.) To capture the viewpoint of the receiver, Merhabian asked other college students to watch another person and *de*code, or interpret, how much liking the other person wanted to show. (The receiver's viewpoint corresponds to you when you are listening to another person speak and are trying to figure out how much he—your boss, say—likes you.)

Five attributes have been found to be associated with *greater* liking from both the sender's and the receiver's viewpoints.

1. *Closer distance.* We get closer to the other person the more we like her (him). Hall has even proposed that four zones of closeness exist in North American culture.[19]

| | |
|---|---|
| 0–1½ | feet means an intimate distance. |
| 1½–4 | feet means a personal distance. |
| 4–12 | feet means a social distance. |
| over 12 | feet means a public distance. |

The conclusion that closer distance means more liking really amounts to a general tendency that usually holds. However, our common sense tells us that there will always be exceptions; for example, fighters have to get close together to slug it out in a barroom brawl.

ACTIVITY 12.11.

Try to measure the approximate distances you and your associates naturally keep during the course of one day. If you can, report on distances at work and at home related to specific activities, such as working at your desk, consulting with the boss, dinner at home, lunchtime, and so on.

ACTIVITY 12.12.

Choose a situation in which you will take an inappropriately close distance to the other person. For example, talking with a co-worker would normally occur at 3 feet; so stand 1 foot away. Keep all other aspects of the interaction as normal as you can. Does the other person adjust the distance? What other reactions does the other person make? Afterward, be sure to explain the whole procedure to the other person.

____________________________________

____________________________________

____________________________________

____________________________________

ACTIVITY 12.13.

Choose a situation as in the preceding activity, but this time take an inappropriately far distance. Remember to explain to the other person afterward.

____________________________________

____________________________________

____________________________________

____________________________________

In the two preceding activities, your task involved taking clearly inappropriate distances. In your mind now, vary the distance that you actually stood. For instance, if you changed a normal distance of 4 feet to 1 foot, suppose now that you only moved from 4 feet to 3 feet. What message would you be sending? Would your other person be able to verbalize the message? Such are the subtleties of ordinary conversation.

2. *More touching.* When we like more, we touch more.[20] Desmond Morris has even gone so far as to virtually equate touching and intimacy in his best-selling *Intimate Behavior.*[21] A slightly less extreme view is taken by Leonard and Natalie Zunin, who agree that "the most powerful impressions you make will be by touch."[22] My own view is one notch less extreme, emphasizing the certain importance and possible dominance of touching for expressing liking and loving. It may be that no words convey what sexual intercourse conveys, for instance.

There are two other aspects of touching that bear mention and these have not yet been studied. Have you ever noticed how some people rub, caress, groom, or fondle *themselves* in public? Also, have you ever noticed people handling the *personal objects of others in public?* I have seen people caressing their own thighs or handling someone's desk paperweight at length. It may be that such touching in public conveys the message "I'm a toucher and giver of liking and other positives." If so, the actions of touching ourselves and personal objects are available to us when we want to convey this message.

3. *More eye contact.* More eye contact means liking.[23] People who say they love another person more have been found to gaze into the loved one's eyes, as we would expect.[24]

4. *Leaning forward.* Leaning forward means more liking. Reclining back does not.

5. *Body torso facing other person.* The more your body torso faces the other person directly, the more liking is conveyed.

The five numbered attributes complete our list of firmly established means to convey liking. Any one or all of them can thus be used as rewards to increase depth of a topic or length of a whole conversation. As always, no one is writing guarantees that any one action will surely work, but these five comprise our best guess at present.

Moving on to semisolid findings, we now consider investigations of leakage, whereby information slips out unintentionally. Research by Ekman and Friesen, Merhabian, and Libby and Yaklevich indicates that persons who are actively trying to lie and deceive suffer leakage of information.[25] The leakage seems to be reflected in less smiling, slower speech, more speech errors, and less liking conveyed from *the neck down.* Ekman and Friesen speculate that the positions of our bodies about which we are least aware are those positions through which leakage occurs (e.g., leaning forward, body torso position, actions of our feet). Perhaps we have most control over the words we speak, less control over facial expression and tone of voice, and least control over our body from the neck down.

A fascinating new idea about emotional communications comes from Ernest Haggard and Kenneth Isaacs, who wrote "Micromomentary Facial Expressions as Indicators of Ego Mechanisms in Psychotherapy."[26] These abrupt changes in facial expression were found to last only a split second. The researchers had to run motion pictures of conversation in slow motion to detect these expressions, and their occurrence was nicely tied into the case history of the various patients. However, users are going to have to wait for a lot more research before practicality looms large. For now, we can only try to detect them.

Another fascinating semisolid idea was proposed by Argyle and Dean.[27] They say that any conversation you have carries an assumed degree of liking or intimacy. The total degree of liking that, say, you and your best friend share can be seen as more or less an equilibrium state. Furthermore, you and your best friend will achieve that equilibrium or total degree of liking by *balancing out* the total messages about liking that you send. Specifically, if you move much closer together, you will likely drop your eyes to the floor. If you give your best friend a friendly rub on the back or grab on the arm (more liking conveyed), you will likely do something else to convey *less* liking. In this case, you might align your body torsos in a more indirect way. Another way to see the Argyle and Dean idea is to make a comparison with the idea of "advertising mix." Advertisers trying to sell a new toothpaste will decide on some *total mixture* of different messages that will hopefully be most persuasive. In a similar way, Argyle and Dean say that you will try to convey a particular degree of liking by juggling and balancing the messages you send in various ways to your other person. To me, Argyle and Dean's idea conjures up the vision of two lovers wrapped around each other discussing platonic philosophy and similarily removed matters.

As a postscript to the Argyle and Dean idea, we note that Albert Scheflen points out different kinds of kisses in public. According to him, the intensity of a kiss in public is affected by whether the parties' pelvises are apart (low-intensity ritual kisses) or together (higher intensity, more sexual kisses).[28]

Finally, I claim that there is a whole realm of communication that conveys more about liking than all the communication we have discussed so far. The most convincing and powerful information about liking, loving, and intimacy comes from the *sharing of scarce personal resources.* Some resources are common to most people and some are unique. The most common and probably most precious resource is time because each of us is issued just 24 hours of it per day. Intense affection is also scarce. For nearly all of us, money and valuable possessions (e.g., automobiles) are scarce. Sexual intimacy is scarce, but to varying degrees. In all cases, you convey more liking and loving and intimacy by sharing more of your scarce personal resources. To the extent that personal resources are not scarce, they lose their value. The rich do not convey much liking by giving away a few thousand dollars. The playboys or playgirls and swingers do not convey much liking by doing it one more time. I only briefly state these points here because Chapter 5 was devoted largely to expanding on the argument I have sketched in this paragraph.

ACTIVITY 12.14.

Why did I not include smiling as a solid or even semisolid means to convey liking? Would *you* have included it?

______________________________

______________________________

______________________________

### Responsiveness

Our other kind of message relevant to the communication of emotions concerns how responsive, or active, we are. More responsiveness means more words spoken, louder speech, and longer utterances by you or your other person. Being more responsive also means greater nonverbal activity, more shifts in position, and more nonverbal expressions of *any* kind. Responsiveness is clearly tied into liking. If we assume that more liking and greater rewardingness usually go together, then higher responsiveness in the form of sheer volume of rewards you give should generally accompany increased liking between you and anyone else. On the opposite extreme, Longabaugh and his associates say that schizophrenics are distinguished by providing zero rewardingness.[29]

In *How to Talk with Practically Anybody About Practically Anything,* Barbara Walters offers an insightful speculation about responsiveness in job interviews: "The main element in landing the job is, believe it or not, how badly you want it. Employers these days put a premium on enthusiasm and zeal because they are fed up with employees who regard their jobs as places to display their wardrobe while waiting for life to begin at five o'clock."[30] She goes on to warn against overdoing your display of ambition, as illustrated in Case 12.5.

**Case 12.5.** "Well, tell me a bit about yourself, Mr. Tweney. Why do you think a manager's job with our firm would be a good thing?" "To tell the truth, Freddy, my whole life has convinced me that management is my bag. In every case from the junior high school newspaper to the county agency I work at now, I have risen through the ranks. Look, if you put me in charge of that department, they'll be doing half again as much work as they're doing now and loving it. And I'll be on my way up again. . . ." "Yes, Mr. Tweney, yes. That's what I'm afraid of. . . ."

In this case high responsiveness conveyed overambition, which was threatening.

We have now considered the nonverbal expression of emotions. Alas, we could only scratch the surface. And reading about nonverbal expressions is a far cry from experiencing them.

### Regulators

Nonverbal *regulators* determine who speaks and for how long. Consider Case 12.6, in which the parties in a conversation regulate their conversation verbally rather than nonverbally.

**Case 12.6.** Sam and Mary are in the snack bar taking their morning coffee break.

Sam: *Let us begin to talk.*

Mary: *Ok, let us converse together.*

Sam: *You start, because I'm having trouble thinking of something to say.*

Mary: *That's all right. I will start. I now have something to say. Hi, Sam, what do you think of the Watkins deal? There, now I've said it. I don't have any more to ask you. Rather, I want you to reply to this very first question. You may talk.*

Sam: *Very good, I will answer. My reply is that BC Corporation should never have got mixed up with the Watkins deal. Ok, there is my answer. It is now your turn to talk.*

(Time passes; a *lot* of time passes.)

Sam: *I will talk now. Our break is almost over, so it is time for us to stop talking. To get back to work, it is first necessary for me to rise out of my chair. I am now doing that. I have enjoyed this conversation, but the demands of my job require me to increase the distance between us. Do you agree? Your turn.*

Mary: *I will now talk. Yes, Sam. That's the way it is. I will do likewise. It is now appropriate to terminate this conversation.*

**Case 12.7.** Here is the same conversation again with the words spoken as might actually happen. After you read each sentence, close your eyes and visualize what Sam and Mary are doing *nonverbally* to regulate the conversation.

Mary: *Hi, Sam, what do you think of the Watkins deal?* (She looks up at Sam, who is ready to talk.)

Sam: *The BC Corporation should* never *have got mixed up with the Watkins deal.* (He says, shaking his head and looking back at her.)

(Time passes.)

Sam: *Bye, Mary.* (He rises from his chair, flashes a warm smile, and backs away waving.)

Mary: *See ya.* (She winks, waves, and looks down at the table while finishing her coffee.)

Do Cases 12.6 and 12.7 indicate that nonverbal communication is efficient; that is, can you communicate a lot of information easily using nonverbal channels?

Scheflen has been concerned mainly with regulators. According to his work, we can view regulation as coming after a sentence, topic, or whole conversation and as always addressing the question, "Do we want to continue or switch or stop?" After you have spoken a sentence, for example, how would you and I determine if *you* have anything more to say? To shed some light on this point, Kendon filmed conversation in slow motion to see if we send out signals that convey "I am finished with this utterance" very quickly.[31] He found that, about two seconds before they stopped talking, speakers shifted their gaze toward the listener's eyes and continued to look toward them during the final moments of an utterance. About two seconds before beginning to talk, the listener starts to look away from the speaker. Then the speaker ends his utterance and the listener begins to talk.

ACTIVITY 12.15.

Assume that the findings of Kendon on his limited sample reflect a general tendency in all of us. Just before we begin to talk, we look away. Just before we stop talking, we look at the other person's eyes. What functions, or *purposes,* might these actions serve for the speaker?

---

---

For the listener?

---

---

Scheflen thinks that any marked change in the pattern of communication can serve as a *terminal marker,* which says, "It is time to stop."[32] Examples include change in pitch of voice, lowering of head, lowering of hands, brushing palms together as if dusting hands off,[33] blocking one's face with hands for a second or more,[34] and rubbing one's eyes.[35] All these terminal markers are speculated to be usually unintentional. You might try to be alert to see if his speculations apply at the end of your conversations.

Scheflen's mammoth contribution to the study of nonverbal communication will probably turn out to be his discovery of *transcontextuals.* Being an astute psychiatrist, Scheflen's broad vision detected a feature of nonverbal communication that is somewhat more general than those we have discussed up to this point. Transcontextuals are "not . . . appropriate to the context and thus have the effect of disturbing the orderly progression of the transaction."[36]

What do you do when your other person is performing a transcontextual? The transcontextual probably means "switch topics or quit talking." It also might mean "I have a problem." To answer the practical question of what to do when faced with a transcontextual, three courses of action come to mind: switch topics, shut up, or gently bring the transcontextual into conversation together with your feelings about it.

Since transcontextuals depend entirely on the *context,* they can assume almost any form. Nowhere will we find a better illustration of the complexity of ordinary conversation. A transcontextual here may earn a promotion there, or get one fired. Some of Scheflen's transcontextuals follow:

*looking at the floor when keen attention is appropriate*[37]
*addressing your remarks to the ceiling*[38]
*laughing at an inappropriate time*[39]
*continuously pulling off and putting on one's wedding band*[40]
*talking too much*[41]
*courting too obviously at a business meeting*[42]
*sudden anger*[43]
*exaggerated emotions*[44]

Also, the Zunins claim that picking at one's eyes or nose in the first 4 minutes of conversation is transcontextual.[45]

**Case 12.8.** Bill says, "When are you going to help me tune up my car? Do you think maybe this afternoon?" John says, "What do you think about that awful test we had in school today? Did you ever see such a hard exam?" What is the transcontextual here?[46]

ACTIVITY 12.16.

Create a situation, from a situation that you encounter daily, in which a transcontextual is being displayed to you by your other person. Be prepared to act it out in class, showing several courses of action you could take.

---

---

---

### Adaptors

*Adaptors* generally maintain smooth interaction with the environment. We will briefly describe adaptors, but that is all, because adaptors are not really communicative; rather, they are directed toward task activities. Ekman and Friesen see *self-adaptors* as self-maintaining actions including eating, scratching, shifting positions, brushing one's teeth, putting on makeup, or changing one's path to avoid an open manhole.[47] *Object adaptors* involve the manipulation of objects, such as playing a piano, fixing supper, tuning a car, or turning the next page of this book.

**LISTENING**

What is the best strategy for building up a topic in conversation? At least two experts would advise us to say as little as possible and to listen actively. From both Elliot Russell and Larry Barker, we can compile a compelling list of advantages obtained by letting our other person do much of the talking.[48]

1. Listening covers our weaknesses.
2. Listening allows us to think.
3. Listening permits us to gather more information about the other person.
4. Listening a lot increases the emphasis and value of what we say. Thoughts offered only rarely probably carry more credibility because they are moderately scarce.
5. Listening allows us to learn more useful facts in general.
6. Listening allows us to evaluate the other person's message. (Such evaluation does not mean that we render a public judgment of what we are thinking.)
7. Listening is usually less stressful than speaking.
8. Listening allows far more opportunity to attend to the other person's nonverbal communication and to behave in a more socially skilled manner.

One major problem looms for the listener, as Barker makes clear.[49] Suppose you are listening to a droning monotone that bores you stiff? Two solutions may lessen the agony if terminating is out of the question. For one, shift your attention mainly to the vocal and nonverbal channels of communication, and start concentrating on the emotional relationship connoted by your nonverbal actions. When thinking such thoughts becomes a drag, do something to *change* his or her nonverbal acts. The other solution is to think ahead and anticipate what he will say. If all else fails, I start putting the other person on by introducing grossly untruthful information presented as factual (unless it will get me fired or rejected).

In cases when you want to listen but encounter difficulty, Thomas Gordon's P.E.T. *Parent Effectiveness Training* approach is helpful.[50] It emphasizes listening skills. Specifically, Gordon warns us that when trying to build up rapport, certain actions are transcontextuals and can derail a relationship—especially a relationship across generations. In the paragraphs to follow, three transcontextuals are first stated and then followed by case examples. These cases are examples of transcontextuals exhibited by the *listener.*

1. Beginning a reply about 0.000001 seconds after the other person finishes speaking.

**Case 12.9.** Johnny comes home dejected and says, "My problem with grades, yes I got one and that's how I see it. Oh yes and we need to talk so much more about it," Bill says. (We could not squeeze quotation marks in the microsecond between Johnny's "it" and Bill's "Oh.")

2. Not responding to the other person's thoughts before going on to other points.

**Case 12.10.** Shiela says, "What do you think about Johnny and me? Do you think it's love?" Beth says, "One thing I think is that we should go shopping next Saturday morning and. . . ."

3. Making clumsy attempts to "reflect" back or restate the other person's thoughts to draw him (her) out. The tried and true procedure of getting the other person to talk about himself (herself) instead means using techniques made famous by Carl Rogers in his client-centered therapy. Rogers's goal was to keep the other person talking. The techniques involve "reflecting" or restating the same thought back to the other person or by uttering a contentless remark such as "mmm." Clumsy reflecting means mechanically parroting back nearly the exact words used by the sender, which conveys the message from the original receiver that "I did not even bother to decode your message and reply in my own words."

**Case 12.11.** Danny says, "Oh that Tasmanian sauerkraut soufflé tasted terrible and I feel just *awful!*" His mother replies, "Oh, does that Tasmanian sauerkraut soufflé taste terrible and make you feel just *awful?*" In this example, the attempt to "reflect" his thought back was clumsy because the other person's statement of feeling was parroted back word-for-word. The unspoken implication is that Danny's thoughts were not

**Figure 12.8.** A transcontextual in progress, similar to that described in Case 12.12. (Photograph by Charles Blakey.)

processed or acted on by his mother. She mechanically and clumsily applied a tool.

**Case 12.12.** Suzie enters the kitchen as you are washing some lettuce in the sink. She says, "I think I'm in bad with the crowd just because I had a talk with Martha's boyfriend." You say, "Oh, is that so?" without turning around, making eye contact, or in any way taking yourself away from the lettuce. In this case, your statement "Oh, is that so?" is fine, but it is accompanied by transcontextual nonverbal communication indicating you are not interested. (See Figure 12.8.)

Before leaving the topic of trancontextuals, I must say a word about the so-called double bind theory of schizophrenia. Originally proposed in a classic paper by Bateson, Jackson, Haley, and Weakland, this theory maintains that schizophrenics grow up in families in which transcontextuals and other *conflicting messages* exist to an abnormal degree.[51] For example, the mother says she loves her children; but her nonverbal behavior and not giving them much of her time tell her children she dislikes them. If the theory is true, we should all become a little worried because conflicting messages and transcontextuals are obviously all around us. In a careful study of communication from parents of disturbed adolescents to their children, Beakel and Merhabian found differences in degree of conflicting messages sent from parents to children to be either nonexistent or opposite to what the theory would predict.[52] The results further indicated that in a more disturbed relationship, communications were simply more negative, *not* more conflicting or inconsistent. Thus it appears that sending inconsistent messages does not put us on the road to schizophrenia. Still, Beakel and Merhabian's subjects were not schizophrenic, but only "disturbed," so the theory might hold for extremely sick families. Also, Beakel and Merhabian studied only communications in a therapy setting, not the home situation. Nevertheless, I am still intrigued by the clinical observations of Scheflen, who discusses familiar conflicting messages we see everyday.[53] There is the boss who screams and rants and raves, but who is really a prince of a guy because he will loan you a few bucks or hear you out when you want to talk. There are women who give you a zero on the liking dimension from the neck up but act flirtatious and seductive from the neck down.

ACTIVITY 12.17.

Spend a day in which you are especially on the lookout for conflicting messages in all you meet. Report here.

______________________________

______________________________

______________________________

______________________________

______________________________

______________________________

ACTIVITY 12.18 (optional).

Using an ordinary conversation as the situation, go back through Chapters 7 through 10 and, for each principle, give an example of where that principle can be clearly applied in conversation. Do this on a separate paper.

**ENDING THE CONVERSATION: FAREWELLS**

"The enthusiasm of greetings compensates for the weakening of the relationship caused by the absence just terminated, while the enthusiasm of farewells compensates the relationship for the harm that is about to be done to it by separation." So says Erving Goffman, the insightful sociologist, in his *Interaction Ritual,* where he discusses greetings and farewells.[54] If we wish to focus on the final moments of a conversation, you and I as active agents can add a special positive touch to farewells.

Suppose your other person is going to be affected more by your farewell than by the body of your conversation. Indeed, memory studies show a tendency to remember first and last words in an otherwise uniform series better than what comes in between.[55] It is possible that, more than any other part of a conversation, the farewell *you* give to your other person captures and summarizes the emotional relationship between you.

In addition to your farewell summarizing the relationship, I speculate that your farewell conveys real meaning about the next contact. While Goffman claims that the usual farewells (e.g., "See ya") inevitably leave open future meetings by chance, I claim that willfully departing from the usual conveys special meaning. Specifically, if we want to convey that we would enjoy another meeting, we can depart from ritual farewell in two ways. First, we can add detail. With more detail, "See you later," becomes "I hope I'll get to see you on Wednesday night." Second, we can indicate that we will spend some scarce personal resources in order to arrange another meeting. By offering such resources, "Come see us again" becomes "Do you think you might be able to come over for a big Sunday dinner real soon?"

ACTIVITY 12.19.

Create a situation from your own social life (not your job) in which adding detail and/or personal resources in the few seconds it takes to bid farewell connotes your desire to meet again.

Situation:

______________________________

Usual farewell:

______________________________

Added detail farewell:

______________________________

______________________________

Added personal resources farewell:

______________________________

______________________________

Added detail and added resources farewell:

______________________________

______________________________

______________________________

### NONVERBAL ACTIONS AS A COMMON INTEREST FOR INITIATING AN INTERACTION

We covered meeting new people and initiating interactions in the previous chapter. In this chapter, you may have acquired a valuable tool for initiating interaction, namely, making opening comments about nonverbal actions in the immediate situation. For example, "You look like you're on top of the world. What are you so happy about?" One variation on this opening comprises what authors of popular books have called "character reading" about the other person. As such, this variation comes under the "common interest" opening category discussed in Chapter 11. If directly speculating about a person you do not yet know seems a bit forward, there is another variation. The newly acquainted other person is immediately enlisted in the fascinating task of interpreting something about, say, the gentleman with the cane over there. In this variation, the common interest category is also used.

### CONVERSATION PATTERNS THAT REPEAT THEMSELVES OVER TIME

#### Berne's Games

In recent years, transactional analysis has captivated millions around the world, largely because of the tremendous success of Eric Berne's *Games People Play* and Thomas Harris's *I'm OK—You're OK.*[56] In these books, the authors present a theory that allows readers to see destructive communication patterns in their own lives and to chuckle at the familiarity of the close-to-home situations described. The so-called games delightfully described by Berne deserve our attention because they reflect a kind of conversational pattern we have not yet considered.

Caution: The longer-range patterns of conversation we will be discussing here are not all bad. In his *Games People Play,* Berne devoted 94 pages to "bad" games and a paltry 6 to "good" games. Thus it is common to jump from 'long-term pattern" to "destructive long-term pattern" of conversation. Don't. Berne was especially attuned to patterning that involves problems in living. And his games involved life events far more serious than most conversations (e.g., alcoholism). He was a therapist, and that was his business.

According to Berne, we are always trying to structure time. In trying to fill up the time, we wish—ideally—to achieve intimacy (social communion) with other persons. However, there are barriers to social communion. One not-so-obvious barrier consists of the ingenious ways we dream up to *avoid intimacy.* We often structure time in four ways to avoid social communion: We engage in withdrawal, rituals, activities (tasks), and pastimes (trivial conversation). When we engage in any of these four to avoid social communion, an opportunity to pursue intimacy is lost and harm results.

A fifth way we can ward off intimacy is to play games. If you play a *game,* you repeat a pattern of action that leads to a *predictable outcome* over time. For Berne the game's outcome is usually destructive and usually hidden from the players. Games are all around us.

Because games reflect complex patterns of conversation over time, we must change our perspective considerably. In most of this chapter, we have considered aspects of conversation that last instants or minutes, such as hand gestures or topics in a conversation. Berne stretches our minds to view patterns that occur over hours, days, and weeks. In a game, the "players" move through a well-defined series of moves toward a payoff that is dishonest, predictable, and usually destructive. From a short-range view, games look like simple conversations, arguments, and decisions. A psychology researcher conducting an hour-iong observation would not often be able to detect a game in progress, let alone trace its course. From a longer-range view, both parties seem caught up in a perverted pattern of immediate rewards that usually works to their ultimate disadvantage over the years.

In the game "Why Don't You—Yes But," one player presents a problem while other players offer solutions.[57] Case 12.13 illustrates.

**Case 12.13.**

Carl: *Y'know? The spring weather coming on makes me wanta just hop in the car and drive down country roads for a whole day or so.*

Carlotta: *Why don't you do just that?*

Carl: *Yes, but I've got a lotta writing to do that's gotta be done by next Wednesday.*

Carlotta: *If you spread the writing out over a few days, you'll get it done.*

Carl: *Yes, but I also have to practice my guitar for the next lesson.*

Carlotta: *Why don't you spread the guitar practice out over time and do a little bit of it every day too?*

Carl: *Yes, but it takes me a half hour just to get my fingers loose so I can get past the warm-up and start practicing for real.*

In this case, the pattern becomes clear over time. Carl presents a problem; Carlotta offers a solution; and Carl rejects the solution with a "Yes but." By playing "Why Don't You—Yes But," the players accomplish several short-range goals. Most important, conversation fills up the time, which might otherwise become deadly silence. Carl gets rewarded with reassurance, which Carlotta provides in the form of solutions. Carlotta gets to play a game of her own, which Berne calls "I'm Only Trying to Help You." However, over the long haul, the payoff of the game "Why Don't You—Yes But" constitutes a self-destructive pattern, and the players avoid intimacy.

Berne also shows us the game "Harried," which he claims is "played by the harried housewife."[58] We can expand this game to include the conversational decision-making patterns of the millions of men and women today who overbook their daily schedules ahead of time without a thought. Here is Berne's description of the game:

**Case 12.14.** The thesis of this game is simple. She [housewife or main player] takes on everything that comes, and even asks for more. She agrees with her husband's criticisms and accepts all her children's demands. If she has to entertain at dinner, she feels she must function impeccably as a conversationalist, chatelaine over the household and servants, interior decorator, caterer, glamour girl, virgin queen and diplomat; she will also volunteer that morning to bake a cake and take the children to the dentist. If she already feels harassed, she makes the day even more harried. Then in the middle of the afternoon, she justifiably collapses, and nothing gets done. . . . The husband is carefully chosen; he is an otherwise reasonable man who will criticize his wife if she is not as efficient as he thinks his mother was.

(From Eric Berne, *Games People Play,* pp. 102–103. Reprinted by permission of Grove Press, Inc. Copyright © 1964 by Eric Berne.)

The wife described could just as well be a modern businessman who overbooks his schedule with club and community service, only to find himself fatigued, denied a promotion, and deserted by his family.

ACTIVITY 12.20.

In Case 12.14, what are the immediate, short-run rewards exchanged in conversation by the wife? By the husband? By the children?

Given and received by the wife:

________________________________________

________________________________________

Given and received by the husband:

________________________________________

________________________________________

Given and received by the children:

________________________________________

________________________________________

If played as a deadly serious or "third degree" game, "Harried" puts the central player in the divorce court, state hospital, or morgue.[59] According to Berne, the solution requires (1) the participants to recognize the deadly ultimate payoff and (2) the central player to somehow take on just one role at a time.

Games can also be unique and personal. In one of my classes, I asked if anyone had ever encountered a unique and personal game. One student came up with an interesting case. Whenever she and a certain man went out to eat, the man would invariably refuse to express even the slightest preference about the restaurant. Once inside, however, he became a tiger—finding everything wrong with the restaurant, food, service, and so on.

Berne's fascinating catalog of games goes on and on with other insightful games. To beat a game in one's own life requires, first, recognition of the destructive pattern. Then the task becomes one of change, perhaps best tackled with the aid of friends, user information, and therapists. Of special importance is user information for reducing unwanted communications (e.g., wife saying yes to added tasks) and for building up desired actions (e.g., wife saying no to added tasks and actually beginning conversation for social communion).[60]

### Perspective on Berne's Games

Berne's games are actually a subvariety of *social traps.* John Platt, recently wrote an article entitled "Social Traps," destined to become a classic. He says: "The term [social trap] refers to situations in society that contain traps normally like a fish trap, where men or organizations or whole societies get themselves started in some direction or some set of relationships that later prove to be unpleasant or lethal and that they see no easy way to back out or avoid."[61] How do we intelligent humans get trapped like fish? Social traps operate like this:

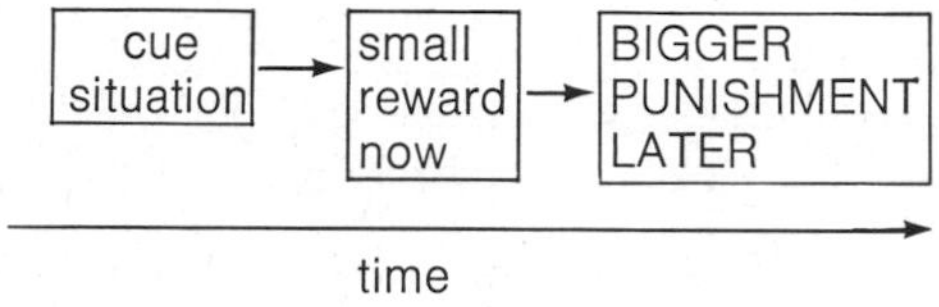


What are some social traps? Berne's game of Harried is a social trap. Sexual intercourse with someone you don't care for is a social trap. Gambling for random jackpots is a social trap. Calorie-laden food is a social trap. Buying a showroom car loaded with $1000 of worthless accessories on it is a social trap. You get the car now, but later your payments contain a portion spent for those accessories that could be better spent for, say, 100 meals eaten out at restaurants. Alcoholism is a social trap. Excessive commercial consumption as discussed in Chapter 5 is a social trap. Telling off your boss is a social trap. Rushing into marriage is a social trap. Getting a divorce too hastily is a social trap. *Repeatedly* withdrawing from other people after a day of social overstimulation on the job is a social trap that leads to loneliness.

ACTIVITY 12.21.

List two social traps you have seen in operation.

Social trap at the interpersonal level:

Social trap at the national level:

Platt also goes on to detail *social fences,* which operate in the opposite way. Fences keep you from acting, like these:

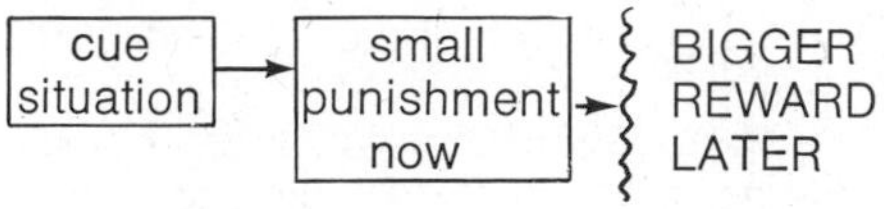


What are some social fences? Not initiating an interaction when you are just about to is a social fence. Fear is the small punishment now, and emotional intimacy is the bigger reward later. Failing to scout out all your options when buying a house is a social fence. Taking the trouble to check out the 5 houses you have not seen is the small punishment now. A possible better house is the bigger reward later. Ordering a car with only the accessories you want and waiting for delivery from the factory is a social fence. You wait a while for the car now, but you have all that money later. Not disclosing yourself to another can be a social fence (it can also be wise, of course). Waiting to build a subsidized, top-notch nationwide railroad system is a social fence for the United States.

ACTIVITY 12.22.

List two social fences you have seen in operation.

Social fence at interpersonal level:

Social fence at national level:

### USING TELEVISION COMMERCIALS AS LEARNING AIDS FOR SELF-IMPROVEMENT

Perhaps more concentrated brainpower from socially skilled individuals is crammed into television commercials than any other persuasive medium. Hundreds of thousands of dollars are often spent to make the persuasive most of the few, fleeting seconds taken by a single commercial on television. I propose that, with a little ingenuity, the powerful professionally mediated information that goes into the making of television commercials can be converted into user information. As a result, we should be able to turn television commercials into teaching and learning devices that serve our own purposes as users.

The Dade County Public Schools have just completed a program of instruction aimed at teaching young people to recognize 10 commonly used persuasive techniques in television commercials. When this program became public, it was attacked by the Florida Association of Broadcasters, a statewide association of radio and television stations.[62] This association argued that the emphasis on television commercials was unfair, because children are also exposed to persuasion on other media. In this regard, the association was on thin ice, because the average child in the United States logs more hours watching television than in school by the time he or she graduates from high school.[63] However, the association is perfectly right in their claim that persuasion attempts are not limited to just television commercials. In fact, we will assume the general effectiveness of the persuasion techniques for the interpersonal area.

We will consider the 10 persuasion techniques in a moment. Going even further than the claim of generality, I encourage you to watch television commercials to learn the techniques as only an animated display can teach, and I encourage you to apply them in your daily life. At this point there will surely be a terrible outcry that I am not only teaching manipulation, but I am glorifying it as well. This anticipated outcry is naive and wrong. It is naive because truly effective persuasion techniques are more properly viewed as descriptions about how people function than tools that can somehow only be applied toward evil goals. The anticipated outcry is wrong for four reasons: (1) Effective interpersonal techniques can be applied for good or ill; (2) Your goals are worthy (I assume); (3) With a working knowledge of these techniques you can better resist persuasion attempts on you, whether they come from television or in conversation; and (4) Power can be abused only when unduly concentrated, and making these strategies public is reducing the concentration by spreading the knowledge around.

With these preliminary remarks, we now consider the 10 techniques of persuasion. Each is listed below, followed by examples.

1. Appealing to authority: "Doctors agree . . . ," "Mom says . . . ," "Thomas Jefferson would surely like . . . ," and "Recent studies have shown that. . . ."

2. Bandwagon approach: "All the other kids are doing it," "My neighbors have one," "More people buy Crashmobile than . . . ," "It's the latest, it's the greatest, it's sweeping the country, it's . . . ," and "To be with it, you gotta. . . ."

3. Transfer technique: This one could also be called the classical conditioning technique, because the technique is to associate an already-effective cue with the product. Examples include a pretty girl using toothpaste, a sexy man driving a shiny new Crashmobile, public figures giving product testimonials, husband and wife madly embracing with product in full view, funny joke or situation portrayed with product in full view, and the furrowed brows of excruciating misery that vanishes upon taking the product.

4. Labelling: "Smoke Spring Waterfall Cigarettes," "My opponent in this has made several hysterical claims . . . ," "The position of my opponent can only be described as radical . . . ," and "I endorse our entrance into this preventive war (instead of aggression). . . ."

5. Ego building: "Since you probably will choose only the best for your children . . . ," "Gentlemen of discriminating taste . . . ," "Choosey mothers pick . . . ," "Barfer's Beer is not for everyone . . . ," "Be the first on your block to own a plobber . . . ," "Let the toolshed look as nice as the rest of your house . . . ," and "You deserve. . . ."

6. Identification: "I'm Irish too . . . ," "Joe Smith is running for mayor, but he had to take time out for his initiation into the Raccoon's Lodge, which we bring you now from the treehouse . . . ," pictures of political candidate with sleeves rolled up, and products endorsed by common folk with just the slightest trace of the local accent.

7. Oversimplification: This technique appeals to the lazy thinker. "In your heart you know he's right . . . ," "After taking just one each day I feel better all over . . . ," "In the pursuit of excellence . . . ," "The ABC Party, the party of the working man . . . ," and "Only people like you can stop pollution."

8. Image making: "You'll feel devilish in the Crashmobile Demona . . . ," "Come to where the tough guys live, smoke Manly Cigarettes . . . ," "You're in safe hands when you elect Governor (father image) . . . ," "The Crashmobile Gazelle will make you feel 10 years younger . . . ," and "Get in the swing with Swinger Soda. . . ."

9. Hypnotism: Mild forms of trance are induced through smooth, resonant verbiage, often through repetition of key words and phrases. This technique may be most effective in television and interpersonal contexts where nothing exciting or thought-provoking is happening. "Sleep, sleep, sleep, sleeeep, ssssleep with Cyanide, the soooothing relaxer . . . ," "I stand of the people, by the people, and for the people . . . ," "(clock ticks and ticks and ticks). In 60 seconds Buttered Beanies can be in your bloodstream, bringing you . . . ," and "It's Buggo for those nasty bugs that bug you, Buggo, Buggo, B-u-g-g-o!"

10. Sophistry: Sophistry means half-truths dominate the appeal. "Research proves our product reduces cavities 60 percent (as compared to exactly what?) . . . ," "Wash the gray right out of your hair (versus dye your hair) . . . ," "It just plain makes sense to drive a Crashmobile Guzzler, the family car (despite the gas rationing likelihood when everyone drives them) . . . ," "They're scrumptious in your tummy (despite the empty calories and resulting cavities) . . ." and "Buy an Evil Primevil Sidewalk Slaughter kit and be the first on your block (to wind up in the emergency room)."

(The list above was adapted from a similar list in "Persuasion Techniques Used on Television," 1975, pp. 4–5, a written set of specifications designed to guide the production and utilization of the 10 15-minute videotape programs that constitute the learning program. Reproduced with the permission of the Department of Education, State of Florida. The specifications were created by Dr. Castelle Gentry, Director of Instructional Media Center, Michigan State University, under a contract with the Florida Department of Education, while the videotape programs were produced in Media Programs, Dade County Public Schools.)

Well, there they are, probably more sophisticated than most of us would guess and certainly beyond the ken of quite young children. Take them for what they are, outward actions. The truest lover and the most untrue will both use them, the difference between sincerity and insincerity being visible only over time.

Let me conclude by saying once more that these techniques are valuable learning aids for self-improvement. You can be on the lookout for them yourself. You can apply them toward the personal goals you hold most dear. You can teach them to your children. And you can probably add to the list.

ACTIVITY 12.23.

At home tape record the commercials in an hour's worth of television viewing. Then go through each one individually and see if all the techniques were used during the hour you sampled. Were other techniques used that are not in the list of ten? Share in class.

ACTIVITY 12.24.

Imagine that you are in a clearly persuasive situation, such as sales, seduction, or a similar setting. Imagine that in this interpersonal situation there are just two people present. The other person is trying to convince you to do something. What might the other person say to you to persuade you *in the normal course of conversation?* For each of the persuasive techniques we have just covered, supply a statement that might be made by the other person in trying to persuade you.

Appealing to authority

________________________________________

________________________________________

Bandwagon approach

________________________________________

________________________________________

Transfer technique

________________________________________

________________________________________

Labelling

______________________________

______________________________

Ego building

______________________________

______________________________

Identification

______________________________

______________________________

Oversimplification

______________________________

______________________________

Image making

______________________________

______________________________

Hypnotism

______________________________

______________________________

Sophistry

______________________________

______________________________

**SUMMARY**

Conversation was defined as two or more people talking to each other or otherwise communicating on a moment-to-moment basis. The Russell thought drift was proposed as a way to think of something to say. Major categories of nonverbal communication include body words, illustrators, nonverbal emotions, regulators, and adaptors. Several advantages of listening to your other person were listed, and some pitfalls in listening were discussed. The importance of farewells that terminate a conversation was emphasized, along with suggestions for effectively conveying the parting idea "Let's meet again, really." We discussed conversation patterns that repeat themselves over time. Eric Berne's "games people play" and similar patterns that repeat themselves were held to be a special instance of social traps. A social trap means a pattern of action in which a smaller, immediate reward tricks one into doing something again and again that is harmful over the longer run, as when we nag in conversation or eat fattening foods. A social fence means a pattern of action in which a small, immediate punishment keeps us from a larger reward over the longer run, as when fear keeps us from initiating an interaction that might lead to a valuable friendship. Finally, we considered the use of ten techniques common in television commercials as they apply to persuasive attempts in the course of everyday conversation.

**FINAL REQUEST**

If you, dear reader, have gained some benefit from or wish to make a comment on this book, please do *me* a favor. Complete and mail the questionnaire at the end of the book. It will be appreciated and used. Thank you.

*Curiously, the good conversationalist does not have to speak with apparent ease or lack of effort. It is human nature to distrust the "born orator." He usually has too much conviction and too little concern for others. A sincere belief, no matter how tortured the manner in which it is delivered, is apt to be accepted at face value.*

MELVIN POWERS

# EPILOGUE ON SURVIVAL

The emphasis throughout this book has centered around positive human contact and practical means for achieving it. Only in Chapter 5, "values," did we depart from the interpersonal level of social interaction to look at the effects of the larger, surrounding economic system. In this epilogue, I shall briefly expand the perspective to the international level to address the knottiest problem of all: the surivival value of human contact and kindness.

As I wrote Chapters 2 through 5, my mind filled with utopian visions of "a good life" (as described in Chapter 5) for all the world's peoples. However, lurking in the background were some nagging questions about harsh reality. At the national level, could a nation realistically attain a good life filled with kind, positive people functioning in the range of optimal intimacy? Or would it starve? Would it collapse economically? Does not the capitalistic economic system institutionalize the law of the jungle? Does not competition lead to survival of the fittest? At the international level, has anyone ever found an effective response to savage aggression other than more savage counter-aggression? Are kind people and kind customs doomed to be "selected out" eventually by social evolution? Is human contact nothing more than the glue that binds us together to fight outsiders? Is there hope?

At the national level, there would seem to be no prior reason why a nation could not shift to functioning largely on the energy of positive emotions, rewards, and feelings. The great power of these positive forces indicates as much. In fact, James Prescott makes a good case for the heavy influence of positive body contact through touching in infancy to enhance specific brain development and later functioning on the basis of positive rewards, emotions, and feelings.[1] Conversely, babies deprived of cuddling or who experience fear may well grow into adults who give out and respond to aversive punishments, emotions, and feelings.

The real problem concerns the international level. Armed to the teeth and steeped in a history of world violence, nations still live by the sword. I see no effective response to armed force other than countering with superior armed forces. Thus, paradoxically, the stratospheric nobility of a good life for a whole nation currently depends on being able to effectively close with and destroy the enemy. In other words, the very atmosphere of domestic tranquility necessary for a nation's citizens to do the nicest things for one another depends on the nation's ability to do the nastiest things to other nations who might attack. The only hope lies in reducing the disposition to use armed force in the first place.

The only hope for reducing the dispositions of adults to use negative control lies in disposing young people to use positive rather than negative control. The only hope for disposing young people to function using positive control (rewards, emotions, feelings) is to find some way to *shift* their functioning from the current both-negative-and-positive to positive. The only way to do this is to experiment. The only way to experiment is with whole communities because anything less than whole social systems would have little generality to other communities and to nations. The only suitable communities are fairly isolated, small towns willing to voluntarily undertake temporary experiments, of the sort sketched in Case 5.11, in improving the quality of life.

Sleepy little towns hold the key to the future because the people in them can do something no other people can. With only modest effort, temporary experiments for better living can be undertaken. Similar undertakings would be far more difficult in urban areas. Before long a rich variety of relaxed community life-styles might come to be, each approaching a good life in the particular town's own individual style. In other words, with some thoughtful (and courageous) fine tuning, small communities can approach the apparent ideal level of intermediate productivity because (1) they are nearly there already and (2) their environment has not yet been devastated. The ultimate future for all of us may well rest with such places.

Because "positive functioning" includes the whole range of human functioning with emphasis on positive emotions, all three kinds of information in psychology (discussed in Chapter 1) are essential. For example, detailed knowledge about the human brain and the physiological processes of emotion would constitute necessary *basic research information.* The specific effects of vehicle traffic or the hours kept by businesses upon social relations inside the family would constitute necessary *professionally mediated information,* which could be applied by professional city and county managers. And, of course, *user information* is required for reasons given throughout this book. Information of all three kinds is currently in extremely short supply when compared to the existing commercial and military technologies. Thus I see ample justification for the evolvement of a "Golden Age of Psychology" if mankind's vision is to truly come to rest on the quality of life and human survival over the long run.[2]

In short, an advanced state of psychological knowledge probably holds the only realistic hope for world peace, let alone "a good life" for everyone in the world. The technology of war is just as advanced as modern commercial technology, and effective measures to counter armed aggression after the outbreak of war do not exist. The only hope is to exert influence before the fact.

Therefore, in addition to the two strategies of environmentalism and creating a viable body of user information, we should probably add a third. The third is research on how to shift human functioning from negative-and-positive to positive. All three strategies deserve support in the form of votes and money. The rest is up to you.

# APPENDIX A

# A Manual for Self-Administered Progressive Relaxation

**GERALD M. ROSEN**
**University of Arizona**

This manual presents all the rules you need to know in order to self-administer progressive relaxation training. The procedures you will be following are based on the work of Dr. Edmund Jacobson, and they are relatively easy to learn. When working on your program, it is important that you follow the instructions step-by-step. Also, remember that progressive relaxation, like any other skill, can be learned only through continued practice. For this reason, you should try to hold regularly scheduled sessions just as if you were seeing a professional therapist. Two sessions a week (45 to 60 minutes each) are usually adequate, although more can always be held if you like.

In progressive relaxation, you learn how to identify feelings of muscular relaxation by alternately tensing and relaxing various muscle groups in your body. The best way to illustrate what this means is to have you practice a demonstration trial right now. Take your dominant hand (if you're right-handed use your right hand, if left-handed use your left hand) and make a loose fist without applying any pressure. Continue to read these instructions. When you come across the word "now" in big capital letters, slightly tighten your fist and notice the tension you produce. You'll probably feel tension in your knuckles, in your fingers, and in other parts of your hand. You may also feel tension spreading into the lower part of your arm. When you make the first, hold it for about 5 to 7 seconds. Then, when you see the word "relax" in capital letters, throw away the tension by quickly opening your hand and relaxing the muscles.

All right, get ready by making yourself comfortable. Have your arm resting on the chair you are in and NOW tighen your fist and hold it. Do you feel tension in your fingers? In your knuckles? Does the tension spread to your wrist and forearm? Briefly study the tension in your hand and now RELAX your fist. Rest your hand comfortably on the chair or in your lap and experience tension leaving your muscles. Don't expect your hand to feel totally relaxed. That takes practice. But you should experience some of the tension you purposefully put into your muscles leaving the tense areas. It doesn't matter if the effects are large or small, and it doesn't matter if your hand still feels a little tense. The purpose of this demonstration was just to help you learn the basic procedural components of relaxation training. *By alternately tensing and relaxing muscles you will learn how to identify tension and bring about a state of relaxation.*

## MUSCLE GROUPS

At this point it would be helpful to review the various muscle groups involved in a standard relaxation program. Notice that there are 15 muscles combined into four major groups. If necessary, additional muscles can always be added later on. Let's say, for example, that you have finished your training program and still experience tension in the lower-back region. In this case, you would try different positions for tensing the particular muscles in question. Then, you would follow the same procedural rules that apply to all muscle groups.

As you read down the following list, try to briefly create a little tension in each muscle group to identify what methods are best suited for your individual needs. Do not, however, actually begin to practice in earnest. There are still more things to learn before your training program gets under way.

You may find it helpful to take some notes on a separate piece of paper. That way you can have a convenient list of the various muscles and how you prefer to tense them.

MAJOR GROUP 1: THE HANDS AND ARMS

A. *Dominant Hand and Forearm:* This is the muscle group you just tensed by making a fist and holding it tight.

B. *Dominant Biceps:* Tense this group by keeping your arm flat on the chair and pushing down with your elbow. If this doesn't work, bend your arm at the elbow so your hand faces toward your shoulder. Then apply what is called a "counterforce." To do this, try touching your shoulder with your hand while at the same time opposing this movement. Your hand will seem to be frozen in the air.

C. *Nondominant Hand and Forearm:* Just like before, make a fist but this time use your nondominant hand.

D. *Nondominant Biceps:* Follow the same procedures described for the dominant biceps.

MAJOR GROUP 2: THE HEAD, FACE, AND THROAT

A. *Forehead:* To tense the muscles in your forehead, try lifting your eyebrows high as if you want to touch the top of your head. An alternative method is to frown or "knit your brows."

B. *Upper Cheeks and Nose:* Squint your eyes and wrinkle your nose. Don't be afraid of making funny faces when you're practicing!

C. *Lower Cheeks and Jaws:* These muscles can be tensed by clenching your teeth together hard and pulling back the corners of your mouth.

D. *Lips and Tongue:* Press your tongue against the top of your mouth while at the same time pressing your lips together.

E. *Neck and Throat:* Pull your chin down as if trying to touch your chest. Now apply a counterpressure to stop your chin.

MAJOR GROUP 3: THE CHEST AND STOMACH

A. *Chest:* To tense the muscles in your chest, take a deep breath and hold it. Then exhale slowly. You will notice during your practice sessions that controlled breathing is an extremely useful way to increase general levels of relaxation throughout your body.

B. *Shoulders and Upper Back:* Pull your shoulders up as if they are being held by strings attached to the ceiling. Then arch them back as if trying to touch your shoulder blades together.

C. *Abdominal or Stomach Area:* These muscles are most easily tensed by either making your stomach hard, pulling your stomach in and holding it tight, or pushing your stomach out.

MAJOR GROUP 4: THE LEGS AND FEET

A. *Thighs and Buttocks:* Tense the muscles in these areas by pressing your heels into the ground and tightening the muscles in your buttocks. An alternative "counterforce" method involves pressing your knees toward each other while at the same time applying pressure to keep them apart. If neither method produces noticeable tension in your thighs and buttocks, try lifting your legs straight out in front of you.

B. *Calves:* Point your toes up toward your head. Alternatively, you can point your toes down away from your head.

C. *Feet:* These muscles can easily cramp. So, rather than holding tension for 5 to 7 seconds, use a shorter 3-second period. Tense your feet by pointing your toes slightly down, turning your feet in, and curling your toes.

## POSSIBLE PROBLEMS

A useful manual for professionals interested in progressive relaxation has been written by Drs. Bernstein and Borkovec. These authors note a number of difficulties that people can sometimes experience while developing relaxation skills. Among the major problems discussed are (1) distractions in the environment, (2) distracting behaviors such as laughing, sneezing, coughing, and fidgeting, (3) intrusive thoughts that are unpleasant or arousing, (4) muscle cramps, and (5) unpleasant sensations that may accompany relaxation.

For each of these potential problems, there are things you can do. In regard to distractions, it goes without saying that you want to keep them to a minimum. Find a place that is private and comfortable. Keep down distracting behaviors by closely monitoring yourself and refraining from unnecessary movements. If at times you have a cold and find yourself coughing or sneezing, it might be a good idea to postpone a session. In general, use your own judgment to arrange the environment so distracting factors are kept to a minimum.

Anxiety-producing or anxiety-arousing thoughts that disrupt feelings of relaxation are not uncommon. Generally, their distracting influence lessens over time. One approach for actively counteracting disruptive thoughts is to purposefully call to mind a pleasant image. For example, if you can't stop thinking about a particular incident that makes you tense, try concentrating your mind on a different scene that is more relaxing. You could imagine yourself sitting under a tree on a beautiful spring day. Let this scene capture your full attention by adding details and making it as real as possible.

Several sensations that many people initially find uncomfortable or strange can accompany feelings of relaxation. These may include tingling or floating sensations, dizzy feelings in your head, and small muscle spasms or jerks. If it's any comfort to you, these types of reactions are not unusual. In fact, they signal that you are getting better at relaxing your muscles. With practice these reactions will either diminish or become familiar. Some sensations, such as the experience of "floating," can even become enjoyable when associated with deep relaxation. Naturally, small muscle spasms are to be distinguished from uncomfortable muscle cramps. When the latter occur, it is important that you reduce the time interval for tensing muscles and/or apply less force when making the muscles tense.

One last problem needs to be mentioned. If you find yourself dozing off, you can be sure your efforts to relax are successful. Unfortunately, once you are asleep, you can no longer practice. And, effectively developing relaxation skills requires continued effort and hard work. So try to stay awake!

## LEARNING THE INSTRUCTIONS

Learning appropriate expressions for tensing and relaxing muscles is important since you need to "instruct" yourself during practice sessions. Here is a sample set of instructions that persons might use when practicing the muscles in their forehead.

*Relax your entire body to the best of your ability. Settle back and, as you are relaxing, wrinkle up your forehead. NOW . . . keep your forehead wrinkled . . . tighter . . . experience the tightness take over your muscles and now . . . RELAX . . . throw away the tightness in your muscles and do the opposite of tension . . . relax . . . let go of all the tension and spread the feelings of relaxation all over . . . experience the contrast between tension and relaxation . . . once again, NOW wrinkle your forehead . . . that's right, put tension back into your muscles and again study this tension . . . hold the tension in your muscles and now RELAX again and enjoy the contrast . . . spread the relaxation over your face further . . . continue this process . . . relax . . . relax.*

Try reading the above example again. Practice creating an initial sense of tension as you read along. Then experience a lazy, calm feeling of restfulness as you read the sections instructing you to relax.

Professionals tend to use a number of standard phrases during relaxation training, some of which are included in the above example. Common expressions associated with relaxation phases of your program include:

Note how you feel as relaxation takes place.
More and more relaxed, more than ever before.
Completely relaxed, warm and relaxed.
Feel the relaxation and warmth flow through your muscles.
Throw away the tension.
Notice the difference between tension and relaxation.
Feel the relaxation come into those muscles.
Relax and smooth out the muscles.
Let yourself relax to the best of your ability.
Feel calm, rested.
Experience the contrast between tension and relaxation.
Continue letting go . . . relax . . . relax.
Let the tension dissolve away.

Expressions for tension phases of your training program are generally less varied. The ones listed below should prove helpful.

Feel the muscles pull . . . hold it.
Tighten your muscles.
Pay attention to these muscles and identify the tension.
Study (attend to) the tension.
Notice where the tightness is.
Put tension into your muscles.

Expressions for tension and relaxation can be used interchangeably with any individual muscle group. It is probably a good idea to spend some time between now and your next regularly scheduled session practicing the varied phrases so you really know them by heart. One last point should also be made. When you instruct yourself during relaxation training, you want to do it SILENTLY. Saying instructions out loud would require muscle exertion and interfere with deep relaxation.

**PRACTICING RELAXATION**

When first practicing a particular group, you should tense the appropriate muscles for a 5–7-second period. The only exceptions to this rule are your feet and other muscle groups that may have a tendency to cramp. When practicing these groups, you should decrease the tension period to about 3 seconds. Naturally, you don't want to tense your muscles so hard that it hurts. You simply want to use sufficient pressure to allow you to identify each distinct point of muscle tension.

After the 5–7-second tension period, you should actively reduce tension by quickly releasing your hold on the muscles. Then, for a period of 20 to 30 seconds, spend your time consciously extending feelings of relaxation throughout your muscles. During this relaxation period, concentrate on the contrast between tension and relaxation. Remember that even when muscles feel relaxed, some fibers may still be contracted. Relaxing is an active process of undoing tension.

*Practice tensing and relaxing each muscle group at least twice before proceeding on to a new group.* If after two trials you feel a deep sense of relaxation, you can proceed to the next muscle group in your list. If, however, residual tension remains in your muscles, you should continue to practice the same group for as many as five trials in a single session. Then stop and go on to the next group.

Don't be concerned or worried about "failures" even if you feel tension in several muscle groups after practicing them five times each. Learning progressive relaxation skills takes time and hard work. Some of you will need to spend as many as six sessions or more. A reasonable goal to be setting for this first session is to simply acquire the idea, or "swing" of things. Expecting to be instantly relaxed in a single session is unrealistic.

One other procedural point should be made at this time. Whenever you finish all the muscles in a particular major group, take some time to more fully relax them before moving on to new muscles. For instance, when you have finished practicing your hands, forearms, and biceps (Major Group 1), spend a minute or so to extend relaxation further and further and experience even greater levels of comfort. Say to yourself relaxing expressions, and use to your advantage the calming effects of exhaling slowly. Each time you exhale, think to yourself the words "relax, calm." Exhaling slowly and evenly seems to carry people into deeper levels of relaxation. It's a good feeling and, with practice, you can learn to take full advantage of it.

Now let's review the rules again. First, you practice each muscle group at least twice. If you feel tension, you can practice the same group up to five times in a single session. When you have finished all the muscles in a major group, take some time and extend relaxation to deeper and deeper levels. After taking this break, go on to the muscles in the next major group and practice them in the same way. Follow this procedure for about 45 minutes each session until you have completed all the muscles in all the major groups.

### Practicing Between Your Regular Sessions

When people are taught progressive relaxation by therapists in a clinic, they are told to practice at home twice a day for 15 to 20 minutes each time. Since your regularly scheduled sessions are equivalent to meeting with a therapist, it's important that you also "practice at home" for short periods each day. Practice sessions give you a chance to work on muscles with which you may have been having trouble. They also allow you to improve your skills and get better at relaxing muscles you're already pretty good at.

During practice sessions, you follow the same rules as before. Tense and relax each muscle group at least twice but no more than five times. Also, be sure to work only on muscles that have been completed during your regular 45-minute sessions. For example, if today you work on muscles in Major Group 1, then between now and your next regular session you should just practice the muscles in your hands, arms, and biceps.

### After Today: Sessions 2 Through 4 and Maybe Even 6!

Today you are having your first regularly scheduled session for actually practicing relaxation training. If your progress is rapid, you may experience little difficulty working through all the muscle groups on your list. In fact, some people only need to spend one or two sessions to complete their program. These individuals, however, are the exception, and most of you will spend at least four regularly scheduled sessions learning to adequately relax. Gradual progress is not at all uncommon and should not cause concern.

What you practice on a particular day will depend, of course, on the progress you have made in your program. Use your regularly scheduled sessions to practice each muscle in its listed order. Use practice sessions to work on especially difficult groups and to increase your general skills. In general, your regular sessions should begin with a review of already completed muscle groups before new ones are attempted. If difficulties are encountered during any session, you may want to refer back to this manual's section on possible problems.

# APPENDIX B

## Checklist of Principles

*This checklist is for tearing out of this book and putting in your wallet or pocketbook. It is a mind-jogger.*

*Remember the H-E-N guidelines.*

*Remember that principles are best* used together *in harmony.*

**PRINCIPLES FOR ELICITING**

**Principles for Eliciting Action Before Modeling**

- Suggestion Principle
- Request Principle
- Opening Principle
- Surroundings Principle
- Timing Principle

**Modeling Principles for Eliciting Action**

- Reward to Model Principle
- Emotions of Model Principle
- Control of Resources by Model Principle
- Status of Model Principle

**Principles for Eliciting Action after Modeling**

- Priming Principle
- Coercion Principle

**PRINCIPLES FOR BUILDING UP ACTION**

**Basic Reward Principle**

**General Principle**

**Reward Selection Principles**

- Other Person Preference Principle
- High Frequency Principle
- Equal Interval Between Participation Principle

**Reward Administration Principles**

- Immediate Reward Principle
- Continuous Reward Principle
- Open Reward Principle
- Reward Contract Principle
- Token Reward Principle
- Sacrifice Principle

**PRINCIPLES FOR MAINTAINING AND REDUCING ACTION**

**Thyself Principle**

**Principles for Maintaining**

- Intermittent Reward Principle
- Unpredictable Principle
- Surprise Principle
- Arabian Nights Principle
- Least Powerful Reward Principle

**Principles for Reducing Unwanted Action**

- Constructive Alternatives Principle (always needed for change)
- Request Principle
- Distraction Principle
- Incompatible Principle
- Extinction Principle
- Unchaining Principle
- Time Out Principle
- Overcorrection Principle
- Punishment Principle
- Group Surrender Principle
- General Principle

**PRINCIPLES FOR CHANGING EMOTIONS**

**Classical Conditioning Principle**

**Desensitization Principle**

**STOP!**

Do not continue on
to the next section of instructions
until you can
successfully relax
all of the muscles on your list.

## INCREASING YOUR EFFICIENCY

These instructions should be practiced only after you have successfully learned how to relax each muscle group as previously instructed. Once you have done that, you can begin combining muscles in a single major group to shorten the time it takes for you to relax. Start with Major Group 1 by simultaneously tensing both fists and both biceps for the usual 5-to-7-second period. Then, all together, release your hold on these muscles and experience comfortable feelings of relaxation take over. Spend a good 30 to 60 seconds during this period spreading relaxation throughout your muscles.

People often feel some residual tension when they first try to combine groups. If this happens, all you need to do is practice in the usual way those muscles that still feel tense. For example, when combining the muscles in Major Group 1, you may find that your left biceps remain tense after the relaxation period. In that case, you should pay individual attention to your left bicep muscles and practice them alone. When your left biceps felt fully relaxed, you could again go back to tensing and relaxing the entire major group.

As you get better at combining muscle groups, you will probably notice that you can sometimes identify tension without having to even tighten your muscles. Being able to do this is a useful skill that is worth developing more fully. Try at times to concentrate on identifying tension in your muscles without actually tightening them. Then recall to yourself what it is like to release the tension and enjoy relaxation. It helps to think to yourself words like "relax" and "calm" while exhaling slowly and evenly. "Relax" and "calm" can eventually serve as cue words that signal you to eliminate tension and deeply relax.

Once you have developed the ability to combine muscle groups, your relaxation program is over. If you were at a clinic, your therapist would certainly pause to mention the significance of your accomplishment. He would point out how you have developed new skills that can be employed to your advantage. Since you are your own therapist, this is probably a good time to stop and congratulate yourself. But don't forget, keep practicing now and then to keep up your newly acquired skills.

### REFERENCES

**Bernstein,** D. A., & **Borkovec,** T. D. *Progressive relaxation training: A manual for the helping professions.* Illinois: Research Press, 1973.

**Jacobson,** E. *You must relax.* New York: McGraw-Hill, 1934.

## CHAPTER ONE NOTES

**1.** An interesting discussion about the hidden curriculum in modern schools is found in Silverman (1971).

**2.** These proverbs are used here as Altman and Taylor (1973, p. 8) used them. The corresponding proverbs follow: Out of sight, out of mind; birds of a feather flock together; to know him is to love him; you can't teach an old dog new tricks.

**3.** National Science Foundation (1969).

**4.** Maslow (1970b); Rogers (1959, 1961); see Sherwood (1970) for a more explicit conceptualization of self-actualization.

**5.** Baer, Wolf, and Risley (1968); Bühler and Allen (1972), chap. 3.

**6.** For a debate on the control of behavior issue, see Matson (1973).

**7.** Skinner's major statements are in Skinner (1948, 1953, 1971).

**8.** Even though the dominant humanistic view emphasizes that you act on your surroundings, Bugenthal (1971) writes of the humanistic ethic: "A second tenet of the humanistic ethic is that the ideal for relationships between people is one of mutuality between persons each of whom values and recognizes the subjecthood of the other" (p. 14). In *The Mystery of Being,* Marcel (1960) writes: "The fact is that we can understand ourselves by starting from the other, or from others, and only by starting from them; . . . it is only in this perspective that a legitimate love of self can be conceived." Maslow (1970b, p. 28) claims that "we must certainly grant at once that human motivation rarely actualizes itself in behavior except in relation to the situation and to other people." Clearly, then, the humanistic psychologists have been doing some thinking about how surroundings affect individuals with external forces. They are coming to view human relations as shown in the bicycle model. They even use groups as the primary means to aid the individual!

On the other hand, behavior modifiers have long emphasized the effects of surroundings and external forces on people. Curiously, a subliterature has grown up within behavior mod emphasizing self-choice and self-control. See Goldfried and Merbaum (1973) for an edited collection of readings on self-control. See Thoresen and Mahoney (1974) for a review of the area.

**9.** Bem (1965, 1967).

**10.** Cooley (1902).

**11.** Argyle (1969), chap. 5; Argyle (1972), chap. 3.

**12.** Libet (1973). See also Libet and Lewinsohn (1973).

**13.** Libet (1973), pp. 58–63. Also, in a test situation where fewer than 92 percent of elicited reponses would be positive, a more detailed structure of social skill (than the three factors Libet detected) and better predictive validity would likely obtain.

**14.** Swensen (1973), p. 418, credits Goffman (1967) with this idea.

**15.** Warga (1974), p. 8.

**16.** Swensen (1973), p. 418.

**17.** Hepner (1973), p. 160; italics in the original.

**18.** Bradburn (1969).

**19.** Jahoda (1958).

**20.** See, e.g., Laing, Phillipson, and Lee (1966).

**21.** Overall psychological well-being was measured by responses to the question, "Taken together, how would you say things are these days . . . would you say you are very happy, pretty happy, or not too happy?" (Bradburn, 1969, p. 39). This question was found to produce extremely stable response patterns across 19 National Opinion Research Center samples with a total of 16,381 interview respondents (Bradburn, 1969, Table 3.1, p. 40).

**22.** Bradburn (1969), p. 97.

**23.** Bradburn (1969), pp. 58, 267.

**24.** Bradburn (1969), pp. 58, 267.

**25.** Bradburn (1969), p. 201.

**26.** Bradburn (1969), p. 125, and Appendix 3, Wave 1 questionnaire.

**27.** Wilson (1967), p. 304.

**28.** Argyle (1972), p. 11.

## CHAPTER TWO NOTES

**1.** Hesse (1971), pp. 100–102.

**2.** Hesse (1971), p. 90.

**3.** Hesse (1971), p. 64.

**4.** Hesse (1971), p. 65.

**5.** Hesse (1971), pp. 110–114.

**6.** Moustakas (1972), chap. 4.

**7.** Lopata (1969), p. 250. Note that I am using her defnition of "presently experienced" loneliness.

**8.** Weiss (1973), pp. 13–14.

**9.** Rules of correspondence are discussed by Deutsch and Krauss (1965, pp. 8–10) and Margenau (1950).

**10.** Weiss (1973), p. 18.

**11.** Weiss (1973), p. 21.

**12.** Weiss (1973), p. 19.

**13.** Weiss (1973), p. 20. Other, more complex, systems of loneliness are discussed in Braceland (1967), D'Aboy (1973), Fromm-Reichman (1959), Lopata (1969), Moustakas (1972, pp. 18–20), and Sermat (1974).

**14.** Bowlby (1973a), pp. 44–45. This incident was told to John Bowlby by James Anderson via personal communication.

**15.** The discussion in this paragraph closely follows that of Bowlby (1969).

**16.** Bowlby (1973b), chap. 21.

**17.** Bowlby (1973b), p. 362.

**18.** Described in Bowlby (1969), p. 27. Bowlby (1969, 1973b) cites scores of studies, but space allows only the briefest summary.

**19.** See, e.g., Ainsworth and Wittig (1969). For a review, see Ainsworth, Bell, and Stayton (1972) and Bowlby (1973b), chap. 3.

**20.** Newson and Newson (1968).

**21.** Evidence from Cairnes (1966); quote here is from Bowlby (1969), chap. 12.

**22.** Harlow and Zimmerman (1959).

**23.** Harlow (1958).

**24.** Bowlby (1969), p. 216.

**25.** Bowlby (1973b), p. 180.

**26.** Tobias (1965). But have humans not changed their genetic makeup in the 10,000 years since agriculture started and we started to shape our own environment? It is possible but not likely, argues Tobias, because man existed at least a couple of million years ago; this means that the last 10,000 years constitute only half of 1 percent of man's existence—not much time to "select out" a basic process.

**27.** Bowlby (1973b), pp. 113–114.

**28.** Bowlby (1969), p. 199.

**29.** Bowlby (1969), p. 357. What other researchers call "dependency," Bowlby prefers to call "anxious attachment."

**30.** Bowlby (1973a), p. 52.

**31.** Keyes (1973).

**32.** I. Taviss, *A Survey of Popular Attitudes toward Technology,* p. 3. Harvard Program of Technology and Society.

**33.** For updated figures on divorce and mobility, check the latest almanac.

**34.** Unseem, Unseem, and Gibson (1960); quote from Keyes (1973), p. 32.

**35.** Keyes (1973), p. 40.

**36.** Keyes (1973), p. 101.

**37.** Pepper (1974).

**38.** Elizabeth Taylor, quoted in *McCalls* by Pepper (1974), p. 112.

**39.** Keyes (1973), p. 141.

**40.** Keyes (1973), p. 147.

**41.** Keyes (1973), p. 211.

**42.** Keyes (1973), p. 193.

**43.** Alexander (1967), p. 60.

**44.** For additional material on primary groups, see Homans (1950), Cooley (1929), or current issues of *Sociological Abstracts.* For purposes of clarity, the following are definitions of Alexander's three primary groups.

(1) The Extended Family: A group of individuals that includes at least one nucleus of two or more adults who have previously or are currently cooperating in the care and rearing of their own or adopted children, who are related to each other, and who are characterized by face-to-face association and cooperation.

(2) The Neighborhood Group of Adults: A group of adults who live near one another and who are characterized by face-to-face association and cooperation.

(3) The Children's Play Group: A group of children who are playmates and who are characterized by face-to-face association and cooperation.

**45.** Alternative methods of relieving the stress include expression of feelings to intimates, drugs (e.g., marijuana, alcohol), physically leaving the stressful situation or area, and manifesting neurotic and psychotic symptoms.

**46.** Lesy (1973).

**47.** Bettman (1974).

**48.** Personal communication, 1974. George Talbot, Curator of Iconography, State Historical Society of Wisconsin, was helpful in supplying the photograph in Figure 2.10 and background information about such memorial photographs of infants.

**49.** Bradburn (1969), p. 56. The number of participants in this particular sub-sample was 1,469. This sample was independent from the sample with 2,787 participants. The italics in the question are mine.

**50.** Sermat (1974). See also Collier and Lawrence (1951), although their data are dated now.

**51.** Personal communication of unpublished data from Vello Sermat, 1974. Sermat's respondents were young; the average age of the respondents to *Homemaker's Digest* was 26.6 years.

**52.** Munnichs (1964).

**53.** Duvall (1945).

**54.** Duvall (1945).

**55.** Wold (1970).

**56.** Bradburn (1969), p. 60. Table 4.3. These correlations represent responses of the 1,259 males and 1,528 females in Bradburn's sample of 2,787.

**57.** Jacobs (1971).

**58.** Jan-Tausch (undated, p. 3).

**59.** Jacobs (1971), p. 1.

**60.** Blanc, Bourgeois, and Henry (1966). The quote is from *Psychological Abstracts,* 1967, *41,* no. 12150.

**61.** Bock (1972), p. 45. Bock (1972) reviews his previous findings and others.

**62.** Sermat (1973), p. 1.

**63.** Personal communication from Vello Sermat, 1974.

**64.** Abrahams (1972), p. 56.

**65.** Kammeyer and Bolton (1968).

**66.** Kammeyer and Bolton (1968), p. 493.

**67.** Lowenthal and Haven (1968).

**68.** Lantz (1956). The accuracy of memory in this study needs to be checked by repeating the research.

**69.** Bock (1972); Bradburn (1969); Wilson (1967).

**70.** For recent reviews and method suggestions, see Cohen (1974) and Masters and Wellman (1974).

## CHAPTER THREE NOTES

**1.** Alexander (1967), p. 62.

**2.** Toffler (1970).

**3.** Packard (1972).

**4.** Jourard (1971b), p. 32; italics in the original deleted.

**5.** Alexander (1967), p. 62; italics in the original deleted.

**6.** Alexander (1967), pp. 67–68; italics in the original deleted.

**7.** Solomon and Corbit (1974).

**8.** Keyes (1973), p. 203.

**9.** Lowenthal and Haven (1968).

**10.** Bradburn (1969).

**11.** Jourard and Lasakow (1958); Jourard (1959).

**12.** Levinger and Senn (1967).

**13.** Taylor, Altman, and Sorrentino (1969). I base this claim about causality only on the continuous positive and continuous negative groups. For a partial correlational analysis, see Jourard and Landsman (1960) and Worthy, Gary, and Kahn (1969).

**14.** Worthy, Gary, and Kahn (1969). This finding held up even when the influence of "initial liking before the experiment proper began" was removed using statistical procedures.

**15.** For a handy collection of Jourard's research in one volume, see Jourard (1971a). For comprehensive reviews, see Cozby (1973) and Cozby and Keding (1975). Jourard measured self-disclosure using questionnaires he developed.

**16.** Jourard (1961a), Jourard and Lasakow (1958), and Jourard and Richman (1963).

**17.** Jourard and Richman (1963).

**18.** Jourard and Lasakow (1958).

**19.** Jourard and Lasakow (1958).
**20.** Jourard (1961b).
**21.** Kaplan, Firestone, Degnore, and Moore (1974). Similar results were found by Cozby (1972).
**22.** Kaplan, Firestone, Degnore, and Moore (1974), p. 638.
**23.** Altman and Taylor (1973).
**24.** Altman and Taylor (1973), pp. 17–19.
**25.** For a detailed treatment of trust of other people, see Wrightsman (1974).
**26.** Taylor (1968).
**27.** Altman and Haythorn (1965).
**28.** Frankfurt (1965); Colson (1968).
**29.** Cozby (1973), p. 89.
**30.** Jourard (1971b), chap. 20.
**31.** Job success may, however, be greater for those who disclose less to clients because informational superiority is a kind of power, as French and Raven (1959) claim in their discussion of expert power, a similar concept.
**32.** Morris (1971).
**33.** Montagu (1971).
**34.** Prescott (1971, 1974).
**35.** Prescott (1974), p. 6; for reviews, see Ainsworth (1972), Bowlby (1969), and Prescott (1971).
**36.** Prescott (1974); Prescott and Pisanic (1974); Kagan and Klein (1973).
**37.** Prescott (1974); Prescott and Pisanic (1974). In current research, Prescott, Wallace, and Vandervoot (1974) are trying to discover similar patterns in U.S. society.
**38.** Levine (1960).
**39.** Harlow and Harlow (1965); Harlow (1971).
**40.** Manson (1968).
**41.** This description is from Prescott (1972), p. 20.
**42.** Berkson (1974).
**43.** Prescott (1971).
**44.** It can be argued that touching can be judiciously and effectively used in psychotherapy with the lonely, as Marita De Thomaso argues in " 'Touch Power' and The Screen of Loneliness" (1971).
**45.** Thibaut and Kelley (1959).
**46.** Rubin (1973), pp. 162–172.
**47.** Rubin (1973), p. 171.
**48.** Altman and Taylor (1973), p. 163.
**49.** Altman and Taylor (1973), p. 172.
**50.** Walster, Berscheid, and Walster (1973); Adams (1965).
**51.** Homans (1961).
**52.** Jourard (1971a, 1971b); Altman and Taylor (1973); Rubin (1973).
**53.** See Walster, Berscheid, and Walster (1973) for a review.
**54.** For reviews of evidence, see Cozby (1973), pp. 81–82, and Altman and Taylor (1973), pp. 52–56; for specific articles, see Jourard (1971a), chap. 3, or Rubin (1973), pp. 163–168.
**55.** Rubin (1973), p. 165.
**56.** Rubin (1973), p. 165.
**57.** Rubin (1973), p. 165.
**58.** Some of the different systems for theorizing about love are found in Fromm (1956) and Otto (1972).
**59.** For the early research, see Swenson (1961) and Swenson and Gilner (1964). For a review of all his research, see Swensen (1972). The six dimensions discussed in this section come from an unpublished dissertation (Gilner, 1967), summarized in Swensen (1972).
**60.** Fromm (1956).
**61.** Fromm (1956), p. 83.
**62.** Fromm (1956), p. 128; italics in the original.
**63.** Fromm (1956), p. 105.
**64.** Fromm (1956), pp. 127–128.
**65.** Fromm (1956), p. 131.
**66.** Butler (1975).

### CHAPTER FOUR NOTES

**1.** Keyes (1973), p. 207.
**2.** Taylor and Altman (1966). This item pool seems superior to others (e.g., Jourard, 1971a, Ap-

pendixes 1, 4–6, 8, 12, 20) because Taylor and Altman (1) studied a comprehensive range of disclosure topics, (2) included a large number of items for scaling, and (3) provided empirical analyses of judges' agreement of items into categories. Permission to reproduce intact items from the Taylor and Altman (1966) research is gratefully acknowledged.

**3.** Table 4.2 was created in the following way: From each of the 13 topic areas in Taylor and Altman (1966), I selected three items using the responses of college-student judges. The criteria for selection were (1) high agreement by judges that a given item belongs to the given topic area, (2) applicability to both sexes, married and unmarried (i.e., not outdated), in 1975, (3) inclusion by Taylor and Altman in the 48-item "Taylor-Altman Self-Disclosure Scale," and (4) appropriate variance in intimacy level. All criteria were met only partially.

**4.** Taylor and Altman (1966). For nearly all items from topic areas, the low, medium, and high intimacy-values approximated 3.5, 6, and 8.5 on their 11-point scale, where 11 means highest intimacy value. However, on topic areas 6, 8, and 12, the respective scale values of items used here reflect trichotomized ranges at the low end of the 11-point scale, due to floor effects. In topic area 2, a ceiling effect required trichotomizing a range from 6 to 10. In all cases, my overall objective was to provide a reasonably wide dispersion of (1) items over topic areas and (2) scale scores across the range of scale scores within each topic area. Avoiding items with high Q-values was not a primary concern here, although the 39 items selected do avoid high quartile values.

**5.** Taylor and Altman (1966).

**6.** The second number before each item in the Taylor and Altman (1966) report indicates the item's intimacy value (1 = low; 2 = moderate; 3 = high) relative to the range of scale values displayed by other items in that scale. These intimacy values were used in my selection process to maximize the range of intimacy within each topic area.

**7.** Foa and Foa (1974).

**8.** Walster, Berscheid, and Walster (1973). For related theories of social exchange, see Homans (1961), Blau (1964), and Thibaut and Kelley (1959).

**9.** Walster, Berscheid, and Walster (1973), p. 151.

**10.** Walster, Berscheid, and Walster (1973), pp. 153–154.

**11.** Flesch (1957), p. 156.

**12.** Flesch (1957), p. 157.

**13.** Boris Levinson's (1972) *Pets and Human Development* is available from the publisher (Charles C. Thomas, 301–327 East Lawrence Avenue, Springfield, Illinois 62703) for $10.50.

**14.** Mussen's (1970) revision of the Carmichael manual is cited here.

**15.** Levinson (1972), pp. 219–220; italics mine.

**16.** Ladd (1971).

**17.** Rogers (1961), p. 62; italics are added.

**18.** See Bradford, Gibb, and Benne (1964); Howard (1970); Schein and Bennis (1965); and Burton (1969).

**19.** Campbell and Dunnette (1968).

**20.** Altman and Taylor (1973), pp. 182–189.

**21.** Altman and Taylor (1973), p. 185.

**22.** Altman and Taylor (1973), p. 187.

**23.** Maslow (1970b), p. 258.

**24.** Lieberman, Yalom, and Miles (1973).

**25.** Koch (1971), p. 112.

**26.** Maslow (1970a), pp. 5–6.

**27.** Keyes (1973), p. 184.

**28.** Keyes, personal communication, 1974.

**29.** Rappaport, Gross, and Lepper (1973).

**30.** Rappaport, Gross, and Lepper (1973), p. 106.

**31.** Johnson, Kavanagh, and Lubin (1973). A discussion of the hidden curriculum of unwritten social learning in schools is given in Silberman's *The Experience of Schooling* (1971).

**32.** Presently you contact national-level offices for both Big Brothers of America and Big Sisters International (1) by writing to either at 220 Suburban Station Building, Philadelphia, Pennsylvania 19103, or by (2) calling 215-567-2748 (the Philadelphia office). In Great Britain, contact the National Council of Social Service, 26 Bedford Square, London WC1. See also Appendix i in their book *Loneliness, a New Study,* where social service organizations are listed.

**33.** Dwight Flanders, personal communication, 1974.

**34.** See, e.g., Ittelson, Proshansky, Rivlin, and Winkel (1974).

**35.** Alexander (1967), p. 91.

**36.** Alexander (1967), p. 88.

**37.** Weiss (1973), pp. 212–224.
**38.** This paragraph paraphrases Weiss (1973), pp. 234–235.
**39.** Riesman (1973), p. xxi.

**CHAPTER FIVE NOTES**

**1.** A necessary question is whether it is even appropriate to consider time as a resource. Foa and Foa have argued that "time, however, is not a resource *per se,* although it is needed for giving and receiving resources . . ." [1973, p. 22]. I agree that time is needed for giving and receiving other resources; but time is a resource in its own right. Time can be allocated or spent. It can undeniably be subjected to economic analysis, as several economists have already done (e.g., Becker, 1965; Linder, 1970). For a review, see Ferber (1973), pp. 1322–1323. Moreover, the more specific, lower-level system of resources proposed by Foa and Foa (1973), including love, status, information, money, goods and services, is just one system that we do cover later when considering personal resources. In contrast, the more general system of time allocation proposed by Linder (1970) is needed to understand the forces of the larger economic system; the resources proposed by Foa and Foa (1973) are far too specific for such an analysis. It should be noted that the systems of both Foa and Foa (1973) and Linder (1970) are conceptually independent from the life satisfactions of the individual. Life satisfactions (i.e., "I enjoy a high quality of life") is a subjective feeling not always linked to reality, as illustrated by happy slaves and successful but despondent people. Unfortunately, a really sophisticated theory of personal resource allocation would require a full-length book that applies theories in economics to interpersonal interaction. For one such attempt, see Foa and Foa (1974). We can lay some practical groundwork in this chapter by concentrating on the use of personal time.

**2.** For a more complete definition of economics, consult a good introductory economics text, such as Lipsey and Steiner (1969), pp. 1–9.

**3.** Linder (1970).

**4.** This principle is familiar to economists as the principle which states that the buyer's utility will be maximized when the ratio of marginal utility to price per last penny spent will be equal. Let x stand for anything exchanged, and

$$\frac{\text{MUx}}{\text{price x}} = \frac{\text{MUy}}{\text{price y}}.$$

**5.** According to Linder (1970, chap. 3), complex forces operate to both increase and decrease your working day, especially if you have a moderate or high income. You want to earn more money (longer hours), but you also want to consume and rest (shorter hours). It is not yet possible to predict whether you or I will work longer hours than our ancestors. It is possible to say that increasing yield from nonworking hours is higher nowadays. Otherwise, we would work all the hours we comfortably could, because the higher productivity from working hours would induce us to work.

**6.** Staikov (1972), p. 464.

**7.** Robinson and Converse (1972), p. 114.

**8.** May 4, 1974, pp. 70–72.

**9.** "Cheaper Ways to Reach the Consumer" (1972), p. 121.

**10.** "Are Executives Efficient?" (1973), p. 54.

**11.** Linder (1970), chap. 2.

**12.** Linder (1970), pp. 78–79.

**13.** Students interested in doing such a project should consult their instructor and assure all participants of total anonymity, not just confidentiality. Cross-cultural comparisons can, of course, be made across ethnic groups in the same city. It would be important to note social customs, family income, and average family income when making comparisons.

**14.** Linder (1970), p. 134. For a discussion of the leisure activities available to take up our time, see DeGrazia (1962).

**15.** Linder (1970), p. 145.

**16.** Szalai (1972).

**17.** Robinson and Converse (1972), p. 114.

**18.** Staikov (1972).

**19.** Cseh-Szombathy (1972), p. 309, Table 1.

**20.** This definition borrows some words from, but changes the meaning of, Murray's (1938, p. 24) definition.

**21.** Maslow (1970b).

**22.** Maslow (1970b), p. 43.

**23.** Maslow (1970b), p. 45.

**24.** Maslow (1970b), p. 46; italics added.

**25.** Maslow (1970b), p. 46.

**26.** These characteristics are paraphrased and reorganized from Maslow's discussion in chap. 11 of Maslow (1970b) and from his list in Table 1 of chap. 23 of Maslow (1971).

**27.** Bugental (1971).

**28.** Fromm (1956), p. 105.

**29.** See, e.g., Graham and Balloun (1973).

**30.** See, e.g., Hall and Nougaim (1968), and Lawler and Suttle (1972).

**31.** Lawler and Suttle (1972).

**32.** Maslow's claim was quoted by Hall and Nougaim (1968), p. 32. The time span used in the Lawler and Suttle (1972) research was 1 year; for Hall and Nougaim (1968), it was 5 years.

**33.** Keys, Brozek, Henschel, Mickelsen, and Taylor (1950).

**34.** Wolf (1958).

**35.** For a review, see Cofer and Appley (1964).

**36.** Technically, it is not possible to separate safety needs from physical needs because when danger from an external source finally takes its toll, a vital body process is always disrupted. For example, when the butler finally does in the lord of the castle with a stab to the heart, interference with the circulatory process causes death. Nevertheless, it is useful to distinguish physical from safety needs because the methods of satisfying these needs are different.

**37.** Weiss (1973), pp. 99–100.

**38.** Photographer James Rackwitz was helpful in procuring the photos in Figure 5.8.

**39.** Commoner (1971).

**40.** "The Third Force" (1974).

**41.** Bell (1973).

**42.** Maslow (1970b), p. 6, italics in original deleted; Bronowski (1965), pp. 83–84, more pointedly states "Those who think that science is ethically neutral confuse the findings of science, which are, with the activity of science, which is not."

**43.** Examples are *Mother Earth News,* Box 70, Hendersonville, N.C. 28739; *Lifestyle,* P.O. Box 2300, Hendersonville, N.C. 28739; and *Blair & Ketchum's Country Journal,* Box 8, Pittsford, Vt. 05763.

**44.** Barker (1968).

**45.** Barker and Gump (1964); Wicker (1968, 1969).

**46.** Wicker, McGrath, and Armstrong (1972); Wicker and Kauma (1974).

**47.** Wicker (1972, 1973); Wicker, McGrath, and Armstrong (1972).

**48.** Community experiments for better living require, among other things, procedures to assess the quality of life. A good beginning toward this end is being made by community psychologist J. R. Newbrough at George Peabody College in his studies on the quality of life in the household (e.g., Newbrough et al., 1973).

**49.** Goslin (1970).

## CHAPTER SIX NOTES

**1.** Merhabian (1970), p. 143.

**2.** Bowers (1973); see also Ekehammar (1974).

**3.** In the Bowers article, the relative contribution of each source of influence is broken down into percentages. However, the experiments he reviews make up an extremely limited set of situations. Thus we shall assume that relatively equal influence comes from each of the three sources until several hundred more studies are added to the handful now available.

**4.** Trotter and Warren (1974).

**5.** See Skinner (1971).

**6.** An interesting twist to the control-of-behavior controversy is provided by William Powers in *Behavior: The Control of Perception* (1973); see also Laing (1966), chap. II. Both these authors reverse the behavior mod perspective by subordinating behavior as an intermediate process leading up to an experiential event as the main focus of their theories.

**7.** D'Zurilla and Goldfried (1973). For a more expanded version, see D'Zurilla and Goldfried (1971).

**8.** Skinner (1953), p. 246.

## CHAPTER SEVEN NOTES

**1.** Students opting to do a project may be interested in exploring the topic of doing formal research in psychology. For an introduction to formal research methods, several good introductory works are available (e.g., Johnson and Solso, 1971; Leedy, 1974), as well as more advanced treatments (e.g., Plutchik, 1973; Runkel and McGrath, 1972). There are also books on research methods as applied to social behavior (e.g., Crano and Brewer, 1973; Lindzey and Aronson, 1968).

**2.** Weitzenhoffer (1953).

**3.** See London (1967) and Weitzenhoffer (1957) for techniques.

**4.** See Barber (1969, 1970), Gordon (1967), Hilgard (1965), and Weitzenhoffer (1953) for reviews of research. See *American Journal of Clinical Hypnosis* and the *International Journal of Clinical and Experimental Hypnosis* for firsthand research reports.

**5.** Weitzenhoffer (1953), p. 8.

**6.** Barber (1969).

**7.** See Barber (1969) for the Barber Suggestibility Scale. See also Barber and Glass (1962).

**8.** Barber (1969); Spanos and Barber (1974).

**9.** Quote from Barber (1970), p. 288; research reported in Barber (1969).

**10.** For alternate views, see Hilgard (1965, 1967) and Weitzenhoffer (1953).

**11.** This claim is made in full view of the fact that in Barber's normal suggestion procedures, the suggestions are usually made firmly. Despite the firmness of the normal suggestions, the similarity of responsiveness across many tasks is compelling.

**12.** From here on out I shall leave many of the details in each case up to your imagination and emphasize the generating of options.

**13.** Landauer, Carlsmith, and Lepper (1970).

**14.** See, e.g., Bandura (1965) as an example.

**15.** Langer and Abelson (1972).

**16.** Langer and Dweck (1973), chap. 5.

**17.** Leventhal and Fischer (1970).

**18.** These descriptions are from Asch (1952).

**19.** See, e.g., Anderson and Barrios (1961) and Luchins (1958).

**20.** Asch (1946) and Luchins (1957) hold this view.

**21.** Anderson and Barrios (1961) hold this view; also, Tagiuri (1969) favors it in his major "person perception" review in *The Handbook of Social Psychology,* which is sort of the Bible of social psychology.

**22.** Similar findings exist for primacy effects in the ordering of arguments to change attitudes. Primacy effects exist, but they can be easily counteracted. For a review, see McGuire (1969).

**23.** Zunin and Zunin (1972).

**24.** Weinstein (1969), p. 755.

**25.** Weinstein (1965).

**26.** Weinstein (1965). Such rules can include rules about the flexibility of other rules.

**27.** Giblin (1956), p. 79.

**28.** Giblin (1956), p. 139. Although Giblin and other popular writers are not producers of user information, their helpful hints are often useful as condensed folk wisdom.

**29.** Schachter and Singer (1962).

**30.** Schachter and Wheeler (1962).

**31.** See, e.g., Barker (1968), Barker and Gump (1964), and Barker and Schoggen (1973).

**32.** Barker (1969), p. 35; italics are in the original.

**33.** See Bowers (1973), Caplan and Nelson (1973), and Mischel (1968, 1973).

**34.** This case was suggested by Rodrigo J. Marulanda, a former student of the author.

**35.** Berkowitz and Geen (1966); Hanratty, O'Neal, and Sulzer (1972).

**36.** Kimbrell and Blake (1958).

**37.** Flanders (1968).

**38.** This case was suggested by Brian Levi, a former student of the author.

**39.** This case was suggested by Janet Schusheim, a former student of the author.

**40.** See, e.g., Mausner and Bloch (1957) and Rosenbaum, Chalmers, and Horne (1962).

**41.** See, e.g., Marston and Kanfer (1963).

**42.** See, e.g., Bandura, Grusec, and Menlove (1967).

**43.** See, e.g., Walters and Parke (1964) and Walters, Parke, and Cane (1965).

**44.** Flanders (1968).

**45.** Kazdin (1973).

**46.** See, e.g., Bryan, Redfield, and Mader (1971).

**47.** See, e.g., Slaby and Parke (1971).

**48.** Determining the underlying mechanisms that play a role in the powerful influence exerted by vicarious reward is a matter for the scientists to battle out among themselves. A convenient framework for classifying such mechanisms is proposed by Bandura (1971), p. 9.

**49.** Berger and Johansson (1968). This study likely met Standard 2 as well, but the researchers did not provide data bearing on that standard.

**50.** Berger and Johansson (1968), p. 54.

**51.** Berger and Johansson (1968), p. 55. In the study, reward to model consisted of telling subjects that they had chosen correctly.
**52.** Slaby and Parke (1971).
**53.** Mischel (1973), pp. 272–273. See also Bandura (1969), pp. 136–143, and Bandura (1971).
**54.** Rapaport (1971).
**55.** Rapaport (1971); Holmes (1974).
**56.** Bandura, Ross, and Ross (1963).
**57.** Grusec (1966).
**58.** Grusec and Mischel (1966).
**59.** This case was suggested by Joey O'Neill, a former student of the author.
**60.** Rosenkrans (1967).
**61.** Harvey and Rutherford (1960).
**62.** Lefkowitz, Blake, and Mouton (1955).
**63.** Klinger (1967).
**64.** Ayllon and Azrin (1968a).
**65.** Skinner (1972).
**66.** Caplan and Nelson (1973), p. 207.

**CHAPTER EIGHT NOTES**

**1.** This case was suggested by Candy Hadler, a former student of the author.
**2.** This case was suggested by Pat Franklin, a former student of the author.
**3.** Thorndike (1911), p. 244.
**4.** This definition is a composite from Verplanck (1957), White (1971), and Flanders's (1968) elaboration of Verplanck.
**5.** This distinction is suggested by White (1971), p. 138.
**6.** For a more extended discussion, see Flanders (1968), p. 317, where I discuss the issue of circularity.
**7.** See, e.g., Clarizo (1971), chap. 2, and Meacham and Wiesen (1969), chap. 4.
**8.** Foa and Foa (1974).
**9.** Foa and Foa (1974), p. 36.
**10.** See Foa and Foa (1974), chaps. 2 and 3, for evidence about the development sequence of interpersonal resources.
**11.** Foa and Foa (1974), p. 82.
**12.** This definition is from Turner, Foa, and Foa (1971), p. 169.
**13.** Foa and Foa (1974), p. 81.
**14.** These examples are from Foa and Foa (1974), p. 159. The research discussed here is reviewed in Foa and Foa (1974), chaps. 5, 6, and 9. Recall that mental events are being researched here, so questionnaire research is quite appropriate.
**15.** Foa and Foa (1974), p. 188.
**16.** Foa and Foa (1974), chap. 9.
**17.** These examples are from Foa and Foa (1974), p. 164.
**18.** Indirect support for this contention is cited in Foa and Foa (1974), p. 168.
**19.** Foa and Foa (1974) treat this topic on pp. 161–162.
**20.** See, e.g., research articles in the *Journal of Applied Behavior Analysis.*
**21.** See, e.g., McGinnies and Ferster (1971).
**22.** Miller (1969).
**23.** Bindra (1974). See also Timberlake and Allison (1974) and Bolles (1972).
**24.** See Bowers (1973). For conceptualizations of the relevant personality dimensions, see Rotter's (1966) treatment of internal versus external control of reinforcement and Kurtines's (1974) treatment of autonomy.
**25.** This case was suggested by Priscilla Schwartz, a former student of the author.
**26.** For behavior mod buffs, Gewirtz (1971) postulates that both reward to model and reward to the other person involve the identical "matching-to-sample" process of discrimination learning. Reward to model is merely a more efficient method, he says.
**27.** This case was suggested by Lorelei Starkman, a former student of the author.
**28.** Premack (1971).
**29.** Homme, C'deBaca, Devine, Steinhorst, and Rickert (1963).
**30.** Goldiamond (1965), p. 859.
**31.** See, e.g., Perin (1943) and Grice (1949).
**32.** See Lawler (1971), pp. 117–124, for a review of this evidence.
**33.** Viteles (1953).

**34.** Giblin (1956), pp. 29–30.
**35.** MacPherson, Candee, and Hohman (1974).
**36.** Tharp and Wetzel (1969), p. 138.
**37.** This case was suggested by Ilene Graditor, a former student of the author.
**38.** See, e.g., Ayllon and Azrin (1968b).
**39.** See, e.g., Becker (1971), Part IIc.
**40.** For a comprehensive review, see Kazdin and Bootzin (1972).
**41.** See Kazdin and Bootzin (1972).
**42.** See, e.g., Deci (1971, 1972).
**43.** Collins and Hoyt (1972).
**44.** Lepper, Greene, and Nisbett (1973).
**45.** Levine and Fasnacht (1974).
**46.** Tighe and Elliott (1968).
**47.** Jones (1964).
**48.** Bach and Deutsch (1970).
**49.** Bach and Deutsch (1970), pp. 246–247.
**50.** Foa and Foa (1974), p. 166.

**CHAPTER NINE NOTES**

**1.** Rehm and Marston (1968).
**2.** Goldfried and Merbaum (1973).
**3.** Thoresen and Mahoney (1974).
**4.** Mahoney and Thoresen (1974); Watson and Tharp (1972).
**5.** Homme (1969).
**6.** Johnson (1970) and Johnson and Martin (1973).
**7.** This case was suggested by L. D. Losada, a former student of the author.
**8.** This case was suggested by Rick Briz, a former student of the author.
**9.** Ferster and Skinner (1957). See also, e.g., Schoenfeld, Cole, Blaustein, Lachter, Martin, and Vickery (1972), Morse (1966), and Reynolds (1968), chap. 3. These references are given in order of decreasing difficulty and scope.
**10.** Lewis and Duncan (1958).
**11.** D. Whaley, S. Sibley, and T. Risley. Conditioning of appropriate verbal duration in a young boy. Unpublished research, Human Development Clinic, Florida State University (1965); described in Whaley and Malott (1971), pp. 110–114.
**12.** This case was suggested by Carlos del Amo, a former student of the author.
**13.** Ferster and Perrott (1968), p. 246.
**14.** Goffman (1967a).
**15.** Bachrach (1962).
**16.** Jourard (1971b), pp. 150–151.
**17.** See Olmsted (1962) and Wagner (1972).
**18.** Nord (1969).
**19.** Goffman (1967b).
**20.** This case was created by Rosemary Connors, a former student of the author.
**21.** This case was suggested by James H. Butler, a former student of the author.
**22.** This case was suggested by Jeff Dorian, a former student of the author.
**23.** This case was suggested by Diane Paull, a former student of the author.
**24.** Scott and Bushell (1974).
**25.** O'Leary, Kaufman, Kass, and Drabman (1970).
**26.** Kopel and Arkowitz (1975).
**27.** Collins and Hoyt (1972), p. 586.
**28.** See Jones, Kanouse, Kelley, Nisbett, Valins, and Weiner (1972) and the topic "attribution" in *Psychological Abstracts* for the latest research on this subject.
**29.** Goldiamond (1965), p. 859.
**30.** Maas (1968).
**31.** See O'Dell (1974).
**32.** This case was suggested by Mike Feldman, a former student of the author.
**33.** Berne (1964), chap. 1.
**34.** Ferster, Nurnberger, and Levitt (1962).
**35.** Harris (1969).
**36.** See, e.g., Ferster, Nurnberger, and Levitt (1962).
**37.** Steinman (1970a, 1970b).

**38.** See Baron, Baron, and Miller (1973).
**39.** Hart, Allen, Buell, Harris, and Wolf (1964).
**40.** This case was suggested by Joey O'Neill, a former student of the author.
**41.** Zeilberger, Sampen, and Sloane (1968), p. 47.
**42.** See Foxx and Azrin (1973) and Epstein, Doke, Sajwaj, Sorrell, and Rimmer (1974).
**43.** Keller (1969), chap. 10; Skinner (1971).
**44.** See Sears, Whiting, Nowlis, and Sears (1953).
**45.** Sandler and Davidson (1973).
**46.** Holtz and Azrin (1961); for a review, see Azrin and Holtz (1966). A tangential issue concerns whether punishment, functioning as a discriminative stimulus that strengthens behavior, can still be called punishment. Azrin and Holtz (1966, p. 381) initially confuse the issue by defining punishment as both a consequence (arranged by experimenter) and as the result or effect of that consequence (exhibited by the organism or subject). The best terminology is supplied later by Azrin and Holtz (1966, p. 381), when they say that "the stimulus [per se] is designated as a *punishing stimulus.*"
**47.** Fenicel (1945), p. 357.
**48.** Wallace (1971), chap. 8.
**49.** Goldiamond (1965), p. 273.
**50.** Goldiamond (1965), p. 274.
**51.** Goldiamond (1965), p. 276.
**52.** See Berkowitz (1974) on the topic of aggression.

**CHAPTER TEN NOTES**

**1.** Bowlby (1969), p. 209.
**2.** Bowlby (1969), p. 212; italics are mine.
**3.** Scott (1963).
**4.** A detailed review is provided by Cairnes (1966).
**5.** Bowlby (1969, 1973b).
**6.** Nunnally and Faw (1968).
**7.** See, e.g., Kendall and Nunnally (1968), Wilson and Nunnally (1971), and Rileigh and Nunnally (1970).
**8.** Solomon, Kamin, and Wynne (1953).
**9.** For detailed analyses, see Hendry (1969) and the Bible of learning theory, Hilgard and Bower (1975).
**10.** White (1971), p. 30.
**11.** Miller (1969).
**12.** See Rosen (1974).
**13.** Rosen (1974), p. 10. Rosen also suggests that standards be set by a nongovernment agency. If so, I feel that standards should include at least the five I suggested.
**14.** Wolpe (1973), p. 17; the original italics are omitted.
**15.** Wolpe (1958, 1973).
**16.** See, e.g., Locke (1971), Wilkins (1971, Morgan (1973), and Wilkins (1973).
**17.** See Bandura (1969), Paul (1969), and Rachman (1967).
**18.** An excellent program is available on tape or record from Cybersystems, Box 3365, Huntsville, Alabama 35810; instructions about the program's use are provided. Instructional Dynamics, 166 East Superior Street, Chicago, Illinois 60611, sells cassettes by Arnold Lazarus (I recommend "Relaxation I"). A tape cassette is also available from Biomonitoring Applications, Inc., Suite 1506, 271 Madison Avenue, New York, New York 10016. A good book on relaxation is *You Can Learn to Relax,* by Gutwirth (1968), available in bookstores or directly from Wilshire Book Company. However, to save yourself some money, it would be wise to use Appendix A in its written form or make your own cassette of it before turning to supplementary programs that will cost you extra money.
**19.** Donner and Guerney (1969).
**20.** See Lang (1969), "The Mechanics of Desensitization and the Laboratory Study of Human Fear."
**21.** McGlynn (1972); McGlynn, Gaynor, and Puhr (1972); McGlynn and Mapp (1970); McGlynn, Mealiea, and Nawas (1969); McGlynn, Reynolds, and Linder (1971b); McGlynn and Williams (1970); and Lang, Melamed, and Hart (1970, Experiment I).
**22.** McGlynn (1971); McGlynn, Reynolds, and Linder (1971a).
**23.** McGlynn and O'Brien (1972); Rardin (1969).
**24.** McGlynn and Linder (1971).
**25.** Phillips, Johnson, and Geyer (1972) reduced fears of public speaking, driving, and authority figures.

**26.** All the McGlynn studies already cited, Rardin (1969), and the Lang et al. (1970, Experiment I) study used such a behavioral approach measure of fear.

**27.** Lang, Melamed, and Hart (1970, Experiment I).

**28.** See, e.g., Baker, Cohen, and Saunders (1973), Clark (1973), and Rosen, Glasgow, and Barrera (1975).

**29.** Wolpe (1973).

**30.** Wolpe (1973); Arkowitz's suggestions by personal communication; the numbers in a through e in item 8 of the checklist comprise Arkowitz's modifications of the numbers originally proposed by Wolpe. The phrasing is mine.

**31.** Kopel and Arkowitz (1975).

**32.** See McGlynn studies listed in footnotes 21–24.

**33.** Greer and Silverman (1967).

**34.** Goldfried (1971), p. 228.

**35.** Kopel and Arkowitz (1974).

**36.** Lazarus (1968).

**37.** Bem (1965, 1967).

**38.** Bem (1965, Study III).

**39.** Bandura, Blanchard, and Ritter (1969), p. 180.

**40.** For a review, see Epley (1974).

**41.** Borkovec, Stone, O'Brien, and Kaloupek (1974), p. 504.

**42.** Borkovec, Stone, O'Brien, and Kaloupek (1974).

**43.** Lader (1967).

**44.** Lader, Gelder, and Marks (1967).

**45.** Sermat (1973); for a literary argument, see Tanner's (1973) *Loneliness: The Fear of Love.*

**46.** Alberti and Emmons (1970), p. 7

**47.** Wolpe (1973), p. 81.

**48.** Alberti and Emmons (1970).

**49.** Laws and Serber (1971), p. 1.

**50.** Martinson and Zerface (1970), p. 40.

**51.** Arkowitz (1973); Glasgow and Arkowitz (1975); Hines (1973).

**52.** Valentine and Arkowitz (1974).

**53.** O'Banion and Arkowitz (1974). In a related finding, Lewinsohn, Lobitz, and Wilson (1973) found depressed subjects to exhibit greater bodily responsiveness to shock. In other words, depressed people became more upset after something painful happened to them.

**54.** Arkowitz (1973), p. 7.

**55.** Gambrill (1973), p. 1.

**56.** Alberti and Emmons (1970).

**57.** For research, see Eisler, Hersen, and Miller (1973), Eisler, Hersen, Miller, and Machum (1973), and Hersen, Eisler, Miller, Johnson, and Pinkston (1975).

**58.** Wolpe (1973), p. 85.

**59.** Salter (1949). I have rewritten the list given by Wolpe (1973), pp. 85–86, who derived the ideas for the six items in the list from Salter's (1949) work.

**60.** Eisler, Miller, and Hersen (1973).

**61.** For reviews, see Bandura (1969), chap. 8, Rimm and Masters (1974), chap. 9, and Sandler and Davidson (1973), pp. 201–204.

**62.** Rachman and Teasdale (1968).

**63.** Anant (1967).

**64.** Cautela (1966, 1967).

**65.** Bandura (1969) makes this point.

**66.** Stampfl and Levis (1967, 1973). My apologies to Stampfl and Levis for omitting many of the finer points in their rationale, such as their dynamic interpretation and the use of graded hierarchies.

**67.** Wolpe (1973), p. 195.

**68.** Morganstern (1973, 1974); Rimm and Masters (1974), chap. 8.

**69.** Levis (1974a, 1974b).

**70.** See footnotes 7 and 8.

**71.** Paul (1969); Wolpe (1973).

### CHAPTER ELEVEN NOTES

**1.** Davis (1973), p. *xxii;* italics are in the original.

**2.** Zunin and Zunin (1972), pp. 9–10.

**3.** Borkovec, Stone, O'Brien, and Kaloupek (1974), p. 504.

**4.** Zimbardo, Pikonis, and Norwood (1974, 1975).

**5.** These lists of outward and inward characteristics were derived from data presented by Zimbardo, Pilkonis, and Norwood (1974) on p. 12.

**6.** Zunin and Zunin (1972), pp. 31–43.

**7.** See, e.g., Brown (1970), Gray (1969), Schaukowitsch (1964), and Weber (1970). Peck (1969) is not a sex book, but rather a social guide for teens.

**8.** Schegloff (1968). Chap. 1 in Davis (1973) treats picking up people of the opposite sex, a special case of initiating interactions.

**9.** Bach and Deutsch (1970), p. 35.

**10.** Initiating interactions by written letter is not treated here. However, with minor changes, the present pretheory could be made to apply.

**11.** Davis (1973), Chap. 1.

**12.** Davis (1973), Chap. 1.

**CHAPTER TWELVE NOTES**

**1.** Russell (1965).

**2.** Russell (1965), p. 38; italics and emphases are in the original.

**3.** This hypothesis is amenable to empirical test. The appropriate test would involve comparing the output of conversation topics from persons who (1) are told they must think very hard to create appropriate conversation topics, (2) are told nothing and given no training, (3) are given (placebo) training unrelated to the Russell thought drift, and (4) are given training on using the Russell thought drift in a standard task for creating topics of conversation.

**4.** Russell (1965), p. 44.

**5.** See the discussion by Arnold (1960).

**6.** See, e.g., Hamburg, Sabshin, Board, Grinker, Korchin, Basowitz, Heath, and Persky (1958).

**7.** Ekman, Friesen, and Tomkins (1971).

**8.** Ekman and Friesen (1969b).

**9.** Body words are called "emblems" by Ekman and Friesen (1969b).

**10.** Scheflen (1972).

**11.** Scheflen (1972).

**12.** Ekman and Friesen (1972), p. 360. I chose not to include the last three of the original list of eight illustrators given by Ekman and Friesen (1972), p. 360.

**13.** This example suggested was by Jack Ortiz, a former student of the author.

**14.** Merhabian and Ferris (1967); Merhabian and Wiener (1967).

**15.** Dittman (1972); Strongman (1973).

**16.** Dittman (1972), pp. 68–69.

**17.** This conclusion is drawn from Dittman (1972), pp. 68–69.

**18.** Merhabian (1969); Merhabian and Williams (1969).

**19.** Hall (1966). For a more recent treatment, see Sommer (1969).

**20.** See, e.g., Scherer and Schiff (1973).

**21.** Morris (1972).

**22.** Zunin and Zunin (1972), p. 81.

**23.** See, e.g., Scherer and Schiff (1973). For a review, see Exline (1972).

**24.** Rubin (1970), gazing experiment.

**25.** See Ekman and Friesen (1969a), Merhabian (1971), and Libby and Yaklevich (1973).

**26.** Haggard and Isaacs (1966).

**27.** Argyle and Dean (1965).

**28.** Scheflen (1972), p. 64.

**29.** Longabaugh, Eldred, Bell, and Sherman (1966).

**30.** Walters (1970), p. 171.

**31.** Kendon (1967).

**32.** Scheflen (1972), p. 48.

**33.** Scheflen (1972), p. 56.

**34.** Scheflen (1972), p. 69.

**35.** Scheflen (1972), p. 79.

**36.** Scheflen (1972), p. 76.

**37.** Scheflen (1972), p. 76.

**38.** Scheflen (1972), p. 76.

**39.** Scheflen (1972), p. 77.

**40.** Scheflen (1972), p. 78.

**41.** Scheflen (1972), p. 80.

**42.** Scheflen (1972), p. 80.
**43.** Scheflen (1972), p. 81.
**44.** Scheflen (1972), p. 102.
**45.** Zunin and Zunin (1972), p. 74.
**46.** This case was written by Stan Adelman, a former student of the author.
**47.** Ekman and Friesen (1969b).
**48.** Russell (1965); Barker (1971).
**49.** Barker (1971).
**50.** Gordon (1970).
**51.** Bateson, Jackson, Haley, and Weakland (1956).
**52.** Beakel and Merhabian (1969).
**53.** Scheflen (1972), p. 174.
**54.** Goffman (1967a), p. 41.
**55.** See, e.g., Hovland (1938).
**56.** Berne (1964); Harris (1967).
**57.** Berne (1964), p. 116.
**58.** Berne (1964), p. 101.
**59.** Berne (1964), p. 64.
**60.** Our attention focuses on Berne's ingenious games rather than his TA or on Harris's popular application of transactional analysis theory to communication patterns. The theory claims that within each of us there is a rational *parent,* a control-hungry *adult,* and a selfish *child* fighting for the control of our actions. The intriguing theory describes how we can come to recognize each of those three and then put control mostly in the hands of the parent. Despite all the popular attention TA has received, Swensen subjects the theory to the glaring searchlights of scientific inquiry in his *Introduction to Interpersonal Relations* (1973), the first review of theories of human relations. Swensen (p. 138) correctly observes that TA "has had relatively little impact upon serious students of interpersonal interaction." Despite claims to the contrary, parent, adult, and child are in fact Freud's ego, superego, and id applied to human speech in everyday life. Unfortunately, rather than doing empirical, quantitative research to support a rather believable theory, advocates of TA have gone into the business of running workshops and institutes. Thus I choose to pass over the parent-adult-child applications (of the untested theory) to briefly consider Berne's fascinating concept of "games." (Drat! TA as a theory is fairly *crying* to be tested and supported with evidence.)
**61.** Platt (1973), p. 641.
**62.** "Lessons on TV Ads Attacked" (1975).
**63.** Schramm, Lyle, and Parker (1961).

**EPILOGUE NOTES**

**1.** Prescott (1971, 1972); Prescott and Pisanic (1974).
**2.** Good, solid research is assumed to underlie all three kinds of information. The creation of such research information can be accomplished only by professional researchers or in consultation with them. Experiments concerning the quality of life must be carefully designed before they begin to properly assess the effects. Otherwise the whole effort may provide only worthless data. I add this postscript because, if massive funds are provided in the near future for psychological research, a lot of unqualified individuals will surely try to cash in on the Golden Age of Psychology. The best guarantee that the fruits of research will not be spoiled beforehand through improper design is consultation with a researcher who has been rigorously schooled in research design at the graduate level.

## BIBLIOGRAPHY


**Abrahams,** R. B. 1972. Mutual help for the widowed. *Social Work* 17:54–61.

***Adams,*** J. S. 1965. Inequity in social exchange. In L. Berkowitz, ed., *Advances in experimental social psychology, vol. 2,* pp. 267–299. New York: Academic.

**Ainsworth,** M. D. S. 1972. Attachment and dependency: A comparison. In J. L. Gewirtz, ed., *Attachment and dependency,* pp. 97–137. Washington, D.C.: V. H. Winston & Sons.

**Ainsworth,** M. D. S., **Bell,** S. M., and **Stayton,** D. J. 1972. Individual differences in the development of some attachment behaviors. *Merrill-Palmer Quarterly,* 18:123–143.

**Ainsworth,** M. D. S., and **Wittig,** B. A. 1969. Attachment and exploratory behavior of one-year-olds in a strange situation. In B. M. Foss, ed., pp. 233–253. *Determinants of infant behavior IV.* London: Methuen.

**Alberti,** R. E., and **Emmons,** M. L. 1970. *Your perfect right: A guide to assertive behavior.* San Luis Obispo, Calif.: Impact.

**Alexander,** C. 1967. The city as a mechanism for sustaining human contact. In W. R. Ewald, Jr., ed., *Environment for man,* pp. 60–102. Bloomington, Ind: Indiana University Press. Also in R. Gutman, ed., 1972. *People and buildings,* pp. 406–434. New York: Basic Books.

**Altman,** I., and **Haythorn,** W. W. 1965. Interpersonal exchange in isolation. *Sociometry,* 23:411–426.

**Altman,** I., and **Taylor,** D. 1973. *Social penetration: The development of interpersonal relationships.* New York: Holt, Rinehart & Winston.

American Psychological Association. 1973. Guidelines for psychologists conducting growth groups. *American Psychologist,* 28:933.

**Anant,** S. 1967. A note on the treatment of alcoholics by a verbal aversion technique. *Canadian Psychologist,* 8:19–22.

**Anderson,** N. H., and **Barrios,** A. A. 1961. Primacy effects in personality impression formation. *Journal of Abnormal and Social Psychology,* 63:346–350.

Are executives efficient? 1973. *Business Week,* December 1. Pp. 52–55.

**Argyle,** M. 1969. *Social interaction.* Chicago: Aldine-Atherton.

**Argyle,** M. 1972. *The psychology of interpersonal behaviour.* 2nd ed. Baltimore, Md.: Penguin.

**Argyle,** M., and **Dean,** J. 1965. Eye contact, distance, and affiliation. *Sociometry,* 28:289–304. Reprinted in M. Argyle, ed., 1973, *Social encounters,* pp. 173–187. Chicago: Aldine-Atherton.

**Arkowitz,** H. 1973. College dating inhibitions: assessment and treatment. Paper presented at the meeting of the American Psychological Association, Montreal, Canada.

**Arkowitz,** H. 1974. Desensitization as a self-control procedure: A case report. *Psychotherapy: Theory, Research and Practice, 11,* 172–174.

**Arnold,** M. B. 1960. *Emotion and personality.* Psychological aspects, vol. 1. New York: Columbia University Press.

**Asch,** S. 1946. Forming impressions of personality. *Journal of Abnormal and Social Psychology,* 41:258–290.

**Asch,** S. 1952. *Social psychology.* New York: Prentice-Hall.

**Ayllon,** T., and **Azrin,** N. H. 1968a. Reinforcer sampling: A technique for increasing the behavior of mental patients. *Journal of Applied Behavior Analysis,* 1:13–20.

**Ayllon,** T., and **Azrin,** N. 1968b. *The token economy.* New York: Appleton.

**Azrin,** N. H., and **Holtz,** W. C. 1966. Punishment. In W. K. Honig, ed., *Operant behavior: Areas of research and application.* New York: Appleton.

**Bach,** G. R., and **Deutsch,** R. M. 1970. *Pairing.* New York: Wyden.

**Bachrach,** A. J. 1962. An experimental approach to superstition behavior. *Journal of American Folklore,* 75:7–9.

**Baer,** D. M., **Wolf,** M. M., and **Risley,** T. R. 1968. Some current dimensions of applied behavior analysis. *Journal of Applied Behavior Analysis,* 1:91–97.

**Baker,** B. L., **Cohen,** D. C., and **Saunders,** J. T. 1973. Self-directed desensitization for acrophobia. *Behaviour Research and Therapy,* 11:79–89.

**Bandura,** A. 1965. Influence of models' reinforcement contingencies on the acquisition of imitative responses. *Journal of Personality and Social Psychology,* 1:589–595.

**Bandura,** A. 1969. *Principles of behavior modification.* New York: Holt, Rinehart & Winston.

**Bandura,** A. 1971. *Social learning theory.* New York: General Learning Press.

**Bandura,** A., **Blanchard,** E. B., and **Ritter,** B. 1969. Relative efficacy of desensitization and modeling approaches for inducing behavioral, affective, and attitudinal changes. *Journal of Personality and Social Psychology,* 13:173–199.

**Bandura,** A., **Grusec,** J. E., and **Menlove,** F. L. 1967. Some social determinants of self-monitoring reinforcement systems. *Journal of Personality and Social Psychology,* 5:449–455.

**Bandura,** A., **Ross,** D., and **Ross,** S. A. 1963. A comparative test of the status envy, social power, and the secondary reinforcement theories of identificatory learning. *Journal of Abnormal and Social Psychology,* 67:527–534.

**Barber,** T. X. 1969. *Hypnosis: A scientific approach.* New York: Van Nostrand Reinhold. (Also as paperback in Van Nostrand Insight series.)

**Barber,** T. X. 1970. *LSD, marijuana, yoga, and hypnosis.* Chicago: Aldine.

**Barber,** T. X., and **Glass,** L. B. 1962. Significant factors in hypnotic behavior. *Journal of Abnormal and Social Psychology,* 64:222–228.

**Barker,** L. L. 1971. *Listening behavior.* Englewood Cliffs, N.J.: Prentice-Hall.

**Barker,** R. G. 1968. *Ecological psychology.* Stanford, Calif.: Stanford University Press.

**Barker,** R. G. 1969. Wanted: An eco-behavioral science. In E. P. Willems and H. L. Raush, eds., *Naturalistic viewpoints in psychological research,* pp. 31–43. New York: Holt, Rinehart & Winston.

**Barker,** R. G., and **Gump,** P. V. 1964. *Big school, small school.* Stanford, Calif.: Stanford University Press.

**Barker,** R. G., and **Schoggen,** P. 1973. *Qualities of community life.* San Francisco: Jossey-Bass.

**Baron,** R. S., **Baron,** P. H., and **Miller,** N. 1973. The relation between distraction and persuasion. *Psychological Bulletin,* 80:310–323.

**Bateson,** B., **Jackson,** D. D., **Haley,** J., and **Weakland,** J. 1956. Toward a theory of schizophrenia. *Behavioral Science,* 1:251–264.

**Beakel,** N. G., and **Merhabian,** A. 1969 Inconsistent communications and pschopathology. *Journal of Abnormal Psychology,* 74:126–130.

**Becker,** G. S. 1965. A theory of the allocation of time. *Economic Journal,* 75:493–517.

**Becker,** W. C. (Ed.) 1971. *An empirical basis for change in education.* Chicago: Science Research Association.

**Bell,** D. 1973. *The coming of post-industrial society.* New York: Basic Books.

**Bem,** D. J. 1965. An experimental analysis of self-persuasion. *Journal of Experimental Social Psychology,* 1:199–218.

**Bem,** D. J. 1967. Self-perception: An alternative interpretation of cognitive dissonance phenomena. *Psychological Review,* 74:183–200.

**Berger,** S. M., and **Johasson,** S. L. 1968. Effect of a model's expressed emotions on an observer's resistance to extinction. *Journal of Personality and Social Psychology,* 10:53–58.

**Berkowitz,** L. 1974. Some determinants of impulsive aggression: Role of mediated associations with reinforcements for aggression. *Psychological Review,* 81:165–176.

**Berkowitz,** L., and **Geen,** R. G. 1966. Film violence and the cue properties of available targets. *Journal of Personality and Social Psychology,* 3:525–530.

**Berkson,** G. 1974. Social responses of animals to infants with defects. In M. Lewis and L. E. Rosenblum, *The origins of behavior: The effect of the infant on its care giver.* New York: Wiley-Interscience.

**Berne,** E. 1964. *Games people play.* New York: Grove.

**Bettman,** O. L. 1974. *The good old days—they were terrible!* New York: Random House.

**Bindra,** D. 1974. A motivational view of learning, performance, and behavior modification. *Psychological Review,* 81:199–213.

**Blanc,** M., **Bourgeois,** M., and **Henry,** P. 1966. La tentative de suicide: Aspects actuels (à propos de 500 observations). [Suicide attempts: Current aspects (apropos of 500 cases).] *Annales Médico-Psychologiques,* 1:554–559.

**Blau,** P. 1964. *Exchange and power in social life.* New York: Wiley.

**Bock,** E. W. 1972. Aging and suicide: The significance of marital, kinship, and alternative relations. *Family Coordinator,* 21:71–79.

**Bolles,** R. C. 1972. Reinforcement, expectancy, and learning. *Psychological Review* 79:394–409.

**Borkovec,** T. D., **Stone,** N. M., **O'Brien,** G. T., and **Kaloupec,** D. G. 1974. Evaluation of a clinically relevant target behavior for analog outcome research. *Behavior Therapy* 5:503–513.

**Bowers,** K. S. 1973. Situationism in psychology: An analysis and critique. *Psychological Review* 80:307–336.

**Bowlby,** J. 1969. *Attachment and loss.* Attachment, vol. 1. New York: Basic Books.

**Bowlby,** J. 1973a. Affectional bonds: Their nature and origin. In R. Weiss, 1973. Pp. 38–52.

**Bowlby,** J. 1973b. *Attachment and loss.* Separation, vol. 2. New York: Basic Books.

**Braceland,** Francis. 1967. Análisis psisiológico de la soledad. [Psychological analysis of solitude.] *Actas Luso-Espanõlos de Neurologia y Psiquiatría* 26:12–23.

**Bradburn,** N. M. 1969. *The structure of psychological well-being.* Chicago: Aldine.

**Bradford,** L. P., **Gibb,** J. R., and **Benne,** K. D. 1964. *T-group theory and laboratory method: Innovation in reeducation.* New York: Wiley.

**Bronowski,** J. 1965. *Science and human values.* 2nd ed. New York: Harper & Row.

**Brown,** H. G. 1970. *Sex and the new single girl.* Greenwich, Conn.: Fawcett Crest.

**Bryan,** J. H., **Redfield,** J., and **Mader,** S. 1971. Words and deeds about altruism and the subsequent reinforcement power of the model. *Child Development* 42:1501–1508.

**Buchanan,** E. 1974. Alone and evicted, Rose finds haven for Mother's Day. *Miami Herald,* May 12, pp. 1A, 2A.

**Bugental,** J. F. T. 1971. The humanistic ethic—the individual in psychotherapy as a societal change agent *Journal of Humanistic Psychology* 11:11–25.

**Bühler,** C., and **Allen,** M. 1972. *Introduction to humanistic psychology.* Monterey, Calif.: Brooks/Cole.

**Burton,** A., ed. 1969. *Encounter: Theory and practice.* San Francisco: Jossey-Bass.

**Butler,** R. N. 1975. *Why survive? Being old in America.* New York: Harper & Row.

**Cairnes,** R. B. 1966. Attachment behavior of mammals. *Psychological Review* 73:409–426.

**Campbell,** J. P., and **Dunnette,** M. D. 1968. Effectiveness of T-group experiences in managerial training and development. *Psychological Bulletin* 70:73–104.

**Caplan,** N., and **Nelson,** S. D. 1973. On being useful: The nature and consequences of psychological research on social problems. *American Psychologist* 28:199–211.

**Cautela,** J. R. 1966. Treatment of compulsive behavior by covert sensitization. *Psychological Record* 16:33–41.

**Cautela,** J. R. 1967. Covert sensitization. *Psychological Reports* 20:459–468.

Cheaper ways to reach the customer. 1972. *Business Week,* September 9, pp. 120–124.

**Clarizo,** H. F. 1971. *Toward positive classroom discipline.* New York: Wiley.

**Clark,** F. 1973. Self-administered desensitization. *Behaviour Research and Therapy* 11:335–338.

**Cofer,** C. N., and **Appley,** M. H. 1964. *Motivation: Theory and research.* New York: Wiley.

**Cohen,** L. J. 1974. The operational definition of human attachment. *Psychological Bulletin* 81:207–217.

**Collier,** R. M., and **Lawrence,** H. P. 1951. The adolescent feeling of psychological isolation. *Education Theory* 1:106–115.

**Collins,** B. E., and **Hoyt,** M. F. 1972. Personal responsibility-for-consequences: An integration and extension of the forced compliance literature. *Journal of Experimental Social Psychology* 8:558–593.

**Colson,** W. N. 1968. Self-disclosure as a function of social approval. Unpublished master's thesis, Howard University, Washington, D.C.

**Commoner,** B. 1971. *The Closing Circle.* New York: Bantam.

**Cooley,** C. H. 1902. *Human nature and the social order.* New York: Schribner. Reprinted in E. H. Misruchi, ed. 1967. *The substance of sociology.* New York: Appleton. Also reprinted in W. S. Sahakian, ed. 1972. *Social psychology.* Scranton,Penn.: Intext.

**Cooley,** C. H. 1929. *Social organization.* New York: Charles Schribner's Sons.

**Cozby,** P. C. 1972. Self-disclosure, reciprocity, and liking. *Sociometry* 35:151–160.

**Cozby,** P. C. 1973. Self-disclosure: A literature review. *Psychological Bulletin* 79:73–91.

**Cozby,** P. C., and **Keding,** A. C. 1975. *Self-disclosure.* New York: MSS Publishing Corp.

**Crano,** W. D., and **Brewer,** M. B. 1973. *Principles of research in social psychology.* New York: McGraw-Hill.

**Cseh-Szombathy,** L. 1972. International differences in the types and frequencies of social contacts. In A. Szalai, (ed.), 1972. Pp. 307–333.

**D'Aboy,** J. E. 1973. Loneliness: An investigation of terminology. *Dissertation Abstracts International* 33(7-B):3281.

**Davis,** M. S. 1973. *Intimate relations.* New York: Free Press.

**Deci,** E. L. 1971. The effects of externally mediated rewards on intrinsic motivation. *Journal of Personality and Social Psychology* 18:105–115.

**Deci,** E. L. 1972. Intrinsic motivation, extrinsic motivation and inequity. *Journal of Personality and Social Psychology,* 22:113–120.

**DeGrazia,** S. 1962. *Of time, work, and leisure.* New York: Anchor.

**DeThomaso,** M. T. 1971. "Touch power" and the screen of loneliness. *Perspectives in Psychiatric Care* 9:112–118.

**Deutsch,** M., and **Krauss,** R. M. 1965. *Theories in social psychology.* New York: Basic Books.

**Dittman,** A. T. 1972. *Interpersonal messages of emotion.* New York: Springer.

**Donner,** L., and **Guerney,** B. G., Jr. 1969. Automated group desensitization for test anxiety. *Behaviour Research and Therapy* 7:1–13.

**Duvall,** E. M. 1945. Loneliness and the serviceman's wife. *Marriage and Family Living* 7:77–81.

**D'Zurilla,** T. J., and **Goldfried,** M. R. 1971. Problem solving and behavior modification. *Journal of Abnormal Psychology* 78:107–126.

**D'Zurilla,** T. J., and **Goldfried,** M. R. 1973. Cognitive processes, problem solving, and effective behavior. In M. R. Goldfried and M. Merbaum, eds., 1973. Pp. 183–194.

**Eisler,** R. M., **Hersen,** M., and **Miller,** P. M. 1973. Effects of modeling on components of assertive behavior. *Journal of Behavior Therapy and Experimental Psychiatry* 4:1–6.

**Eisler,** R. M., **Hersen,** M., **Miller,** P. M., and **Machum,** J. 1973. Shaping components of assertive behavior with instructions and feedback. Paper presented at the meeting of the Association for the Advancement of Behavior Therapy, Miami. (Available from authors.)

**Eisler,** R. M., **Miller,** P. M., and **Hersen,** M. 1973. Components of asertive behavior. *Journal of Clinical Psychology* 29:295–299.

**Ekehammar,** B. 1974. Interactionism in personality from a historical perspective. *Psychological Bulletin* 81:1026–1048.

**Ekman,** P., and **Friesen,** W. V. 1969a. Non-verbal leakage and clues to deception. *Psychiatry* 32:88–105. Reprinted in M. Argyle, ed., 1973. Pp. 132–148.

**Ekman,** P., and **Friesen,** W. V. 1969b. The repertoire of nonverbal behavior: Categories, origins, usage and coding. *Semiotica* 1:49–98. (Available from authors at Langley Porter Neuropsychiatric Institute, San Francisco, Calif.)

**Ekman,** P., and **Friesen,** W. V. 1972. Hand movements. *Journal of Communication* 22:353–374.

**Ekman,** P., **Friesen,** W. V., and **Tomkins,** S. S. 1971. Facial affect scoring technique: A first validity study. *Semiotica* 3:37–58.

**Epley,** S. W. 1974. Reduction of the behavioral effects of aversive stimulation by the presence of companions. *Psychological Bulletin* 81:271–283.

**Epstein,** L. H., **Doke,** L. A., **Sajwaj,** T. E., **Sorrell,** S., and **Rimmer,** B. 1974. Generality and side effects of overcorrection. *Journal of Applied Behavior Analysis* 7:385–390.

**Exline,** R. V. 1972. Visual interaction: The glances of power and preference. *Nebraska symposium on motivation, 1971.* Lincoln, Neb.: University of Nebraska Press.

Exploiting the aged. 1974. *Time,* June 3, pp. 60–61.

**Fenicel,** O. 1945. *The psychoanalytic theory of neurosis.* New York: Norton.

**Ferber,** R. 1973. Consumer economics, a review. *Journal of Economic Literature* 11:1303–1342.

**Ferster,** C. B., **Nurnberger,** J. I., and **Levitt,** E. E. 1962. The control of eating. *Journal of Mathetics,* 1:87–109. Reprinted in M. R. Goldfried and M. Merbaum, eds., 1973. Pp. 195–212.

**Ferster,** C. B., and **Perrott,** M. C. 1968. *Behavior principles.* New York: Appleton.

**Ferster,** C. B., and **Skinner,** B. F. 1957. *Schedules of reinforcement.* New York: Appleton.

**Flanders,** J. P. 1968. A review of research on imitative behavior. *Psychological Bulletin* 69:316–337.

**Flesch,** R. 1957. *The book of unusual quotations.* New York: Harper & Row.

**Foa,** U. G., and **Foa,** E. B. 1973. Measuring the quality of life: Can it help the ecological crisis? *International Journal of Environmental Studies* 5:21–26.

**Foa,** U. G., and **Foa,** E. B. 1974. *Societal structures of the mind.* Springfield, Ill.: C. C Thomas.

**Foxx,** R. M., and **Azrin,** N. H. 1973. The elimination of autistic self-stimulatory behavior by overcorrection. *Journal of Applied Behavior Analysis* 6:1–14.

**Frankfurt,** L. P. 1965. The role of some individual and interpersonal factors in the acquaintance process. Unpublished dissertation, The American University, Washington, D.C.

**French,** J. R., Jr., and **Raven,** B. 1959. The bases of social power. In D. Cartwright, ed., *Studies in social power.* Ann Arbor: University of Michigan Press. Reprinted in numerous books of readings in social psychology.

**Fromm,** E. 1956. *The art of loving.* New York: Harper & Row. (Available as paperback by Bantam.)

**Fromm-Reichman,** F. 1959. Loneliness, *Psychiatry* 22:1–15.

**Gambrill,** E. D. 1973. A behavioral training program for increasing social interaction. Paper presented at the seventh annual meeting of the Association for Advancement of Behavior Therapy, Miami.

**Gewirtz,** J. L. 1971. The roles of overt responding and extrinsic reinforcement in "self-" and "vicarious reinforcement" phenomena in "observational learning" and imitation. In R. Glaser, ed., *The nature of reinforcement,* pp. 279–309. New York: Academic.

**Giblin,** L. 1956. *How you can have power and confidence in dealing with people.* Hollywood, Calif.: Wilshire.

**Gilner,** F. 1967. Self-report analysis of love relationships in three age groups. Unpublished Ph.D. dissertation, Purdue Univ.

**Glasgow,** R. C., and **Arkowitz,** H. 1975. The behavioral assessment of male and female social competence in dyadic heterosexual interactions. *Behavior Therapy.*

**Goffman,** E. 1967a. *Interaction ritual.* New York: Doubleday Anchor.

**Goffman,** E. 1967b. Where the action is. In E. Goffman, *Interaction ritual.* New York: Doubleday Anchor.

**Goldfried,** M. R. 1971. Systematic desensitization as training in self-control. *Journal of Consulting and Clinical Psychology* 37:228–234. Reprinted as chap. 21 in M. R. Goldfried and M. Merbaum, eds. 1973.

**Goldfried,** M. R. and **Merbaum,** M., eds. *Behavior change through self-control.* New York: Holt, Rinehart & Winston.

**Goldiamond,** I. 1965. Self-control procedures in personal behavior problems. *Psychological Reports* 17:851–868.

**Gordon,** J. E., ed. 1967. *Handbook of experimental and clinical hypnosis.* New York: Macmillan.

**Gordon,** T. 1970. *P. E. T. Parent effectiveness training.* New York: Wyden.

**Goslin,** D. A., ed. 1970. *Guidelines for the collection, maintenance, and dissemination of pupil records.* New York: Russell Sage.

**Graham,** W. K., and **Balloun,** J. 1973. An empirical test of Maslow's need hierarchy theory. *Journal of Humanistic Psychology* 13:97–108.

**Gray,** F. 1969. *Scoremanship.* New York: Bantam.

**Greer,** J. H., and **Silverman,** I. 1967. Treatment of a recurrent nightmare by behavior modification procedures: A case study. *Journal of Abnormal Psychology* 72:188–190.

**Grice,** G. R. 1949. Visual discrimination learning with simultaneous and successive presentation of stimuli. *Journal of Comparative and Physiological Psychology* 42:365–373.

**Grusec,** J. 1966. Some antecedents of self-criticism. *Journal of Personality and Social Psychology* 4:244–252.

**Grusec,** J., and **Mischel,** W. 1966. The model's characteristics as determinants of social learning. *Journal of Personality and Social Psychology* 4:211–215.

**Gutwirth,** S. W. 1968. *You can learn to relax.* Hollywood, Calif.: Wilshire.

**Haggard,** E. A., and **Isaacs,** K. S. 1966. Micromomentary facial expressions as indicators of ego mechanisms in psychotherapy. In L. A. Gottschalk and E. H. Auerbach, eds., *Methods of research in psychotherapy.* New York: Appleton.

**Hall,** D. T., and **Nougaim,** K. E. 1968. An examination of Maslow's need hierarchy in an organizational setting. *Organizational Behavior and Human Performance* 3:12–35.

**Hall,** E. T. 1966. *The hidden dimension.* Garden City, N.Y.: Doubleday. (Available in paperback by Anchor.)

**Hamburg,** D. A., **Sabshin,** M. A., **Board,** F. A., **Grinker,** R. R., **Korchin,** S. J., **Basowitz,** H., **Heath,** H., and **Persky,** H. 1958. Classification and rating of emotional experiences. *Archives of Neurological Psychiatry* 79:415–426.

**Hanratty,** M. A., **O'Neal,** E., and **Sulzer,** J. L. 1972. Effect of frustration upon imitation of aggression. *Journal Personality and Social Psychology* 21:30–34.

**Harlow,** H. F. 1958. The nature of love. *American Psychologist* 13:673–685.

**Harlow,** H. F. 1971. *Learning to love.* San Francisco: Albion.

**Harlow,** H. F., and **Harlow,** M. K. 1965. The affectional systems. In A. M. Schrier, H. F. Harlow, and F. Stollnitz, eds., *Behavior of nonhuman primates,* vol. 2. New York: Academic.

**Harlow,** H. F., and **Zimmerman,** M. K. 1959. Affectional responses in the infant monkey. *Science* 130:421–432.

**Harris,** M. B. 1969. Self-directed program for weight control: A pilot study. *Journal of Abnormal Psychology* 74:263–270.

**Harris,** T. A. 1967. *I'm OK—you're OK.* New York: Harper & Row. (Available in paperback by Avon.)

**Hart,** B. M., **Allen,** K. E., **Buell,** J. S., **Harris,** F. R., and **Wolf,** M. M. 1964. Effects of social reinforcement on operant crying. *Journal of Experimental Child Psychology* 1:145–153.

**Harvey,** O. J., and **Rutherford,** J. 1960. Status in the informal group: Influence and influencibility at differing age levels. *Child Development* 31:377–385.

**Hendry,** D. P. 1969. *Conditioned reinforcement.* Homewood, Ill.: Dorsey.

**Hepner,** H. W. 1973. *Psychology applied to life and work.* 5th ed. Englewood Cliffs, N.J.: Prentice-Hall.

**Hersen,** M., **Eisler,** R. M., **Miller,** P. M., **Johnson,** M. B., and **Pinkston,** S. G. 1975. Effects of practice, instructions and modeling on components of assertive behavior. *Behaviour Research and Therapy.*

**Hesse,** H. 1971. *Knulp.* New York: Farrar, Straus & Giroux. (Translated from the German, *Knulp: Drei Geschichten aus dem Leben Knulps,* Copyright S. Fischer Verlag, 1915; Copyright 1949 by Suhrkamp Verlag, Frankfurt/Main.)

**Hilgard,** E. R. 1965. *Hypnotic susceptibility.* New York: Harcourt Brace Jovanovich.

**Hilgard,** E. R. 1967. Individual differences in hypnotizability. In J. E. Gordon, ed. 1967. Pp. 391–443.

**Hilgard,** E. R., and **Bower,** G. 1975. *Theories of learning.* 4th ed. Englewood Cliffs, N.J.: Prentice-Hall.

**Hines,** P. A. 1973. Social competence and incompetence. Unpublished master's thesis, University of Oregon.

**Holmes,** D. S. 1974. Investigations of repression: Differential recall of material experimentally or naturally associated with ego threat. *Psychological Bulletin* 81:632–653.

**Holtz,** W. C., and **Azrin,** N. H. 1961. Discriminative properties of punishment. *Journal of the Experimental Analysis of Behavior* 4:225–232.

**Homans,** G. C. 1950. *The human group.* New York: Harcourt Brace Jovanovich.

**Homans,** G. C. 1961. *Social behavior: Its elementary forms.* New York: Harcourt Brace Jovanovich.

**Homme,** L. E. 1969. *How to use contingency contracting in the classroom.* Champaign, Ill.: Research Press.

**Homme,** L. E., **C'deBaca,** P., **Devine,** J. V., **Steinhorst,** R., and **Rickert,** E. J. 1963. Use of the Premack principle in controlling the behavior of nursery school children. *Journal of the Experimental Analysis of Behavior* 6:544.

**Hovland,** C. I. 1938. Experimental studies in rote-learning: III. Distribution of practice with varying speeds of syllable presentation. *Journal of Experimental Psychology* 25:622–633.

**Howard,** J. 1970. *Please touch.* New York: McGraw-Hill.

**Ittelson,** W. H., **Proshansky,** H. M., **Rivlin,** L., and **Winkel,** G. H. 1974. *An introduction to environmental psychology.* New York: Holt, Rinehart & Winston.

**Jacobs,** J. 1971. *Adolescent suicide.* New York: Wiley.

**Jahoda,** M. 1958. *Current concepts of positive mental health.* New York: Basic Books.

**Jan-Tausch,** J. Undated. Suicide of children 1960–63, New Jersey Public School Studies. Bulletin published by Department of Education, State of New Jersey.

**Johnson,** D. W., **Kavanagh,** J. A., and **Lubin,** B. 1973. Comparison of anxiety level of students taking an examination and participating in a laboratory training group. In D. W. Johnson, ed., *Contemporary social psychology.* Philadelphia: Lippincott.

**Johnson,** H. H., and **Solso,** R. L. 1971. *An introduction to experimental design in psychology: A case approach.* New York: Harper & Row.

**Johnson,** S. M. 1970. Self-reinforcement vs. external reinforcement in behavior modification with children. *Developmental Psychology* 3:147–148.

**Johnson,** S. M., and **Martin,** S. Forthcoming. Developing self-evaluation as a conditioned reinforcer. In B. Ashem and E. G. Poser, eds., *Adaptive learning: Behavior modification with children.* New York Pergammon.

**Jones,** E. E. 1964. *Ingratiation.* New York: Appleton.

**Jones,** E. E., **Kanouse,** D. E., **Kelley,** H. H., **Nisbett,** R. E., **Valins,** S., and **Weiner,** B. 1972. *Attribution.* Morristown, N.J.: General Learning Press.

**Jourard,** S. M. 1959. Self-disclosure and other cathexis. *Journal of Abnormal and Social Psychology* 59:428–431. Reprinted in S. M. Jourard, ed., 1971b. Pp. 13–18.

**Jourard,** S. M. 1961a. Age and self-disclosure. *Merrill-Palmer Quarterly* 7:191–197. Reprinted in S. M. Jourard, ed., 1971b. Pp. 45–52.

**Jourard,** S. M. 1961b. Self-disclosure and grades in nursing college. *Journal of Applied Psychology* 45:244–247. Reprinted in S. M. Jourard, ed., 1971b. Pp. 59–64.

**Jourard,** S. M. 1971a. *The transparent self.* 2nd ed. New York: Van Nostrand Reinhold.

**Jourard,** S. M., ed. 1971b. *Self-disclosure: An experimental analysis of the transparent self.* New York: Wiley.

**Jourard,** S. M., and **Landsman,** M. J. 1960. Cognition, cathexis, and the "dyadic effect" in man's self-disclosing behavior. *Merrill-Palmer Quarterly* 6:178–186. Reprinted in S. M. Jourard, ed., 1971b. Pp. 19–27.

**Jourard,** S. M., and **Lasakow,** P. 1958. Some factors in self-disclosure. *Journal of Abnormal and Social Psychology* 56:91–98. Reprinted in S. M. Jourard, ed., 1971b. Pp. 3–12.

**Jourard,** S. M. and **Richman,** P. 1963. Disclosure output and input in college students. *Merrill-Palmer Quarterly* 9:141–148. Reprinted in S. M. Jourard, ed., 1971b. Pp. 28–35.

**Kagan,** J., and **Klein,** R. E. 1973. Cross-cultural perspectives on early development. *American Psychologist* 28:947–961.

**Kammeyer,** K., and **Bolton,** C. D. 1968. Community and family factors related to the use of a family service agency. *Journal of Marriage and the Family* 30:488–498.

**Kaplan,** K. J., **Firestone,** I. J., **Degnore,** R., and **Moore,** M. 1974. Gradients of attraction as a function of disclosure probe intimacy and setting formality: On distinguishing attitude oscillation from attitude change—study one. *Journal of Personality and Social Psychology* 30:638–646.

**Kazdin,** A. E. 1973. The effect of vicarious reinforcement on attentive behavior in the classroom. *Journal of Applied Behavior Analysis* 6:71–78.

**Kazdin,** A. E., and **Bootzin,** R. R. 1972. The token economy: An evaluative review. *Journal of Applied Behavior Analysis* 5:343–372.

**Keller,** F. S. 1969. *Learning: Reinforcement theory.* 2nd ed. New York: Random House.

**Kendall,** K. A., and **Nunnally,** J. L. 1968. Effects of reward schedules on the acquisition of conditioned reward value. *Psychonomic Science* 12:239–240.

**Kendon,** A. 1967. Some functions of gaze-directions in social interaction. *ACTA Psychologica* 26:22–47. Reprinted in M. Argyle, ed., 1973. Pp. 76–92.

**Keyes,** R. 1973. *We the lonely people: Searching for community.* New York: Harper & Row.

**Keys,** A., **Brozek,** J., **Heneschel,** O., and **Taylor,** H. 1950. *The biology of starvation,* vol. 2. Minneapolis: University of Minnesota Press.

**Kimbrell,** D., and **Blake,** R. R. 1958. Motivational factors in the violation of a prohibition. *Journal of Abnormal and Social Psychology* 56:132–133.

**Klinger,** E. 1967. Modeling effects on achievement imagery. *Journal of Personality and Social Psychology* 7:49–62.

**Koch,** S. 1971. The image of man implicit in encounter group theory. *Journal of Humanistic Psychology* 11:109–128.

**Kopel,** S. A., and **Arkowitz,** H. S. 1974. Role playing as a source of self-observation and behavior change. *Journal of Personality and Social Psychology* 29:677–686.

**Kopel,** S. A., and **Arkowitz,** H. 1975. The role of attribution and self-perception in behavior change. *Genetic Psychology Monographs.*

**Kruglanski,** A. W., **Friedman,** I., and **Zeeri,** G. 1971. The effects of extrinsic incentive on some qualitative aspects of task performance. *Journal of Personality* 39:606–617.

**Kurtines,** W. 1974. Autonomy: A concept reconsidered. *Journal of Personality Assessment* 38:243–246.

**Ladd,** P. B. 1971. Book facts. *Directory of publishers.* Association of American Publishers: Oberlin, Ohio.

**Lader,** M. H. 1967. Palmar skin conductance measures in anxiety and phobic states. *Journal of Psychosomatic Research* 16:271–281.

**Lader,** M. H., **Gelder,** M. G., and **Marks,** I. M. 1967. Palmar skin conductance measures as predictors of response to desensitization. *Journal of Psychosomatic Research* 11:283–290.

**Laing,** R. D., **Phillipson,** H., and **Lee,** A. R. 1966. Interpersonal perception. New York: Springer.

**Landauer,** T. K., **Carlsmith,** J. M., and **Lepper,** M. 1970. Experimental analysis of the factors determining obedience of four-year-old children to adult females. *Child Development* 41:601–611.

**Lang,** P. J. 1969. The mechanics of desensitization and the laboratory study of human fear. In C. M. Franks, ed., *Behavior therapy: Appraisal and status.* New York: McGraw-Hill.

**Lang,** P. J., **Melamed,** B. G., and **Hart,** J. 1970. A psychophysiological analysis of fear modification using an automated desensitization procedure. *Journal of Abnormal Psychology* 76:220–234.

**Langer,** E. J., and **Abelson,** R. P. 1972. How to succeed in getting help without really dying: The semantics of asking a favor. *Journal of Personality and Social Psychology* 24:26–32.

**Langer.** E. J., and **Dweck,** C. S. 1973. *Personal politics.* Englewood Cliffs, N.J.: Prentice-Hall.

**Lantz,** H. R. 1956. Number of childhood friends as reported in the life histories of a psychiatrically diagnosed group of 1000. *Marriage and Family Living* 18(May):107–108.

**Lawler,** E. E. III. 1971. *Pay and organizational effectiveness.* New York: McGraw-Hill.

**Lawler,** E. E., III, and **Suttle,** J. L. 1972. A causal correlational test of the need hierarchy concept. *Organizational Behavior and Human Performance* 7:265–287.

**Laws,** D. R., and **Serber,** M. 1971. Measurement and evaluation of assertive training with sexual offenders. Paper presented at the meeting of the Association for the Advancement of Behavior Therapy, Washington, D.C., September. (Available from authors.)

**Lazarus,** A. A. 1968. Behavior therapy and graded structure. In R. Porter, ed., *The role of learning in psychotherapy.* Boston, Mass.: Little, Brown.

**Leedy,** P. D. 1974. *Practical research: Planning and design.* New York: Macmillan.

**Leftkowitz,** N. M., **Blake,** R. R., and **Mouton,** J. S. 1955. Status factors in pedestrian violation of traffic signals. *Journal of Abnormal and Social Psychology* 51:704–706.

**Lepper,** M. R., **Greene,** D., and **Nisbett,** R. E. 1973. Undermining children's intrinsic interest with extrinsic reward. *Journal of Personality and Social Psychology* 28:129–137.

Lessons on TV ads attacked. 1975. *Miami Herald,* May 22, page B-2.

**Lesy,** M. 1973. *Wisconsin death trip.* New York: Pantheon.

**Leventhal,** H., and **Fischer,** K. 1970. What reinforces in a social reinforcement situation—words or expressions? *Journal of Personality and Social Psychology* 14:83–94.

**Levine,** F. M., and **Fasnacht,** G. 1974. Token rewards may lead to token learning. *American Psychologist* 29:816–820.

**Levine,** S. 1960. Stimulation in infancy. *Scientific American* 202:80–86. May. Reprinted in J. L. McGaugh, N. M. Weinberger, and R. E. Whalen, eds., *Psychobiology: The biological basis of behavior,* pp. 92–98. San Francisco: Freeman.

**Levinger,** G., and **Senn,** D. J. 1967. Disclosure of feeling in marriage. *Merrill-Palmer Quarterly 13:237*–249.

**Levinson,** B. M. 1972. *Pets and human development.* Springfield, Ill.: C. C Thomas.

**Levis,** D. J. 1974a. Implosive therapy: A critical analysis of Morganstern's review. *Psychological Bulletin* 81:155–158.

**Levis,** D. J. 1974b. Implosive therapy: A review and critical analysis of Morganstern's review. Unpublished supplement of Levis, 1974a. Available from author, State University of New York at Binghamton.

**Lewinsohn,** P. M., **Lobitz,** C., and **Wilson,** S. 1973. "Sensitivity" of depressed individuals to aversive stimuli. *Journal of Abnormal Psychology* 81:258–263.

**Lewis,** D. J., and **Duncan,** C. P. 1958. Vicarious experience and partial reinforcement. *Journal of Abnormal and Social Psychology* 57:321–326.

**Libby,** W. L., Jr., and **Yaklevich,** D. 1973. Personality determinants of eye contact and direction of gaze aversion. *Journal of Personality and Social Psychology* 27:197–206.

**Libet,** J. M. 1973. The construct of social skill: An empirical study of several behavioral measures on temporal stability, internal structure, validity and situational generalizability. Ph. D. dissertation, University of Oregon. (Available from University Microfilms in Ann Arbor, Mich. as dissertation #73-28,610).

**Libet,** J. M., and **Lewinsohn,** P. M. 1973. Concept of social skill with special reference to the behavior of depressed persons. *Journal of Consulting and Clinical Psychology* 40:304–312.

**Lieberman,** M. A., **Yalom,** I. D., and **Miles,** M. B. 1973. Encounter: The leader makes the difference. *Psychology Today* 6:69–76. Exerpted from M. A. Lieberman, I. D. Yalom, and M. B. Miles. 1973. *Encounter groups: First facts.* New York: Basic Books.

**Linder,** S. B. 1970. *The harried leisure class.* New York: Columbia University Press.

**Lindzey,** G., and **Aronson,** E., eds. 1968. *The Handbook of social psychology,* vol. 2. 2nd ed. Reading, Mass.: Addison-Wesley.

**Lipsey,** R. G., and **Steiner,** P. O. 1969. *Economics.* New York: Harper & Row.

**Locke,** E. A. 1971. Is "behavior therapy" behavioristic? *Psychological Bulletin* 76:318–327.

**London,** P. 1967. The induction of hypnosis. In J. E. Gordon, ed., 1967. Pp. 44–79.

**Longabaugh,** R., **Eldred,** S. H., **Bell,** N. W., and **Sherman,** L. J. 1966. The interactional world of the chronic schizophrenic patient. *Psychiatry* 29:78–99.

**Lopata,** H. Z. 1969. Loneliness: Forms and components. *Social Problems* 17:248–262. Reprinted in R. S. Weiss, 1973. Pp. 102–115.

**Lowenthal,** M. F., and **Haven,** C. 1968. Interaction and adaptation: Intimacy as a critical variable. *American Sociological Review* 33:20–30.

**Luchins,** A. S. 1957. Primacy-recency in impression formation. In C. Hovland, A. Cohen, W. McGuire, I. Janis, R. Feierabend, and N. Anderson, *The order of presentation in persuasion,* pp. 33–61. New Haven, Conn.: Yale University Press,

**Luchins,** A. S. 1958. Definitiveness of impression and primacy-recency in communications. *Journal of Social Psychology* 48:275–290.

**Maas,** H. S. 1968. Preadolescent peer relations and adult intimacy. *Psychiatry* 31:161–172.

**McGinnies,** E., and **Ferster,** C. B., eds. 1971. *The reinforcement of social behavior.* Boston: Houghton Mifflin.

**McGlynn,** F. D. 1971. Experimental desensitization following three types of instructions. *Behaviour Research and Therapy* 9:367–369.

**McGlynn,** F. D. 1972. Systematic desensitization under two conditions of induced expectancy. *Behaviour Research and Therapy* 10:229–234.

**McGlynn,** F. D., **Gaynor,** R., and **Puhr,** J. 1972. Experimental desensitization of snake avoidance after an instructional manipulation. *Journal of Clinical Psychology* 28:224–227.

**McGlynn,** F. D., and **Linder,** L. H. 1971. The clinical application of analogue desensitization: A case study. *Behaviour Therapy* 2:385–388.

**McGlynn,** F. D., and **Mapp,** R. H. 1970. Systematic desensitization of snake-avoidance following three types of suggestion. *Behaviour Research and Therapy* 8:197–201.

**McGlynn,** F. D., **Mealiea,** W. L., Jr., and **Nawas,** M. M. 1969. Systematic desensitization of snake-avoidance under two conditions of suggestion. *Psychological Reports* 25:220–222.

**McGlynn,** F. D., **O'Brien,** L. 1972. The semi-automated treatment of a phobia: A case study. *Journal of Clinical Psychology* 28:228–230.

**McGlynn,** F. D., **Reynolds,** E. J., and **Linder,** L. H. 1971a. Experimental desensitization following therapeutically oriented and physiologically oriented instructions. *Journal of Behavior Therapy and Experimental Psychiatry* 2:13–18.

**McGlynn,** F. D., **Reynolds,** E. J., and **Linder,** L. H. 1971b. Systematic desenetization with pre-treatment and intra-treatment therapeutic instructions. *Behaviour Research and Therapy* 9:57–63.

**McGlynn,** F. D., and **Williams,** C. W. 1970. Systematic desensitization of snake-avoidance under three conditions of suggestion. *Journal of Behavior Therapy and Experimental Psychiatry* 1:97–101.

**McGuire,** W. J. 1969. The nature of attitudes and attitude change. In G. Lindzey and E. Aronson, eds., *The handbook of social psychology,* vol. 3. 2nd ed. Reading, Mass.: Addison-Wesley.

**MacPherson,** E. M., **Candee,** B. L., and **Hohman,** R. J. 1974. A comparison of three methods for eliminating disruptive lunchroom behavior. *Journal of Applied Behavior Analysis* 7:287–297.

**Mahoney,** M. J., and **Thoresen,** C. E. 1974 *Self-control: Power to the person.* Monterey, Calif.: Brooks/Cole.

**Manson,** W. A. 1968. Early social deprivation in the non-human primates: Implications for human behavior in environmental influences. In D. C. Glass, ed., *Environmental influences.* New York: Rockefeller University Press and Russell Sage Foundation.

**Marcel,** G. 1960. *The mystery of being.* Chicago: Gateway.

**Margenau,** H. 1950. The nature of physical reality. New York: McGraw-Hill.

**Marston,** A. R., and **Kanfer,** F. H. 1963. Group size and number of vicarious reinforcements in verbal learning. *Journal of Experimental Psychology* 65:593–596.

**Martinson,** W. D., and **Zerface,** J. P. 1970. Comparison of individual counseling and a social program with nondaters. *Journal of Counseling Practice* 17:36–40.

**Maslow,** A. H. 1970a. Humanistic education vs. professional education: Further comments. *New Directions in Teaching* 2 (2, Spring): 3–10.

**Maslow,** A. H. 1970b. *Motivation and personality.* 2nd ed. New York: Harper & Row.

**Maslow,** A. H. *The farther reaches of human nature* New York: Viking, 1971.

**Masters,** J. C., and **Wellman,** H. M. 1974. The study of human infant attachment: A procedural critique. *Psychological Bulletin* 81:218–237.

**Matson,** F. W. (ed.) 1973. *Without/within: Behaviorism and humanism.* Monterey, Calif.: Brooks/Cole.

**Mausner,** B., and **Bloch,** B. L. 1957. A study of the additivity of variables affecting social interaction. *Journal of Abnormal and Social Psychology* 54:250–256.

**Meacham,** M. L., and **Wiesen,** A. E. 1969. *Changing classroom behavior: A manual for precision teaching.* Scranton, Pa.: Intext.

**Mead,** M. (ed.) 1953. *Cultural patterns and technical change.* Paris: UNESCO.

**Merhabian,** A. 1969. Significance of posture and position in the communication of attitude and status relationships. *Psychological Bulletin* 71:359–372.

**Merhabian,** A. 1970. *Tactics of social influence.* Englewood Cliffs, N.J.: Prentice-Hall.

**Merhabian,** A. 1971. Nonverbal betrayal of feeling. *Journal of Experimental Research in Personality* 5:64–73.

**Merhabian,** A. 1972. *Nonverbal communication.* Chicago: Aldine-Atherton.

**Merhabian,** A., and **Ferris,** S. R. 1967. Inference of attitudes from nonverbal communication in two channels. *Journal of Consulting Psychology* 31:248–252.

**Merhabian,** A., and **Wiener,** M. 1967. Decoding of inconsistent communications. *Journal of Personality and Social Psychology* 6:109–114.

**Merhabian,** A., and **Williams,** M. 1969. Nonverbal concomitants of perceived and intended persuasiveness. *Journal of Personality and Social Psychology* 13:37–58.

**Miller,** G. A. 1969. Psychology as a means for promoting human welfare. *American Psychologist* 24:1063–1075. Reprinted in G. A. Miller and R. Buckhout, 1973. *Psychology: The science of mental life,* Appendix C. New York: Harper & Row.

**Mischel,** W. 1968. *Personality and assessment.* New York: Wiley.

**Mischel,** W. 1973. Toward a cognitive social learning conceptualization of personality. *Psychological Review* 80:252–283.

**Montagu,** A. 1971. *Touching.* New York: Columbia University Press. (Available in paperback by Perennial Library.)

**Morgan,** W. G. 1973. Nonnecessary conditions or useful procedures in desensitization: A reply to Wilkins. *Psychological Bulletin* 79:373–375.

**Morganstern,** K. P. 1973. Implosive therapy and flooding procedures: A critical review. *Psychological Bulletin* 79:318–334.

**Morganstern,** K. P. 1974. Issues in implosive therapy: Reply to Levis. *Psychological Bulletin* 81:380–382.

**Morris,** D. 1971. *Intimate behavior.* New York: Random House. (Available in paperback by Bantam.)

**Morse,** W. H. 1966. Intermittent reinforcement. In W. K. Honig, ed., *Operant behavior,* pp. 52–108. New York: Appleton.

**Moustakas,** C. 1972. *Loneliness and solitude.* Englewood Cliffs, N.J.: Prentice-Hall (Spectrum).

**Munnichs,** J. M. A. 1964. Loneliness, isolation and social relations in old age: A pilot survey. *Vita Humana* 7:228–238.

**Murray,** H. A. 1938. *Explorations in personality.* New York: Science Editions.

**Mussen,** P., ed. 1970. *Carmichael's manual of child psychology,* vols 1 and 2, 3rd ed. New York: Wiley.

National Science Foundation. 1969. *Knowledge into action: Improving the nation's use of the social sciences.* Washington, D.C.: GPO.

**Newbrough,** J. R., **Berger,** M., **Greentree,** I., **McMillan,** D., **Simpkins,** C., **Smith,** S., **Smith,** W., and **Wuescher,** L. 1973. *Quality of life in the household.* CMHE Working Paper No. 51. Unpublished manuscript, Center for Community Studies, George Peabody College, Nashville, Tenn. (Available from first author.)

**Newson,** J., and **Newson,** E. 1968. *Four years old in an urban community.* Chicago: Aldine

**Nord,** W. R. 1969. Beyond the teaching machine: The neglected area of operant conditioning in the theory and practice of management. *Organizational Behavior and Human Performance* 4:375–401. Reprinted in G. W. Dalton and P. R. Lawrence, eds. 1971. *Motivation and control in organizations,* pp. 352–377. Homewood, Ill.: Irwin-Dorsey.

Not much time for anything but work. 1974. *Business Week,* May 4, pp. 70–72.

**Nunnally,** J. C., and **Faw,** T. T. 1968. The acquisition of conditioned reward value in discrimination learning. *Child Development* 39:159–166.

**O'Banion,** K., and **Arkowitz,** H. 1974. *Social anxiety and selective memory for affective information about the self.* Manuscript submitted for publication. (Available from authors.)

**O'Dell,** S. 1974. Training parents in behavior modification: A review. *Psychological Bulletin* 81:418–433.

**O'Leary,** K. D., **Kaufman,** K. F., **Kass,** R. E., and **Drabman,** R. S. 1970. The effect of loud and soft reprimands on the behavior of disruptive students. *Exceptional Children* 37:145–155.

**Olmsted,** C. 1962. *Heads I win, tails you lose.* New York: Macmillan.

**Otto,** H. A. (ed.) 1972. *Love today.* New York: Delta.

**Packard,** V. 1972. *A nation of strangers.* New York: McKay.

**Paul,** G. L. 1969. Psychological effects of relaxation training and hypnotic suggestion. *Journal of Abnormal Psychology* 74:425–437.

**Peck,** E. 1969. *How to get a teen-age boy & what to do with him when you get him.* New York: Geis. (Available in paperback by Avon.)

**Pepper,** C. B. 1974. I don't ever want to be that much in love again. *McCall's,* January, 112–113.

**Perin,** C. T. 1943. A quantitative investigation of delay-of-reinforcement gradient. *Journal of Experimental Psychology* 32:37–51.

**Phillips,** R. E., **Johnson,** G. D., and **Geyer,** A. 1972. Self-administered systematic desensitization. *Behaviour Research and Therapy* 10:93–96.

**Platt,** J. 1973. Social traps. *American Psychologist* 28:641–651.

**Plutchik,** R. 1973. *Foundations of experimental research.* 2nd ed. New York: Harper & Row.

**Powers,** W. T. 1973. *Behavior: The control of perception.* Chicago: Aldine.

**Premack,** D. 1971. Catching up with common sense or two sides of a generalization: Reinforcement and punishment. In R. Glaser, ed., *The nature of reinforcement,* pp. 121–150. New York: Academic.

**Prescott,** J. W. 1971. Early somatosensory deprivation as an ontogenetic process in the abnormal development of the brain and behavior. In *Medical primatology.* New York: Karger Basel. Pp. 356–375.

**Prescott,** J. W. 1972. Before ethics and morality. *The Humanist,* Nov./Dec., 19–21.

**Prescott,** J. W. 1974. James Prescott: Touching. *Intellectual Digest* 4:6–10.

**Prescott,** J. W., and **Pisanic,** C. 1974. Pleasure or pain: Paths toward peace or violence. Paper presented at the meeting of the Society for Cross-Cultural Research, Boston, Feb. 22–24. Under revision for publication.

**Prescott,** J. W., **Wallace,** D., and **Vandervoort,** H. E. 1974. Drugs are better than sex: Consequences of parental affectional deprivation. Paper presented at the meeting of the National Council on Family Relations, St. Louis, Oct. 23–26.

**Rachman,** S. 1967. Systematic desensitization. *Psychological Bulletin* 67:93–103.

**Rachman,** S., and **Teasdale,** J. D. 1968. Aversion therapy. In C. L. Franks, ed., *Assessment and status of behavior therapies and associated developments.* New York: McGraw-Hill.

**Rapaport,** D., 1971. *Emotions and memory.* 5th ed. New York: International Universities.

**Rappaport,** J., **Gross,** T., and **Lepper,** C. 1973. Modeling, sensitivity training, and instructions: Implications for the training of college student volunteers and for outcome research. *Journal of Consulting and Clinical Psychology* 40:99–107.

**Rardin,** M. W. 1969. Treatment of a phobia by partial self-desensitization: A case study. *Journal of Consulting and Clinical Psychology* 33:125–126.

**Rehm,** L. P., and **Marston,** A. R. 1968. Reduction of social anxiety through modification of self-reinforcement: An instigation therapy technique. *Journal of Consulting and Clinical Psychology* 32:565–574.

**Reynolds,** G. S. 1968. *A primer of operant conditioning.* Glenview, Ill.: Scott, Foresman.

**Riesman,** D. 1973. Foreward. In R. S. Weiss, 1973. Pp. ix–xxii.

**Rileigh,** K. K., and **Nunnally,** J. C. 1970. A new measure of semantic appraisal for studies of secondary rewards. *Psychonomic Science* 18:203–205.

**Rimm,** D. C., and **Masters,** J. C. 1974. *Behavior Therapy: Techniques and empirical findings.* New York: Academic.

**Robinson,** J. P. 1973. Life satisfactions and happiness. In J. P. Robinson and P. R. Shaver, (eds.), 1973. Pp. 11–43.

**Robinson,** J. P., and **Shaver,** P. R. 1973. (Eds.) *Measures of social psychological attitudes.* Ann Arbor, Mich.: Institute for Social Research.

**Robinson,** J. P., and **Converse,** P. E. 1972. In A. Szalai, (ed.), 1972. Pp. 113–144.

**Rogers,** C. R. 1959. A theory of therapy, personality, and interpersonal relationships, as developed in the client-centered framework. In S. Koch, ed., *Psychology: A study of a science,* vol. 3, pp. 184–241. New York: McGraw-Hill.

**Rogers,** C. R. 1961. *On becoming a person.* Boston: Houghton Mifflin.

**Rosen,** G. M. 1974. On the development and use of "nonprescription behavior therapies." University of Oregon, unpublished manuscript.

**Rosen,** G. M., **Glasgow,** R., and **Barrera,** M. 1975. A controlled study to assess the effectiveness of a manual for self-administered desensitization. Unpublished research, University of Oregon.

**Rosenbaum,** M. E., **Chalmers,** D. K., and **Horne,** W. C. 1962. Effects of success and failure and the competence of the model on the acquisition and reversal of matching behavior. *Journal of Psychology* 54:251–258.

**Rosenkrans,** M. 1967. Imitation in children as a function of perceived similarity to a social model and vicarious reinforcement. *Journal of Personality and Social Psychology* 7:307–315.

**Rotter,** J. 1966. Generalized expectancies for internal versus external control of reinforcement. *Psychological Monographs* 80 (1, Whole No. 609).

**Rubin,** Z. 1970. Measurement of romantic love. *Journal of Personality and Social Psychology* 16:265–273.

**Rubin,** Z. 1973. *Liking and loving.* New York: Holt, Rinehart & Winston.

**Runkel,** P. J., and **McGrath,** J. E. 1972. *Research on human behavior.* New York: Holt, Rinehart & Winston.

**Russell,** E. 1965. *Conversation made easy.* 2nd ed. Kingswood, Tadworth, Sy., England: Elliot Right Way Books. (Available in paperback by Wilshire.)

**Sachs,** R. 1974. Mother feels lonely amid 300 partygoers. *Miami Herald,* May 13, p. 1-B.

St. Louis: Pride on "The Hill." 1974. *Time,* April 29, p. 27.

**Salter,** A. 1949. *Conditioned reflex therapy.* New York: Farrar, Straus & Giroux.

**Sandler,** J., and **Davidson,** R. S. 1973. *Psychopathology: Learning theory, research, and applications.* New York: Harper & Row.

**Sarton,** M. 1961. *Cloud, stone, sun, vine, Poems selected and new.* New York: Norton.

**Schachter,** S., and **Singer,** J. E. 1962. Cognitive, social, and physiological determinants of emotional state. *Psychological Review* 69:379–399.

**Schachter,** S., and **Wheeler,** L. 1962. Epinepherine, chloropromazine, and amusement. *Journal of Abnormal and Social Psychology* 65:121–128.

**Schaukowitsch,** F. J. 1964. *How to avoid marriage.* New York: Ace Star.

**Scheflen,** A. 1972. *Body language and social order.* Englewood Cliffs, N.J.: Prentice-Hall (Spectrum).

**Schegloff,** E. A. 1967. The first five seconds: The order of conversational openings. Unpublished dissertation, Department of Sociology, University of California, Berkeley.

**Schegloff,** E. A. 1968. Sequencing in conversational openings. *American Anthropologist* 70:1075–1095. Summarized as "Opening conversations" in J. Helmer and N. A. Eddington, eds. 1973. *Urbanman,* pp. 142–169. New York: Free Press.

**Schein,** E. H., and **Bennis,** W. G. 1965. *Personal and organizational change through group methods: A laboratory approach.* New York: Wiley.

**Scherer,** S. E., and **Schiff,** M. 1973. Perceived intimacy, physical distance, and eye contact. *Perceptual and Motor Skills* 36:835–841.

**Schoenfeld,** W. N., **Cole,** B. K., **Blaustein,** J., **Lachter,** G. D., **Martin,** J. M., and **Vickery,** C. 1972. *Stimulus schedules.* New York: Harper & Row.

**Schramm,** W., **Lyle,** J., and **Parker,** E. B. 1961. *Television in the lives of our children.* Stanford, Calif.: Stanford University Press.

**Scott,** J. P. 1963. The process of primary socialization in canine and human infants. *Monographs of the Society for Research in Child Development* 28:1–47.

**Scott,** J. W., and **Bushell,** D., Jr. 1974. The length of teacher contacts and students' off-task behavior. *Journal of Applied Behavior Analysis* 4:39–44.

**Sears,** R. R., **Whiting,** J. W. M., **Nowlis,** V., and **Sears,** P. S. 1953. Some child-rearing antecedents of aggression and dependency in young children. *Genetic Psychology Monographs* 47:135–234.

**Sermat,** V. 1973. Loneliness and interpersonal competence. Paper presented at the Western Psychological Association meeting, Santa Barbara, Calif., July. (Available from author.)

**Sermat,** V. 1974. Personal correspondence to Patricia Middlebrook, 1972. In P. Middlebrook, *Social psycology and modern life,* pp. 250–251. New York: Knopf.

**Sherwood,** J. J. 1970. Self-actualization and self-identity theory. *Personality* 1:41–63. Also available as Reprint No. 326, Krannart School of Industrial Administration Reprint Series, Purdue University.

**Silberman,** M. L., ed. 1971. *The experience of schooling.* New York: Holt, Rinehart & Winston.

**Skinner,** B. F. 1948. *Walden two.* New York: Macmillan.

**Skinner,** B. F. 1953. *Science and human behavior.* New York: Macmillan.

**Skinner,** B. F. 1971. *Beyond freedom and dignity.* New York: Knopf. (Available in paperback by Bantam.)

**Skinner,** B. F. 1972. Humanism and behaviorism. *The Humanist,* July/August. Reprinted in F. W. Matson, ed., 1973. Pp. 47–53.

**Slaby,** R., and **Parke,** R. D. 1971. Effect of resistance to deviation of observing a model's affective reaction to response consequences. *Developmental Psychology* 51:40–47.

**Solomon,** R. L., and **Corbit,** J. D. 1974. An opponent-process theory of motivation: I. Temporal dynamics of affect. *Psychological Review* 81:119–145.

**Solomon,** R. L., **Kamin,** L. J., and **Wynne,** L. C. 1953. Traumatic avoidance learning: The outcomes of several extinction procedures with dogs. *Journal of Abnormal and Social Psychology* 48:291–302.

**Sommer,** R. 1969. *Personal space.* Englewood Cliffs, N.J.: Spectrum.

**Spanos,** N. P., and **Barber,** T. X. 1974. Toward a convergence in hypnosis research. *American Psychologist* 29:500–511.

**Staikov,** Z. 1972. Time budgets and technological progress. In Szalai (ed.), 1972. Pp. 461–482.

**Stampfl,** T. G., and **Levis,** D. J. 1967. Essentials of implosive therapy: A learning-theory-based psychodynamic behavioral therapy. *Journal of Abnormal Psychology* 72:496–503.

**Stampfl,** T. G., and **Levis,** D. J. 1973. *Implosive therapy: Theory and technique.* Morristown, N.J.: General Learning Press.

**Stanley,** F. 1962. Gamblers anonymous. *Saturday Evening Post* 235:44–46.

**Steinman,** W. M. 1970a. Generalized imitation and the discrimination hypothesis. *Journal of Experimental Psychology* 10:79–99.

**Steinman,** W. M. 1970b. The social control of generalized imitation. *Journal of Applied Behavior Analysis* 3:159–167.

**Strongman,** K. T. 1973. *The psychology of emotion.* New York: Wiley.

**Swensen,** C. H., Jr. 1961. Love: Self-report analysis with college students. *Journal of Individual Psychology* 17:167–171.

**Swensen,** C. H., Jr. 1972. Manual and test booklet for the "Love Scale." In J. W. Pfeiffer and J. E. Jones, eds., *Group facilitators handbook.* Iowa City, Iowa: University Associates.

**Swensen,** C. H., Jr. 1973. *Introduduction to interpersonal relations.* Glenview, Ill.: Scott, Foresman.

**Swensen,** C. H. Jr., and **Gilner,** F. 1964. Factor analysis of self-report statements of love relationships. *Journal of Individual Psychology* 20:186–188.

**Szalai,** A. (ed.) 1972. *The use of time.* The Hague, Netherlands: Mouton.

**Tabor,** E. 1950. *The cliff's edge: Songs of a psychotic.* New York: Sheed & Ward.

**Tagiuri,** R. 1969. *Person perception.* In G. Lindzey and E. Aronson, eds., *The handbook of social psychology* vol. 3. 2nd ed. Reading, Mass.: Addison-Wesley.

**Tanner,** I. J. 1973. *Loneliness: The fear of love.* New York: Harper & Row.

**Taylor,** D. A. 1968. Some aspects of the development of interpersonal relationships: Social penetration processes. *Journal of Social Psychology* 75:79–90.

**Taylor,** D. A., and **Altman,** I. 1966. Intimacy-scaled stimuli for use in studies of interpersonal relations. *Psychological Reports* 19:729–730. Also available as Research Report MF 022, 01, 03–1002; Report No. 9. Bethesda, Md.: Naval Medical Research Report Institute, April, 1966. (Available from authors.)

**Taylor,** D., **Altman,** I., and **Sorrentino,** R. 1969. Interpersonal exchange as a function of rewards and costs and situational factors: Expectancy confirmation-disconfirmation. *Journal of Experimental Social Psychology* 5:324–339.

**Taylor,** D. A., and **Oberlander,** L. 1969. Person-perception and self-disclosure: Motivational mechanisms in interpersonal processes. *Journal of Experimental Research in Personality* 4:14–28.

**Tharp,** R. G., and **Wetzel,** R. J. 1969. *Behavior modification in the natural environment.* New York: Academic.

The third force. 1974. *Time,* December 30, p. 13.

**Thibaut,** J. W., and **Kelley,** H. H. 1959. *The social psychology of groups.* New York: Wiley.

**Thoresen,** C. E., and **Mahoney,** M. J. 1974. *Behavioral self-control.* New York: Holt, Rinehart & Winston.

**Thorndike,** E. L. 1911. *Animal intelligence.* New York: Macmillan.

**Tighe,** T. J., and **Elliott,** R. 1968. A technique for controlling behavior in natural life settings. *Journal of Applied Behavior Analysis* 1:263–266.

**Timberlake,** W., and **Allison,** J. 1974. Response deprivation: An empirical approach to instrumental performance. *Psychological Review* 81:146–164.

**Tobias,** P. V. 1965. Early man in East Africa. *Science* 149:22–33.

**Toffler,** A. 1970. *Future shock.* New York: Random House.

**Trotter,** S., and **Warren,** J. 1974. Behavior modification under fire. *APA Monitor* 5:1, 4.

**Turner,** J. L., **Foa,** E. B., and **Foa,** U. G. 1971. Interpersonal reinforcers: Classification, interrelationship, and some differential properties. *Journal of Personality and Social Psychology* 19:168–180.

**Unseem,** R. H., **Unseem,** J., and **Gibson,** D. L. 1960. The function of neighboring for the middle-class male. *Human Organization* 19 (Summer): 68–76.

**Valentine,** J., and **Arkowitz,** H. 1974. *Social anxiety and the self-evaluation of interpersonal performance.* Manuscript submitted for publication. (Available from authors.)

Valley of horrors. 1974. *Time,* Aug. 5, p. 47.

**Verplanck,** W. S. 1957. A glossary of some terms used in the objective science of behavior. *Psychological Review* 64 (6, pt. 2).

**Viteles,** M. S. 1953. *Motivation and morale in industry.* New York: Norton.

**Wagner,** W. 1972. *To gamble or not to gamble.* New York: World Publishing.

**Wallace,** J. 1971. *Psychology: A social science.* Philadelphia: Saunders.

**Walster,** E., **Berscheid,** E., and **Walster,** G. W. 1973. New directions in equity research. *Journal of Personality and Social Psychology* 25:151–176.

**Walters,** B. 1970. *How to talk with practically anybody about practically anything.* Garden City, N.Y.: Doubleday. (Available in paperback by Dell.)

**Walters,** R. H., and **Parke,** R. D. 1964. Influence of response consequences to a social model on resistance to deviation. *Journal of Experimental Child Psychology* 1:269–280.

**Walters,** R. H., **Parke,** R. D., and **Cane,** V. A. 1965. Timing of punishment and the observation of consequences to others as determinants of response inhibition. *Journal of Experimental Child Psychology* 2:10–30.

**Warga,** R. G. 1974. *Personal awareness a psychology of adjustment.* Boston: Houghton Mifflin.

**Watson,** D. L., and **Tharp,** R. G. 1972. *Self-directed behavior.* Monterey, Calif.: Brooks/Cole.

**Weber,** E. 1970. *How to pick up girls.* New York: Bantam.

**Weinstein,** E. A. 1965. The applied art of one-downsmanship. *Trans-Action* 2 (July/August): 36–38. Reprinted in E. Aronson and R. Helmreich, eds. 1973. *Social psychology,* pp. 96–98. New York: Van Nostrand Reinhold.

**Weinstein,** E. A. 1969. The development of interpersonal competence. In D. A. Goslin, ed., *Handbook of socialization theory and research,* pp. 753–775. Skokie, Ill.: Rand McNally.

**Weiss,** R. S. 1973. *Loneliness: The experience of emotional and social isolation.* Cambridge, Mass.: MIT Press.

**Weitzenhoffer,** A. M. 1953. *Hypnotism: An objective study in suggestibility.* New York: Wiley.

**Weitzenhoffer,** A. M. 1957. *General techniques of hypnotism.* New York: Grune & Stratton.

**Whaley,** D. L., and **Malott,** R. W. 1971. *Elementary principles of behavior.* New York: Appleton.

**White,** O. R. 1971. *A glossary of behavioral terminology.* Champaign, Ill.: Research Press.

**Wicker,** A. W. 1968. Undermanning, performances, and students' subjective experiences in behavior settings of large and small high schools. *Journal of Personality and Social Psychology* 10:255–261.

**Wicker,** A. W. 1969. Cognitive complexity, school size, and participation in school behavior settings: A test of the frequency of interaction hypothesis. *Journal of Educational Psychology* 60:200–203.

**Wicker,** A. W. 1972. Processes which mediate behavior-environment congruence. *Behavioral Science* 17:265–277.

**Wicker,** A. W. 1973. Undermanning theory and research: Implications for the study of psychological and behavioral effects of excess populations. *Representative Research in Social Psychology* 4:185–206.

**Wicker,** A. W., and **Kauma,** C. E. 1974. Effects of a merger of a small and a large organization on members' behaviors and experiences. *Journal of Applied Psychology* 59:24–30.

**Wicker,** A. W., **McGrath,** J. E., and **Armstrong,** G. E. 1972. Organization size and behavior setting capacity as determinants of member participation. *Behavioral Science* 17:499–513.

**Wilkins,** W. 1971. Desensitization: Social and cognitive factors underlying the effectiveness of Wolpe's procedure. *Psychological Bulletin* 76:311–317.

**Wilkins,** W. 1973. Desensitization: A rejoinder to Morgan. *Psychological Bulletin* 79:376–377.

**Wilson,** W. 1967. Correlates of avowed happiness. *Psychological Bulletin* 67:294–306.

**Wilson,** W. H., and **Nunnally,** J. C. 1971. A naturalistic investigation of acquired meaning in children. *Psychonomic Science* 23:149–150.

**Wold,** C. I. 1970. Characteristics of 26,000 suicide prevention center patients. *Bulletin of Suicidology* 6:24–28.

**Wolf,** A. V. 1958. *Thirst: Physiology of the urge to drink and problems of water lack.* Springfield, Ill.: C. C Thomas.

**Wolpe,** J. 1958. *Psychotherapy by reciprocal inhibition.* Stanford, Calif.: Stanford University Press.

**Wolpe,** J. 1973. *The practice of behavior therapy.* 2nd ed. New York: Pergammon.

**Worthy,** M., **Gary,** A. L., and **Kahn,** G. M. 1969. Self-disclosure as an exchange process. *Journal of Personality and Social Psychology* 13:59–64.

**Wrightsman,** L. 1974. *Assumptions about human nature.* Monterey, Calif.: Brooks/Cole.

**Yufit,** R. 1956. Intimacy and isolation: Some behavioral and psychodynamic correlates. Unpublished doctoral dissertation, University of Chicago. (University Microfilms, Ann Arbor, Mich., 1956, BF 698, 9 S6Y8.)

**Zeilberger,** J., **Sampen,** S. E., and **Sloane,** H. N., Jr. 1968. Modification of a child's problem behaviors in the home with the mother as therapist. *Journal of Applied Behavior Analysis* 1:47–53.

**Zimbardo,** P. G., **Pilkonis,** P., and **Norwood,** R. 1974. The silent prison of shyness. Unpublished manuscript, Stanford University.

**Zimbardo,** P. G., **Pilkonis,** P. A., and **Norwood,** R. M. 1975. The social disease called shyness. *Psychology Today* 8:69–72.

**Zunin,** L., and **Zunin,** N. 1972. *Contact: The first four minutes.* Los Angeles: Nash.

# INDEX

**T**

*Dear Student*

*I would greatly appreciate your help. I would like to consider your reactions to PRACTICAL PSYCHOLOGY in future editions of the book. Please answer this questionnaire and return it to me, care of Harper & Row. No postage is required. Thank you very much.*

*Sincerely,*

*JAMES FLANDERS*

**1.** What is your overall impression of PRACTICAL PSYCHOLOGY? How do you rate the book in terms of the following:

| | ALL OF THE BOOK | A GREAT AMOUNT OF THE BOOK | A MODERATE AMOUNT OF THE BOOK | NONE OF THE BOOK |
|---|---|---|---|---|
| Had personal relevance | ( ) | ( ) | ( ) | ( ) |
| Supplied practical information | ( ) | ( ) | ( ) | ( ) |
| Was readable | ( ) | ( ) | ( ) | ( ) |
| Had a clear organization | ( ) | ( ) | ( ) | ( ) |
| Explained concepts clearly | ( ) | ( ) | ( ) | ( ) |
| Held my interest | ( ) | ( ) | ( ) | ( ) |
| Photographs were helpful | ( ) | ( ) | ( ) | ( ) |
| Cases were helpful | ( ) | ( ) | ( ) | ( ) |
| I did the activities | ( ) | ( ) | ( ) | ( ) |
| Activities were helpful | ( ) | ( ) | ( ) | ( ) |
| I read the chapter notes | ( ) | ( ) | ( ) | ( ) |
| I liked the book | ( ) | ( ) | ( ) | ( ) |
| It is a good book | ( ) | ( ) | ( ) | ( ) |

**2.** What chapters were you required to read? (Circle chapters and materials assigned)

1 2 3 4 5 6 7 8 9 10 11 12 Epilogue Appendix A

**3.** What chapters did you read that were not assigned? (Circle below)

1 2 3 4 5 6 7 8 9 10 11 12 Epilogue Appendix A

**4.** What chapters did you like the best? ______________________________

**5.** What chapters did you like the least? ______________________________

**6.** Did your instructor use other learning aids in addition to PRACTICAL PSYCHOLOGY? (circle all that apply)

| | | |
|---|---|---|
| films | optional projects, papers | readings (please list) ______________ |
| audiotapes | required projects, papers | ______________ |
| videotapes | guest speakers | other text(s) ______________ |
| workbook | field trips | ______________ |
| | small groups in class | other ______________ |

**7.** What topics did your instructor cover in your class that were not in the text? (circle all that apply)

| | | | |
|---|---|---|---|
| personality | learning theory | prejudice | the self |
| motivation | perception, sensation | alienation | dreams |
| frustration, stress | sex | neurosis | biofeedback |
| conflict, aggression | drugs | abnormal behavior | management |
| | nursing | religion | |

other (please list) ______________________________

**8.** Your comments and suggestions. Please be as specific as you can.

**9.** Your school ______________________________

**10.** Size of your class___ 11. Age___ 12. Sex ☐ Male ☐ Female

***THANK YOU, PLEASE FOLD, STAPLE, AND MAIL.***

*first class*
*permit no. 247*
*new york, n.y.*

*business reply mail*

*no postage stamp necessary if mailed in the united states*

*postage will be paid by*

Harper & Row, Publishers
Att: George A. Middendorf
10 East 53d Street
New York, New York 10022